Revitalizing Russian Industry: The Road Ahead after Fifteen Years of Transition

REVITALIZING RUSSIAN INDUSTRY: THE ROAD AHEAD AFTER FIFTEEN YEARS OF TRANSITION

JAMES D. GAISFORD
VLADIMIR MAYEVSKY
AND
WILLIAM A. KERR
EDITORS

Nova Science Publishers, Inc.
New York

Copyright © 2007 by Nova Science Publishers, Inc.

All rights reserved. No part of this book may be reproduced, stored in a retrieval system or transmitted in any form or by any means: electronic, electrostatic, magnetic, tape, mechanical photocopying, recording or otherwise without the written permission of the Publisher.

For permission to use material from this book please contact us:
Telephone 631-231-7269; Fax 631-231-8175
Web Site: http://www.novapublishers.com

NOTICE TO THE READER

The Publisher has taken reasonable care in the preparation of this book, but makes no expressed or implied warranty of any kind and assumes no responsibility for any errors or omissions. No liability is assumed for incidental or consequential damages in connection with or arising out of information contained in this book. The Publisher shall not be liable for any special, consequential, or exemplary damages resulting, in whole or in part, from the readers' use of, or reliance upon, this material. Any parts of this book based on government reports are so indicated and copyright is claimed for those parts to the extent applicable to compilations of such works.

Independent verification should be sought for any data, advice or recommendations contained in this book. In addition, no responsibility is assumed by the publisher for any injury and/or damage to persons or property arising from any methods, products, instructions, ideas or otherwise contained in this publication.

This publication is designed to provide accurate and authoritative information with regard to the subject matter covered herein. It is sold with the clear understanding that the Publisher is not engaged in rendering legal or any other professional services. If legal or any other expert assistance is required, the services of a competent person should be sought. FROM A DECLARATION OF PARTICIPANTS JOINTLY ADOPTED BY A COMMITTEE OF THE AMERICAN BAR ASSOCIATION AND A COMMITTEE OF PUBLISHERS.

LIBRARY OF CONGRESS CATALOGING-IN-PUBLICATION DATA

Revitalizing Russian industry : the road ahead after fifteen years of transition / James D. Gaisford, Vladimir Mayevsky, and William A. Kerr, editors.
    p. cm.
Includes index.
ISBN-13: 978-1-60021-778-4 (hardcover)
ISBN-10: 1-60021-778-8 (hardcover)
 1. Industrial policy--Russia (Federation) 2. Industrial management--Russia (Federation) I. Gaisford, James D. II. Maevskii, V. I. (Vladimir Ivanovich) III. Kerr, William A. (William Alexander)
 HD3616.R93R49   2007
 338.947--dc22
                                                      2007021135

Published by Nova Science Publishers, Inc. ✧ New York

CONTENTS

List of Contributors		vii
Acknowledgements		ix
Preface		xi
Chapter 1	Russian Industry after Fifteen Years of Transition *William A. Kerr*	1
Chapter 2	Transition to What?: Institutional Change and the Evolution of Economic Systems *Edward MacKay and William A. Kerr*	5
Chapter 3	From the Soviet Union to the Russian Federation: An Economy in Transition *Inna Iourkova*	19
Chapter 4	The Rocky Path of Transition: Institutions and Transaction Costs in the Russian Economy *Jill E. Hobbs*	39
Chapter 5	Thin Markets and Under-investment in the Russian Economy *James D. Gaisford*	57
Chapter 6	Economic Policy to Foster Russian Industrial Development: A State Centred Approach *Vladimir Mayevsky*	73
Chapter 7	Investment Aspects of Public Industrial Policy *Alexander Amosov*	85
Chapter 8	International Trade Policy and Re-investment in the Russian Economy *James D. Gaisford and Inna Iourkova*	97

Chapter 9	The Economics of Foreign Investment Law and Business Practice in the Russian Federation: "Learning to Share the Golden Eggs and not to Kill the Goose that you were Lent" *William A. Kerr and Kristal M. Bessel*	**111**
Chapter 10	Piracy, Property and Productivity: The Case for Protecting the Results of Intellectual Activity *William A. Kerr and Shari L. Boyd*	**131**
Chapter 11	Transformation and Reform in the Russian Energy Sector: The Upstream Petroleum Industry *Jennifer I. Considine*	**149**
Chapter 12	Transformation and Reform in the Russian Energy Sector: Natural Gas and Oil Transmission *Wilfred Barke*	**177**
Chapter 13	The Role of Household Demand in the Expansion of Russian Industrial Production *Alla Chebanova*	**197**
Chapter 14	From Farm to Fork: Food Supply Chains in the Russian Federation *Jill E. Hobbs and Shari L. Boyd*	**221**
Chapter 15	The Road Ahead for Industry in the Russian Federation *William A. Kerr and Jill E. Hobbs*	**237**
Index		**241**

LIST OF CONTRIBUTORS

Alexander Amosov	Professor, Centre for Evolutionary Economics, Moscow, Russia.
Wilfred Barke	Research Associate, Revitalizing Russian Industry Project, University of Calgary, Calgary, Canada.
Kristal M. Bessel	Research Associate, Estey Centre for Law and Economics in International Trade, Saskatoon, Canada.
Shari L. Boyd	Research Associate, Estey Centre for Law and Economics in International Trade, Saskatoon, Canada.
Alla Chebanova	Research Scientist, Centre for Evolutionary Economics, Moscow, Russia.
Jennifer I. Considine	Senior Lecturer, The Centre for Energy, Petroleum and Mineral Law and Policy, University of Dundee, Dundee, United Kingdom.
James D. Gaisford	Professor of Economics and Associate Dean, Faculty of Social Sciences, University of Calgary, Calgary, Canada.
Jill E. Hobbs	Professor and Head, Department of Agricultural Economics, University of Saskatchewan, Saskatoon, Canada.
Inna Iourkova	Research Associate, Department of Economics, University of Calgary, Calgary, Canada.
William A. Kerr	Van Vliet Professor, University of Saskatchewan, Saskatoon, Canada.
Edward MacKay	Research Associate, Department of Economics, University of Calgary, Calgary, Canada.
Vladimir Mayevsky	Professor and Vice President, Centre for Evolutionary Economics, Moscow, Russia.

ACKNOWLEDGEMENTS

The authors in this series gratefully acknowledge the financial support of the University of Calgary Gorbachev Foundation and the Canadian International Development Agency. The analysis, views and opinions expressed in this book are those of the authors and are *not* necessarily representative of the University of Calgary Gorbachev Foundation or the Canadian International Development Agency.

The authors would also like to express their thanks to Mr. Mark Kazhdan of the Centre for Evolutionary Economics in Moscow for his sterling work as translator and in making the Canadian team's visit to Russia a truly memorable experience.

PREFACE

In spite of a daunting array of impediments to the revitalization of Russian industry, there are also important opportunities for constructive policy that will encourage and sustain reinvestment. Growth and economic performance in Russia, after many setbacks through the first decade of economic transition, has finally been promising in recent years. Nevertheless, there are well-founded concerns that the foundation for this recent success is precarious, particularly with respect to investment-related policies. The high energy prices of the middle years of the first decade of the twenty-first century have allowed serious difficulties to be partially masked and the Russian economy has been given a breathing space as a result of strong resource revenues. Economic transition in Russia and other transition economies has often been a difficult road; market and related institutions did not initially exist, competitive pressures have often been weak and transaction costs have been high. In this context, the "frictionless-markets paradigm" frequently associated with neoclassical economics has often provided an incomplete and even misleading guide to economic policy formulation in general and investment policy issues in particular. To capitalize on the opportunities available to Russia and sustain its recent success, it is important that economic policy addresses issues concerning deficient market institutions and existing market power and transaction costs.

This book on revitalizing Russian industry is the outcome of a joint research project undertaken over the period 2001-2006 by a "teams" of Canadian economists centred at the University of Calgary and the University of Saskatchewan and a "team" of Russian economists based at the Centre for Evolutionary Economics in Moscow. While the Canadian and Russian economists participating in the project have widely divergent backgrounds and perspectives, they share a determination to conduct the policy debate over reinvestment issues in a manner that recognizes the importance of transaction costs and the existence and evolution of institutions.

The collaborative work on this project has been very worthwhile in many dimensions. On the one hand, for outside analysts including the Canadian participants, the project provided an opportunity to share in the inside knowledge of the operation of the Russian economy. Indeed, to some degree experiencing the dynamism of Russian society is a necessary antidote for the academic pessimism that tends to arise from a serious analysis of the difficulties facing Russia. On the other hand, the Russian economics profession, as well as the Russian economy, is in a state of transition. Consequently, the outside perspective and the rigours of "western" economic research that the Canadian economists have brought to the table have also been important. As is often the case with international projects, the dialogue on a broader mix of ideas and experience has extended the understanding and expertise of both sets of participants.

A roundtable research meeting in held in Moscow in November 2002 provided an important focal point for the dialogue between all of the economists participating in the project. At a broad level, the research efforts of the Russian economists, which have a more macroeconomic point of departure, have balanced and dovetailed nicely with those of the Canadian economists, which have been more microeconomic in thrust. Nevertheless, in the discussions leading to this volume, the research teams have not attempted to artificially achieve a full consensus on the details of policy directions between or even within the Russian and Canadian teams. Rather, the magnitude and complexity of the problems confronting reinvestment in Russia are such that a diversity of opinions concerning the formulation of policy appears both natural and constructive.

James Gaisford
Calgary ,Canada
Vladimir Mayevsky
Moscow, Russia
William Kerr
Saskatoon, Canada

Chapter 1

RUSSIAN INDUSTRY AFTER FIFTEEN YEARS OF TRANSITION

William A. Kerr

ABSTRACT

With the fall of the Soviet empire in Central and Eastern Europe and the disintegration of the Soviet Union a number of countries, including the Russian Federation, began the process of transition to modern market economies simultaneously. Progress in the process of transition has been mixed with the Russian Federation currently somewhere in the middle of the pack. A great deal has been learned by economists in Russia and modern market economies over the last fifteen years yet Russia, and particularly its vital but lagging industrial sector, has not made the transition to a well functioning market system. This book explores the process of transition in the Russian industrial sector and seeks to provide insights into how more rapid progress can be achieved.

INTRODUCTION

More than fifteen years have now past since the momentous events that brought an end to the Soviet Union and its system of central planning and resource allocation by bureaucratic command. Of course, the demise of the Soviet Union was preceded, but only just, by the disintegration of the Soviet empire in Central and Eastern Europe. The Russian Federation, the other former constituent nations of the Soviet Union and the countries of Central and Eastern Europe all entered into a process of economic transition at approximately the same time. The paths of transition have been unique to each country and have met with varying degrees of success. This result should not have been unexpected given that there were no "roadmaps" to provide directions for how to become a modern market economy. Although the Russian Revolution in the early part of the twentieth century and the subsequent establishment of a non-market economy by Lenin and his Bolsheviks is often touted as the greatest large scale economic experiment of all time, the process of transition set in motion by the abandonment of central planning and allocation by command in the last decade of the same century is an equally ambitious economic experiment.

PROGRESS TOWARD TRANSITION

It is not clear whether any former communist country has fully made the transition to a modern market economy. Certainly, the degree of success has varied considerably with a number of countries having become sufficiently market oriented to gain membership in the European Union while others such as Belarus, Ukraine and some Central Asian countries have made much less progress. The process of transition has not been anywhere easy, even where the resources available have been bountiful as in the case of the former East Germany much less in impoverished countries such as Albania or Moldova. Certainly the process of transition has been much more difficult than anyone in the transition countries expected, or for that matter by those residing in, and providing advice from, modern market economies.

Economists from both transition economies and modern market economies have learned a great deal in fifteen years. The latter, in particular, have gained a far greater appreciation of the importance of market institutions and the need to better understand them. Economists from transition economies have had to learn to appreciate the power of market forces and how difficult it is to predict the outcomes that they will produce. Debates continue to rage over how to best foster the institutional environment that underpins the efficient operation of a market economy and the degree to which intervention in the economy by governments is desirable.

An examination of the evolving economy of the Russian Federation is important both for assessing the process of transition to date and to gain insights into the prospects for the future. The Russian Federation is the second largest transition economy after China and its relative success or failure will have considerable ramifications for its neighbours, Western Europe and the global economy. Its transition record is mixed and progress toward becoming a modern market economy is somewhere in the middle of the pack of the countries that began the process fifteen years ago. Russia's progress exceeds that of Belarus or Tajikistan but it lags behind Slovenia or the Czech Republic. It has vast resources and a well educated labour force, hence its ability to grow and prosper is not constrained by these factors as is the case in a number of other transition economies. One must look elsewhere for explanations for why Russia has not progressed as far as other countries and for how it will fare in the future.

One of the most visible manifestations of the failure of the Russian Federation to make the transition to being a modern market economy is the malaise that affects its industrial sector. Hence, the revitalization of Russian industry will be central to the full transition of its economy. The stagnation of Russia's industrial base, of course, predates the transition era by at least fifteen years beginning in the long tenure of Leonid Brezhnev (Considine and Kerr, 2002). As a result, Russia's industrial infrastructure was far from modern when the transition process began meaning that investment in excess of that expected for normal depreciation was required simply to maintain industrial productivity. To foster additional economic growth would have required even greater amounts of investment. In the early years of the transition period, of course, public investment funds dried up and neither income levels nor financial institutions existed to fill the investment gap. Hence, fifteen years later much of Russia's industrial sector can be characterized as being in a "rust belt", lacking dynamism and modern plant and equipment.

SCOPE OF THE BOOK

This book attempts to provide insights into what needs to be done to revitalize Russian industry. It does this through a number of mechanisms from discussions of macroeconomic policies, to detailed examinations of institutional arrangements, to case studies of particular industries. While industry coverage is far from universal, the industries chosen are both important and representative of the broader industrial base in the Russian Federation. It is clear that while transition has been very disruptive, there remain considerable systemic problems that sap the vitality of the industrial sector and limit its desirability as a home for investment. It is far clearer now what must be done than it was fifteen years ago when the process of transition had just begun.

REFERENCES

Considine, J.I. and Kerr, W.A. (2002). *The Russian Oil Economy*, Cheltenham: Edward Elgar Press.

In: Revitalizing Russian Industry
Eds: J. Gaisford, V. Mayevsky et al., pp. 5-18
ISBN 978-1-60021-778-4
© 2007 Nova Science Publishers, Inc.

Chapter 2

TRANSITION TO WHAT?: INSTITUTIONAL CHANGE AND THE EVOLUTION OF ECONOMIC SYSTEMS

Edward MacKay and William A. Kerr

ABSTRACT

The transition from a command economy to a modern market economy is neither deterministic nor linear. It involves a complex institutional change that pits those with vested interests in the status quo against those that can benefit from change. Well defined property rights are central to the functioning of a modern market economy and to the low transaction costs that underpin its smooth functioning. Poorly defined property rights allow corruption to flourish. Corruption can be a major source of transaction costs. The Russian economy has poorly defined property rights and exhibits considerable corruption. If the vested interests in corruption are able to inhibit the further development of property rights the full transition to a modern market economy may not be achieved.

INTRODUCTION

There has been an implicit (and often explicit) assumption that the process of economic transformation initiated by the political collapse of communist regimes would ultimately lead to economic systems based on markets.[1] The reasons why this assumption has been made are complex. The rivalry between command and market economies that comprised the economic content of the *Cold War*, defined the world in terms of only two systems. The political demise of communist governments was, in the context of rival systems, taken as a sign of victory for a system based on markets. It is an easy *leap of faith* to assume that the *victor's* economic system would become the ruling paradigm in post-command economies. For most of those living in what had been command economies, the obvious material wealth produced in

---

[1] Certainly, mixed form economies where the government plays a significant role have also been envisioned. However, the role of government is expected to be an adjunct to the market system, its primary function being to deal with problems of market failure or income redistribution.

modern market economies suggested it was a desirable system. Those from modern market economies involved in advising on the process of transition concurred with those desires as they were not contradicted by their own experience. Many neoclassically trained economists, in particular, while having a market based paradigm as a model, poorly understood the institutional basis of modern market economies.[2]

While the desired endpoint of the transition process can at least be envisioned, the process by which it can be achieved is not well understood. Many economists have gone through a progression in thought which started with the belief that, by freeing prices and privatizing assets, a market system would (rapidly) evolve and ended with a realization that institutions do, indeed, matter. A great deal of effort has been put into thinking and learning about institutions over the last few years. Institution building has become a major focus for those directly involved in the providing advice on the process of transition.

While institutions can be created or transformed, they are not static entities. They respond to the changing institutional environment that defines the wider economy. Hence, even if the major institutions that currently underpin modern market economies could be duplicated in the former command economies, there is no assurance that they will work as envisioned or that they, collectively, will evolve into a set of institutions which operationally mirror those in modern market economies.

It seems clear that to obtain a fuller understanding of the process of economic transition, a theory of institutional change is required. While a model of institutional change may not necessarily predict stable institutional equilibria, if it does then the possibility of economies transforming to market systems exists. The process of transition is proving far more difficult than was originally expected. While some former command economies, most of which are in close geographic proximity to modern market economies, appear to be well on the way to a market based system, many are not. Hence, the central question in current discussions regarding the former command economies should not be: what is the rate at which transition to a market economy is progressing?, but rather it should be: *transition to what?*

This chapter puts forward a simple model of institutional change and then attempts to provide some insights into answering the question: *transition to what?* While the insights may not be conclusive, or even compelling, at the very least they should suggest that more effort should be spent understanding the process of institutional change.

TRANSACTION COSTS

Coase (1988) suggests that economics is *the science of human choice* (p. 2). By viewing economics as the study of choice, Coase implies that the economic approach can be used to examine much more than consumer preferences and production functions of firms - the basis of neoclassical economics. Economic systems are founded on institutional structures that are comprised of firms, markets and legal rules and regulations which govern exchanges between economic agents. Institutional structures can change, however, and since politico-economic systems are founded in these institutions, they can also change.

---

[2] Given the cursory treatment given institutions in curricula that focus on the neoclassical paradigm, this is not surprising.

Each economic system is governed by the institutional arrangements which are the laws and regulations that define the property rights in the society (Cheung, 1982). Further, these arrangements establish the rules under which individuals compete and interact. In most modern market economies the rules of the game are established by a constitution. If the rules of the game are not clear and/or are not enforceable, then opportunities exist to take advantage of the lack of rules. One of the problems with the current constitutions of the former command economies is that, rather than establishing a structure of rights for economic interaction, they serve only to confuse. While some constitutions in the former command economies have been revised to provide better-defined rights, the absence of effective enforcement of those rights is endemic. The legal and police institutions do not function well enough to effectively and transparently enforce civil law. This void allows government officials (including the continuing managers of privatized state enterprises), who operate within an existing set of rather vague constraints, to advance their own self-interest. It also allows entrepreneurs who operate outside the law to do so with impunity.

According to Cheung (1982), the postulate of constrained maximization asserts as a *universal truth that each individual will constantly seek to benefit himself as much as possible subject to constraints and limitations he faces* (p. 30). Cheung also assumes that Pareto optimality holds for politico-economic institutions - i.e. communism, socialism and capitalism. Combining constrained maximization with Pareto optimality yields an equilibrium condition whereby:

> if constraints permit, people will not interact to harm themselves; if they can accomplish something of benefit at sufficiently low cost, they will work toward that end. It follows that when the constraints or limitations facing them change, individuals will make adjustments until no further improvements are possible (Cheung, 1982, p. 30)

This equilibrium has two key elements. First, the limitations imposed by the constraints determine the citizens' ability to maximize their benefits. Second, individuals will act in their own self-interest. We will examine each of these elements more closely below. It is, however, sufficient to state that we have an equilibrium from which agents can move.

Maximization is constrained by transaction costs. There are two categories of transaction costs:

a) Execution Costs (ECs) - those incurred in the operation of an institutional arrangement.
b) Modification Costs (MCs) - those incurred in adopting or changing institutions.

Execution costs refer to costs which result from using the current institutional arrangement while modification costs refer to costs which must be borne to change any institutional arrangement. It is the combined incidence of these transactions costs that determines economic institutions. In the absence of modification costs, society will always evolve towards an institutional arrangement which reduces execution costs. If ECs are lowered, then by definition we can assume that society is better off. This process becomes the driving force of institutional change. Execution costs can be lowered in two ways: (1) by promoting competition with the institutional arrangement fixed, and (2) lowering the costs of adopting alternative institutions.

When MCs are positive, those who would benefit from change must assess the stream of benefits which are likely to arise from the lowering of ECs against the MCs which must be incurred to bring about change. If the MCs are high - i.e. if the information costs regarding alternative systems and the costs of negotiating or forcing change are large - then institutional choices will be fewer and ECs may be high. The crucial question then becomes, what determines the level of MCs? This will be discussed in greater detail below, but it should be clear that when MCs exceed the stream of benefits expected to arise from lowering ECs, an equilibrium institutional arrangement can be reached. Cheung (1982) suggests that ECs will be lowest under a system of well defined, transferable and enforced private property rights because:

> private property rights are unique in that (a) they permit the largest range of institutional choice and (b) competition to reduce transaction costs is enforced by the right to transfer or sell (p. 40).

THE ROLE OF PROPERTY RIGHTS

When one thinks of private property rights in modern market economies, the material things owned by individuals often come to mind – one's house, car or business. In today's liberal democracies one forgets that the right to work (or not to work) is a valuable property right. Armed with this property right, one can make investments in skills that will allow one to get a better job with a higher salary. Similarly, employers have the right to hire the worker they believe will be the most productive for a particular position. If a worker is no longer deemed to be sufficiently productive, they can fire that person. Certainly, these ideas are not new, and they are generally accepted as rights in liberal democracies. However, if you take away the ability to contract one's own labour, the major means of accumulating wealth is removed.

Prior to the reforms associated with transition, workers in command economies did not have property rights to their labour. Employment was to a large degree allocated by the state. Workers were told where and at what rate - usually low - they would be paid.

In societies where individual choice is not allowed - where property rights are not held by individuals - activities must be planned. In planned economies, enterprises were not allowed to sell goods at prices they would have chosen, nor could they decide where to sell or even who to hire. If governments could allocate all resources so as to maximize everyone's preferences subject to resource constraints, then their ECs would be zero (Cheung, 1982). The information costs associated with national level planning are, however, enormous.

It is generally recognized that high information costs prevent state planners from being able to effectively allocate resources to provide for sustained increases in economic growth. This led to the ever-widening gap between the living standards in modern market economies and those in Central and Eastern Europe and the Soviet Union.

Well-defined private property rights, on the other hand, can be expected to lead to low ECs over the long run. Property rights induce the development of markets and competitive forces, which seek lower cost institutional arrangements and minimize ECs (Freedman and Freedman, 1980). It is the case that:

> Any productive resource is a private property; if within well defined limits its owner has: (a) the right to exclude others so that he alone may decide on its use; (b) the right to extract exclusive income from its use; and (c) the right to transfer or sell the property or resource to anyone he sees fit (Cheung, 1982, p. 32)

Having these rights, however, is not sufficient. What goes unsaid is that these rights must be enforced. If enforced, these clearly-defined rights allow individuals in society to accumulate wealth. The basic premise is that if one owns something of value, one should be able to extract the value by selling it or using it in such a way to produce value for oneself. Implicit in the system of property rights is the right to make choices. Further, property rights act to restrain competition among individuals who want more of the same economic good - it removes the common property problem of over-use of resources. The ownership of property rights along with the right to chose defines societies' winners and losers. If one chooses to use the assets over which one has property rights correctly, one will be a winner. Bad choices create losers.

If property rights define winners and losers in a society, what determines the distribution of the rights? In a centralized regime dominated by a Communist Party, the winners and losers are determined by their place in the hierarchy. The Party controls placement in the hierarchy. The rents, arising from the Party's control of virtually all of the property rights in society, are distributed to members of the hierarchy. Of course, the high ECs associated with planned economies mean that the total rents available are much smaller than in modern market economies.

In countries such as India and Indonesia, property rights are allocated indirectly to the bureaucracy. Government officials are given considerable leeway to extract income from private citizens. For example, a bureaucrat may not own the capital to start a business, but does control business licensing. If he has a monopoly in providing licenses, he can take a bribe for approval.

This is the system that has evolved in Russia according to Vaksberg (1995):

> It is these former functionaries who have full control of real estate; they sell, allocate, and lease land and buildings for bribes that may be in money, assets, or reciprocal favours ... Those who have something to offer in return for bribes — for example, managers of assets that they have a right to sell - are for the most part the middle ranks of the former party nomenclature who have learned the modern market jargon... (p. 211).

In liberal democratic societies, winners and losers are determined by many criteria. Market prices are, however, one of the most effective criteria by which winners and losers can be decided (Cheung, 1992). Individuals in these societies compete for economic goods by paying a price that reflects scarcity.[3] The individual who can pay the highest price gets the good. An institutional arrangement not predicated on price competition with clearly defined property rights leads to rents being dissipated or wasted. This waste is reflected in Execution Costs. Lack of market pricing remains one of the major obstacles to economic growth in the former command economies. The absence of market pricing allows the continuation of large state monopoly enterprises, fosters rent extraction by privileged officials and keeps income in the hands of those in command instead of entrepreneurs and workers (Cheung, 1989).

---

[3] Even if the scarcity is artificially created by the exercise of market power.

The rapid and widespread growth of organized crime in the former command economies is also a reflection of poorly defined and enforced property rights. In the absence of well defined property rights, a well functioning commercial legal system and an effective criminal justice system, it is not surprising that individuals with the private ability to appropriate and enforce property rights have chosen to do so. Those operating outside the law already had the embryo of enforcement organizations when the state enforcement organizations were stripped of their power. Ethnic minorities with strong family allegiances and a long history of mutual support when resisting oppression were well poised to fill the vacuum created by the end of Party rule. While organized crime groups are involved in high profile criminal activities as they are in the West - drugs, prostitution, smuggling, extortion - this is not the reason they have become so widespread in the former command economies. They are involved in, or control, a wide range of commercial activities in what would be considered legitimate endeavors in modern market economies. Where they are directly involved, they have appropriated the property rights and use coercion or violence to defend them. As a result, they are able to capture any economic rent. Entry is controlled and, hence, the dissipation of rents prevented. What had become common property with the demise of the state's willingness to control all aspects of economic activity has become the property of organized crime. The ECs associated with maintaining separate private enforcement establishments are, however, high.[4] When organized crime does not have a direct stake in a business activity it has tended to act as the regulator of business affairs - competition is controlled so that rents are available, payments for goods and services are enforced so that businesses can prosper and make their payments to organized crime, and petty crime is controlled so that customers feel safe. Of course, the cost of this system of property rights protection is very high for businesses - making their EC's much higher than the taxes businesses in modern market economies pay for a secure legal environment.

It is unlikely, however, that organized crime will continue in its role as the regulator of legal economic activity to any significant degree. Without the legitimacy of state sanction, their property rights are vulnerable. As the *legitimate* but corrupt licensing and regulating officials become more secure in their positions, they will be able to extract greater amounts of rent from organized crime. Over time, the *legitimate* police authority will become more effective, if for no other reason than it will facilitate their ability to extract rents. Organized crime will retreat to those truly illegal activities where they traditionally operate in both modern market economies and licensing and regulating economies such as India or Indonesia.

This does not mean that organized crime in the former command economies will be vanquished in a direct confrontation with legitimate enforcement authorities.[5] Rather, as the *legitimate* licensing and regulating authorities gain greater rent capturing abilities over the long run:

> We are witnessing something more than simply a merger of the criminal world and government structures. A fierce struggle for power is taking place, involving the use of criminal groups and criminal methods on the one hand, and on the other, the attempts of

---

[4] Organized crime is able to operate in illegal areas of the economy because property rights are not legally defined and enforced for these activities. The *territories* of Mafia families in the U.S. can be seen simply as a low cost means of dividing up the property rights. The high cost of Mafia turf wars attests to the expenses associated with defending property rights.

[5] Such as those glorified on U.S. television in shows such as the *Untouchables*.

criminal groups to put their own people in command position where true and not token power lies (Vaksberg, 1995, pp. 208-209)

These vested interests will not be easily convinced to relinquish the ability they have acquired to extract rents.

ALTERNATIVE INSTITUTIONAL ARRANGEMENTS

There are two major types of modification costs: (1) the costs of gathering information concerning alternative institutional arrangements, and (2) the costs of persuading, or compelling acquiescence from, those members of society whose real income would be reduced by change. Communist parties were able to ensure that both these costs were very high in the former command economies. The Berlin Wall served as a focal metaphor for how high the costs associated with achieving alternative institutions could be in communist countries.[6] While there was much optimism regarding the transition of the former command economies, it will be the ability of the citizens in post-command economies to reduce these costs which will determine the pace and path of economic evolution.

The costs associated with acquiring information regarding alternative institutional arrangements have been greatly reduced in the former command economies. Travel restrictions have been removed, interactions with foreigners are allowed, radio signals are no longer jammed, satellite television receivers abound, the press has considerably more freedom than in the past, etc. One benefit of the former regime is that education levels are high.[7] Probably the major remaining constraint to the acquisition of information is low income levels, which limits mobility. Further, countries in close geographic proximity to modern market economies will have a distinct cost advantage in acquiring information on alternative institutions - the Czech Republic and Poland versus Tadzhikistan or Mongolia.

Assuming that factions in society have gained the information necessary to want change to happen, they then must incur the costs associated with persuading and/or compelling those who would lose as a result of change, to change. In countries where those in power are not accountable to the people, such as in communist regimes, agitating for change can be fatal. Stalin's purges, the Gulag, Hungary in 1956, Czechoslovakia in 1968, Tiananmen Square in 1989, and numerous other examples attest to the fact that the cost can be high and the struggle not always successful.

When the MCs which must be incurred to accomplish change appear to exceed the benefits likely to arise from lowering ECs, an equilibrium will exist in institutional arrangements. This discussion of alternative institutional arrangements and their evolution postulates that there is a relationship between ECs and the degree to which private property rights are defined and enforced. Figure 2.1 represents a stylized representation of four scenarios which lie along a continuum of possible institutional arrangements, and which can be summarized as follows:

---

[6] And still are in Cuba and North Korea.
[7] Which is not the case in China where the legacy of the cultural revolution's effect on the education system will be felt for generations. As a result, the cost of acquiring and using information remains high in China. These high costs will act as a break on the pace of reforms. Low levels of education can also slow the rate of reform in developing countries (Kerr and MacKay, 1997).

1. Point A - property rights are common and, as a result, all rents will be competed away. This may be the case in some very underdeveloped countries. The nomadic cultures of the Sahel, where there has been large-scale degradation of the land resource come to mind. Other nomadic cultures in East and Southern Africa may have similar common property problems (Sommerville and Kerr, 1988). Of course, high seas fishing in the absence of effective international regulation is the best known example of rent dissipation where property rights are not defined. As no one has property rights, transactions cannot take place. As all rents are dissipated, the costs of organizing transactions must exceed the benefits that could accrue from organizing them.
2. Point B - the communist state based on central planning and transactions organized on the basis of command. This is a hierarchical system where rents accrue to those near the top of the hierarchy. There are only very limited private property rights. The ECs in the system are very high when strict central planning is followed, and are due to the information requirements of the planners and the monitoring costs associated with command. The prohibitive cost of the information required for effective planning prevents efficient allocation of resources (von Mises, 1981). The lack of individual property rights to labour – leading to an incomplete set of incentive mechanisms and an absence of labour markets – means that the costs of monitoring labour are too high to prevent shirking on a grand scale. This leads to poor productivity levels and low quality products and services.
3. Point C - a system where licensing and regulation are endemic. Rents accrue to those who license and regulate. This type of economy is characterized by corruption. The freeing of (some) prices from central control reduces the information costs associated with comprehensive economic planning. Hence, the efficiency of resource allocation improves.
4. Point D - a capitalist system. Property rights are exclusive and well defined. Rents accrue to the owners.

The two zones in the centre of Figure 2.1, containing points B and C, are institutional arrangements where the government and/or the administration are able to extract rent. These are the institutional arrangements where the cost of inducing institutional change are very high. Seeking to maximize their own self-interest, Party members, government officials and bureaucrats will seek to protect their ability to extract rent. This form of rent seeking is commonly referred to as corruption.

Schleifer and Vishny (1993) describe both of these institutional arrangements. The first set of arrangements, containing B, can be characterized as monopolistic corruption. This normally involves a bribe which is taken once and then *divided between all relevant government bureaucrats, who agree not to demand further bribes from the buyer of the package of government goods, such as permits* (Schleifer and Vishny, 1993, p. 605). Examples of this type of state include not only communist regimes, but also dictatorships like those of Ferdinand Marcos in the Philippines and corrupt monarchies.[8] Under this type of regime, the bribe need only be paid once and the buyer gets the goods and services he/she wants. In discussing the Brezhnev era in the Soviet Union, Vaksberg (1995) suggests:

---

[8] The House of Saud and other Gulf monarchies are extremely effective at extracting rents.

The people who took bribes then were different, and the bribes have assumed new forms. In those days, they were called "overstatement of profits", which were shared equally by those who did the "overstating" and those who shut their eyes to it. In the Brezhnev days, there were "gifts presented from the bottom of the heart" on the anniversaries of the Bolshevik Revolution or for the birthday of a distant relation. In those days, bribes and favours were euphemistically called "solicitude" and "reciprocal solicitude" (p. 213).

A second system described by Schleifer and Vishny (1995) characterizes the institutional arrangements containing point C. These institutional arrangements allow government officials to act as independent monopolies over the goods or government services they control. The sellers of complimentary goods, such as permits and licenses, each individually attempt to maximize their own revenues independently. The buyer must pay multiple bribes and may have to pay for the same services more than once. India, Indonesia, Nigeria and a number of other African countries are plagued by these types of institutional arrangements. Two distinctive features of Russian corruption are described by Vaksberg (1995):

First, it has spread across the nation with lightening speed like an epidemic (pandemic is perhaps a more accurate term) that blights every sphere of activity and penetrates every pore of society to the point where it becomes the rule rather than the exception in business relations.

Second, the main carriers of the virus have been the former apparatchiks, members of the nomenclature at various levels, who for years had instructed us in right living and had exacted compliance with the rules of party ethics ... the former functionaries once appointed by the party to be "captains of industry" hold all the key position in the central and regional administrations and in the economy generally (p. 210).

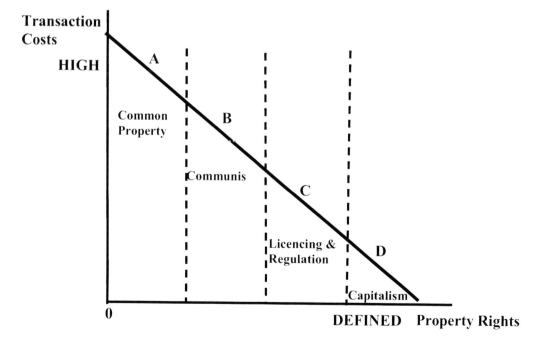

Figure 2.1. Property Rights and Transaction Costs.

When the countries of Central and Eastern Europe and the New Independent States of the former Soviet Union moved to liberalize their economies, we suggest that they may have moved from point B to point C in 2-1. In doing so, the economies in transition may have also entered into an institutional arrangement that can cause stagnation.

The shift from comprehensive central planning and Party control meant that economic decision making was no longer monopolized at the centre but, rather, decentralized (Considine and Kerr, 2002). This shift in institutional arrangements loosened the centralized control and allowed many former Party members and bureaucrats to go into the business they knew best, *trafficking in influence*. Large-scale extraction of rent is now taking place. This is best documented in the frustration expressed by firms from modern market economies that have attempted to invest in the former command economies (Hobbs, et al, 1997). In particular, there is frustration not so much with paying bribes, but with not receiving the government services for which payments have been made. No sooner has one set of officials have extracted their rents than a new group of officials show up with an additional set of licenses and permits which are required. In some industries, such as the Russian oil and gas industry, many foreign firms have decided to cut their losses and withdraw (Considine and Kerr, 1993). While the economies in transition are often perceived as having tremendous growth potential, it is possible that future growth may be stifled by the corruption associated with the current institutional arrangements.

The corruption problem, which to a greater or lesser degree, affects all former command economies, is endemic in India, Indonesia and a host of other developing countries. Some lessons may be gleaned from the experience of these latter countries. Whether or not adverse institutional arrangements are the only cause of these countries' failure to develop, it is clear that they do not contribute to economic growth. Moreover, it may be very difficult to move to another equilibrium with better defined property rights and lower Execution Costs because of persistent resistance from those in the government and the bureaucracy who are protecting their vested interests.

India is often cited as an example of how corruption impedes development. Unlike many developing countries, India does not have a shortage of highly educated people. They may, however, actually hinder the process of development. This is because their self-interest may best be served by occupying one of the public service positions where it is possible to extract large rents (Wade, 1985). Thus, those who might be expected to advocate alternative institutions become part of the problem. In Africa, Sandbrook (1986) suggests that *pervasive corruption as well as political instability and the inability to prevent widespread evasion of laws* (p. 321) are important reasons for Africa's poor record of development. The MC's associated with altering this form of institutional arrangement may be extremely high because it is not sufficient to topple the political hierarchy to institute change. The cost of rooting out endemic corruption may simply be too high. African governments change often, but corruption continues unabated.

To summarize, in order for institutions to change, two types of MC's must be reduced: (1) those associated with gathering and disseminating information about alternative arrangement, and (2) those involving persuading or compelling change among the members of society who stand to lose if the change occurs. In the economies in transition, it would appear that the former costs have been considerably reduced with the demise of the communist regimes that expended large amounts of resources to prevent the acquisition of information regarding alternative institutional arrangements. In the case of the latter, however, the costs may actually have increased relative to those that existed in communist regimes. Hence, movement beyond the zone of licensing and regulation may not be possible without a further liberalization of property rights.

Constitutions generally set out the boundaries and definition of property rights in developed countries. How do the constitutions of successful modern market economies foster the reduction of transaction costs as a prerequisite to development? One such constitution is that of the United States.

That the U.S. constitution protects property rights should not come as a surprise given the basic assumption of self-interest that underlies this discussion. All of the *founding fathers* of the United States were private property owners who sought institutional arrangements to entrench their rights. Beard (1929) suggests that all of the framers of the constitution were property owners who sought to correct the existing institutional arrangement known as the Articles of Confederation. The Articles of Confederation adversely affected the owners of capital, although land ownership was reasonable well protected. In an effort to reform a system which provided little protection for their capital, they assembled a convention to replace the Articles.

After the break from the British monarchical system, the U.S. found itself floundering with a system of ill-defined property rights. Without well-defined property rights, those lacking property were willing to lay claim to it. Beard (1929) quotes a letter from General Knox to General Washington:

> They feel at once their own poverty, compared with the opulent, and their own force, and they are determined to make use of the latter in order to remedy the former. Their creed is "That the property of the United States has been protected from the confiscations of Britain by the joint exertions of all, and therefore, ought to be the common property of all. And he that attempts opposition to this creed is an enemy to equity and justice, and ought to be swept from the face of the earth". In a word, they are determined to annihilate all the debts public and private and have agrarian laws, which are easily effected by means of unbounded paper money which shall be tender in all cases whatever (p. 59).

The framers of the U.S. Constitution were able to protect their property rights by designing a constitution that not only protected their interests, but also balanced the concerns of opposing groups.

The fact that the U.S. Constitution has been described as a system of checks and balances is no accident; it had to be otherwise the losers from the arrangement could have risen up against the winners. Therefore, while the designers of this liberal document developed it with the sole purpose of protecting their property rights, the genius of their collective minds was to design a document which could gain willing compliance; a feature which Sandbrook (1986) suggests is essential for development. James Madison, in a letter to Thomas Jefferson, wrote:

> In our Government, the real power lies in the majority of the community, and the invasion of private rights is chiefly to be apprehended, not from acts of Government contrary to its constituents, but from acts in which the Government is the mere instrument of the major number of constituents (as cited in Beard, 1929, p. 18).

The realization that *willing compliance* is a strength of government and, hence, its institutions, led to a very flexible and workable arrangement of property rights, chiefly because the founders realized that cooperation was in their best interest. Voluntary compliance greatly reduced Execution Costs. In the constitutions of the Russian Federation, property rights remain poorly defined and costly coercion, rather than willing compliance with institutional arrangements, remains the norm.

CONCLUSION

The central question regarding the transition process which is taking place in the former command economies is whether the existing institutional arrangements can lead to a modern market economy and, if they cannot, can they be reformed? The evidence suggests that the former command economies may be moving from a point such as B in Figure 2.1 to an equilibrium at point C. The very high ECs associated with central planning – costs of operating within the institutional arrangements – are being reduced as individuals receive additional property rights and decision making authority. The new institutional arrangement, however, allows for large scale corruption by those who hold the ability to license and regulate economic activity – largely the officials who held these positions in the previous hierarchy but were not able to individually extract large rents due to the power of the Party and the secret police.

The move away from central planning and command has decreased the very high information costs associated with operating within the set of institutional arrangements that characterized command economies. The move to licensed-based institutional arrangements, however, adds to ECs due to the need to pay multiple bribes. The net effect, however, has been a decrease in total transaction costs. Opportunities have been created by the transaction cost reducing reforms initiated by the government, but the ability of those engaged in commerce to capitalize on those opportunities will be reduced as corruption becomes formalized. The important question is whether significant additional reforms can be accomplished.

Before this question is answered, the question of the political popularity of *reformed communists* needs to be addressed. Can they move the system back from C to B? Their supporters are, by and large, the old and others who were significant losers as a result of liberalization. What they have lost is not the ability to extract rents, but rather they are not receiving the government services, pensions, low consumer prices, freedom from crime, etc., which they paid for (mostly in the form of low wages) over their lifetime. To the extent that the reformed communists can find resources to provide those paid-for-but-not-received services, they will be politically popular. Will they be able to reinstate the command system? This seems unlikely because it would require that the reformed communists induce or compel those who have acquired the power to extract rents from licensing and regulating to give up that power to a system able to centrally collect the rents and distribute them. This is probably not possible for two reasons: (1) the total amount of the bribes were probably less than in the current decentralized system; and (2) those who would have to give up the power to extract rents directly would then be subject to the whims of those at the centre for their share of the bribes. Further, those who provide support to *reformed communists* are not interested in the institutional arrangements of the past, but rather in a set of services. Given their exposure to alternative institutional arrangements since the fall of communist regimes, they are unlikely to support a return to an institutional arrangement that exceeds that necessary to provide the services they expect. Of course, this is the exact political line of *reformed communists*.

It would seem that the licensing and regulation system creates vested interests that will be very costly to induce to change. As a result, an equilibrium at point C may well be created. The end point of transition may be economies similar to India or Nigeria rather than the U.S. or Germany. Of course, our stylized points in Figure 2.1 are too simple, with combinations likely to lie along a continuum. This is true for modern market economies as well. Each economy defines and enforces property rights to a different degree. It is unlikely that all former command economies will transform into the same institutional arrangements.

What will be the determining factors? The first is the cost of acquiring information on alternative institutional arrangements. For the citizens of the Czech Republic,[9] for example, the ease of travel to modern market economies will make comparisons easy. There is little doubt that having a nearby example where government services can be had without paying a bribe will lead to greater agitation for change. Foreign businesses wishing to enter into transactions with Czechs also have two choices, operate in the Czech Republic or have Czech citizens visit their establishments in a modern market economy. Distances are short and transportation systems good. Competition will simply reduce the ability of officials to extract rents. The smaller the available rents, the less inducement required for change.

Of course, the citizens of many other former command economies will not benefit from being in close proximity to modern market economies. There transformation may well be arrested at equilibrium such as point C in Figure 2.1 which is well short of the configuration of property rights and transaction costs which characterizes modern market economies. Development may then be as illusive as it has been for many licensing and regulatory economies in what used to be called the *Third World*.

REFERENCES

Beard, C.A. (1929). *An Economic Interpretation of the Constitution of the United States*. New York: MacMillan.

Cheung, S.N.S. (1982). *Will China Go Capitalist?* London: Institute of Economic Affairs.

Cheung, S.N.S. (1989). Privatization vs. Special Interest: The Experience of China's Economic Reforms. *CATO Journal*, 8, 585-596.

Cheung, S.N.S. (1992). On the New Institutional Economics. In L. Werin and H. Wykander (Eds.), *Contract Economics*. (pp. 82-111). London: Blackwell.

Coase, R.H. (1988). *The Firm, The Market and The Law*. Chicago: The University of Chicago Press.

Considine, J.I. and Kerr, W.A. (1993). Russian Recentralization of Energy. *Geopolitics of Energy*, 15, 7-10.

Considine, J.I. and Kerr, W.A. (2002). *The Russian Oil Economy*. Cheltenham: Edward Elgar.

Freedman, M. and Freedman, R. (1980). *Free to Choose*. London: Secker and Warburg.

---

[9] Also, in the Czech case, because the market system was well advanced before the communist take-over, the memory of alternative arrangements is better developed.

Hobbs, J.E., Kerr, W.A. and Gaisford, J.D. (1997). *The Transformation of the Agrifood System in Central and Eastern Europe and the New Independent States*. Wallingford: CAB International.

Kerr, W.A. and MacKay, E. (1997). Is Mainland China Evolving into a Market Economy? *Issues and Studies*, 33 (9), 31-45.

Sandbrook, R. (1986). The State and Economic Stagnation in Tropical Africa. *World Development*, 14, 319-332.

Schleifer, A. and Vishny, R. (1993). Corruption. *Quarterly Journal of Economics* 18, 599-617.

Sommerville, M.F. and Kerr, W.A. (1988). The Common Property Dilemma and Alternative Policy Prescriptions for Spatially Restricted Users of Sub-Saharan Rangelands. *Quarterly Journal of International Agriculture*, 27, 136-149.

Vaksberg, G.A. (1995). Fitting the Punishment to the Crime, and Politics Too. In H. Isham (Ed) *Remaking Russia* (pp. 207-217) New York: M.E. Sharpe.

von Mises, L. (1981). *Socialism*. Indianapolis, Liberty Classics.

Wade, R. (1985). The Market for Public Office: Why the Indian State is not Better at Development. *World Development*, 13, 467-497.

Chapter 3

From the Soviet Union to the Russian Federation: An Economy in Transition

Inna Iourkova

Abstract

The history of the transition path of the Russian economy is outlined. Starting with a brief description of the operation of the Soviet-style command economy to set the stage for reform, the process of dismantling the command system both in the last – Gorbachev – years of the Soviet Union and in the early post-Soviet period are then described. This is followed by a discussion of the, often chaotic, management of the economy of the Russian Federation in the later Yeltsin years. This era was characterised by hyperinflation, deflation, debt crises, capital flight, bank failures, rigged privatization, unemployment, wage arrears and general industrial malaise. The economy staggered from one crisis to the next without coming to grips with reform and was lumbered with rising corruption. The final section examines the reforms in the post-Yeltsin period and suggests that the economy has exhibited relative macroeconomic stability – aided by high energy prices – but suggests that significant structural problems remain.

Introduction

The economy based on central planning and command put in place in the Soviet Union in the 1930s remained relatively unaltered "until the system virtually collapsed under simultaneous pressure for change from above and below in the late 1980s,"(Smith, 1993, p.36). To fully understand the challenges presented by the desire to transform the Russian economy into a modern market economy, it is necessary to understand how the command economy operated in the Soviet Union and the role that central planning played in it. Thus, before going on to discuss the challenges and record of the economic reforms put in place in post-Soviet Russia, a brief description of the Soviet era economy is provided.

THE COMMAND ECONOMY AND CENTRAL PLANNING IN THE SOVIET UNION

Each sector of the Soviet economy was carefully monitored by the central planning authority and plans establishing priorities for resource use and allocation drawn up. Lower level state planning authorities added progressively more detail and enterprise specific growth targets. Implementation of these plans was carried out by state enterprises. The enterprises, however, received strict instructions regarding all possible aspects of their activities, including wages, revenue and profit levels. Costs were based on artificial prices established by government fiat.

Planning provided perverse incentives for enterprises to understate their potential to planners so that they could easily achieve their productivity targets. Similarly, estimations of required inputs tended to be exaggerated to ensure that the enterprise received adequate supplies. Inputs were often over-consumed, since excess input, if reported, would alter resource allocations in future plans. Hence, planners were dependent on information provided by enterprises that had a clear incentive not to provide accurate information. Further, central planners never had sufficient information to accurately assess consumer demand.

The monetary and financial governance structures within which socialist enterprises operated further contributed to the long-term decay of the command economy by ignoring basic market principles for inter-enterprise relations. Individual enterprises were not required to ensure that revenues from output sold were sufficient to buy inputs and pay wages – how could they when the state set both input and output prices. Payments between enterprises were reflected on special accounts in the State Bank, the sole bank to administer and maintain financial affairs, and did not bear any relationship to the enterprise's financial reality. The State Bank credited or debited enterprises with the estimated value of outputs supplied or inputs received and had no power to declare an enterprise bankrupt. As a result, Soviet enterprises operated under a "soft budget constraint", whereby, irrespective of demand for the end product, credit was guaranteed to achieve a given plan.

Similarly, consumer demand had no direct impact on the level or structure of investment. Prices remained unchanged between the early 1950s and April 1991, with any shortfall between production cost and output revenues covered by subsidies from the state budget. Relatively low prices for subsidised goods increased demand for these goods, although the authorities did not automatically increase the supply to meet demand at fixed state-set prices. Lack of supply and fixed low prices meant shortages and consumers were forced to hold more savings, relative to income, than they desired. Such involuntary savings resulted in a form of "repressed inflation".

Disequilibria in goods markets were manifest in long line-ups for those wishing to purchase high-demand (mostly light industry) goods at the low "state" price. Further, to satisfy their demand, people had to use black markets, where the same goods were available at much higher so-called "market" prices rather than the "state" prices. Access to any kind of "luxury" was a privilege, which could be exchanged for numerous favours and or monetary bribes. Corruption and nepotism were a way of life.

The all encompassing regulation of market responses to consumer demand was made possible by complete state control over foreign trade that prevented any inflow of imports becoming available to individuals or enterprises. On the other hand, having no demand (or a "soft demand") constraint, Soviet era enterprises did not welcome export additions to their output targets because they would require higher quality specifications to be met and unwanted alterations in product engineering. Soviet era enterprises preferred to concentrate production on low quality goods sold in domestic markets. Soviet exports consisted primarily of raw materials; such as crude oil, gas, and unprocessed goods and gold, rather than sophisticated manufactured goods.

It was, however, necessary to finance a certain level of imports of machinery for the industrial and military sectors, foodstuffs, and consumer goods to compensate for the deficiencies of those available in domestic market. The inability of the Soviet economy to generate the exports required to obtain sufficient imports from western economies led to the realisation among some Soviet official that a deep structural reorganisation would be required before there could be any significant improvement in the economic situation. As Smith (1993, p. 73) predicted; "This could, in turn, considerably extend the period over which large sectors of the population suffer from the cost of the reform process before experiencing any benefits".

It became increasingly clear years before the system collapsed that the command mechanism for resource allocation not only trapped the Soviet consumer in a stagnant environment consisting of low quality products, but had also inhibited technological advancement. The planners had no method for integrating new technology into the economy nor any way to encourage its development. A point was reached when the better performance of capitalist economies could no long be ignored. By the early 1980s the Soviet economy was crying out for fundamental reforms

REFORMS UNDER GORBACHEV

The first phase of reforms, from 1985 through 1987 started with the appointment of Mikhail Gorbachev as the General Secretary of the Communist Party of the Soviet Union (CPSU). The conceptual basis for the reforms in this period, in fact, had been introduced by Yurii Andropov, who was General Secretary from November 1982 till his death on February 9 1984. Andropov's coming to power was welcomed with a sigh of relief after Leonid Brezhnev's "era of stagnation". Chernenko, who immediately preceded Gorbachev as General Secretary, was frequently absent from official functions due to his deteriorating health, which made him unfit to govern effectively much less oversee a major reform of the economy. He died in office on March 10, 1985. The fifty-four year old Gorbachev who succeeded him, started by insisting that the command system was still a viable economic model, albeit with considerable operational deficiencies.

During the crucial first years of Gorbachev's reforms, the main efforts were focussed on such general issues as corruption, nepotism and economic lethargy and sloth. Beyond a number of catchy slogans, however, there was not much that could be linked to a consistent economic reform program. The seriousness and depth of the problems facing the Soviet economy were underestimated by many, and Gorbachev was not an exception. One of the most important goals set by Gorbachev was a focus on the acceleration of economic growth, which required enterprises to achieve higher output with a given supply of inputs. Since there was no quick solution to improve technologies, this declared goal only aggravated existing supply constraints and was not achievable in the short-term simply by trying to use fewer inputs. Gorbachev addressed many of the problems in a superficial manner. Such cosmetic changes, however, often caused deep disturbances within the entire system or sector he was focusing on. Often, he was unwilling to admit, or was not able to foresee, the depth of the problem and the full extent of the changes required.

A prominent feature of the period was an attempt to deal with chronic alcohol abuse through the reduction in production and availability of alcohol. This policy was targeted at increasing labour productivity and the elimination of drinking in the workplace. Perhaps, one the most serious consequence of this campaign was that thousands of hectares of vineyards in Georgia and Moldova were destroyed. "Symptomatically enough, both Georgia and Moldova were among the first of the Soviet republics to proclaim their sovereignty" (Hedlund, 1999, p.83). The anti-alcohol campaign resulted in the loss of a major source of budget revenue, increased excess demand in retail markets, and was effectively abandoned in 1988.

The second phase of the Gorbachev reforms, from 1988 through 1990, was concerned with the reorganisation of the planning system, leaving enterprises to make day-to-day decisions while central authorities were left to concentrate on long-term plans. Simultaneously, the creation of a competitive environment was recognised to be important, and the non-state sector comprised of private firms, cooperatives, and foreign owned and joint-venture firms started to expand.

Gorbachev's proposals were not restricted to rebuilding the enterprise system; they incorporated changes to banking sector, foreign trade, taxation, the organisation of labour allocation, property rights, and retail and wholesale prices. These are dealt with in turn in what follows.

Enterprises

The most important feature during this period was the adoption of the State Enterprise Law. The activity of an enterprise was now expected to be based on the central principles of self accounting, self management and self financing through an independent financial institution. The enterprises now had to make decisions about their assets, as well as having to cover their variable costs with sales revenue (self accounting). The system of subsidies and investments as "free gifts" from the state was replaced by the bank loans on which interest was to be paid (self financing). The self management principle was intended to weaken the principle of enterprise's subordination to a ministerial authority, and provided workers the right to elect managers, supervisors and foremen, who would become responsible to workers for enterprise net income (profit). Workers' wages were to be directly connected to the enterprise's profits, and determined at the enterprise level.

Pricing

Potentially, pricing was the most critical area to reform. Under the condition of excess demand, liberalisation of the system of fixed and highly subsidised state retail prices was potentially a highly inflationary process. Gorbachev suggested retail prices remain centrally determined (but subject to increase) while the system of wholesale prices was replaced with "contract prices" determined by negotiation between enterprises and their customers. To mitigate hostility to price increases, Gorbachev promised that living standards and purchasing power of the population would be preserved by an equivalent increase in a per capita payment from the central budget.

Initially, the introduction of "contract prices" was considered as a tool to create an incentive for enterprises to switch their production to "new goods", (i.e. higher quality goods) by improving technologies. In practice, enterprises often adjusted their existing production mix to more profitable goods with higher prices without any major changes to technologies. This resulted in the withdrawl of "non-profitable" goods (such as matches, soap, socks and underwear) from the market, and contributed to the rapid growth of illegal secondary markets for these goods.

New enterprise managers appointed by workers paid higher wages following profit increases (while retail prices remained fixed) from production of "new" high-priced goods. These reforms, on one hand, resulted in a rapid increase in the rouble surplus held by consumers and an aggravation of suppressed inflation as well as an erosion of confidence in the Soviet currency. In order to get rid of roubles, consumers bought almost anything that became available, hoping to exchange their purchases for what they actually desired at some later period. More expensive items, such as TV sets, washing machines, stereos, irons, food, and cheap "non-profitable goods" (if one was lucky enough to find them), were bought in large quantities as a hedge against future shortages.

In an attempt to deal with food shortages and to ensure provision of food to the population on a constant and regular basis, a system of coupons was introduced. This system was not new and had been used by the Soviets during 1980s mostly for agricultural goods (bread, butter, sugar, poultry and meats). Monthly and three month coupons were distributed among households.[10] Further, as the "state" winter food supply in Soviet grocery shops consisted of dirty half rotten basic vegetables grown domestically, and little fruit, almost every Russian family had to support itself by cultivating extensive gardens, often located at little cottages or "dacha's", to ensure a fresh supply of potatoes, carrots, onions, cabbages, etc. Large "dacha" communities started to grow up around every Russian city during this period.[11]

Banking

Inflationary pressure was aggravated by banking system reforms, which started in 1988 with division of the Central Bank into 5 state-owned banks (departments), each with its own specialisation – agriculture, construction, foreign trade, savings and investments. In addition, 1988 saw the beginning of the commercial and co-operative banking system in Russia.

The idea behind the banking reforms was to loosen central state control over cash and credit but, in fact, these reforms just aggravated inflationary pressure. Commercial and co-operative banks initiated a poorly founded expansion of credit by accumulating excess liquidity from one enterprise and lending it to another with cash problems. There was always a guarantee that the loan would be repaid: banks knew that the enterprise would not be

---

[10] The denomination of these coupons restricted consumers to buying, for example, 2 kg of sugar per family member per month, or 2 kg of butter, or 2 bottles of vodka, 2 pieces of soap and so on.
[11] Such unreported activities of the Russian population and the black market turnover seriously affected any economic statistics issued during the Soviet era.

allowed to go bankrupt by the state. Enterprises with cash flow problems managed pay wage increases to their workers using funds lent to them by the banking system.

Joint Venture Enterprises

Major difficulties were faced by joint ventures with market economy firms from the moment they were allowed to be established on the territory of the USSR. At the first stage of joint venture creation an approval of the USSR Council of Ministers had to be obtained. The enterprise then was detached from Soviet planning process and, as a result, it experienced major difficulties in obtaining inputs from Soviet suppliers, and selling goods in Soviet markets. The further legal restrictions and meddling by Soviet authorities clearly indicated to western companies that the primary reason for allowing joint ventures was to stimulate hard currency earnings for the state budget, and not to satisfy the domestic market or to create competition for domestic producers.

Many of the major western companies operating in the Soviet market were interested in expanding sales to the Soviet Union, but not in establishing production facilities in the Soviet Union for exports to market economies. The lack of control over prices and quality of inputs and outputs meant that Soviet joint ventures offered western partners a far less easily controlled and less competitive environment than wholly owned subsidiaries in, for example, many developing countries.

Foreign Trade

In 1989 export and import licenses were instituted for a wide range of goods, and by the end of 1989 the new legislation resulted in a major expansion of the number of organisations empowered to conduct foreign trade. The efficient decentralisation of foreign trade required that enterprises be able to make a comparison between domestic production costs and world market prices. Arbitrary differences between the structure of Soviet relative prices and world market prices meant that a single exchange rate could not be used to evaluate the profitability of imports and exports, which resulted in a complicated system of differentiated valuation coefficients. This measure was introduced, in part, to address the problem of the artificial exchange rate that existed for the rouble and not to deal with the irrational relative values that the long-term use of domestic prices established by government fiat produced.[12]

The final stage of Soviet era reforms began in 1991. This round of reforms started with "Pavlov's reform", named after the Prime Minister who introduced it. This was a populist move based on a general belief that large denomination bank notes were not earned legally and had to be taken out of the monetary overhang. This strategy, however, turned out to be a very unpopular decision since many pensioners and ordinary people also suffered an arbitrary confiscation, having built their savings in high-denominated notes. The measure had no effect on the economy, because almost all savings ended up being converted into smaller denominated notes.

---

[12] For more details on the issues of exchange rates introduced in 1990 see Smith (1993, p.135).

Secondly, an increase in producer and agricultural prices at the beginning of January 1991 required an increase in subsidies to consumers. By April 1991, retail prices were increased by 60 percent, but the official level of increased compensation only accounted for 85 percent of the expected increase in expenditure resulting from the price reform. Increased tax collection was not sufficient to match the level of compensation required: the overall effect on the budget was, therefore, negative.

Before 1991, inflation was low but the large wage increases arising from attempts to reform state-owned enterprises from 1988 to 1990 created a large monetary overhang. This overhang was eliminated in the beginning of price reform, as average real wages fell back to their 1987 level in the second quarter of 1991. Retail prices remained more or less stable after April 1991, but real wages rose again and by the end of the year more than doubled compared to their 1987 level. As worker's productivity did not grow nearly as much as the increase in rouble wages, excess demand continued to expand. An increasing rouble surplus aggravated the erosion of domestic confidence in the Soviet currency. In attempt to get rid of their roubles, jewellery, rags, extra useless TV sets, household appliances, anything that could be stored was bought (Hedland, 1999). Western experts observing empty shelves in Soviet shops attributed the situation to a production failure rather than to a monetary phenomenon. During winter of 1991-1992, the Russian population was surprised by a large operation called "Food Aid", as rumours of coming food shortages in the Soviet Union were spread in the West.

The existence of a large monetary overhang allowed a much higher level of monetary financing in the Soviet economy than in a market economy where consumers can easily escape inflation by diversifying their portfolio so that only their monetary holdings will be affected. In the case of Soviet Union in the second half of the 1980s, large monetary holdings could not be avoided. As a result, the ratio of financial assets to GDP rose from 30 percent in the mid-1980s to 45 percent by 1990.

Other factors contributing to the deteriorating economic situation in 1991 included a decline in exports of 40 percent in US dollar terms. Imports declined approximately 80 percent. At the end of 1991, foreign-exchange deposits were frozen.[13] The only way to respond to such a catastrophic situation was to reduce the budget deficit and to end the repressed inflation by liberalising prices.

Many of Gorbachev's policies were introduced by combining mutually inconsistent individual reforms into one single package. Many Soviet economists argued that reforms should be delayed until the next planning period that was to begin in 1991, since the reform proposals were in direct conflict with 1986 five-year plan for accelerated investment and output and where the production potential of enterprises had already been determined. "Thus, elements of new system had to co-exist with parts of the old central planning system, which together lead to a failure in the central control over basic magnitudes such as the money supply, the budget balance, the balance between supply and demand for consumption, and ... balance of payments." (Smith, 1993, p.101). In the end, the reforms were "too little, too late" and the deteriorating economic situation contributed to the ouster of the Soviet regime and Gorbachev.

---

[13] See more detailed analysis in Granville (1995, p.17).

REFORMS UNDER YELTSIN

Gorbachev was the last General Secretary of the Communist Party and the last President of the Soviet Union. Besides his inability to foresee the significance of the economic change required, to the greatest disappointment of the Russian democratic forces, Gorbachev invested all his political capital in keeping the Communist Party in power. He was no longer popular with the Russian people by 1989. A small group of senior Communist Party officials, headed by one of those closest to Gorbachev, attempted to take over the country in August 1991. They isolated Gorbachev for three days at a secluded resort. While the coup the failed, Gorbachev had lost his power base. Boris Yeltsin was able to secure the presidential power while Gorbachev remained General Secretary of the failing Communist Party. On December 21, 1991 eleven of the fifteen constituent Soviet republics agreed to the formation of a Commonwealth of Independent States (CIS) (Georgia and three Baltic republics stayed out), the Soviet Union became a history. The Communist Party was removed from power ending the last vestiges of Gorbachev's regime. The Russian Federation, as the largest of the new post-Soviet States, became the new regional power and the focus of economic reforms.

The early post-Soviet era was characterised by myths surrounding Boris Yeltsin, the Russian leader who dared to stand on a tank and defy the August 1991 "putschists". Yeltsin launched radical economic reform in 1992 under Yegor Gaidar's program, and its anti-communism stance complemented his image as a liberal reformer.

According to Hedlund (1999, p. 101): "Thus it was time for Russia to step forth, outwardly at least freed from both communists and Soviet power. For Boris Yeltsin, this meant moving from destruction to construction. Given the prominence of Russia within the CIS it was largely for him to decide on the future course.

"Russia First", the 1992 Gaidar Period

By choosing the economic program of a young economist, Yegor Gaidar, Yeltsin put an end to all talk about reforming the Soviet economy. Yeltsin's choice was based on establishing a clear priority in political power rather than the question of further economic development. An alternative, "Yabloko" ("An Apple"), was proposed by a prominent Russian economist, Yavlinskii, and his team. This program was believed to be a more sophisticated and comprehensive economic plan, which supported the preservation of some elements of the centralised Soviet structure. Gaidar pushed the strategy "Russia first", which better suited Yeltsin political need for a break with the past.

Ashland (1997, p.46) noted: "… the Yeltsin-Gaidar cabinet never published any clear formulation of the government program. ...(but) only made general statements in …public presentations. Indeed, the (comprehensive) concept (for economic reforms) was drafted by Gaidar's team just before its nomination to government."

The policy introduced by the Gaidar's team focused on the liberalisation of economic activity and dismantling of the remnants of command system of resource allocation. In 1992, changes to the Soviet system began with wide ranging price liberalisation and internal convertibility of the rouble as well as new policies encouraging private entrepreneurial activity and foreign investment. During this year a classic two-tier banking system was also introduced, and a program of mass privatisation of state property was started.

Price liberalisation started on January 2, 1992, although price controls remained on food and energy despite Gaidar's determination to free all prices. The resulting huge subsidies to these sectors were a major cause of a continuing budget deficit. "For example, housing rents – which typically represents a large share of consumer expenditure in market economies – were controlled and would thus be given an artificially low weight in such a calculation," (Granville, 1995, p.19).

Price liberalisation triggered inflation, which at times bordered on hyperinflation, and assisted the Russian government with its budgetary shortfalls. Some statistics show that during 1992 the inflation tax was about 10-15 per cent of GDP. Bank accounts in Sberbank, the only state savings bank in the Soviet Union, were effectively expropriated, with insignificant compensation from the government and lifetime savings were reduced to nothing, which was particularly painful for the retired population with un-indexed pensions. People, who had enough roubles in their accounts to pay cash for a new car two month ago, could not buy a pair of shoes for the same amount of money after the inflation. Thus, ordinary wage earners and savers, whose standards of living dramatically decreased, became the main losers during this period.

Inflationary expectations were built into any delayed payments. A series of bank failures followed because the government had lost the confidence of Russian savers. This left the Russian economy without a major source of credit and investments, and this market failure remains an important economic constraint on Russian development.

A flight from rouble began when current account convertibility for residents was formally introduced in November 1992. Negative real interests rates further discouraged households from saving money in Sberbank and encouraged dollar deposits. With the crisis in the banking system people stopped using banking services and started to save dollars at home as a hedge against inflation.

Liberalisation of the exchange rate and foreign trade began in July 1992 when the Central Bank of Russia introduced a unified floating exchange rate with 125.26 roubles to the dollar initially quoted. The number of exporters began to grow. Almost everyone who wanted to acquire the necessary permission to export goods could obtain it – exporting was subject to licensing. Another source of bribes and corruption was the result. Ashland (1995 p.65) has noted that, "... any obstacle to economic activity, especially one which assumes the existence of a discretionary choice, will be circumvented in Russia, and therefore this country has to be more liberal than any other". Even with the number of exporters increasing, "because of export quotas, exports fell in 1992 from US$51 bn in 1991 to US$41.6 bn ... despite the sharp depreciation of the exchange rate," (Granville, 1995, p.90).[14]

The problem of firms being arrears in their payments was not new. It had already emerged in 1987 when many enterprises started to deliver products against payments guaranteed by the state at a later date. The introduction of hard budget constraints in 1992

---

[14] Any statistics should be treated with caution, especially those where the exchange rate is involved because of its instability and the general inability to measure the true reflection of the parity relation to world prices. One often finds significant statistical discrepancies when referring to different sources. These statistics were sometimes officially reported to please IMF in hopes obtaining additional credits; sometimes they were reported to show the government's performance in a better light. Many types of unreported economic activity were also growing very rapidly.

took place almost "overnight" but was not taken seriously by state enterprises. The consequences of the hard budget constraint were hardly understood and bankruptcy legislation was not adopted. Enterprises simply continued to function through a "financial system" of using mutual non-interest credits, i.e. non-payment of their bills.

Enterprises, unable to pay their suppliers, managed to pay and even increase wages to their workers by borrowing from private commercial banks, often owned by enterprise's directors. Commercial banking was in its infancy, and was fully supported by government policies through access to the cheap credit from the Central Bank. Military enterprises were unable to obtain credit since there was little demand for their outputs. Thus, they could pay neither suppliers nor their workers, although they maintained production as usual.

From a macroeconomic point of view, the main stimulus for inter-enterprise arrears was the combination of relatively easy credit in the non-cash enterprise sector and a cash shortage in the household sector. In January 1992, the Russian government was already behind in paying wages, pensions and benefits, and by June 1992 these arrears rose by more than ten fold.[15] The cash shortage was reflected in the building up of arrears by the government. With the purchasing power of rouble falling, additional credits to enterprises only further increased inventories.

Attempt were also made to reform the monetary, financial and banking systems. At the beginning of 1992, each of the 15 newly independent states of the former Soviet Union had its own central bank issuing money without co-ordination. Further, the former Soviet republics were still using credits from the Russian budget, although they failed to pass on taxes to the central government.[16]

Subsidies continued to be the largest item of government spending in 1992. The Central Bank still issued credits to commercial banks, the Ministry of Finance, and to the other governments in the rouble zone. There were also import subsidies due to the large depreciation of the rouble. There were also interest-rate subsidies designed for state enterprises, since they undertook a large proportion of social expenditure for their workers (housing, kindergartens, medical care, etc.) as well as providing employment insurance. These interest subsidies were channelled through commercial banks by the Central Bank of Russia (CBR). These, so-called, 'directed credits' did not appear in the budget and were financed by money creation. The justification was lowering the unemployment rate. In total, financial transfers to state enterprises amounted to almost 45 percent of GDP in 1992.[17]

Another general feature of the early post-Soviet reforms was that many enterprises had their own pocket commercial banks, which greatly enhanced the wealth of their owners.[18] Hedlund (1999, p. 163) suggests that; "Creating ones own bank was, in the circumstances of the time, a way of softening one's budget constraint and escaping policy makers' attempt to impose market discipline on firms." By the end of 1991, there were already about 2000 small commercial banks, which opened a back door to the CBR through which subsidies to industry

---

[15] See statistics in Granville (1995, p.48)
[16] Examples of contradictory policy decisions can be found in Granville (1995, p.p.45-46) and discussion on the government-central bank relationship in Hedlund (1999, p.162-165).
[17] See Granville (1995, p.66-68).
[18] They were making tremendous profits during high inflationary periods when the CBR refinance rate was much lower than the inflation rate. Another source of income for banks included speculative games on the exchange rate markets. The CBR credits were not passed immediately to the point of designation: instead, the US dollars were bought, held for a few days, and sold as the rouble depreciated rapidly.

were continued. The pocket banks applied for credits at subsidised rates from the Central Bank, and then passed this money to their owners.

A major tax avoidance problem also manifest itself in 1992. According to Granville (1995, p. 49); "In principle, with high inflation, taxes are simply reduced by delaying collection on receivables or by using inter-enterprise arrears to avoid the commercial banking system, which was responsible for collecting taxes. If delays lower tax collection and lower tax collection increases money creation, then inflation will result, which ratifies the expectation of inflation that starts the process." Another way to evade taxes was, of course, not to pay them at all or not to report all the enterprise's activities.[19]

Widespread privatisation of large and medium size enterprises started with the distribution of shares of state enterprises free of charge, or at a minimum charge through vouchers. The idea behind privatisation was to transform enterprises into public joint companies, allowing the free sales of shares. The first tranche of vouchers was distributed amongst the population in the forth quarter of 1992. Anatoly Chubais[20], the 'father' of the Russian privatisation, stated: "The GKI (The State Committee for State Property Management) estimate is about 40-50 per cent of the property in Russia can be privatised by means of vouchers." (as quoted in Ashlund, 1995, p.73).

The cost of the 1992 reforms turned out to be very high. First, a very deep recession occurred (GDP dropped by 14.5%). Second, the country entered a phase of extremely high inflation. Consumer prices increased by 26.1 times, and the real supply of money diminished considerably, which is a characteristic of a period of hyperinflation. Third, living standards went down dramatically: household expenditures in real terms were cut by 31.6% (Nekipelov, 1999 p.1).

As Gaidar notes, (quoted in Granville, 1995, p.103):

We began the reforms in a very interesting situation when you could have listed many absent preconditions, making reforms impossible to implement at the time. I myself could have given a perfect explanation of why in 1992 the reforms should not have been launched. There was no stable support in the parliament; there were no normal functioning institutions of governance (the army, customs, the police) - they were staggering from a crisis of power that had begun in the earlier 1990s. There were sixteen central banks instead of one; there were no traditions of private enterprise; there was no strong private sector as in Poland. There wasn't a kopeck to be had of hard currency or gold reserves, nor the opportunity to attract free investment from the international financial market. But aside from all that, we could not wait any longer. We could not just keep doing nothing, or keep explaining why it was impossible to do anything.

The Chernomyrdin Reforms (1993-1998)

The second stage of reforms under Yeltsin started in the beginning of 1993 and lasted until March, 1998 when Victor Chernomyrdin, a representative of the arms industry, became prime minister of Russia. The main reforms during this period entailed, first and foremost, the

---

[19] This partly explains the poor reliability of output statistics.
[20] Chubais was Minister of Privatization from November, 1991 until November, 1994 as well as Deputy Prime-Minister, after that he was the Head of President Yeltsin's administration. He was one of the key political figures during these times of change.

creation of the non-government sector of the economy through voucher privatisation in 1993-1994 and the institution loans-for-share 'auctions' in 1996. Further, direct loans from the CBR to the government were replaced by borrowing from the market as government securities started to trade and the stock market emerged. A floating exchange rate regime was also introduced during this period. The fight against inflation became the main concern for the Chernomyrdin's government, in part in order to satisfy the IMF to obtain international credits. All of these initiatives helped set the stage for the economic catastrophe of August 1998, when the rouble devaluation exceeded 200 per cent overnight followed by a default on the government debt.

During the previous stage of privatisation a substantial volume of state property was transferred into private hands, which represented a transfer of wealth to a rather large group of new owners. This was, of course, an anticipated outcome being a price to pay in order to create a private ownership sector in the economy. Privatisation during the earlier period had one specific feature: auctions were often run by local authorities where the buyers were agreed upon beforehand through widespread bribery.

Privatisation during Chernomyrdin's tenure was linked to the rapidly deteriorating financial position of the government, and resulted in the creation of a special program of "loans-for-shares" auctions in 1995. Officially, the intent of the "loans-for-shares" auctions was that the winner of the auction would grant a credit to the government for a period of three years at the bank rate plus 0.5 per cent. The government, in turn, reserved the right to repay credits and thus to reclaim the collateral. It was specifically stated that there was to be more than one bidder at each auction, and that there was to be a broad competition between domestic and foreign investors. In fact, the number of investors was often limited to a small group of very large banks. In two auctions foreign investors were explicitly excluded, in five auctions there was only one bidder. The scandalous nature of these deals was uncovered when Russia's independent accounting office undertook an investigation, revealing massive fraud.

Peter Reddaway (quoted in Hedlund, 1999, p.165) summarised the investigation's findings: "Not only were the assets undervalued and the winners predetermined, but the government actually deposited its own funds in the banks that won the auctions. So the banks made the loans using the government's own money, and the whole transaction was, for the Kremlin, not a major infusion of cash but a net loss. Since it was obvious at the moment of transaction that the government would not be able or willing to pay back loans, in practice the collateral was forfeit at the moment of transaction…". Following the scandals, loans-for-shares auctions were temporary discontinued.

In 1997 the focus of government reforms changed concentrating on the restructuring of the country's many monopolies. In effect, the result was often limited to enforcement of tax payments and the government exerting indirect control over firms.

At the start of the transition process, Russia was not a member of IMF, and thus was not eligible for IMF assistance. In 1993, a "Systematic Transformation Facility" was initiated by the IMF in order to facilitate lending to post-communist economies by offering softer rules. In May 1993, the IMF reached an agreement with Russian representatives on a program of stabilisation, and on July 1, 1993 Russia received a transfer of $1.5 billion.[21]

To satisfy the IMF requirements, Russia had to agree to enforce unrealistic or difficult to achieve targets. According to Hedlund (1999, pp. 169-170); "So keen is the fund to help

---

[21] See Hedlund, 1999, p.167 for more details.

Russia that it often turns a blind eye when its supposedly stringent lending conditions are infringed on... (S)ome western advisers have come to act more as advocates than analysts. Once they give advice they have a vested interest in that reform and therefore are reluctant to be critical of the results. These really are textbook illustrations of the problem of moral hazard...".

By the end of 1995, the IMF had finally managed to put an effective break on the Russian printing presses and financing through money creation was greatly curtailed. Inflation came down and the rouble stabilised.

During the Chernomyrdin reforms, the Central Bank of Russia assumed a more independent status as a result of a new budget law. Lending to the government in 1995 was significantly reduced. However, the role of the CBR was not restricted to solely monitoring interest rates and money supply as is common in modern market economies. The new budget law, in fact, changed only the form of acquiring the CBR credits from direct credits to borrowing through secondary market for government securities. Hence, the CBR was still able to use credit to cover up half of the budget deficit. Since operating through the secondary market was more costly than direct borrowing, the period was marked by an increase in the cost of government debt management.

Without direct injections from the government and a sharp increase in reserve requirements, commercial banks began to face major difficulties. Beginning in January 1995, the CBR raised its refinance rate to 200 percent, which by the end of the year fell to 160 percent with inflation having fallen to 3.2 percent in December 1995. Already in May, the CBR credits to commercial banks were practically zero, and in spite of the high revenues obtained from the securities market, with low inflation, and a stable rouble, which altogether stopped easy speculative gains for commercial banks, the banking sector as a whole was depressed.

Government borrowing could not make up the revenue shortfall. The Ministry of Finance started issuing promissory notes known as KOs. KOs were used as subsidies and credits to local authorities. Local authorities, in turn, issued their own promissory notes to local enterprises leading to *money surrogates (vekselya)* being issues. The problem was that local authorities eventually had to accept KOs as a payment of taxes, which only aggravated their budgetary problem.

As a result, the Russian government eventually sacrificed tax discipline in order to gain more financial leeway during major political campaigns. Further, very substantial tax exemptions were granted for political reasons. As Hedlund (1999, pp.210-211 noted: "It was not primarily a question of refusal to pay taxes, but of conscious government actions designed to allow tax breaks and/or tax deferrals... Yeltsin's struggle against communist leader Gennadii Zuganov (and the war in Chechnya) required substantial handouts from the budget, handouts that could not be remotely covered by current revenues."

Meanwhile, many newly private firms were keeping two sets of books and not reporting the bulk of their business activities to the tax authorities. Taxes were very high, and bribing tax service workers to defer payments was much more convenient and, of course, less costly for firms. Tax service workers, who were paid out of the budget, were happy to receive such handouts in addition to their poor and not regularly paid salaries.

After Yeltsin had been successfully re-elected in July 1996, the IMF finally felt it necessary to voice its dissatisfaction with the poor performance of the Russian tax system and eventually withheld a monthly tranche of US$10.1 billion in March 1997. As a result, it appeared that reported tax collections during the second quarter of 1997 improved significantly rising to 85 percent of the target. A closer look, however, showed more than half of those payments were in money surrogates. This paved the way for a general economic collapse in 1998.

Arrears in payments continued to be a major problem. While the budgets for 1992 and 1993 were approved at the end of the respective years, the 1994 budget was approved in June of that year. Showing some improvement, the budget for 1995 was approved in February 1995 and the budget for 1996 in December 1995. Then the budget process began to break down. In the budget law for 1997 it was stated that if tax revenue during any quarter were to fall below 90 percent of target, the government would have to submit a revised budget. In the first quarter of 1997, tax revenue fell below 60 percent. Massive spending cuts had to be made. Meanwhile, total outstanding unpaid wages had grown to a stunning 50 trillion roubles. The government owed about one fifth of this sum, the rest was owed by enterprises.

On the other side, Russian employees continued to work every day having not been paid for months or years. The population was simply accustomed to the idea of being dependent on the state and this mentality was hard to change. Similar to the idea of "suppressed inflation", there was also a "suppressed unemployment" in the Soviet era, whereby everyone had to be employed. This system made everyone "equal" and guaranteed a small source of income, enough to survive at least, for everyone who participated in the inefficient "employment game". The handouts, called salary were centrally distributed to every single citizen. This system continued in the post-communist era. Thus, the workforce largely continued to function as usual, hoping to be paid some time in the future.

In addition to the tradition of relying on the state for support, it also became virtually impossible to switch jobs for some professional people employed in sectors which remained fully under state control, such as schools, universities, health care facilities, mining and utilities. They had too large a stake in the payments owing. Worst of all was pension arrears. With the value of pensions eroded by inflation and saving having been wiped out, when the meagre pensions were not paid on time many of Russia's elderly population were literally forced onto the streets to beg for money.

In the autumn of 1994, US dollar deposits started to offer a higher return that the state treasury bills (GKO). To attract investors, the government had to offer yields up to 500 percent per annum in real terms. The dollar doubled in value against the rouble every six months. Despite declining inflation and a high CBR refinance rate, inflationary expectations remained very high due to developing arrears on public sector payments, fiscal policy and expansion of credits by the CBR. The "Black Tuesday" of October 11, 1994 was a perfect illustration of how monetary factors affect the exchange rate: the 27 percent fall in the exchange rate in a single day was the result of an excessive increase in M2 to finance the agriculture and defence sectors.

Following the events of October, 1994, the Russian authorities turned to a solution that lay between adopting a fixed and a floating exchange rate regime by choosing the interest rate peg "corridor" regime, in which the interest rate remained, in fact, fixed and the exchange rate was allowed to fluctuate insignificantly within the chosen numerical interval assigned by the CBR for a certain period, usually a year. The exchange rate climbed constantly, despite attempts by the CBR to keep it down.

Interestingly, Granville (1995, p.97) predicted:

Advocates of a fixed peg argue that the adoption of an official parity prevents the monetary authorities from allowing excessive growth of the money supply, thereby imposing a degree of financial discipline. This discipline is absent if a country's currency floats freely and the domestic inflation rate is free to deviate permanently from that of its trading partners. Under a fixed exchange rate regime, the monetary authorities are committed to certain parity, while credit expansion is restricted by the availability of international reserves and the capacity to borrow internationally. If the authorities do not control the expansion of credit and therefore the way in which the budget deficit is financed, they will have to devalue and so loose credibility, thus compromising the whole stabilisation attempt. In the context of loose credit policies, an exchange rate target would inevitably end in a succession of financial crises followed by devaluation. This would introduce a high degree of instability into the behaviour of the real exchange rate. This instability would in turn generate macroeconomic uncertainty and disrupt trade and investment flow.

All the efforts in 1995-1998 to prevent rouble devaluation and attempts to maintain the exchange rate corridor were dashed in August 1998.

The Russian government began issuing domestic bonds, denominated in hard currency in 1992. Although they were an important source of revenue, they did not affect the way in which the domestic money market was functioning. It was the introduction of rouble denominated domestic debt instruments that changed the money market dramatically.

The first three-month treasury bills were introduced in May 1993, six-month GKO followed in October, but the turning point arrived in June 1995 when long-term government bonds (OFZ) with a quarterly coupon were introduced. The period of inflationary financing was practically over by the summer of 1995. Those who had already made a fortune on currency speculation began moving their capital into the security market, where yields were rising rapidly. The impact of such a transformation would be every bit as destructive as that under the previous era of high inflation.

In October 1995 the OECD published its first report on Russia suggesting that the economy was improving. Monthly inflation was brought down during the year, from 17.8 per cent to merely 3.8 per cent in December. The federal budget deficit was reduced from 11.2 per cent of GDP in 1994, to an acceptable 3.7 per cent. There was, however, a problem that only a few recognised through taking a closer look at how the "improvements" were achieved. As a result of market interventions to hold down the decline in the international value of the rouble, a substantial increase of money supply in 1995 was observed. With the CBR credits cut, and with the market now monopolised by large commercial banks, the government willingly entered into a vicious spiral, in which larger and larger issues of securities at higher and higher yield were made. The reason behind this development was that all receipts from the sales of securities went straight into an expanding black hole in the budget meaning that no money was still available for current payments, much less payment arrears. The expenditure required for this type of debt servicing was rapidly increasing but not accounted for in the budget.

It was becoming obvious that the system of borrowing, having acquired a life of its own, went far beyond any macroeconomic rationality. In the short term, the government was winning and the commercial banks were winning, but not in the long term, and not the financial system as a whole. With annual inflation of 40 per cent in 1996, the GKO annual yield varied from 60 per cent to 150 per cent, while yield on long-term OFZs increased from 150 percent to 600 percent.

Hoping to change this situation, the CBR opened the government securities market to non-residents in 1996. As a result, gross inflow of foreign investments in Russia equalled US$46 billion in 1997, which brought a reduction in nominal GKO yield to 26 percent, or down to 15 percent in real rouble terms. Transformation of the national economy into a hostage of foreign speculative capital turned out to be another side consequence of this policy.

During a single year the foreign exchange position of the Russian commercial banks radically changed: their foreign liabilities exceeded considerably their foreign assets, which made them extremely vulnerable to a possible outflow of short-term foreign capital from the country and a resultant drop in the rouble exchange rate. A sharp reduction in yields forced a wave of bankruptcies among the banks, which had become dependant on revenues from the securities market. On the other hand, maintaining the pyramid game would force everything else out of the financial markets, making a crash inevitable.

In the autumn of 1997 the idyllic picture of economic stabilisation began to fall into pieces. Rescuing the rouble became the main goal of the Central Bank. To accomplish this task the Central Bank redeemed foreign exchange reserves and raised the refinancing rate. As a result, high interest rates prevented money from flowing into the real sector of the economy, and the domestic state debt crisis assumed catastrophic proportions. A panic flight from the rouble and rouble denominated assets continued. Further, the world oil prices collapsed meaning the loss of one of Russia's major sources of foreign exchange.

In March 1998, Chernomyrdin was asked to step down. Sergei Kirienko, a 35-year-old former banker and energy minister, was appointed as prime minister. Yeltsin justified the move by saying he needed a new team to boost Russia's flagging reforms. Political analysts expected Kirienko to assemble a Cabinet dominated by pro-reform professionals.

The Kirienko interlude (March 1998 – August 1998)

Kirienko recognised the critical situation and attempted to restore fiscal equilibrium through a set of measures defined in "The program for Stabilisation of the Economy and Finances" which was approved by the Russian government in July 1998. An unprecedented degree of financial assistance from international organisations and Japan was requested. However, it was impossible to make market participants believe in the ability of the authorities to save the situation, since many of them had finally come to realise the true nature of the pyramid games that had been played in the securities market. Outflows of capital belonging to non-residents and flight of residents from the rouble and rouble-denominated assets continued apace.

In the night between August 16 and 17, 1998, financial collapse became a reality. The government defaulted on its GKOs and the rouble depreciated sharply by 200-300 percent in the next few weeks. All major commercial banks found themselves in default, the payment system collapsed and tax revenues dried up. Expectations were that Russia would either devalue the rouble or default on its debt, and the Russian government chose to do both. A three-month moratorium on short-term debt was announced. A little later the foreign exchange corridor was sharply broadened, and the rouble was allowed to float freely. Prices immediately rose sharply and continued climbing following the declining rouble exchange rate and a consumer panic.

Although it was obvious that the last years of reforms had lead to such a failure in the system, and not the short attempt of Kirienko's new team to prevent it from happening, following the August events Kirienko was asked to step down. After Yeltsin attempted to have Chernomirdin come back as a prime minister in August 1998, we can only guess if Kirienko's appointment was only a planned action in the Kremlin's political games, or a true attempt to find the "right" reforms to stave off the impending economic catastrophe.

The Primakov Government (August 1998- May 1999)

Yeltsin eventually chose the 68-year-old former foreign minister and intelligence chief Yevgeniy Primakov as a compromise candidate after his previous choice for prime minister, Viktor Chernomyrdin, was rejected twice by the Communist-dominated Duma. In contrast with past governments, which had largely ignored the State Duma, the government of Prime Minister Primakov was dramatically different from the cabinets assembled by his predecessors Chernomyrdin and Kirienko. Primakov expanded the political diversity of the cabinet including representatives from the Communist Party among many others.

The Primakov government pursued a series of *ad hoc* measures rather than a coherent overall economic strategy, and together with the CBR, managed to prevent a return to hyperinflation. Primakov's measures to improve the economic situation included a fight against corruption and an extremely restrictive federal budget for 1999. It also included cuts in imports, while import-substituting domestic production was promoted. On this foundation, beginning in October 1998, a positive industrial production growth on a month to month basis was reported, and from April 1999, the economy achieved a positive growth level compared to the same period of the previous year.

There were also costs that could not be avoided. The policy pursued by Primakov's government was accompanied by significant decline in the standard of living. Maintaining a system of payments and preventing the banking system from collapsing totally was very expensive for the government: numerous commercial banks, which by any normal criteria had gone bankrupt were allowed to function as usual. There was also a sharp decline in government expenditures and a contraction in government services. In spite of the hardships imposed, Primakov's approach to stabilising the economy received grudging support among the Russian population.

The Stepashin Government (May 1999 – August 1999)

Sergei Stepashin, a forty-seven year old former Interior Minister, continued the economic course that had been agreed with IMF and World Bank and pursued by the Chernomyrdin and Kirienko governments. Stepashin stressed the need to push laws through the Duma to meet the IMF's conditions for the promised multibillion-dollar credit. The requirements included raising gasoline and alcohol taxes, postponing a reduction of the valued-added tax, and forcing insolvent large banks into bankruptcy. Like Primakov, Stepashin continued to struggle with "economic crime" promising to strip banking licenses from a group of banks, which he accused of illegally moving capital out of Russia while defaulting on depositors and creditors. Stepashin stressed that he would work to make sure that criminal elements did not gain power through legislative or executive elections.

In June 1999, Prime Minister Stepashin announced that Russia's economic recovery had begun earlier than forecasted. Industrial output increased 1.5 percent during the first five months of the year, the rouble stabilised, and the monthly inflation rate was less than one percent. He also noted that foreign investors were now returning. In the same month, *Trud*, one of the most respected economic newspapers in Russia, reported that industrial output in May 1999 jumped 6.1 percent compared with the same month the previous year, The average wage in May 1999 amounted to 1,465 rubles (US$60) a month, which in terms of real purchasing power represented a decline of more than one third relative to the period prior to the collapse of August 1998.

The Russian stock market performed extremely well in the summer of 1999, which was attributed by westerners to the departure of Prime Minister Yevgeniy Primakov's leftist cabinet. Unemployment rose to 10.44 million as of early June, 1999, which was a 26 percent hike over the same period the previous year and a seven percent increase since January 1999. Almost fifteen percent of the country's economically active population was unemployed. Meanwhile, the number of people officially registered as unemployed with the State Employment Service fell by more than seven percent in June 1999 compared with the previous year.

President Yeltsin fired Prime Minister Stepashin and the entire Cabinet in August 1999, the fourth time in seventeen months he replaced the country's government. Vladimir Putin, who was not well known either in Russia or abroad, the head of the Federal Security Service, was named acting prime minister.

REFORMS UNDER PUTIN

In a televised address to the Russian people at the time of Putin's appointment as prime minister, Yeltsin said that he wanted Putin to succeed him as Russian president next year: As planned, Putin became the second president of Russia in January 2000, when Yeltsin resigned.

President Putin's main focus has been on: (1) establishing targets for increased economic growth; (2) encouraging the flow of investment funds into the real sector; (3) increasing industrial production; (3) improving tax collection (as an alternative to cutting budget expenditure – a flat tax rate of 13 percent was imposed beginning January 2000) (4) reducing the problem of salary and input purchase arrears; (5) stemming capital flight by stabilising the rouble and; (6) keeping inflation and inflationary expectations under control. In short, the economic policy of his administration recognises a wide range of deep-seated Russian problems and is attempting to deal with them. In reality, the Putin regime has been projecting an image of calm stability that is in sharp contrast to the often chaotic image associated with Yeltsin's tenure. This change of image, backed by some sensible economic policies, has considerably raised confidence in the Russian economy for both the Russian people and foreign businesses. By mid-decade high energy prices were temporarily removing some of the constraints on the Russian economy.

Putin's administration is also putting an emphasis on *social-economic reforms* such as raising public sector pay and pensions and developing an insurance policy against poverty and unemployment. The Putin government's program includes resolving issues of fiscal and economic federalism, which focuses on establishing a stronger vertical connection with the local authorities, changing the federal structure (instead of 89 federal units it proposed there be only seven) and centralising the appointment of senior regional officials. In imposing the latter rule, the administration hopes that corrupt elements will not come to a power as easily as has been the case in the past – but little progress has been made.

The monetary and credit policy of the government and the CBR is tightly focused on keeping the inflation rate down, through strict control of M2 and keeping the refinance rate of the CBR at a reasonable level. Throughout 2001, inflation remained at the 18-19 percent level, which is viewed by the government as acceptable. A floating exchange rate remains in place, and gold and currency reserves have been collected so that a sharp devaluation of the currency can be avoided. The CBR introduced a policy to attract commercial banks' deposits by raising deposit interest rate.

The government also established control over consumer goods prices by letting them rise gradually within pre-set intervals. The moderation of price increases in this area still presents a challenge for the government agencies with the result that transportation and utility prices remain regulated. Subsidies in these areas are, however, declining. It is expected that these industries will be fully exposed to the market conditions and that there will be no future subsidies coming from the state to mitigate the expected rise in cost for consumers.

Despite the government's efforts, arrears continue to grow, but the rate of their growth is slowing. GKO and OFZ are back in the market, but they do not offer very high yields. Yields are, however, now distributed more evenly and interest rates are higher on longer term securities. Three-year OFZ offer a yield of about 25 percent, which indicates that the government is now becoming more credible and able to attract investors without providing a substantial premium over inflation. Non-residents percentage of borrowing fell from 24 percent to 15 percent of the total debt by summer 2001.

The process of privatisation is ongoing. More than 500 enterprises listed in the government privatisation program project for 2002 and 2003 were fully transferred into private ownership. Auctions were held and shares distributed through a system of public offering. State ownership is forecast to be only one of two per cent in the most significant industrial (heavy machine building, timber industry, chemical, medical, and metallurgy sectors) enterprises by 2007. Existing monopolies are to be restructured and partly transferred into private ownership. The lucrative energy sector, however, has seen increased government control.

The pace of the reforms slackened in 2003 as the government tried to address more challenging issues. This included the break up of the state-controlled electricity and gas monopolies. The government contended that these monopolies must be split up and sold if the country's ageing power plants are to be kept running and ultimately modernised. In addition, the government has yet to produce a plan to overhaul Gazprom, the state-controlled gas monopoly, or to revamp the banking and housing sectors or to reform the civil service.

Economists from the IMF suggested that Russia speed up the reform program and particularly to lessen the dependence on foreign sales of oil, the country's largest export. They suggest that such changes are now necessary because economic growth in Russia has slowed. After expanding at a remarkable 8.3 percent in 2000, Russia's economy is now growing at only 3.5 percent per year despite continued high international oil prices.

CONCLUSION

During Putin's tenure, Russia has greatly improved its economic stability, parts of the legal system, and appears increasingly committed to the international rules of trade and business – except in the energy sector. It has again become attractive to foreign investment.

President Vladimir Putin has made an impressive start on economic reforms. It seems clear that the great challenge will be finding a way to deepen reforms in the face of the considerable vested interests that now exist in the current economic structure. While impoverishment remains widespread, the current arrangements have allowed some individuals and segments of the population to become very wealthy – largely through corruption and cronyism. Further reforms will threaten their privileged position. While President Putin may have the presence of purpose to take on the vested interests, he also appears to have a predilection to authoritarianism that would mean one barrier to Russia evolving into a modern market economy would only be replaced with another. Hence, while it will take a strong hand to shift the current vested interest, it will take considerable skill to ensure that corruption and cronyism is not replaced by the dead hand of heavy state intervention and control.

REFERENCES

Aslund, A. (1995). *How Russia Became a Market Economy*, Washington: Brookings Institute.
Aslund, A. (ed.) (1997). *Russia's Economic Transformation in the 1990s*, London: Blackwell.
Granville, B. (1995) *The Success of Russian Economic Reforms*, London: The Royal Institute of International Affairs.
Hedlund, S. (1999). Russia's "Market" Economy : A Bad Case of Predatory Capitalism, London: UCL Press.
Nekipelov, A. (1999). *A Set of Measures Aimed at Rationalization of the Russian Economy*, http://www.ecaar-russia.org/nek_e.htm.
Smith, A. (1993). *Russia and the World Economy: Problems of Integration*, London: Routledge.

Chapter 4

THE ROCKY PATH OF TRANSITION: INSTITUTIONS AND TRANSACTION COSTS IN THE RUSSIAN ECONOMY

Jill E. Hobbs

ABSTRACT

Modern market economies rely on a complex set of institutions that support commercial transactions. These institutions did not exist in command economies – they were not needed. Hence, transition to a modern market economy requires much more than the freeing of prices, privatization of assets and a degree of macroeconomic stability. A set of market oriented institutions also needs to be fostered; otherwise transaction costs will remain high and economic growth will be inhibited. The relationship between market institutions and transaction costs in the context of transition in the Russian Federation is discussed and suggestions for future progress provided.

INTRODUCTION

The path of transition from a command economy to a market economy is a difficult one. It is a path likely to be characterized by numerous wrong turns, uphill climbs, unexpected twists, and with by no means a clear vision of where the path is headed or how one will know when it has ended. While there are many facets to unravelling and smoothing the path to transition, one of the most important is the institutional environment within which transition occurs. In most modern market economies, the institutional environment can be taken largely for granted, it exists in the background, serving to facilitate the smooth functioning of market transactions and (usually) the maintenance of a stable investment climate. The transition path involves the establishment and adaptation of institutions, a process fraught with uncertainty. Failure to establish an efficient, credible institutional environment raises the transaction costs of doing business, stunting economic growth and deterring investment. The importance of the

THE MANY PATHS OF TRANSITION

After more than a fifteen years of 'transition', it is clear that the Russian experience is quite different in many respects to that of other transition countries, particularly some of the Central and Eastern European countries (CEEC). The widening gulf between the Russian Federation and other members of the Commonwealth of Independent States (CIS) and CEEC countries is evidenced by a number of measures of economic performance. A comparison of gross domestic product (GDP) growth over the first decade of transition, for example, reveals that Russian GDP fell by 40 percent between 1990-99, compared with a 40 percent growth in Polish GDP over the same period (World Bank, 2002)[22]. Inequality, as measured by Gini coefficients that relate the proportion of income earned to the proportion of the population, increased markedly in the Russian Federation over the first decade of transition, compared to more modest increases in most CEEC countries. Rather than educational premiums and wage dispersion, this inequality has been attributed to widespread corruption, rent seeking and state capture by vested interests (World Bank, 2002), all of which are symptomatic of a weak institutional environment.

In an analysis of institutional performance in transition economies, Weder (2001) identifies five clusters of countries, grouped by institutional performance[23]. The Russian Federation lies in the third (intermediate) cluster, alongside Azerbaijan, Belarus, Kazakhstan and the Ukraine, among others, while several CEEC countries such as Poland, the Czech and Slovak Republics, Hungary and Estonia lie in the 2nd (high) cluster. Of 31 transition countries, Weder's analysis places the Russian Federation well down the list (21st) in terms of overall average institutional quality. The clear message is that the 'transition' countries, although by no means uniform to start with, have undergone very different transition processes in terms of policy reform and institutional development.

Initial conditions (geography, history, price and output distortions) and the external shocks associated with the break-up of the Soviet Union, war and civil strife may be valid explanations for much of the output decline witnessed in many CIS countries in the early 1990s. However, it has been argued that these are far less persuasive explanations of later economic differences between transition countries. Instead, a key factor has been the effectiveness of policies and the evolving institutional environment in disciplining the 'old' (state) sector and encouraging growth and investment in the new business sector (World Bank, 2002).

For obvious reasons, one of the first steps in the transition process was privatization of state-controlled assets. The privatization process proceeded in the Russian Federation through

---

[22] In more recent times there has been some improvement in key macro-economic indicators, for example, a 15 percent growth in GDP in 2000-2001, pushing GDP back to its 1993 level (OECD, 2002). Nevertheless, the Russian economy lags behind other transition economies.

[23] Weder's measure of institutional performance is an amalgam of various aspects of the economic and business environment, derived from private sector surveys of firms and expert surveys of country risk assessment firms. The variables include evaluations of the rule of law, graft, regulatory burden, government effectiveness, political instability, credibility of government announcements, judiciary reliability, property rights enforcement, bribes, freedom from discretionary bureaucrats, and more.

a number of mechanisms, including voucher privatization, deposit auctions and cash privatization, until by 1999, more than 80 percent of Russian enterprises were privately owned. Almost 90 percent of output was produced by privately held enterprises by 1999 (Nureev and Runov, 2001; OECD, 2002).

The structure of private ownership, however, is markedly different from that observed in most western economies. Insiders (managers, workers) dominated the ownership structure, at least initially, and although post-privatization redistribution of ownership has redressed the balance towards outsiders (individuals, financial and non-financial firms, etc), insiders remain an important ownership group. In 1999, insiders were the most important shareholders in 43 percent of enterprises (OECD, 2002). The imbalance in ownership structure has a number of important implications for corporate governance, where the dominance of insider vested interests weakens the incentive for outside investment. It should also be noted that, in many cases, only partial privatization occurred. Mixed ownership forms, combining state, regional or local government with private ownership, still represented the largest proportion of privatized enterprises at the end of the 1990s (OECD, 2002).

Privatization by itself, while a necessary condition for transition to an efficient functioning market economy, is by no means a sufficient condition. In the absence of an effective, credible and transparent institutional environment, the expected gains from privatization will not be realized. In particular, the absence of an effective, enforceable system of property rights leads to high transaction costs and discourages investment. Thus, observers repeatedly refer to the "informal rights" that pervade the Russian economy, undermining fledgling institutions and stalling the transition process (Nureev and Rudov, 2001; Radaev, 2001).

The neoclassical economic paradigm, with its core assumptions of perfect information, efficient (unhampered) allocation of resources and competitive markets takes as given the institutional environment within which transactions occur. Neoclassical economic analysis concentrates on equilibrium outcomes, without consideration of how transactions occur; by default it assumes a frictionless economic environment. To understand the challenges facing the Russian Federation in encouraging economic growth and establishing a stable climate for business investment, we must augment the traditional neoclassical model of rational self-interested individuals and firms with insights from the Transaction Cost Economics branch of New Institutional Economics.

THE RELEVANCE OF TRANSACTION COSTS

Transaction costs arise whenever there is any form of economic organization, from command economy transactions, to transactions through a market interface, to transactions within a vertically integrated firm. Simply, they are the costs of carrying out a transfer of goods between technically separable phases of production or distribution *when we no longer assume information costs to be zero*. According to Cheung (1987), transaction costs encompass:

> a spectrum of institutional costs including those of information, of negotiation, of drawing up and enforcing contracts, of delineating and policing property rights, of monitoring performance, and of changing institutional arrangements (p.56).

Underlying the notion of transaction costs, and highlighting the fallacy of a frictionless economic environment no matter what the economic system, are four key concepts: bounded rationality, opportunism, asset specificity and information asymmetry. *Bounded rationality* recognizes that people have limited cognitive abilities; while they intend to act rationally, their capacity to evaluate all possible alternative outcomes of a decision is physically limited (Simon, 1961). When combined with situations of uncertainty and complexity, bounded rationality forces agents to incur higher transaction costs and may lead to sub-optimal decisions. Uncertainty and complexity have been characteristics of the transitioning Russian economy as institutions emerge and evolve, the rules change, and new business relationships are formed (and flounder). Indeed, Radaev (2001) argues that far from decreasing transaction costs, the uncertainty that emerged from the development of new institutions increased the transaction costs facing firms due to poorly structured and weakly enforced rules.

> Imposition of formal rules by the (Russian) authorities leads to additional transaction costs. These rules are formulated and enforced in such a way that leaves a large room for uncertainty and even creates uncertainty. The main reason is that legislative and regulatory documents include very general and/or ambivalent statements, which become subject to different interpretations (Radaev, 2001 pp.3-4)

Opportunism – self-interest seeking with guile (Williamson, 1979) – becomes a problem in the presence of small-numbers bargaining when agents can exploit a situation to their own advantage. Bounded rationality implies that other agents cannot identify, with any degree of certainty *ex ante*, the potential for opportunistic behaviour. If the privatization process has resulted in a monopoly or a small number of firms dominating an industry, then a small-numbers bargaining situation exists. It may also exist in industries with an outwardly competitive structure if investments in specific assets, which cannot be contractually safeguarded, reduce a firm's effective transaction partners to a small-numbers bargaining situation. This bring us to the third key concept of transaction cost economics (TCE) – asset specificity.

Asset specificity arises when one party to an exchange has invested in resources specific to that exchange, with little or no value in an alternative use (Klein et al., 1978); examples include the installation of specialized equipment, and the development of specialized infrastructure or specific human capital skills. Having made a specialized investment, the firm or individual is vulnerable to the other party opportunistically attempting to appropriate rent from the investment by altering the pre-agreed terms of a transaction. Bounded rationality and/or a weak institutional environment with poorly defined (and poorly enforced) property rights preclude the development of a fully contingent and enforceable contract to govern this transaction. In the absence of credible contractual protection, the investment is 'held-up' and the transaction does not occur. The hold-up problem is particularly troublesome in a transitioning economy wherein new investments are essential to long-term economic growth.

Finally, TCE relaxes the full or perfect information assumption of the traditional neoclassical model, drawing on the economics of information literature. The assumption of *information asymmetry* underlies the concepts of bounded rationality, opportunism and asset specificity. Ex ante information asymmetry – or adverse selection – occurs when information is hidden prior to a transaction, such that a buyer and seller have unequal access to information. If buyers are not able to determine the true quality of a good prior to purchase –

therefore cannot distinguish high quality from low quality – both qualities must sell for the same price, which reduces the incentive for sellers to supply the market with high quality goods (Akerlof, 1970). Institutions to reduce buyer measurement costs or protect the contractual rights of buyers are necessary to prevent market failure.

Moral hazard arises from ex post opportunism when the actions of agents are not directly observable by other parties. Insurance markets typically are vulnerable to moral hazard if the insured parties are able to make spurious insurance claims that are difficult for the seller of insurance to validate. Bureaucratic rules are also subject to moral hazard if officials can abuse their position of power within the institutional structure. It can also be a problem in shareholder-managerial relations: if actions by management to maximize their own self-interest at the expense of the shareholders are not directly observable by the owners of the enterprise. The practice of "tunnelling" is a prime example of moral hazard. Tunnelling involves the legal expropriation of income and shareholder assets, for example, through diverting cash flows and asset stripping. It has been identified as a particular problem in some transition economies, including the Russian Federation (World Bank, 2002; Nureev and Runov, 2001).

Transaction costs arise in the process of searching for information prior to a transaction, in negotiating the transaction and in monitoring and enforcing the transaction.

Information Costs

Information – or search – costs arise directly from the information asymmetry that characterizes many transactions. Economic agents incur search costs in gathering information about products, prices, the reliability of buyers (suppliers), etc. A raft of private and public sector institutions act to reduce these information costs, for example, communication systems: telecommunications, the Internet, postal systems, electronic (radio, television). Fostering competitive markets in the communications sector is an important role of government policy[24].

The provision and dissemination of business information can also reduce information costs. In many commodity markets, buyers and sellers have easy access to price information through a variety of institutions. These include print media (e.g. agricultural commodity prices are published regularly in the farming press and in local newspapers), commodity futures exchanges, and through industry associations that collate and publish price and market trend information (Hobbs et al., 1997).

Buyers incur information costs in ascertaining the true quality of a good, particularly when the product has experience or credence attributes that are important to the purchase decision[25]. Barzel (1982) argues that buyers use proxy measures of value, leading to measurement errors and a divergence between the price of a product and its valuation by the

---

[24] This has proven to be a challenge in many modern market economies, with the privatization of previously state-owned communication systems (e.g. telephone service). The challenge lies in finding the efficient (non-distortionary) level of regulation for industries that were traditionally viewed as natural monopolies – and increasingly a questioning of whether the 'natural monopoly' label remains valid as technological change generates potential competitors both within and across communication mediums.

[25] Experience attributes are those that a consumer cannot evaluate until after purchasing and consuming the good, for example, the tenderness of a steak. Consumers are unable to detect or evaluate credence attributes even after purchase and consumption, for example, organically produced food.

consumer. For example, buying oranges on the basis of weight, when it is the juiciness of the orange that is the characteristic of interest to the consumer. If buyers incur high measurement costs, the net price they are willing to pay for the product (posted price net of the costs of measurement) is reduced. Typically in consumer markets, multiple buyers must incur information costs as they sort goods to estimate their true value, whereas if a seller were to incur the costs of value measurement, products would be measured once. It may therefore be in the seller's interest to incur product quality measurement costs to reduce the incentive for costly sorting activities on the part of buyers. Barzel concludes that institutions arise to reduce the costs of measurement.

> The problems and costs of measurement pervade and significantly affect all economic transactions. Errors of measurement are too costly to eliminate entirely. The value of equally priced items will differ, then, and people will spend resources to acquire the difference. Such resource expenditure is wasteful, and it is hypothesized that exchange parties will form such contracts and engage in such activities that reduce this kind of resource use (Barzel, 1982, p.48).

The mechanisms to reduce measurement costs through credible quality signals include firm-level strategies such as branding and product warranties. Industry-wide initiatives include commodity grading schemes, quality assurance and certification systems – usually with third party verification to strengthen the credibility of the quality signal. The government's role in this case may be limited to ensuring that the institutional environment is in place to facilitate third party verification of grading schemes, quality assurance and certification systems. Establishing the regulatory environment to protect consumers from fraudulent labelling claims and product adulteration is also an important function of government[26].

Negotiation Costs

Negotiation costs arise from the physical act of the transaction, and include the costs of negotiation and drawing up contractual agreements, the use of an intermediary, such as a broker, etc. In the presence of high levels of uncertainty and a weak institutional environment, drawing up fully contingent contracts is costly, or even impossible. Without an effective set of commercial contract laws, negotiation costs will be higher. Financial institutions reduce negotiation costs by facilitating payment over time and distance and by providing access to a source of credit. In the absence of effective financial institutions, as was the case in the early days of transition, many more transactions must be carried out using cash – a cumbersome, risky and time-consuming method of doing business, only really suited to small-scale, personal business relationships (Hobbs et al., 1997).

---

[26] Law (2001) argues that the origins of food and drug regulation in the US can be traced to consumer concerns about adulteration and misrepresentation of food and drugs in the late 1800s. Asymmetric information between consumers and producers as a result of lengthening supply chains between consumers and producers of food led to uncertainty over product quality and increasing information costs for consumers.

Monitoring and Enforcement Costs

Monitoring and enforcement costs arise after the transaction has been agreed to, and include the costs of monitoring the actions of transaction parties, monitoring the quality of goods and, if necessary, enforcing the terms of the transaction in the event of abrogation by the other party. A transparent and enforceable system of property rights, an effective commercial legal system and judiciary, a reliable financial system and enforceable rules of corporate governance are all components of the institutional environment that help to mitigate monitoring and enforcement costs. In the absence of these institutions, or if they are weak or undermined by vacillating rules, opportunistic bureaucrats and inconsistent enforcement, the resulting uncertainty and high transaction costs will impede business investment and economic growth.

Transaction costs affect the vertical coordination of products along a supply chain – be it via spot markets, contracts, strategic alliances or within a vertically integrated firm. In the presence of asset specificity and uncertainty, economic agents will take steps to safeguard these investments. Without effective contractual safeguards, the transaction will only occur through a vertically integrated firm, or may not occur at all. Thus, transaction costs have direct implications for the incentives to invest, for long-term economic growth and for the structure of industries. The institutional environment within which transactions occur is critically important in determining the nature, level and distribution of those transaction costs. Several facets of that institutional environment have already been alluded to, however, a number deserve closer attention within the Russian context. Legal institutions, particularly the system of property rights, financial institutions and the rules of corporate governance are areas in which considerable institutional uncertainty remains.

BUILDING BETTER INSTITUTIONS

Property Rights

Insecure property rights are a significant constraint on new investment and economic growth. A comprehensive survey of enterprises[27] in 1999 found that over 75 percent of enterprises surveyed in the Russian Federation lacked confidence in the security of property rights, compared to fewer than 30 percent in Estonia and Poland (World Bank, 2002). To a large extent, differences in the security of property rights are determined by the effectiveness of legal drafting systems and the judiciary. Inadequate consultation with enterprises when drafting new laws or policies and failure to publicize new rules before their implementation were identified as major problems by Russian enterprises, with over 90 percent stating that they were seldom or never consulted or informed about new rules (World Bank, 2002). Lack of confidence in the security of property rights and the efficacy of the system of drafting rules that affect property rights is a serious impediment to investment.

Well defined (and enforced) property rights enshrine the right to make choices about a property or resource, the right to extract rents from its ownership and the right to transfer its

---

[27] The Business Environment and Enterprise Performance Survey conducted a survey in 22 transition countries across CEEC and the CIS.

ownership without restriction (Cheung, 1982; MacKay and Kerr, 1997). In this way, resources can be allocated – and reallocated – efficiently among competing users. The economic value of the resource is maximized, and overuse from a common property problem is avoided. Since ownership of property rights confers potential wealth – or loss of wealth depending on the choices made – the distribution and protection of those property rights is crucial in determining whether resources are allocated in response to economic signals or as a result of perverse bureaucratic incentives.

Hanisch et al. (2001) argue that property rights reform in transition should be analyzed as a process. They distinguish between formal and effective property rights. Although the reform process may begin with the establishment of formal property rights, rational actors then bargain to establish the effective rights to land given obscure formal laws or those subject to interpretation. Thus, there are numerous actors involved in the process of establishing effective property rights. Politicians establish the 'rule of law', these rules are implemented by lawyers and bureaucrats, and local actors play a role in determining how property rights are exchanged to become economic rights of action or effective property rights (Hanisch et al., 2001). Rent seeking and corruption cloud the relationship between formal and effective property rights.

The security of property rights is also determined by the credibility of government policies toward private assets. If policy announcements to the effect that governments will not expropriate privately held assets are not believable they will not elicit an increase in private sector investment. In an empirical model linking the institutional environment to the efficacy of property rights protection, Keefer and Knack (2001) find that countries with less secure property rights and with government decision makers less constrained by political institutions had a higher ratio of public to private investment. They conclude that the security of property rights is a direct product of the broad institutional and political environment in which governments make decisions. Institutional arrangements that ensure credibility by constraining decision makers' ability to engage in aggressive or expropriatory action towards investors are deemed essential.

Other institutions that contribute to the establishment and maintenance of secure property rights include property registries, a transparent and effective body of laws, dispute settlement mechanisms, readily available and skilled legal expertise and competent judiciary enforcement (World Bank, 2002).

Contract Law and Dispute Settlement Mechanisms

Long-term business relationships between firms reduce search and negotiation costs and are conducive to investment and economic growth. Regular transactions with raw material suppliers mean that an enterprise does not have to undertake costly search activities each time new supplies are needed. Quality control is made easier by regular supply relationships, where the quality of the input is known from previous experience. Negotiation costs are reduced if a long-standing agreement on price determination can be reached rather than being re-negotiated at each delivery. Similarly, regular business relationships with buyers reduce the search costs of locating new buyers for each transaction and in continuously establishing the trustworthiness and creditworthiness of new players. Monitoring costs are reduced if a long-term relationship with a reliable distributor is developed. The (unobserved) actions of a distributor are particularly important for perishable products as product handling and storage affects product quality throughout the marketing chain. Long-term relationships with a trusted distributor reduce the exposure to moral hazard.

Regular business relationships often evolve naturally as the most efficient vertical coordination mechanism. These relationships take on various degrees of formality in terms of the contractual environment in which they are consummated. In the presence of low levels of uncertainty, information asymmetry and asset specificity, contracts may be self-enforcing. Where reputation is important and both parties have a stake in the long-term survival of the business relationship, contractual terms are honoured even in the absence of third party enforcement (Hobbs et al., 1997). Many business relationships exist on this basis within stable economic climates, where reputations are easily established and maintained, and the potential for moral hazard is low. Of course, even long-term business relationships can fail spectacularly, as was the case with the acrimonious break-up of the 95 year-old supply relationship between Firestone (Bridgestone) Tires and Ford in the US in 2001[28].

Self-enforcing contracts are prone to failure in environments where uncertainty is prevalent. The Russian Federation has exhibited high levels of economic uncertainty during transition, with low growth rates, unemployment and opaque economic policies with respect to key macro-economic variables and business investment policy. Political uncertainty emerges from a bureaucratic system prone to graft, corruption and a bewildering array of informal rules.

If self-enforcing contracts cannot be relied upon, enforceable contract law is necessary for the establishment of long-term stable business relationships and as an inducement to investment. The key phrase here is "enforceable". Enshrined in a system of contract law must be the credible threat that the coercive power of the state will be brought to bear on those parties that abrogate their contractual commitments. This threat, if credible, should discourage post-contractual opportunistic behaviour that attempts to appropriate rents from asset specific investments. Yet it would be naïve to conclude that business disputes would not occur even in the presence of this credible threat. Complex contractual relationships in environments of uncertainty mean that genuine disagreements may arise over the interpretation of contractual clauses. As the transaction environment becomes more complex, attempting to write fully contingent contracts to cover every eventuality leads to ever-increasing transaction costs. Contractual gaps and the potential for legitimate contract disputes also pave the way for opportunistic reneging on contractual obligations (Hobbs et al., 1997). An efficacious dispute-settlement institution fosters long-term business relationships, investment and economic growth.

Arbitration is a private sector institutional alternative to the court system for settling commercial disputes and may be particularly effective in safeguarding (thereby encouraging) foreign investment. A number of different arbitration systems exist and compete internationally. For example, the International Chamber of Commerce has a widely accepted code of arbitration, with arbitration centres located worldwide. The arbitration details are specified in advance in a contractual agreement following well-established, yet flexible, rules

---

[28] Bridgestone/Firestone and Ford were forced to recall the Firestone tires on Ford Explorers in 2000 after a series of fatal accidents caused by tire blow-outs. Both companies were sued in subsequent civil lawsuits. Ford blamed Firestone Tires. The tire company blamed Ford for problems with the design of the vehicle body. Both companies accused the other of withholding information. The dispute brought a long-standing business relationship to an abrupt, and very public, end.

for appointing arbitrators. Thus, two parties to a contractual agreement in the Russian Federation might agree, in the event of a dispute, to use a Swiss arbitration centre, a Canadian arbitrator and follow German arbitration laws.

Arbitrators are usually chosen for their specialist knowledge in the industry concerned. They are more likely to understand what constitutes 'normal business practices' over opportunistic behaviour than a judge who may be trained in law but not trained in the specifics of the industry. In economic terms, arbitration is more likely to result in Pareto efficient outcomes, since compromise is possible and the adversarial "I win, you lose" outcome of a court decision based on precedence is avoided. Compared to pursuing a contractual dispute through the courts the arbitration process is less costly, both in terms of time and money; this is particularly advantageous for perishable goods. Hearings are held in private rather than being part of the public record as is usually the case in most legal systems. Intellectual property may be at risk from the discussion in court of commercially sensitive material, whereas this is not an issue with arbitration (Kerr and Perdikis, 1995; Hobbs et al, 1997).

Parties to a dispute voluntarily agree to be bound by the decision of an arbitrator. As there is no legal enforcement of arbitration decisions per se, it cannot prevent overt opportunism. The same could probably be said of the court system, however, given the complexity of enforcing complex contractual agreements through the courts in an uncertain economic environment. Arbitration is useful in resolving genuine disagreements over contractual terms and obligations in a speedy, transparent and transaction-cost reducing manner. Firms may also use compliance with arbitration decisions (which are a matter of public record) to signal reputation – thus reducing information costs in establishing the credibility of new business partners (Hobbs et al., 1997).

Commercial arbitration centres are usually private sector establishments, part of wider (international) arbitration systems. Policies that foster the development of private sector commercial arbitration centres in the Russian Federation, together with educating the new business sector about the uses of commercial arbitration would be beneficial. It should be noted that arbitration is a complement to - rather than a substitute for - a commercial legal system. In this respect, establishing support for arbitration decisions within the legal system is important; this includes provisions for legal enforcement of arbitration decisions should either party renege on its commitment to be bound by the decision of the arbitrator.

Private sector commercial arbitration systems survive on the basis of their success in resolving commercial disputes. Critical to this success is credibility, which in large part is a function of whether parties to a dispute abide by the decision of the arbitrator. A supportive legal framework that enforces arbitration decisions is important. However, arbitration cannot work if the legal system is used regularly to overturn arbitration decisions – a particular danger when a dispute arises between a domestic firm and a foreign firm. In those situations, national courts might overturn arbitration decisions if they are seen to contravene domestic legislation, if third parties might be adversely affected by the arbitration decision, or if the arbitration decision was not in the national interest (Kerr and Perdikis, 1995). Uncertainty over the enforcement of arbitration decisions deters the use of arbitration, and by default may deter investment and economic growth. Domestic legislation can reduce this uncertainty by avoiding the temptation to place restrictive limits on arbitration awards, and only allowing appeal to domestic courts if compliance with the award would put the party in violation of domestic law (Hobbs et al., 1997).

Corporate Governance

The rules of corporate governance are important in establishing transparency in shareholder-management relationships. Both corporate governance and the procedures for exit and bankruptcy are critical for long-term access to equity and investment. The World Bank (2002) points out that:

> ... rules to protect minority shareholders; rules against insider deals and conflicts of interest; adequate accounting, auditing, and disclosure standards; and takeover, insolvency, and collateral legislation, together with the development of enforcement capacity, are key to preventing asset stripping that reduces the true long-term value and competitiveness of a firm (p.x)

Too little attention has been given to establishing efficient and credible institutions for corporate governance in the Russian Federation. Some of these problems can be traced back to the privatization process that left existing directors of state enterprises or local bureaucrats in charge, effectively making these individuals residual claimants to the assets of the enterprise. Rampant tunnelling activities - such as asset stripping and cash diversion - resulted. Theft and corruption are also major problems.

Nureev and Runov (2001) point to weaknesses in the Russian institutional environment as an explanation for 'privatization inefficiency', which allowed a gap between the *de facto* and *de jure* ownership of property rights to emerge. They argue that informal rights dominate, with considerable control remaining in the hands of regional authorities. They attribute the reduction in the list of enterprises banned from privatization between 1995 and 1998 - particularly in the oil, fuel, aircraft, chemical and petro-chemical industries - to "a strong desire of the new bureaucracy to receive in their private ownership the most profitable objects of former soviet property" (Nureev and Runov, 2001, p.23).

Experience has shown that enterprises sold through transparent tenders or auctions have attracted serious investors and have subsequently outperformed those sold directly to those with a political vested interest (World Bank, 2002). These problems remain endemic, particularly in the 'old' unrestructured enterprises and are a serious impediment to securing financial backing.

Effective legal protection is a prerequisite for inducing suppliers of finance to commit resources to an enterprise for a return on their investment. Specific provision for legal protection of investors and a credible regulatory system for financial intermediaries, such as investment funds, brokers and stock markets is essential (Johnson and Shliefer, 2001)[29]. The predominance of insider-ownership structures creates perverse incentives for managers to act in their own self-interest, thereby deterring outside investment. In a White Paper on corporate governance in the Russian Federation, it is noted that:

> Many investors in Russia remain frustrated in their efforts to confront abusive interested party investors. This has been one of the most pervasive shareholder rights abuses, including in

---

[29] Indeed even modern market economies are vulnerable to weak corporate governance and a failure of regulatory oversight. One only has to recall the dramatic destabilizing effects on world stock markets during 2002 from the revelations of corporate accounting fraud and the apparent failure of the auditing process in the demise of several large US corporations – Enron, WorldCom, etc.

companies with significant state ownership. Lack of a clear definition of an interested party, lack of credible sanctions for failure to disclose interested party transactions and lack of access by injured parties to information about company transactions have all contributed significantly to this problem ... the law still does not contain credible sanctions that may be applied against the individuals who engage in self-dealing and/or fail to follow required procedures in this area. (OECD, 2002, p.13, paragraph 61).

Stock option plans are commonly used in western economies to provide managers with incentives to maximize shareholder return. The success of these plans is contingent upon an appropriate institutional structure, including an efficient capital market, fair and transparent price evaluation and accounting processes and a legal framework governing the establishment and operation of stock-option plans – none of which currently exist in Russia (OECD, 2002). Without the appropriate institutions, the introduction of stock option plans would be open to manipulation and abuse by vested interests. As such, they would likely fail as a device to align the interests of managers with outside shareholders, fail to enhance corporate performance and, ultimately, fail to encourage outside investment.

A system of credible third party *auditing* is necessary for the long-term development of efficient and sustainable capital markets and in maintaining long-term investor confidence. Manipulation of audit statements and widespread fraud have become major problems in the Russian Federation:

> Many independent audit reports are issued fraudulently by so-called "black auditor firms" who know the financial statements are materially misstated and are intended to deceive tax authorities and minority shareholders (OECD, 2002, p.22, paragraph 125).

Recognizing this problem, the Russian government enacted a Federal auditing law in 2001 that includes some sanctions for auditors who do not comply with proper auditing procedures. The enforcement strength of the new law, however, is questionable, with sanctions only extending to the removal of licenses and to fines in limited cases where an audit was conducted by an unlicensed firm or where a required audit has been avoided.

> "...the fines are not high enough to serve as a substantial deterrent to a large firm. Moreover, there are no sanctions on other kinds of violations ... for example, to prevent the preparation of an audit by parties with certain relationships to the audited entity" (OECD, 2002, p.23, paragraph 135).

Thus, although the 2001 audit law is an important institutional development, it appears to be only a partial institutional reform. Strengthening of the audit law to reduce the opportunities for manipulation by insider vested interests would improve investor confidence.

According to the World Bank (2002), powerful insiders with a stake in weak corporate governance frequently have hampered the enforcement efforts of the Securities and Exchange Commission in the Russian Federation. The very real danger is that the transition process becomes stalled at a sub-optimal equilibrium because winners from the early stages of transition have a vested interest in inhibiting further institutional development.

Nevertheless, privatization is a necessary step in the liberalization process and strategies for further privatization of state-owned assets should consider the implications of the privatization process for corporate governance. The World Bank (2002) recommends open, competitive auctions for small enterprises. Sale of controlling shares to carefully screened strategic outside investors is recommended for medium and large size enterprises, rather than mass privatization or privatization to insiders. However, the latter strategy is perhaps easier said than done. It entails a delicate balance between selecting credible market-driven outside investors and succumbing to the very real potential for influence peddling and corruption in this selection process.

Bankruptcy laws are also important in bringing the discipline of the market to bear on poor management, and they have a direct effect on the long run availability of financing in a market system. Gray (1993) points out that in modern market economies, bankruptcy proceedings give first priority to secured creditors, and then to reimbursing owed salaries, tax, supplier credits, etc., leaving shareholders as the residual claimant. In some transition countries, new bankruptcy laws shifted the priorities in favour of salaries and severance pay for workers over secured creditors. In the long run this is likely to limit access to secured credit as a source of enterprise financing. Nevertheless, it is also important to distinguish between appropriate rules during a period of transition compared with a post-transition equilibrium. Giving suppliers who have extended credit priority in bankruptcy proceedings may be necessary as a temporary transition step, given the importance of inter-firm credit and the potential cascade effect of a bankruptcy within a fledgling supply chain (Hobbs et al., 1997). Although cushioning inter-firm credit may be applicable in the short-run, financial intermediaries are a more sustainable institution in the long run; being generally more transaction-cost efficient in terms of evaluating creditworthiness and risk.

The Federal Law on Insolvency (Bankruptcy) was enacted in the Russian Federation on January 8 1998 (No. 6-FZ) (OECD, 2002). A recurring theme, however, is the significant gap between the *de jure* rules governing the commercial environment and *de facto* enforcement of those rules. Bankruptcy procedures appear to be no exception:

> Judicial practice has revealed numerous cases where bankruptcy procedures have been abused as a means to acquire assets or entire companies. They are also used to eliminate competitors, to strip assets or to exclude certain shareholders. These abuses have been facilitated by the bankruptcy administrators' poor supervision. These problems have undermined the credibility of the bankruptcy law. (OECD, 2002, p.19, paragraph 104.)

In the aftermath of privatization, transparent and rigorously enforced *competition laws* can help expose poor management to the disciplines of the marketplace. The challenge lies in designing these laws to encourage competition, without inhibiting investment. Transition economies, in particular, face unique obstacles in this regard. The Russian Federation enacted a law "On Competition and Limitation of Monopoly Activity in the Commodity Markets" in March 1991 (No. 948-1). The law proscribes organisational and legal principles to prevent or limit monopoly activities and unfair competition (OECD, 2002). Enforcement of these laws and further institutional development of competition policies to establish and maintain competitive market environments are ongoing concerns (OECD 2001).

Typically, competition laws deal with industry structure, such as the number and size distribution of firms in an industry, and firm conduct – pricing strategies, strategic creation of entry and exit barriers, etc. It is often difficult in modern market economies to distinguish between predatory behaviour that is contrary to the public interest and firm strategies that are a natural part of the competitive process within that the industry. In the Russian Federation, the structure of industries formerly organized as state enterprises is largely a result of the privatization process. Where that process led to the creation of bilateral monopoly situations, distortions inevitably arise (Gaisford et al., 1994). Strict anti-monopoly laws may inhibit investment at critical junctures of the transition process. Nevertheless, rules outlawing – and penalizing – cartel behaviour are an essential component of market reforms in the Russian Federation, and in maintaining public confidence in the transition process (Hobbs et al., 1997).

The Banking Sector

A competitive, stable and market-driven banking system plays a key role in encouraging long term investment and economic growth. As financial intermediaries, banks lower the negotiation costs of doing business by facilitating payment over time and over distance. The ability to clear cheques through an integrated banking system eliminates the need for costly and risky cash-based transactions. The large amounts of cash required to finance cash-based transactions poses a security risk and raises internal monitoring costs for firms in guarding against pilfering. Inventory management is made easier by the use of delayed payment practices that simply would not be possible in a cash-based transaction environment.

In market economies, banks are also an important source of financing for new investments. As private businesses, banks make loans based on their assessment of the creditworthiness and riskiness of the borrower. Poorly managed firms that subsequently perform poorly are subject to the disciplines of the market through equity and financing constraints. A competitive private commercial banking sector is a key institution in a modern market economy.

In the early years of transition, the Russian Federation introduced a number of reforms to the state banking system; the entry of a relatively large number of new banks was encouraged and old state banks were liquidated. The entry of new banks is fundamental to the building a competitive banking sector in the long run. In the short run, however, rapid entry meant a high level of bank failures and a weakening of depositor confidence in the new Russian banking sector (World Bank, 1996). The Russian banking sector is struggling to recover from its collapse during and after the 1998 financial crisis. Banking licenses were removed from the most problematic banks but a number of the banks restructured by the Agency for Restructuration of Credit Organisation (ARCO) have yet to be sold. The banking sector remains small, fragmented and highly concentrated, with about 1300 banks existing in 2002 but 50 percent of banking capital residing with the top five. The liquidity crisis facing a large number of small banks has resulted in merger and acquisition activity among banks (OECD, 2002).

In general, these factors have led to a low level of trust in the banking system, with only a very low level of deposits (6.6% of GDP). These deposits are primarily short-term. Private deposits in commercial banks are reported to cover only 6 percent of their assets, compared with 31 percent in Poland and 48 percent in the Czech Republic (OECD, 2002). A credible system of deposit insurance would help maintain depositor confidence. High transaction costs for insurance firms in evaluating the sustainability of a commercial bank and the potential size of losses are market failure arguments in favour of public sector provision of deposit insurance. Deposit insurance is also important in preventing widespread depositor panic and spillover effects across the banking sector in the event of a single bank failure.

Failed banks, nonetheless, should be allowed to exit the banking system, particularly if bank failures are a direct result of poor lending and investment decisions. Policies to ensure good corporate governance reduce information and monitoring costs for banks, thereby reducing the risk of bank failure due to information asymmetry rather than simply poor lending decisions. Regulatory oversight of the banking system is also critical in ensuring that banking failures do not destabilize the entire sector. At the same time, regulatory oversight of new banks reduces information and monitoring costs for depositors in requiring that these firms meet certain capital requirement standards. Entry by reputable foreign banks may also provide a source of capital, managerial expertise and competition, provided that foreign banks are subject to the same domestic regulatory environment as Russian banks. Relaxing the restrictions on foreign banks' activities and the adoption of international financial reporting standards may be necessary steps in strengthening the Russian banking sector (OECD, 2002).

Despite new entry, the banking sector remains small relative to its counterpart in western market economies and banks have not been a major source of financing for enterprises. Domestic credit to the private sector as a percentage of GDP is considerably lower in the Russian Federation than the world average, and lower than many other transition countries, particularly those in central and eastern Europe (World Bank, 2002). In 1999-2000, only three percent of total investment was sourced from banks. Commercial bank loans represented 14.6 percent of Russian GDP, compared to over 20 percent of GDP in Hungary and over 40 percent in the Czech Republic (OECD, 2002).

CONCLUSION

Transaction cost economics provides insights into the nature of the firm and the structure of inter-firm relationships. In helping us understand why and how economic transactions occur, it highlights the factors that encourage or impede investment and, by extension, economic growth.

In the presence of uncertainty and asymmetric information, boundedly rational individuals face transaction costs in safeguarding asset specific investments against opportunistic behaviour. Investment is deterred – or may only incur within vertically integrated firms, thus placing capital constraints on long-term investments. Fundamentally, businesses dislike uncertainty; yet high levels of uncertainty characterize an economy in transition with only fledgling market institutions. Getting the institutional environment right is an important prerequisite to lowering transaction costs and facilitating economic growth. Institutional development needs to be backed by policy reforms to ensure clearly defined and enforced property rights. Fears that newly established property rights could be either expropriated or undermined by weak institutional protection that favours entrenched vested interests threatens to stall transition of the Russian Federation to a market economy that is competitive, credible and accountable.

Commercial contract law and effective dispute settlement mechanisms, either through the courts or through commercial arbitration processes, reduce transaction costs and facilitate the development of new supply chains. Weak corporate governance, graft and corruption have undermined investor and public confidence in the new market economy and pose a serious threat to economic growth and investment. Policies that enable the market to discipline poorly managed firms, while encouraging growth and investment in new enterprises are a priority. For the most part, this requires that the state concentrate on establishing the necessary institutions that allow market forces to work, rather than interfering directly in the market.

Clearly there are many institutions that underpin a market economy, and to discuss them all is beyond the scope of this paper. Instead, the focus has been on those institutions that, first and foremost, can be effective in lowering transaction costs. A sustainable commercial banking sector, effective contract law, close attention to the corporate governance, and clear definition and protection of property rights are key components of the institutional environment in the Russian Federation that deserve closer attention.

Although the transition path has been anything but smooth, substantial progress has been made. At this juncture, it is important to continue along this path, rather than be diverted from it by opposition from entrenched vested interests who – while having gained in the early stages of privatization – stand to lose from further strengthening of property rights, corporate governance and the rule of law. The very real danger is that the Russian Federation settles into a partial reform equilibrium, with weak institutions, continuing uncertainty and high transaction costs. Policymakers should be encouraged to continue the institutional reforms necessary to navigating the rocky path of transition.

REFERENCES

Akerlof, G.A. (1970). The Market for 'Lemons': Qualitative Uncertainty and the Market Mechanism. *Quarterly Journal of Economics*, 84, 488-500.

Barzel, Y. (1982). Measurement Cost and the Organization of Markets. *Journal of Law and Economics*, 25 (1), 27-48.

Cheung, S.N.S. (1987). Economic Organization and Transaction Costs. In J. Eatwell, M. Milgate and P. Newmann (Eds.), *The New Palgrave – A Dictionary of Economics* (p. 5057). London: Macmillan Press.

Cheung, S.N.S. (1982). *Will China Go Capitalist?* London: Institute of Economic Affairs.

Gaisford, J.D., Kerr, W.A. and Hobbs, J.E. (1994). Non-Cooperative Bilateral Monopoly Problems in Liberalizing Command Economies. *Economic Systems*, 18, 3, 265-279.

Gray, C.W. (1993). *Evolving Legal Frameworks for Private Sector Development in Central and Eastern Europe*. World Bank Discussion Papers, 209. Washington DC: International Bank for Reconstruction and Development, Washington DC.

Hanisch, M., Beckmann, V., Boger, S. and Brem, M. (2001). In Search of the Market: Lessons from Analyzing Agricultural Transition in Central and Eastern Europe. Proceedings of the 5th Annual Conference of the International Society for New Institutional Economics: Institutions and Governance, Berkeley, CA, September.

Hobbs, J.E., Kerr, W.A. and Gaisford, J.D. (1997). *The Transformation of the Agrifood System in Central and Eastern Europe and the New Independent States*. Wallingford: CAB International.

Johnson, S. and Shleifer, A. (2002). *Privatization and Corporate Governance*. Paper prepared for the 12th Annual East Asian Seminar on Economics, June 28-30, Cambridge, MA: National Bureau of Economic Research.

Keefer, P. and Knack, S. (2001). Boondoggles and Expropriation: When are Property Rights Secure and Public Investment Growth-Promoting? Proceedings of the 5th Annual Conference of the International Society for New Institutional Economics: Institutions and Governance, Berkeley, CA, September.

Kerr, W.A, and Perdikis, N. (1995) *The Economics of International Business*. London: Chapman and Hall.

Klein, B., Crawford, R.G. and Alchian, A.A. (1978). Vertical Integration, Appropriable Rents and the Competitive Contracting Process. *Journal of Law and Economics*, 21 (2), 297-326.

Law, M. T. (2001). The Transaction Cost Origins of Food and Drug Regulation. Proceedings of the 5th Annual Conference of the International Society for New Institutional Economics: Institutions and Governance, Berkeley, CA, September.

MacKay, E. and Kerr, W.A. (1997). Is Mainland China Evolving into a Market Economy? *Issues and Studies*, 33 (9),31-45.

Nureev, R. and Runov, A. (2001). *Russia: Whether Deprivatization is Inevitable? Power-Property Phenomenon as a Path Dependence Problem*. Proceedings of the 5th Annual Conference of the International Society for New Institutional Economics: Institutions and Governance, Berkeley, CA, September.

OECD (2001). *Reforming Russian Infrastructure for Competition and Efficiency*. Paris: Organisation for Economic Cooperation and Development.

OECD (2002). *White Paper on Corporate Governance in Russia*. Paris: Organisation for Economic Cooperation and Development, Paris.

Radaev, V. (2001). Informal Institutional Arrangements and Tax Evasion in the Russian Economy. Proceedings of the 5th Annual Conference of the International Society for New Institutional Economics: Institutions and Governance, Berkeley, CA, September.

Simon, H. (1961). *Administrative Behavior*. 2nd edition, New York: Macmillan.

Weder, B. (2001). *Institutional Reform in Transitions Economies: How Far Have They Come?* Proceedings of the 5th Annual Conference of the International Society for New Institutional Economics: Institutions and Governance, Berkeley, CA, September.

Williamson, O.E. (1979). Transaction Cost Economics: the Governance of Contractual Relations. *Journal of Law and Economics*, 22, 233-262.

World Bank (1996). *From Plan to Market*. World Development Report 1996. Oxford: Oxford University Press.

World Bank (2002). *Transition The First Ten Years: Analysis and Lessons for Eastern Europe and the Former Soviet Union*. Washington DC:, The World Bank.

Chapter 5

THIN MARKETS AND UNDER-INVESTMENT IN THE RUSSIAN ECONOMY

James D. Gaisford

ABSTRACT

Industry in the Russian Federation suffers from poor productivity and chronic underinvestment. The causes for this underproduction and underinvestment are often attributed to poor macroeconomic management but this chapter argues that microeconomic factors also play a considerable role. In particular, thin markets mean that vertical relationships between firms along supply chains can be characterized by bi-lateral monopolies or oligopolies resulting in lower levels of output and subsequently investment than would be the case if Russian markets were more competitive. A formal model that assumes thin markets is developed and the ramifications for the Russian industrial sector examined. Suggestions regarding the policy initiatives that will assist in alleviating the problems identified are presented. Overcoming the problems associated with thin markets will be crucial for the process of revitalizing Russian industry.

INTRODUCTION

Problems of under-production and under-investment are frequently analyzed from a macroeconomic perspective. Without negating the importance of macroeconomic factors, this chapter suggests that there is also a key microeconomic dimension that is at least as important for the Russian Federation (RF) and other former command economies. As shown in Gaisford *et al.* (2001), bilateral market power associated with thin markets coupled with high transaction costs appears to act as a significant microeconomic deterrent not only for production but also for investment. The purpose of this chapter is to provide a systematic but non-algebraic analysis of the investment issues originally explored in Gaisford *et al.* (2001) and to consider the importance of those issues to the Russian Federation.

When transactions between firms take place on competitive markets with many potential buyers and sellers, efficient volumes of transactions and efficient levels of investment are the norm. Prices are disciplined by other potential transactions and the return to investment by one firm is not subject to opportunistic behaviour by a few other firms. Transactions between upstream and downstream firms, however, do not always occur on competitive markets. Even in developed market economies, thin markets with few potential buyers and sellers are often observed, particularly on remote local or regional markets. In Russia thin markets are more widespread. In part this is a direct legacy of the command system, which emphasized large production establishments with relatively few external linkages. While Russia's vast geography will make geographic dispersion a major on-going obstacle, general weakness in transportation and communications infrastructure has often made even nearby markets less economically integrated than would be expected in developed market economies.

On thin markets, under-production and under investment will arise whenever it is most profitable for firms to utilize non-cooperative spot contracts. This is because it will be *individually rational* for both buyers and sellers to resort to restrictive behaviour in order to exercise market power within their bilateral relationship. If transaction costs remained the same, contracts that determine the volume of exchange cooperatively would necessarily result in greater investment by both buyers and sellers as well as efficient volumes of exchange contingent on those investment levels. Further, cooperative contracts that specify performance requirements for investment as well as exchange would serve to place investment as well as exchange on an efficient footing.

Transaction costs, however, do not tend to be equal across contract types. Non-cooperative spot contracts frequently have the virtue of lowest transaction costs, with transaction costs rising in succession for cooperative exchange contracts and cooperative investment and exchange contracts. In developed market economies with well-established systems of commercial and property law and effective procedures for commercial arbitration, cooperative contracts may be frequently observed because they are enforceable at relatively low cost. In Russia, non-cooperative spot contracts appear to be the norm because the transaction costs associated with greater cooperation escalate rapidly.

This analysis suggests that traditional monopoly *busting* through competition policy should proceed with care. Enforced vertical segmentation could exacerbate the problems associated with non-cooperative bilateral transactions. Horizontal division of productive assets may have some scope for success but, given the investments in extremely large-scale integrated production facilities made during the command economy era, the normal strategy of dividing assets may lead to nonviable sub-grouping of the existing assets.

As the problem of thin markets stems largely from the high transaction costs that firms face in broadening markets, government resources will be better spent in providing infrastructure and fostering institutional arrangements to reduce such transaction costs. It becomes readily apparent that such endeavours can have a significant public-good aspect once transaction costs are viewed explicitly. Investment in transportation and, particularly, communications infrastructure for business will reduce the costs of market broadening.

Inadequate and poorly enforced commercial law may lead governments to attempt to re-exert control over inter-firm interfaces along supply chains in an attempt to impose cooperative solutions where they fail to arise from bilateral bargaining. While this may provide a short-term solution, it can only delay the process of transition to a revitalized economy based on market signals. The need to foster the development of a low cost and enforceable commercial legal system is imperative. The analysis suggests that even stepwise improvements in systems of commercial law that allow enforceable exchange commitments will enhance investment as well as production. Further, successive transaction-cost reductions will eventually permit the proliferation of more cooperative types of contracts.

The reform of trade policy would also serve as a market-broadening policy that reduces the problems of high transaction costs and bilateral monopoly. While trade liberalization provides the potential for benefits over the long term, the immediate priority should be a move to more transparent measures such as tariffs and away from non-tariff measures. In particular, state trading agencies serve to drastically reduce the competitive pressures from international trade and preserve the *status quo*.

Transaction costs and thus production and investment are also likely to be directly and profoundly affected by the policy environment set by governments. The stability of the policy regime as well as its economic soundness is important in generating lower transaction costs and greater investment. Providing maximum transparency and simplicity, while minimizing compliance and documentation costs is very important. Variations and asymmetries in the implementation of policy, whether due to corruption or the complexity of regulations, exacerbate risks and may put firms at a competitive disadvantage. A higher probability of policy variations frequently translates into greater risk and, thus serves as a brake on investment. Finally the perceived possibility of direct opportunism by governments can have a large detrimental impact on commercial investment in general and foreign investment in particular.

OVERVIEW OF THE THREE-STAGE BUYER-SELLER GAME

A market can be generally described as situation where m sellers transact related items with n buyers. As m and n both become sufficiently large, or strictly speaking go to infinity, the market becomes competitive. As n becomes large, the market becomes a monopoly if $m=1$ and an oligopoly if m is small but greater than one. Conversely, as m becomes large, the market becomes a monosony if $n=1$. The market is "thin" when m and n are both small and it becomes a bilateral monopoly in the extreme case where both $m=1$ and $n=1$. In principle, both m and n are endogenous such that the net benefits or "profits" of all participants are non-negative while those of all non-participants are non-positive. Where transportation, communications and transaction costs are high such as in sparsely populated regions, developing countries and transition economies, thin markets tend to be pervasive.

We examine a simple bilateral relationship where an *upstream firm* can produce and sell a good that a *downstream firm* can buy and use. The two firms may constitute a bilateral monopoly, where the upstream firm is the only potential seller and the downstream firm is the only potential buyer in a particular regional market for the good in question. For example, a steel mill may sell a particular product to only one auto plant in a particular region. More generally, however, the bilateral relationship between the upstream and downstream firms may be conditioned by the presence of "competition" from a small numbers of other rival buyers and/or sellers in the context of a thin market.

The bilateral relationship between the upstream and downstream firms can be described by a three-stage buyer-seller game (Figure 5.1).

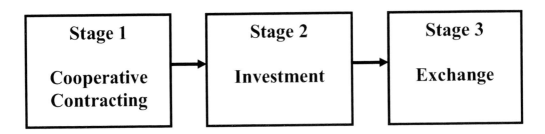

Figure 5.1. The Three State Game.

In the first stage, the firms may elect to bargain towards a partially or fully cooperative contract. Then, in stage two they set investment levels. Finally, stage three involves exchange. More specifically, during stage three the upstream firm produces the output, the good is delivered, and the downstream firm uses the input.

At the investment stage, both firms make capital investments, which enhance the value of the exchange, but they also face fixed entry costs arising from research and development, licensing, etc. While the quantities of capital, unlike entry costs, vary continuously, the subsequent stage-three exchange sub-game calls for a short-run type of analysis because the quantities of capital have become fixed. Further, because of the bilateral relationship between the firms, the quantity of capital acquired by either firm is potentially a specific asset that is subject to opportunism by the opponent (see Williamson, 1975; Klein *et al.*, 1978). In our model, each firm anticipates the investments of the other. Consequently, a sufficiently high entry cost for either firm will cause a Nash equilibrium in which neither firm produces or invests as in Klein *et al.* (1978). The variable investment in productive capital is, however, more complex. While a larger purchase of capital puts more investment on the line, a larger capital stock may also provide a strategic benefit in the exchange sub game, for example by reducing the seller's marginal cost.

Depending on the level of transaction costs, firms can either vertically integrate or seek more permanent relationships, such as long-term contracts, to avoid problems associated with the vulnerability of specific assets to opportunistic behaviour (Coase, 1937; Joskow, 1977). In a cooperative bilateral-monopoly game, the two firms may be able to split the maximum available surplus in accordance with their bargaining positions (e.g., threat points). While *ex post* bargaining will not generate an efficient volume of exchange when information is asymmetric (e.g., Myerson and Satterthwaite, 1983) or when specific investments are involved, efficiency can typically be restored through an appropriate, possibly complex, *ex ante* contract (see Tirole, 1988, 22-27). Nevertheless, it would be rash to expect that efficient long-term contracts will guide all bilateral relationships (Grout, 1984; Tirole, 1986). Particularly in transition economies, opportunism may be widespread because of the absence of effective, low-cost judicial or quasi-judicial mechanisms to enforce such contracts and the presence of high transaction costs related to contracting.

We allow for three types of contracts to guide the relationship between the two firms. The default is a stage-three *spot contract* where there is no initial cooperation at stage one and both the investment and exchange stages are played non-cooperatively. We envisage such contracts as if they were conducted under the auspices of a broker to which each party submits a set of offers concerning prices and quantities. Brokerage fees are included in the transaction costs of each firm. With respect to exchange, each firm must be satisfied with its offers given those of the other firm. Similarly with respect to investment, each firm must be satisfied with its investment level given that of the other. Thus, spot contracts are individually rational and self-enforcing.

Alternatively, the firms may bargain towards either of two types of cooperative contracts at stage one. First, the firms may agree on a relatively simple *exchange contract* with provisions concerning the price and quantity of the good to be transacted. While exchange is determined cooperatively in such a contract, the preceding investments are determined non-cooperatively. Thus, an exchange contract can be said to be partially cooperative. The second type of cooperative contract adds investment commitments by both firms to the exchange commitments concerning price and quantity. Consequently, such an *investment and exchange contract* can be said to be fully cooperative.

Neither of the types of cooperative contracts is directly self-enforcing. In both types of cooperative contracts the efficient quantity is chosen directly, and the price fulfils a distributive, rather than an allocative role. Consequently, the price will virtually never reflect the underlying shadow value of good. Given the price, which is specified in the contract, one of the firms will always have an incentive to renege by reducing the quantity transacted. In addition, in the fully cooperative investment contract, both firms will have an incentive to deviate from their commitments and under invest. Thus, the cooperative contracts require some form of external means of enforcement. For example, the firms may rely on recourse to the judicial system or quasi-judicial mechanisms such as arbitration to enforce their contracts or obtain damages if the contract is breached. Alternatively, the firms could enlist the support of intermediaries and post performance bonds, etc. Either way, however, non-trivial transaction costs are to be expected in addition to the time and effort spent in bargaining *per se*.

In addition to the fixed entry costs, the firms face variable transaction costs that reduce the value of the exchange. While we consider transaction costs explicitly because they are particularly important in transition economies, we abstract from issues of asymmetric information for simplicity. Whatever the institutional arrangements in a particular economy, transaction costs will often be the highest for fully cooperative investment and exchange contracts, lower for partially cooperative exchange contracts and the lowest for spot contracts. Of course, the potential private and social benefits, net of transaction costs, are also the highest for fully cooperative investment and exchange contracts, lower for partially cooperative exchange contracts and the lowest for spot contracts. Thus, the magnitudes of the respective transaction costs are crucial not only because they directly affect the exchange and investment levels that will arise for each type of contract, but also because they influence the decision on whether more cooperative forms of contracts will be chosen.

There are two important differences between the developed market economies and transition economies such as the Russian Federation. The first difference concerns the magnitude of bilateral producer and consumer surpluses and thus the importance of any particular bilateral transaction. In the developed market economies, where there are more substitute customers and suppliers, the bilateral surpluses tend to be smaller and the relationships between firms tend to be more competitive. Each bilateral transaction, therefore, tends to be less important. Second, there are differences in transaction costs. While contracts with investment as well as exchange commitments are quite common in many developed market economies where they are enforceable at low cost, such fully cooperative contracts are rare in transition economies. Higher transaction costs also make partially cooperative exchange contracts less prevalent.

We analyze the spot contracts first because they form the default if the firms are not able to agree on one of the cooperative forms of contract. Further we start at the stage three, the exchange stage, because the firms will anticipate the payoffs or outcomes arising from exchange when they make their investment decisions.

THE EXCHANGE STAGE WITH A NON-COOPERATIVE SPOT CONTRACT

The total surplus generated by exchange is equal to the revenue of the downstream firm minus the cost of the upstream firm. We make fairly innocuous baseline assumptions concerning the configuration of the marginal-revenue and marginal-cost functions to streamline the analysis.[30] Under these assumptions, there are potential net benefits from the exchange provided that the marginal revenue of the downstream firm initially exceeds the marginal cost of the upstream firm. Further, the socially optimal level of exchange, which maximizes the total surplus, equates the marginal revenue of downstream firm with the marginal cost of the upstream firm. In Figure 5.2, the efficient level of exchange of good y is Y^*, and the shadow value is, P^*, as determined by the intersection of upstream firm A's marginal cost curve, MC_A, and downstream firm B's marginal revenue curve, MR_B. Further, the maximum total surplus is the sum of the areas enclosed by MC_A and MR_B. An increase in the capital investment of firm A or a reduction in its transaction costs shifts its marginal cost curve downward and, thereby, increases the socially optimal output and the maximum total surplus, but reduces the shadow value of the good. Meanwhile, an increase in the capital investment of firm B or a reduction in its transaction costs shifts its marginal revenue curve upward, and increases the socially optimal output, the maximum total surplus, and the shadow value.

It will ultimately be assumed that each firm chooses its optimum (marginal) markup — the difference between the price and its marginal valuation — conditional on that of its opponent as in Gaisford et al. (1995). By using markups as the instruments of market power we avoid several modeling difficulties that would otherwise arise in a bilateral context.[31] The markup of the upstream firm is the difference between the price and its marginal cost, while

---

[30] The slope of the marginal cost (revenue) curve of the upstream (downstream) firm is assumed to be positive (negative) and to remain constant or become steeper as the output (input) quantity rises. Either an increase in capital investment by the downstream (upstream) firm or a decrease in its per-unit transaction costs shifts both the total and marginal cost (revenue) curves down (up), and leaves the slope of the marginal cost (revenue) function unchanged or makes it flatter. It is also assumed that each firm faces decreasing returns to scale so as to guarantee non-infinite values of the optimum investment and exchange levels for the full game. For any given levels of transaction costs, if the upstream (downstream) firm doubles its capital investment and output (input), its cost (revenue) more than (less than) doubles.

[31] On the one hand, if one firm were to choose price and the other were to choose quantity, then all of the market power would be arbitrarily assigned to the price setting firm. On the other hand, obvious complications arise if both firms tried to simultaneously choose the price or alternatively the quantity. While it is possible to allow both firms to set quantity or price constraints, the results are not attractive. If both firms are assumed to set price constraints, a competitive volume of exchange is automatic because both firms are effectively price takers. If both firms set quantity constraints, the volume of exchange approaches zero as in quota retaliation games in international trade (Rodriguez, 1974).

the markup of the downstream firm is the difference between its marginal revenue and the price. These markups implicitly define the respective offers that each firm submits to the broker. The markup of the upstream firm gives rise to a restricted supply curve, while that of the downstream firm gives rise to a restricted demand curve. When downstream firm A's markup in Figure 5.2 is $\tilde{M}_A$, its restricted supply function is $\tilde{RS}_A$, and similarly, when upstream firm B's markup is $\tilde{M}_B$, its restricted demand function is $\tilde{RD}_B$. Since these "supply" and "demand" curves are subject to restriction, this bilateral relationship is distinct from a competitive market; neither firm is a price-taker. In Figure 5.2 when the restricted supply and demand functions are $\tilde{RS}_A$ and $\tilde{RD}_B$, the spot quantity determined by the broker is $\tilde{Y}$. An increase in either firm's markup reduces the spot quantity of good y.

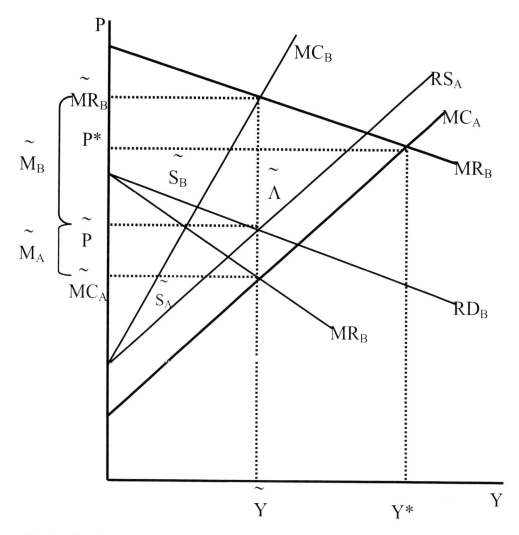

Figure 5.2. Payoffs with Non-Cooperative Spot Contracts.

Each firm chooses its optimum markup contingent on the markup of its opponent. The upstream firm behaves as a standard monopolist. In Figure 5.2, upstream firm A faces the restricted-demand curve of downstream firm B, $R\tilde{D}_B$. Consequently, the associated marginal revenue curve that upstream firm A faces is MR_A. The upstream firm chooses its optimum output where its marginal cost, MC_A, is equated with the marginal revenue that it faces, MR_A. In so doing, the upstream firm implicitly chooses its optimum markup, $\tilde{M}_A$, conditional on the markup of the downstream firm. As shown in Figure 5.3, there is a best-response function for upstream firm A for the third stage of the game, $R3_A$, specifying its optimum markup contingent on each possible value of the downstream firm's markup.

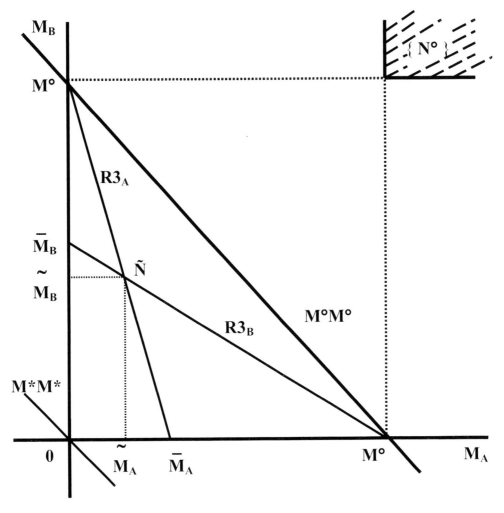

Figure 5.3. Nash-Equilibrium Markups with Non-Cooperative Spot Contracts in the Exchange Sub-Game.

Analogously, the downstream firm behaves as a standard monopsony. In Figure 5.2, the downstream firm B faces the marginal input cost curve, MC_B, which is derived from the restricted-supply curve of upstream firm A, $R\tilde{S}_A$. Since the downstream firm's optimum position equates its marginal revenue, MR_B, with the marginal input cost that it faces, MC_B, its optimum markup is $\tilde{M}_B$. In Figure 5.3, the best-response function for downstream firm B, $R3_A$, shows its optimum markup for each value of the upstream firm's markup.

Figure 5.3 shows a typical configuration of the best response curves of the two firms. Since these best-response functions are negatively sloped, the markups are said to be strategic substitutes (Bulow *et al.*, 1985). Further, an increase in the optimum markup of one firm leads a to a *reduction* in the other firm's optimum markup that is of a smaller magnitude. Consequently, there is a unique stable Nash or "no-regrets" equilibrium involving non-prohibitive markups for the non-cooperative bilateral-monopoly sub-game at $\tilde{N}$ in Figure 5.3 where the two best response functions intersect. The Nash equilibrium markup of the upstream firm is $\tilde{M}_A$, while that of the downstream firm is $\tilde{M}_B$. A higher level of capital investment (transaction costs) for any one firm shifts the reaction functions of both firms away from (toward) the origin. Since having more capital (higher transaction costs) provides a strategic advantage (disadvantage) by making a firm's marginal valuation function flatter (steeper), the other firm's Nash equilibrium markup could fall (rise) but its own markup must rise (fall).

Given that $\tilde{M}_A$ and $\tilde{M}_B$ constitute a Nash equilibrium in Figure 5.3, it follows that $\tilde{Y}$ and $\tilde{P}$ are the Nash equilibrium quantity and price in Figure 5.2. Further, the Nash equilibrium surplus obtained by the upstream firm is $\tilde{S}_A$, that of the downstream firm is $\tilde{S}_B$ and the efficiency or deadweight loss is $\tilde{\Lambda}$. Under the baseline assumptions, a higher level of capital investment (transaction costs) for any one firm, necessarily raises (lowers) the Nash equilibrium surplus of the other firm. The Nash equilibrium total surplus and efficiency loss also rise (fall). The fact that increased investment by one firm increases the surplus of the other firm is indicative of the standard pecuniary external economies that underlie the analysis of opportunism in Klein *et al.* (1978) and Williamson (1955).

Since efficiency requires the aggregate markup, but not the individual markups, to be equal to zero, the M^*M^* line in Figure 5.3 shows the combinations of markups for the two firms that are efficient. As the aggregate markup rises above zero, the volume of exchange and the total surplus fall, while the deadweight loss rises. Finally, if the aggregate markup rises to equate with or exceed the difference between the intercepts of firm B's marginal revenue function and firm A's marginal cost function, then exchange ceases, the total surplus is equal to zero and the deadweight loss is equal to S^*. In 5-3, all combinations of markups lying on, or to the right of, the $M^\circ M^\circ$ line result in the cessation of exchange.

It is useful to compare the results that arise for a non-cooperative bilateral-monopoly with those that would arise, *ceteris paribus*, under pure monopoly or pure monopsony. If firm B were to set its markup equal to zero in Figure 5.3, then firm A would be a pure monopoly and would set its markup equal to $\overline{M}_A$. This is unambiguously smaller than the Nash equilibrium aggregate markup, $\tilde{M} = \tilde{M}_A + \tilde{M}_B$. Thus, the reduction in output and the efficiency loss is larger with a non-cooperative spot contract than it would be under pure monopoly. Similarly, since the Nash equilibrium aggregate markup exceeds the pure monopsony markup of firm B, $\overline{M}_B$, the reduction in output and the efficiency loss is also larger with a non-cooperative spot contract than it would be under pure monopsony.[32]

THE INVESTMENT STAGE WITH A NON-COOPERATIVE SPOT CONTRACT

In the completely non-cooperative (nn) game where the firms decide against bargaining towards a cooperative contract at stage one, a broker will ultimately manage the terms of exchange through a spot contract at stage three. The firms determine investment levels independently and non-cooperatively at stage two and they set markups non-cooperatively at stage three. Of course, the firms make their stage-two investment decisions with an eye toward their stage-three payoffs or surpluses. For each firm, the optimal capital investment arises where its marginal benefit of capital is equal to the marginal cost, which is one. These optimum investment conditions can be interpreted as best response functions for investment levels. For example, the upstream firm's marginal benefit equals marginal cost condition for investment determines its optimal capital investment for the upstream firm conditional on that of the downstream firm.

In Figure 5.4, the best response functions of the upstream and downstream firms for stage two in the completely non-cooperative game are $R2_A^{nn}$ and $R2_B^{nn}$. Consequently, K_A^{nn} and K_B^{nn} are the Nash equilibrium levels of capital investment for the upstream and downstream firms. This configuration of best response functions is typical. The best response functions are positively sloped and the capital investment levels are strategic complements (Bulow et al., 1985) because additional capital investment by one firm makes capital investment by the other firm more productive. Further, in the typical case a firm's optimal capital investment rises by less than one percent when the other firm's capital investment rises by exactly one percent. In the typical case, there is a unique, stable Nash equilibrium involving strictly positive capital investment levels, but in atypical cases there could be multiple equilibria.

An outcome with no investment by either firm and with no subsequent exchange between them can be an equilibrium outcome in the completely non-cooperative game. Such an outcome can arise either because of high transaction costs or high entry costs. First, suppose that transactions costs are sufficiently high that the maximum total surplus available from exchange is equal to zero because the intercept of A's marginal cost function is greater than or equal to that of firm B's revenue function. In this situation, the $M^{\circ}M^{\circ}$ zero-exchange line in Figure 5.3 would go through the origin, and the Nash equilibrium point, $\tilde{N}$, would lie at the origin. Similarly, the best response functions for stage-two capital investment in Figure 5.4, $R2_A^{nn}$ and $R2_B^{nn}$, would intersect at the origin and there would be no investment. Alternatively, suppose that entry costs were such that either or both of the firms would earn negative profit after making investments and setting markups non-cooperatively. In such a situation zero investments and prohibitive markups comprise the equilibrium for the

---

[32] Since chains of product-market monopolies lead to a multiple margin phenomenon (Spengler,1950; Tirole 1988), chains of bilateral monopolies exacerbate the problem. In fact, the constriction of the quantity transacted at each successive stage of production and distribution is one of the most prevalent problems in the former command economies (Hobbs et al., 1997).

completely non-cooperative sub-game. Neither firm regrets setting a mark-up that curtails exchange, given that the other firm has set such a prohibitive markup. Further, neither firm will regret its investment decision if they both have refrained from making capital investments or paying entry costs at stage two.[33] Such no-investment, no-production equilibria are more prevalent in developing countries and transition economies where transaction costs are higher than in the advanced market economies.

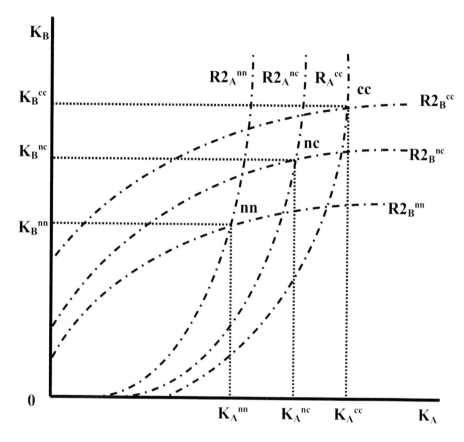

Figure 5.4. Capital Investment Levels in the Various Games Conditional on Equal Transaction Costs

EXCHANGE AND INVESTMENT WITH A PARTIALLY COOPERATIVE EXCHANGE CONTRACT

In the partially cooperative game, nc, firms A and B set their investment levels non-cooperatively in stage two, but their exchange contract sets cooperative terms of exchange for stage three. The efficient quantity conditional on the prevailing capital investments, Y^*, is always transacted under an exchange contract and consequently the underlying markups of

---

[33] Any pair of markups in the set $\{N^o\}$ in Figure 5-3 is an alternative Nash equilibrium to $\tilde{N}$ in the exchange sub-game. If both firms would earn positive profits at $\tilde{N}$, however, they would be expected to focus on that mutually superior Nash equilibrium.

the two firms sum to zero. The price, however, does not generally reflect the shadow value of the good, P^*, and the markup of each firm is not set equal to zero. Rather, the price becomes a purely distributive instrument.

The non-cooperative spot contract from the completely non-cooperative game constrains the cooperative exchange game because the Nash equilibrium surpluses of firms A and B provide the disagreement payoffs. If the firms failed to agree on a cooperative exchange outcome, then they would default into non-cooperative behaviour. Thus, in order to agree each firm must get at least the surplus that would arise in non-cooperative spot contract with whatever capital investments are on hand. In essence, the Nash bargaining solution to the cooperative, stage-three exchange sub-game amounts to splitting in half the net benefits from cooperation adjusted for differences in transaction costs (see Gravelle and Rees, 1992; Grout, 1984; and Hart, 1995). Suppose for a moment that both the capital investments and transaction cost for the non-cooperative spot contract and for the cooperative exchange contract were the same. In this case, the net benefit of cooperation on exchange would amount to recovering the efficiency loss, which would have arisen with non-cooperative play. While higher transaction costs under the cooperative exchange contract serve to reduce the net benefits from cooperation, higher capital investments will push those net benefits up.

The firms will anticipate receiving their spot-contract surplus or disagreement payoff *plus* half the net benefits of cooperation when they make their investment decisions. Each firm's capital investment level continues to be set independently to maximize its own profit at stage two. Once again, best response curves for capital investment can be formulated for each firm based on the marginal benefit equal to marginal cost criterion for profit maximization. In Figure 4, these best response functions for the upstream and downstream firm are shown as $R2_A^{nc}$ and $R2_B^{nc}$, and therefore the Nash equilibrium levels of capital investment for the non-cooperative second stage are K_A^{nc} and K_B^{nc}. The best response functions for the partially cooperative exchange contract differ from those for the non-cooperative spot contract because a firm's capital investment affects its share of the net-benefits of cooperation as well as its spot-contract surplus.

EXCHANGE AND INVESTMENT IN WITH A FULLY COOPERATIVE CONTRACT

We now consider the fully cooperative sub-game, *cc*, where both investment and exchange are cooperative. Since the payoffs are fully transferable simply by adjusting the price at the exchange stage, the fully cooperative investment levels can be determined by choosing K_A and K_B to maximize aggregate or joint profits. The solution to this problem requires that the fully cooperative marginal benefit of capital in each firm be equated with the marginal cost of capital. Given the baseline assumptions, the capital stocks of the two firms are complementary in the sense that one firm's optimal capital investment increases as the other firm's capital investment rises. Since an increase in investment by one firm makes the good available on more advantageous terms to the other firm, the marginal benefit of the other firm's capital rises and the optimal quantity of capital for the other firm rises. Consequently, the fully cooperative investment curves, which are shown by $R2_A^{cc}$ and $R2_B^{cc}$

in Figure 5.4, are positively sloped. The fully cooperative Nash equilibrium capital investments of the upstream and downstream firms are, therefore, K_A^{cc} and K_B^{cc}.

Since the partially cooperative game provides the disagreement payoffs for the fully cooperative game, each firm receives half of the net benefits from setting investment levels cooperatively in addition to its profits from the partially cooperative game. By analogy with the partially cooperative game, the efficient quantity is exchanged in the fully cooperative game, but the price is set so as to split the net benefits of cooperation on investment and exchange. While the underlying markups sum to zero, they are not, in general, individually equal to zero.

THE CHOICE OF CONTRACTS

To completely assess the bilateral transaction game, it is necessary to address the choice of contracts at stage one. The current modeling framework allows three possibilities: (1) a non-cooperative spot contract (i.e., the completely non-cooperative sub-game), (2) a cooperative exchange contract (i.e., the partially cooperative sub-game), and (3) a cooperative investment and exchange contract (i.e., the fully cooperative sub-game). While either firm could potentially veto a move more cooperative forms of contract, both parties will generally agree on the form of contract that is most desirable because each of the cooperative forms of contracts involve splitting the associated net benefits. Transaction and entry costs have an important bearing on the form of contract that they will choose.

To begin, it is helpful to consider the rather unlikely case where variable transaction costs as well as entry costs are the same for all three types of contracts. In this case, the marginal benefit of capital investment would be unambiguously higher in the partially cooperative game than in the non-cooperative game. Further, the marginal benefit of capital investment must be higher still in the fully cooperative game since due consideration is given to the fact that an increase in one firm's capital confers benefits on the other firm. As a result, for any given capital investment by the downstream firm, therefore, the upstream firm's optimum capital investment would be the highest in the fully cooperative sub-game, lower in the partially cooperative sub-game and the lowest in the completely non-cooperative sub game. Thus, in Figure 5.4, the upstream firm's capital investment curve for the fully cooperative game, $R2_A^{cc}$, would necessarily lie to the right of its best-response function for the partially cooperative game, $R2_A^{nc}$, which in turn would lie to the right of its best-response function for the completely non-cooperative game, $R2_A^{nn}$. Analogously, the downstream firm's capital investment curve for capital investment in the fully cooperative game, $R2_B^{cc}$, would lie above its best-response function for the partially cooperative game, $R2_B^{nc}$, which, in turn, would lie above its best-response function for the completely non-cooperative game, $R2_B^{nn}$. Since the best-response curves for the fully cooperative sub-game must be positively sloped, the investment levels of both firms under a cooperative exchange and investment contract would be unambiguously higher than with either a cooperative exchange contract or a non-cooperative spot contract if transaction costs were equal. Further, in the typical case where the reaction functions for the partially cooperative sub-game are positively sloped as shown in

Figure 5.4, the capital investments of both firms would be higher in the partially cooperative game than in the completely non-cooperative game.

Now consider the effect of an increase in transaction costs but, for simplicity, continue to assume transaction costs and entry costs are uniform for all three types of contract. Regardless of the type of contract, higher transaction costs experienced by any one firm reduce its total and marginal benefits of capital investment for both firms and shifts their best response functions curves toward the origin. Since the fully cooperative investment curves must be positively sloped, there is an unambiguous reduction in capital investment by both firms in this sub-game. In the typical case shown in Figure 5.4 where the best-response functions are positively sloped for the partially cooperative and completely non-cooperative sub games, the capital investments of both firms would also be reduced under these sub-games. More generally, the capital investment of at least one of the two firms must decline under the partially cooperative and completely non-cooperative sub-games. Consequently, higher transaction costs tend to be associated with lower overall capital investment, as well as lower total surpluses and lower volumes of exchange, regardless of the contract type.

If the fixed entry costs and variable transactions costs are the symmetric in all three sub-games, then overall profits will be highest in the fully cooperative sub-game, lower in the partially cooperative sub-game and lowest in the completely non-cooperative sub-game. Consequently, only cooperative investment and exchange contracts would be observed. Moreover, gradual increases in entry costs will make non-cooperative spot contracts unprofitable first, cooperative exchange contracts unprofitable next, and finally render investment and exchange contracts uneconomic last. Provided that profits remain positive, however, the size of the entry costs have no impact on either the quantity exchanged or the investment levels in any of the three sub games. If the entry costs are larger in the fully cooperative sub-game, then cooperative investment and exchange contracts may be non-profitable, while cooperative exchange contracts and/or non-cooperative spot contracts remain profitable. Analogously, high entry costs in the partially cooperative sub-game can make profits negative, although profits are positive in the non-cooperative game.

Variable transaction costs, as noted earlier, will generally differ across contract types, and may often be highest for cooperative investment and exchange contracts and lowest for non-cooperative spot contracts. If the transaction costs in the fully cooperative sub-game were sufficiently greater than those in the other sub-games, the levels of capital investment and exchange in the fully cooperative game could be smaller than the corresponding levels in the partially cooperative sub-game and/or the completely non-cooperative sub-game. Similarly, higher transaction costs could lead to lower investment and exchange levels in the partially cooperative sub game than those in the completely non-cooperative sub-game.

CONCLUSION

Under-investment and under-production will be endemic in the Russian Federation and other former command economies as long as markets remain thin and transaction costs remain high. The problem is aggravated by poorly defined and enforced legal systems that inhibit the potential for cooperation between firms along the supply chain (Hobbs, et. al., 1997). These results suggest that a major review of transition policies may be warranted. For example, there have been calls for, but as yet little action by the state to undertake traditional monopoly *busting* activities. While a more vigorous application of competition policy is important, it is at best only a partial strategy that introduces further complications. In particular, enforced vertical segmentation could potentially exacerbate the problems associated with bilateral relations on thin markets. Horizontal division of productive assets may have some scope for success but, given the investments in extremely large scale integrated production facilities made during the command economy era, it may lead to nonviable sub-grouping of the existing assets (O'Neil and Kerr, 1997).

As thin markets stem largely from the high transaction costs, government resources should be directed towards providing infrastructure and fostering institutional arrangements to reduce such transaction costs. It becomes readily apparent that such endeavours can have a significant public-good aspect once transaction costs are viewed explicitly. Investment in transportation and, particularly, communications infrastructure will reduce the costs of market broadening. While a gradual reduction in transaction costs provides an impetus for additional production and investment for any given contract type, eventually successive transaction-cost reductions will permit the proliferation of more cooperative types of contracts. The reform of trade policy would also serve as a market-broadening policy that reduces the problems of high transaction costs and thin markets. While trade liberalization provides the potential for benefits over the long term, the immediate priority should be a move to more transparent measures such as tariffs and away from non-tariff measures and state trading monopolies.

Inadequate and poorly enforced commercial law may lead governments to attempt to re-exert control over inter-firm interfaces in an attempt to impose cooperative solutions where they fail to arise from bilateral interaction. While this may provide a short-term solution, particularly in cases where no-production, no-exchange equilibria arise, it will delay or derail the process of transition to a more efficient economic system based on market signals. The need to foster the development of a low cost and enforceable commercial legal system is imperative. According to Goldman (2000),

> ...reforms will be successful only when there is pressure from the public at large and the business community, not only for a set of more equitable laws but the enforcement of those laws, both from above and below. ... If this can be done, it will lead to the weakening of oligarchs and monopolists and also make it harder for the Russian mafia to maintain its control (p. 39).

The analysis in this paper suggests that even stepwise improvements in systems of commercial law that allow enforceable exchange commitments (i.e., partial cooperation) will enhance investment as well as production.

After a decade and a half of decline and stagnation, the Russian economy has shown very promising signs over the recent period. In spite of a significant rebounding of production and investment, significant structural problems remain. This chapter suggests that a major re-assessment of the initiatives put in place to facilitate transition is in order and a multi-faceted policy framework for broadening thin markets is needed. In addition to sound market-promoting policy, the stability of the policy regime is important in engendering lower transaction costs and greater investment. A higher risk of policy change translates into lower investment regardless of the type of contract. Governments at all levels should to strive to provide policy transparency and simplicity and keep compliance and documentation costs to a minimum.

REFERENCES

Bulow, J.I., Geanakopolos, J.D. and Klemperer, P.D. (1985). Multi-market Oligopoly: Strategic Substitutes and Compliments. *Journal of Political Economy*, 93 (3), 488-511.

Coase, R., (1937). The Nature of the Firm. *Economica*, new series 4, 386-405.

Gaisford, J.D., Hobbs, J.E., and Kerr, W.A. (2001). Making Markets Work: Modeling Agrifood Systems in Transition. *Canadian Journal of Agricultural* Economics, 49 (2), 181-202.

Gaisford, J.D., Hobbs, J.E. and Kerr, W.A. (1995). If the Food Doesn't Come - Vertical Coordination Problems in the CIS Food System: Some Perils of Privatization. *Agribusiness - An International Journal*, 11 (2), 179-186.

Goldman, M. (2000). Reprivatizing Russia. *Challenge* 43 (3), 28-43.

Gravelle, H. and Rees, R. (1992). *Microeconomics*, 2nd edn., London: Longman.

Grout, P.A. (1984). Investment and Wages in the Absence of Binding Contracts: A Nash Bargaining Approach. *Econometrica*, 52 (3), 449-460.

Hart, O. (1995). *Firms, Contracts and Market Structure*. Oxford: Oxford University Press.

Hobbs, J.E., Kerr, W.A. and Gaisford, J.D. (1997). *The Transformation of the Agri-Food Systems in Central and Eastern Europe and the New Independent States*. Wallingford: CAB International.

Joskow, P.A. (1987). Contract Duration and Relationship – Specific Investments: Empirical Evidence from Coal Markets. *American Economic Review*. 77 (1), 168-185.

Klein, B., Crawford, R.G. and Alchian, A.A. (1978). Vertical Integration, Appropriable Rents, and the Competitive Contracting Process. *Journal of Law and Economics*, 28 (2), 297-326.

Myerson, R. B. and Satterthwaite, M.A. (1983). Efficient Mechanisms for Bilateral Trading. *Journal of Economic Theory*, 29, 265-281.

O'Neil, A.O. and Kerr, W.A. (1997). Vertical Coordination in a Post-command Agricultural System - Can Russian Dairy Farms be Transformed? *Agricultural Systems*, 53, 253-268.

Rodriguez, C.A. (1974). The Non-equivalence of Tariffs and Quotas Under Retaliation. *Journal of International Economics*, 4 (3), 295-298.

Spengler, J.J. (1950). Vertical Integration and Anti-trust Policy. *Journal of Political Economy*, 58 (4), 347-352.

Tirole, J. (1988). *The Theory of Industrial Organization*. Cambridge, MA: MIT Press.

Tirole, J. (1986). Procurement and Renegotiation. *Journal of Political Economy*, 94 (2), 235-259.

Williamson, O.E. (1975). *Markets and Hierarchies: Analyses and Anti-trust Implications*. New York: Free Press.

Chapter 6

ECONOMIC POLICY TO FOSTER RUSSIAN INDUSTRIAL DEVELOPMENT: A STATE CENTRED APPROACH

Vladimir Mayevsky

ABSTRACT

Underinvestment is chronic in Russian industry. This means that the existing capital stock is not being replaced as it depreciates. Poor capital markets and limited ability to access credit means that Russian firms cannot take advantage of potentially profitable investment opportunities. This chapter proposes that the state intervene to offset this market failure through a State Industrial Policy (SIP) whose primary aim is to target particular industries that will assist in the modernization of the Russian industrial base. The central elements of a SIP are outlined and suggestions for its implementation are provided.

INTRODUCTION

One of the major observable trends during Russia's transition from a command economy based on central planning to one based on market allocation has been the decline of the industrial sector. Revitalisation of Russia's industrial base has become an important political concern and a subject for considerable economic debate. One position in this debate is that the revitalisation of Russian industry will require a state centred approach that would encourage industrial growth through large-scale strategic investments by the central government. This chapter outlines the case for an interventionist State Industrial Policy (SIP).

THE DEFINITION OF STATE INDUSTRIAL POLICY

In a market oriented economy such as Russia, an interventionist SIP may be considered the aspect economic policy that shapes the structure of industrial production, is essential to the fostering of economic growth and ensuring competitiveness in the world economy, while taking into account the broad social interest. The need for such an approach to industrial policy increases during periods of economic, military, social and environmental shocks when normally self-regulating market mechanisms are unable to ensure a stable economic environment and the growth that flows from it.

The need for a well-formulated SIP also arises during the development and implementation of large-scale projects and programs and when constraints exist in the economy that necessitate the state setting priorities to guide industrial development. An example of this would be Russia's decision to seek membership in the World Trade Organisation (WTO). Russian accession to the WTO will require a considerable revamping of state subsidies to industry and a realignment of industries to international prices. The SIP can assist is such a transition.

In periods when the need for the SIP subsides, the government should concentrate on its usual functions (regulation, legislation, national defence and social policy). Self-regulating market mechanisms, free competition and private enterprise can be relied upon to foster industrial development.

AN ANALYSIS OF THE ECONOMIC SITUATION IN RUSSIA

The current economic situation in Russia's industrial sector differs in some respects from the situations described above when a central approach to SIP is normally required. Russia's economic problems are not caused by the inability of market mechanisms to overcome economic, social and military shocks. In Russia, serious economic shocks have arisen in large part because the Russian government has undertaken the transition from a centrally planned economy to the free market without having a long term, scientifically-based economic and social policy in place. Russian leaders have entirely abolished state planning, the centralised distribution of all resources and privatised a considerable portion of public property. They have failed, however, to create and maintain the necessary conditions for the efficient performance of the Russian financial system and have been unable to foster the full range of institutions that underpin a modern market economy. There are two main reasons for this:

Firstly, Russia's banking system is poorly developed.[34] It cannot adequately finance short-term projects in the real sector and, in practice, does not facilitate investment in long-term projects. The weakness of the Russian banking system is evidenced by fact that the ratio of the bank system's assets to GDP has not exceeded 40 per cent in recent years. By contrast, in most developed countries such as Germany, Japan and Switzerland, this ratio is between 200 to 300 percent. In the US, the ratio between its banking system's assets and GDP is 350

---

[34] Analysis has shown that a key cause reason for the poor lending performance of the Russian banking system is the contraction and subsequent tight control of the money supply (M2). Currently, the rate of monetary expansion is approximately five times less than it was in 1991. The dynamics of M2 depend largely on the policy of the Central Bank of the Russian Federation (CBRF). Given the tight control the government has over the activities of the CBRF, responsibility for the banking sector's difficulties lies directly with the government.

percent (see Ershov, *Voprosi ekonomiki*, 12, 2001, p.7). Hence, it can be argued that Russia's extremely high borrowing cost (more than 20 percent annually) are due to the government's tight monetary policy and its effect on commercial credit. Due to high Russian interest rates, Russian companies must either find foreign banks that offer lower interest rates or forgo investment opportunities.

Secondly, the Russian stock market is poorly developed in comparison to the US and other modern market economies. Table 6.1 shows that although the GDP of the United States is seventeen times greater than the Russian GDP, the US economy is capitalised to a much greater degree, almost 300 times higher, than the Russian economy. This suggests that trust in the stock market is much greater in the US, in part, because there is more confidence in the government's ability to regulate the potential for stock market abuse. The situation is aggravated by the well-known fact that the Russian stock market greatly underestimates the value of companies on its quoting sheets, causing share issues to be an extremely poor source of financing for the activities of these companies.[35]

The comparative efficiency of the system common in Europe where banks finance investments to a greater degree than in the US where capital markets dominate is a subject for debate among economists. In Russia, neither system has been adequately developed. Both the banking system and the stock market are in rudimentary stages of development. Thus, the Russian market is unable to provide sufficient capital to satisfy the demand for investment funds, leading to a lack of fixed capital re-investment in the real sector of the economy. As a result, there has been a significant decline in the renewal of fixed capital and a rise in its economic and physical depreciation. There are many examples of deteriorating plant and equipment. In particular, by the end of 2000, more than 70 percent of electrical power enterprises were employing fixed capital fifteen years past its useful economic life, as were 76 percent of engineering firms, 67 percent of metallurgical firms and 66 percent of chemical and petrochemical enterprises. One explanation for why this physical deterioration in industrial assets has arisen is that unlike modern market economies where more than half of fixed capital investment is financed by credit, share issues, bonds and other securities, these sources of funds financed only 9 per cent of fixed capital investment in Russia in the 2000 (see Table 6.2).

Table 6.1. A Comparison of Stock Markets in 2000

	USA	Great Britain	Poland	Russia
Number of companies in the quoting sheets of the largest national stock exchanges	10100	2200	220	40
Market capitalisation (billions dollars)	14000	2800	32	49
Daily share turnover (million dollars)	130000	29000	75	93

Source: *Voprosi Ekonomiki*, 2001, 7, p. 112.

---

[35] For example, at the outset of 2001 the capitalization of *Gasprom* per barrel of hydrocarbon fuel was 365 times less than that of Exxon (USA), and the capitalization of the Russian corporation "United Power System" was 25 times less than that of Edesa (Spain). See Voprosi Ekonomiki, 2001, 7, p. 112.

Table 6.2. Sources of Financing for Fixed Capital Investment in Russia in 2000

Total investment	100
Own resources of enterprises (amortization and profit)	55
Government	25
Bank credits	4
Bonds	4
Equities	1
Other (including foreign investment)	11

Source: *Voprosi ekonomiki*, 2001, 11, p. 8.

Simple calculations show that an increase in the share of credit, equity and bond financing from 9 to 50 percent would increase total fixed capital investment in Russia by 1.8 times as long as the amount of financing through other sources remained unchanged. Thus, the insufficient development of Russia's financial system is a key deterrent to industrial development. As a result, Russia has difficulty attracting financial resources. The Russian practice has been to solve this problem through external means, such as foreign investment and capital equipment imports.

Russia's investment problems will be resolved when Russian industries can finance projects without government assistance and the financial system is able to generate sufficient capital domestically so that there is no need to rely on foreign investment. This is the direction that all government policies should be oriented towards in order to fully develop a market economy capable sustainable growth. The goal is to form a liberal market economy with an internationally competitive industrial sector where the state's role is largely regulatory.

Table 6.3. Industrial growth rate (per cent of the previous year)

	1998	1999	2000	2001	2001 compared to 1998
Total industry	94.8	111.0	111.9	105.2	130.7
Electrical power engineering	97.7	98.8	102.3	101.4	102.5
Fuel industry	97.4	102.5	104.9	106.2	114.2
Ferrous metallurgy	92.4	116.8	115.7	100.1	135.3
Nonferrous metallurgy	95.7	110.1	115.2	105.2	133.4
Chemical and petrochemical industry	94.0	124.1	113.1	107.3	150.6
Manufacturing engineering and metal-working	91.3	117.2	120.0	108.1	152.0
Wood, woodworking and pulp and paper industry	100.4	117.8	113.4	102.3	136.7
Building materials industry	93.7	110.2	113.1	106.4	132.6
Light industry	89.7	112.3	120.9	105.0	142.6
Food industry	100.8	103.6	114.4	108.2	128.2
Investment in fixed capital (total in the real and housing sectors)	88.0	105.3	117.4	108.4	134.0

Sources: *Goskomstat of RF*, 2001; The Center of Macroeconomic Strategy, the Institute of Economics of RAS (including data for January – October 2001).

Table 6.4. Official Forecasts and Actual Values for Main Macroeconomic Indices (As a Percentage of the Previous Year)

	1999	2000	2001
GDP growth rates			
Government forecast*	97.0-98.0	101.5	104.0
Actual**	105.4	109.0	105.5
Growth rates of industry			
Government forecast*	97.0	104.0	104.5
Actual**	111.0	111.9	105.2
Growth rates of investment in fixed capital			
Government forecast*	95.0-100.0	102.0-103.0	107.0
Actual**	105.3	117.4	108.4

Sources: *Ministry of Economy's Forecast for social and economic development.
**Data of Goscomstat RF.

Before fully developing the model proposed for a SIP in this chapter, the current performance of Russian industry will be explored. A question worthy of particular attention is how Russian industry achieved notable success from 1999 to 2001 despite the difficulties faced by the financial system. Official data show that industrial output increased by 30 percent from 1998 to the end of 2001. Furthermore, output in manufacturing, engineering and metal working, as well as in the chemical and petrochemical industries increased by 50 percent or more (see Table 6.3).

Furthermore, real incomes increased, unemployment fell and inflation declined. Consequently, there were positive effects, such as an increase in the birth rate, a decline in worker unrest and an improvement in the social climate. Even the government forecast more modest results in its official projections for social and economic developmen prepared annually by the Ministry of Economic Development and Trade (known as the Ministry of Economy of Russia before May 2000) (see Table 6.4).

These positive trends arose because of the rouble's devaluation in August 1998, when the rouble to US dollar exchange rate declined 400 percent over a few months. Russian producers took advantage of the situation, resulting in an expansion of the import competing sector in the domestic market. This expansion was not accompanied by large investments in fixed capital, which only increased by 34 percent from 1999 to 2001 and could not compensate for the fourfold decrease in fixed capital investment from 1992 to 1998. The lack of fixed capital investment during the expansion of Russia's import competing sector was mainly due to the availability of a large stock of idle productive capacity that had accumulated during the devastatingly deep recession that lasted from 1992 to 1996.

Increasing world prices for oil and oil products were another significant factor contributing to the revitalisation of the Russian economy from 1999 to 2001. The government was able to mitigate the problem of state debt, increase currency and gold reserves and expand the money supply (M2). Furthermore, there was a reduction in interest rates and growth in income arising as an indirect effect of strong world oil prices.

This period is also interesting because the rate at which the monetary base increased depended mainly on the size of export returns. Thus, growth was driven primarily by the exporting sector, chiefly oil and gas, as well as by metallurgical, petrochemical and timber firms and weapons producers. Although the benefits of such activities cannot be denied, one should be cognisant of the fact that they are driven by vested interests that are concerned with the maintenance, development and improvement of factors that are of importance to the exporting sector only. The exporting sector is indifferent to the problems of other sectors. For example, one can hardly hope that the exporters will engage in the modernisation of machine building for agriculture, or providing financial support for the purchase of agricultural equipment or to carry out research and development in the agricultural sector. Other industries, such as machine-tool manufacturing, instrument-making, machine building for light industry, food processing, pharmaceuticals, medical supplies, sport implements, etc. are also relatively isolated from the exporting sector. Thus, they must find other sources of financing for re-investment and industrial expansion.

The problem of fixed capital modernisation broadly across the economy should be a major concern for government policy along with the development of the Russian financial system. Resolving these problems is possible only if the government pursues a more effective and aggressive industrial policy fostering a highly efficient and liberal economy.

IS THERE A STATE INDUSTRIAL PLAN IN RUSSIA TODAY?

At present, there is no legislatively approved SIP. In fact, there is no SIP at all. In particular, in the document that sets forth the economic priorities of the government, "The Main Direction of Social and Economic Development of Russia towards 2010", there is no mention of an industrial strategy. Furthermore, in "The Declaration by the Government and Central Bank of the Russian Federation on Economic Policy for 2001 and Some Aspects of the Strategy for the Medium Period", industrial policy is mentioned only in the introductory section and is reduced to two objectives: reforming existing monopolies and restructuring non-competitive enterprises. In the "List of Main Social and Economic Problems (Tasks) Which the Policy of the Government of the Russian Federation Will Be Directed at Solving in 2001" prepared by the Ministry of Economic Development and Trade in August 2001, the elaboration of state innovation policy is postponed to some future date.

One should not conclude, however, that the government is not aware of, and attempting to deal with, the problems facing Russian industry. For example, the increase of railway, electric power and gas tariffs at the beginning of 2002 shows the government's active support of some basic industries and their need to modernise their fixed capital. Another example is the government's intention to raise customs for imports of used cars in order to protect the domestic automobile industry from external competitors. The federal budget is also an important tool of industrial policy. For example, in the framework of the 2002 federal budget, the government provided partial compensation for the cost of interest payments on credit to organisations in the fuel and energy complex and the textile industry, among others (see Clause 73). Budget credits were also given to the coal industry so that it can undertake investment projects (see Clause 76). Further, there was the ambitious federal purpose-oriented program "Electronic Russia", among others, that is being partially supported through government expenditures.

Thus, the Russian Federation's government is, *de facto*, actively engaged in industrial policy. However, these activities are conducted without any legislative approval, public discussion and expert examination. Further, how the government determined which industries to assist while leaving many others unsupported is opaque. It is also not clear why such assistance often takes the form of tariff increases rather than the long-term loans. The reason the government is avoiding deficit financing, which is conducive to having funds available for investment, also lacks transparency. Budget deficits have been, and still are, used extensively in fostering economic recovery in developed countries (see Table 6.5).

Table 6.5. US Budget Deficits, GDP Rates, and the GDP Deflator: 1983 - 1998

Years	Budget Deficit (billion $)	GDP rates (%)	GDP deflator (%)	Years	Budget Deficit (billion $)	GDP rates (%)	GDP deflator (%)
1983	-208	3.9	4.3	1991	-269	-1.0	4.0
1984	-185	6.2	4.6	1992	-290	2.7	2.7
1985	-212	3.2	3.8	1993	-255	2.2	2.7
1986	-221	2.9	2.8	1994	-203	3.5	2.2
1987	-150	3.1	2.9	1995	-164	2.0	2.7
1988	-155	3.9	3.5	1996	-108	2.8	2.3
1989	-152	2.5	5.0	1997	-22	3.8	2.0
1990	-221	0.8	4.8	1998	69	4.3	2.1

Source: Ershov, 2001, p. 16.
International Financial Statistics, 1998.

The data in Table 6.5 show that the US ran a budget deficit throughout most of the period from 1983-1998. In all of those years, (except during the crisis in 1991), the US economy was growing and the annual inflation index (the GDP deflator) did not exceed five percent. Thus, the budget deficit by no means hindered normal development in the US experience. The central question is why the Russian government is appears loath to follow the US example and consider the strategic use of deficit financing.

Recently, Russia's attitude toward a SIP began to change. The Ministry of Science, Industry and Technology of the Russian Federation declared in 2002 that its goal was to develop a unified state industrial, scientific and innovation policy, as well as to more efficiently regulate industry in order to secure domestic competitiveness and the stable development of the Russian economy. This was an important step towards the formation of an official SIP. To be fully effective, however, the development of the SIP must be conducted by subdivisions of the Ministry of Economic Development, the Ministry of Finance and the CBRF, as well as the Ministry of Science, Industry and Technology, because the SIP will be linked to the financial system.

A PROPOSAL FOR THE DESIGN OF A STATE INDUSTRIAL POLICY

The Purpose of the SIP

During the previous decade (1992 – 2001), the replacement of worn out or obsolete production equipment simply did not take place and the level of physical and economic depreciation in most industries reached critical levels. Hence, the main purpose of the SIP should be to accelerate the modernisation and renewal of fixed capital in various branches of the economy by utilising the existing industrial capacity of Russia (and possibly Byelorussia) to the greatest extent possible. In other words, industry should not be re-equipped with foreign machinery and other capital goods. The re-investment should be domestically financed to the greatest degree possible. Industrial modernisation should be accompanied by reforms and reorientation of the Russian Federation's financial system. Thus, the main purpose of the suggested SIP will be to strengthen domestic sectors that can contribute materially, technically and financially to economic development. Hence, imports of foreign equipment and foreign investment must be supplanted to the greatest degree possible by those of domestic origin.

This version of the SIP is not just an industrial policy, but combines aspects of financial policy as well. In the framework of this suggested SIP, the financial system is not expected to be a constraint on the replacement and modernisation of fixed capital, but a system whose restrictions must be relaxed in order to overcome the current dearth of investment funds. What is unique about our proposed version of the SIP is that it will not cause spiralling hyperinflation. The problems that may arise from relaxing financial restrictions on fixed capital investment can be avoided if some conventional practices are abandoned. For example, there is no reason to abandon policies involving an increase in government debt if such debt is incurred through long term state bonds (LSB), instead of short term state bonds (SSB), and the borrowed money (mainly from the CBRF) is used specifically to finance modernisation programs for domestic industries.[36] The role of the Development Budget (or Bank) should also be strengthened to promote the modernisation of fixed capital.

The main difficulty with the proposed SIP is not, however, in overcoming the restrictions imposed by conventional practices and policies. Instead, the problem lies in the inability of actors in Russia's investment community to respond objectively to an increase in investment demand if financial restrictions are relaxed. This difficulty arises because some Russian capital goods industries are not competitive with Western producers of similar capita goods, As a result, it is quite possible that if financial restrictions are relaxed sufficiently, many economic actors will attempt to convert investment funds granted in roubles into hard currency in order to purchase equipment and technology from abroad. Such a response could destabilise the Russian foreign exchange market by perpetrating a devaluation of the rouble and possibly an eventual bout of hyperinflation. Thus, total relaxation of financial restrictions may prove to be harmful rather than helpful and is, hence unwise. The question then arises as to how best to renew and modernise fixed capital in the Russian economy. This question will be answered within the context of the details of the SIP outlined in what follows.

Details of the Proposed SIP

The proposed SIP can be implemented once the government acknowledges that non-inflationary relaxation of financial restrictions is possible as long as the replacement and

---

[36] In February 2002, Prime Minister M.Kasianov drew attention of the Ministry of Finance to the expediency of addressing the increase of internal state debt, and this fact suggests some optimism concerning successful reform of the financial system.

modernisation of Russia's fixed capital stock could be achieved by utilising the available capacity of the Russian capital goods industry. This should be the focus of the government's policy despite the fact that some capital goods industry firms are not internationally competitive, particularly in their ability to produce high quality products. There are four possible strategies that conform to the objectives of the SIP outlined above.

The first strategy is to increase the competitiveness of the various segments of the Russian capital goods industry through the revitalisation and modernisation of those industries directly. To achieve this goal, the industries in question must have sufficient potential for development. Examples include the automobile industry, machine-tool manufacture, tool-making and electronic engineering. These industries are key players as they will form the core of modern industrial production in Russia. They do, however, require re-equipping modernisation, which may be accomplished largely through internal development. Imports are not required for these industries since the capital goods in question are composed of industries considered of strategic importance or providers of military equipment in the command era – hence, considerable capacity and experience exists. A deliberate relaxation of financial restrictions for these branches of industry will not involve import expansion or pressure on the rouble. There will also be no inflationary effects. Thus, the first strategy entails revitalisation and modernisation of the central core of Russian industry. It is a long-run strategy that would create a basis for the modernisation of fixed capital in the capital goods sector as a whole and a foundation for fixed capital modernisation in other industries.

The second strategy is to increase the competitiveness of key Russian industries in order to achieve the cutting edge of technology. This involves the re-investment and modernisation of fixed capital in the most advanced industrial branches of the Russian economy; e.g. the aircraft and space industry, the energy industry, watch-making and weapons production, by utilising the existing capacity of the domestic engineering industry. These industries can be competitive in the world market because they are capable of creating new products and developing superior technologies, thus promoting scientific and technical progress. However, these industries often lack the financial resources necessary to undertake the large scale projects that are required. Since government support is limited, they must resort to the services of Western investors. A relaxation of financial restrictions on these industries is equivalent to the substitution of domestic capital for foreign capital. Hence, this strategy will not exert any inflationary effects on the economy.

The third strategy involves investment support through loans to the major exporting industries (oil, gas and metallurgy) for modernising their fixed capital by utilising the current excess capacity available in the Russian engineering industry. Although exporting companies often use their own resources for investment, these resources are scarce because of the lack of capital reserves. Hence, firms in these industries need to borrow funds in order to invest. However, as pointed out above, the Russian banking system is unable to carry out large-scale and long-term financing at low interest rates. Consequently, when, for example, the *Lukoil* Corporation needed capital to reconstruct the oil-processing plant in Perm, it was forced to take out long-term loans from a large Western bank rather than from a Russian institution. This is a common situation in the current Russian capital market. Thus, in a similar fashion to the second strategy, the third strategy involves the relaxation of financial restrictions so that domestic loans become available to these industries. The difference is that this change would be made in order to bring the fuel and energy complex, as well as the Russian metallurgy industry, up to world standards.

The fourth strategy would be to modernise fixed capital in the industries that will not face direct foreign competition in the Russian market in order to prevent excessive capital depreciation in these industries. This type of strategy is necessary to prevent the risk of industrial disruptions caused by outdated procedures and to restore and maintain the production potential of vital industries, such as electrical power, railway transport, agriculture, housing, health care and social services. This strategy may be accomplished through the utilisation of surplus capacities in the energy, transport, agriculture engineering and metallurgy industries, among others. The only necessary condition is non-inflationary relaxation of financial restrictions on credit for the purposes of such modernisation. Domestic firms should not be permitted to purchase more efficient equipment from abroad (perhaps with the exception of Byelorussia). Correspondingly, import duties for such equipment should be raised to protect the domestic market.

The government must be proactive in promoting the fourth strategy, because the desired result will not arise as a spontaneous market outcome. The strategy should be abandoned after the industrial core has been modernised under the first strategy and is engaged in modernising industries such as the metallurgy, energy, transport and agricultural engineering.

These four strategies are different in regard to their functions and purposes. The first strategy provides the prerequisites for the formation of a competitive capital good sector in Russia. The second strategy expands industries that are currently competitive in the world market. The third strategy raises the fuel and energy sector and metallurgy to a higher level of competitiveness. The fourth strategy is oriented towards the maintenance of production capacities in necessary industries, although it will also promote their technological progress to a certain degree. However, all of these strategies are united by their reliance on the Russian capital good industry and in the fact that they can all be implemented with a non-inflationary impact on the economy. Furthermore, although financial capital constraints will be relaxed in the framework of each strategy, the state should actively finance these strategies through the development bank or a development budget. The state's assistance may be extended to enterprises that fall under the first strategy through the development bank. As for enterprises that fall under the second or third strategies, long-term crediting by the development bank is possible. Enterprises that fall under the fourth strategy may receive financing from a variety of sources.

In order to secure non-inflationary state financial support for the proposed SIP, each of the four strategies must be specified as a set of programs and projects for modernising corresponding branches particular industries. Further, within the framework of the first and second strategies, innovative projects are to be encouraged that will lead to the creation of new "crucial" technologies, which may help secure a leading position in the world for Russia. The Ministry of Science, Industry and Technology of the Russian Federation is currently planning such "super projects" (see the article by I. Klebanov in *Expert*, 2002, January 14, pp. 45-47).

The version of the SIP proposed here should not be restricted solely to the four strategies outlined above. There must be a fifth strategy which, contrary to the four previous strategies, deals with foreign factors affecting development rather than domestic factors, and may perhaps be the most important component of the SIP. The first four strategies do not encompass all of the problems surrounding the revitalisation and modernisation of the capital stock in Russia. There are industries in Russia whose fixed capital cannot be renewed through domestic investment, either because the domestic capital good industry lacks the necessary capacity to do so, or the capacities in question are not competitive compared to the rest of the world. In particular, the following industries are insufficiently developed in Russia: engineering for automobile construction, computer production, some sectors in food processing, some light industries, sports equipment and tourism. Therefore, fixed capital in these industries must be modernised through equipment imports (including second-hand equipment) and possibly foreign franchises.

As the rouble is not convertible in external markets, hard currency sold by exporters through the Moscow Interregional Currency Exchange (MICE) is the main financial resource for equipment imports (besides direct investment and borrowing from foreign banks). The state should not assist Russian importers with acquiring hard currency at the MICE. Such financial support might cause the rouble's devaluation and inflation. However, state policy should provide importers access to hard currency (although 50 percent of export returns must be re-converted at the MICE). State safeguards for foreign bank credits are also possible, as well as various legislative and political measures that could facilitate free access to Western capital equipment for importers. One way to accomplish this is through Russia's membership in the WTO.

However, there is a problem that can only be solved with the strategic participation of the state. If the four SIP strategies are implemented successfully, it will cause a notable increase in domestic demand for energy sources, metal and other primary resources whose export is actively promoted. If the Government introduces measures to restrict exports, the value of the rouble will gradually fall. As a result, purchases of Western equipment to modernise Russian fixed capital will also decrease. Thus, the modernisation and renewal of fixed capital in one part of economy will be at the expense of other sectors. Therefore, it is important to fully explore and implement the fifth strategy in order to deal with this trade off. In dealing with policies surrounding Russian exports, the fifth strategy may require that all programs utilise resource-saving technologies in order to deal with the problems caused by the increase in domestic demand for such resources.

Chapter 7

INVESTMENT ASPECTS OF PUBLIC INDUSTRIAL POLICY

Alexander Amosov

ABSTRACT

The considerable disruption to normal investment patterns since Russia began the process of transition is outlined. Based on the shortfall in re-investment the capital stock in Russia is aging and, in many cases, technologically antiquated. An investment strategy to overcome both past shortfalls in investment as well as for modernizing Russian industry is suggested. Particular attention is given to investment in key industrial sectors – power generation, oil and gas, transportation, housing and social infrastructure, capital goods and agricultural machinery. The resources required for research and development are also discussed.

INTRODUCTION

The Russian Government is following the recommendations of free market oriented economic research centres – think tanks – in its formulation of industrial policy. E. Yasin heads the most influential of these economic research centres. Until recently, the State Duma Committee for Economic Policy and Entrepreneurship had charged S. Glaziev with developing an alternative vision for investment policy targeted at revitalising the Russian industrial sector. In conjunction with others at the Centre for Evolutionary Economics, I have been working with analysts in the State Duma of the Russian Federation and the Russian Ministry of Science, Industry and Technologies (RMSIT) to further study the topic of an investment strategy for the re-invigoration and modernisation of Russian industry.

Underinvestment in capital goods and associated industries in Russia over the 1992 - 1998 period was officially declared as having reached crisis proportions. According to annual statistics compiled by RMSIT,[37] the low level of fixed capital investment from 1992 - 1998

---

[37] See Voprosi ekonomiki, 2002, No. 6, p. 92.

increased the average economic life of industrial equipment in Russia from 10.8 years in 1990 to 16 years in 1998 and, if the trend continued, to 30 years by 2002. On average, the normal useful economic life of industrial equipment is expected to be 12 years. There was a similar fixed capital depreciation in the centrally important transportation, agriculture, housing medical and social services as well as other branches of the economy. Although there was an increase in fixed capital investment from 1999-2001, investment growth rates remain insufficient even for the renewal of the fixed capital stock. Fully depreciated industrial machines and equipment in industry as a whole comprised 66.5 percent of the total stock in 2000. In the engineering, chemical and petrochemical industries, the stock of fixed capital that was fully depreciated exceeded 75 percent. It was projected that from 2003-2005, a large portion of production capacity in electrical power engineering as well as agricultural machinery and tractor stocks will be sufficiently decrepit that they can no longer contribute to production. There is also a crisis in the innovation sphere. Budgetary financing for innovative research and development, for example, was by 1998 one-third of the amount in 1992 (in comparable prices) according to data from the RMSIT. This bleak appraisal of investment levels is common to all the proposals pertaining to Russia's new investment policy. There is no disagreement in the various proposals regarding the necessity of increasing the volume of fixed capital investment and funding for innovation, although the proposals do differ in regard to methods of investment financing and the time period over which investment and innovation are to be pursued.

RE-INVESTING IN RUSSIA'S INDUSTRY

As noted above, the government has unofficially adopted the industrial policy formulated by E. Yasin's group. This policy was published in the journal *Voprosi ekonomiki*, and its authors' position has not changed since then.[38] In 2002, Yasin outlined his conceptual approach to industrial policy: first, there must be institutional changes, followed by an increase in investment and afterwards, increased economic output fostered by increased investment. Our principal objections to Yasin's approach is with the content and timing of the stages in his policy, rather than with the consistency of these activities with the goal of increasing investment. Yasin's group suggests the following stages in its investment policy.

Stage I (2000 - 2003): In the first stage, Russia must overcome its investment crisis, which has arisen from the lack of credit, and improve its investment climate. Yasin's group projected annual economic growth during this stage to be between 2-3 percent, but annual growth proved to be much lower in reality. Further, they did not predict significant investment gains during this stage.

Stage II (2004 - 2007): During this stage, the improved investment climate will drive investment growth. Yasin's group predicted GDP growth between 2 - 2.5 percent.

Stage III (2008 - 2010): In the third stage, Yasin's group projects high economic growth rates (between 7-8 percent) and a correspondingly high rate of investment growth.

In 2002, the President of Russia directed the government to foster more "ambitious" growth rates, but this had no impact on either the stages or sequencing of the government's

---

[38] E.Yasin. Perspektivy rossiiskoy ekonomiki: problemi i faktori rosta [Perspectives for Russian Economy: Problems and Factors of Growth.] Voprosi ekonomiki, 2002, No. 5, pp. 4 - 26

investment policy or on the projected and actual rates of investment growth. From 1992 - 1998, the Russian government pursued institutional reform through policies that were ineffective in the opinion of some experts in Russia and abroad. Yasin agreed with this view, although he was one of the principal government officials during the period of institutional reform including accelerated privatisation, which was conducted in gross violation of the existing legal framework and commercial norms. From 2002 to present, the government has not significantly changed its approach to institutional transformation. Hence, it is not clear why Russia's investment climate would benefit from industrial policy based on the work of Yasin's group since it is very similar to policies that were implemented in the 1990s.

Yasin's proposition that institutional reforms are required to create a stable investment climate in Russia is problematic. More than 90 percent of the laws necessary to support transformation of the economy have already been adopted, but there is a lack of political will to enforce these laws and adhere to commercial standards that are followed in many parts of the world. The government had the opportunity to show its commitment to such laws and standards from the beginning of the transitional period, but has failed to do so. Furthermore, if economic revival and rejuvenation of industrial investment is delayed until 2008 – 2010, fixed capital will become non-productive *en mass* due to physical depreciation and the loss of highly skilled workers and professionals.

Yasin's group developing industrial policy includes former and present representatives of the governing bodies of the Central Bank, the Ministry of Economic Development and the Ministry of Finance. This connection is important to keep in mind when examining the Yasin group's solution to the shortfall in financial resources for fixed capital investment and innovation. In a report published by Yasin's group, (see the footnote above), they state the following: "The domination of state investments, as well as investment made by large financial and industrial groups, cannot be allowed to actively participate in the process of transforming savings into investment. Instead, financial markets must dominate. Since securities markets in Russia cannot attract large pools of financial capital, banks should be responsible for providing credit." Yasin's group admits that the banking system in modern Russia is also "very weak and cannot solve the problems hindering modernisation and economic growth, nor meet the requirements on the basis of which securities markets may be built". The group proposes to solve the problem by accelerating the development of the banking system so that it can play a key role in the investment system. Therefore, banks must be increasingly capitalised in order to increase the volume of credit available to investors. Yasin's group also believes it is necessary to increase money demand and money supply without causing inflation as well as in promoting securities markets and attracting foreign capital.

In principle, there is no divergence between Yasin's proposal and its alternatives regarding the necessity of increasing the pool of loan capital in private banks and stimulating growth in money demand and money supply through methods that minimise inflation. At the same time, alternative proposals view different sources of investment financing, whether from the corporations, private banks or capital markets as well as the state, as an integrated system rather than as having conflicting roles. Another important distinction is that alternative proposals place considerable emphasis on the government consistently enforcing existing laws and decrees pertaining to the financial industry and innovative activity.

The proposed industrial policy put forth by Glaziev and the State Duma is more constructive. According to Glaziev's estimate, less than one-third of the capital goods capacity available in the Russian economy is currently being utilised. When exports are accounted for, this estimate declines even further. Furthermore, the total amount of financial capital controlled by Russian private banks is presently comparable to the capital of a single large foreign commercial bank. Thus, Russian banks operate in an environment characterised by an absence of institutions and infrastructure to facilitate investment and innovation.

According to Glaziev, "investment supports the realisation of economic priorities and growth when state banks function as development institutions". Using examples such as as post-war Japan and modern China, India and Brazil, Glaziev shows that an advantage of state banks is that they can be granted exclusive rights to cheap money resources by the government. In a number of cases, state development banks have received direct access to credit provided from government resources. The activation of the Russian Development Bank, as well as other banks connected with investment in the real sector, is an important component of the State Duma's proposed industrial policy. Glaziev pays particular attention to reforming the system and upgrading the technologies used by the Central Bank for money and credit distribution. He proposes "financial balance in the scale and proportion of credit allocation, as well as the enhancement of financial flows through institutions other than development banks." We agree with Glaziev's view and our goal is to reinforce his proposal, as well as to supplement it rather than provide an alternative. Our proposal is linked to the development of public policy measures that will sharply increase domestic investment in the near future.

The government transferred public industrial enterprises to the private sector in order to expand the role of self-financing by firms in the modernisation of industry. It was also expected to free up government resources so that they could be channelled into areas of government priorities. For a number of reasons however, recipients of government financing for industrial investment tend not to use these resources efficiently. Further, in the case of long-term investment projects financed by the state because profitability is expected to be low and self-financing out of profits is insufficient, difficulties arise due to unfavourable borrowing costs and restrictions and the absence of internal company resources to provide a hedge against investment risk. The inefficient use of government funds is also caused by the lack of accounting standards to ensure funds are spent in a manner that reflects the purpose for which they were provided.

In modern market economies, governance institutions exist to support organisations that provide credit and finance long-term projects with low profitability. These organisations benefit from grants of financial resources for fixed capital investment, to support innovative business ventures and provide financing for research and development projects that are significant for the industry as a whole. The Russian government has yet to initiate a system of non-commercial institutions with large pools of capital that can be loaned to high priority but low return sectors. Financial authorities still have not been able to increase the share of investment that is financed by savings accumulated through the securities market. This source of investment financing is virtually non-existent because pension and insurance funds have not developed as they have in modern market economies. As a result, Russian securities markets lack the large institutional investors that are typical in other jurisdictions. Pension funds have experienced little growth because the risks associated with investing in pensions are perceived as being very high because a lack of state control and safeguards in the investment sphere, as well as the underdevelopment and unreliability of the secondary market. In such a situation, the highest priority of government investment policy should be to create a favourable environment for industrial investment.

In a number of countries, national development banks have been established in order to increase financing for industrial investment. In March 1999, a directive of the Government of the Russian Federation established the Russian Development Bank (RDB) as the state credit organisation. However, during the three years of its existence, the RDB has not yet been active because Russian financial authorities have been debating the role of the organisation as a creditor in the investment process and the financial resources to be made available to it. The absence of lending activity by development institutions headed by the RDB has also been caused by contradictions in its statutes regarding the RDB's purpose as a crediting body. In other countries, a common principle with respect to the organisation of national development banks is that such institutions should not seek maximum profits either for credit recipients or for the bank itself. All profits of Western development banks are directed to reserves and other funds. Dividends of non-state shareholders are strictly limited, albeit often exempted from taxes. In Germany, according to federal law, the national development bank is excluded from the category of credit institutions. It is granted the status of a "public rights" corporation, a status that is conferred only on government bodies and their affiliated public policy agencies. By contrast, the RDB's goals and purpose, as formulated in its statutes, include functions that are more appropriate to commercial banks. In addition, the RDB has to fulfil functions such as accumulating state financial resources, developing financial leasing, providing credit, accounting and cash monitoring services to private firms and providing cash resources for executing the development budget. Instead of organising and regulating financial flows in the investment process, the RDB competes with commercial banks for financial resources.

In order to isolate the RDB from the private banking sector, it is necessary to abolish its commercial functions. Instead, it is necessary to create a network of banks affiliated with the RDB so that it can provide support for them rather than acting as a competitor. At the current point in time, Germany's many years of experience with similar credit organisations is probably a good model to follow whereby the national development bank directs credit resources to final borrowers through commercial banks, the latter working directly with customers who meet certain requirements. In this model, the RDB would evaluate the investment project and its degree of risk, search for an intermediary bank, monitor subsequent stages of the lending process and determine the division of risk between itself and the intermediary bank for the project in question.

The State Duma of the Russian Federation is debating whether to adopt the law entitled "On the Russian Development Bank", or to insert amendments into the more general law "On Banks and Banking Activities". In our opinion, a new law is required. The RDB can only assist in the renewal of Russian industry as a formal arm of the state. It is therefore important to define the RDB's status under this new law as a public sector credit corporation responsible for the organisation and control of investment funds that contribute to achieving the industrial policy of the state. In order for the RDB to embark upon its programs and activities, the agencies responsible for conducting industrial policy must also be strengthened through, for example, the development of a State Industrial Policy.

Various governments throughout the world conduct programs and purpose-oriented planning under industrial policy using different models. In the US, for example, the Congress is responsible for considering and accepting purpose-oriented programs and is engaged in this task every year from January to June. Governmental agencies, department and other bodies further give structure to purpose-oriented programs, which are then co-ordinated by the US government's administrative branch. There is no single "Gosplan" in the US. Governments in Japan, France and a number of other countries follow a different industrial policy, in which state planning committees develop and co-ordinate purpose-oriented programs. In Russia, according to the Law "On Federal Purpose-Oriented Programs", the Ministry of Economic Development is responsible for co-ordinating industrial policy. However, current legislation does not strictly regulate the initiation and development of purpose-oriented programs. This approach is ineffective due to the lack of financial resources to put such programs into action. Thus, few of these programs exist and it makes no sense to expand the number of programs if they cannot be executed. Along with the absence of regulations necessary for the expansion of targeted programs, the Ministry of Economic Development does not perform a role as co-ordinator of industrial policy. In 2001, the RMSIT, as well as the Ministry of Fuel and Power Engineering, the Ministry of Transport and a number of other agencies, outlined long-term programs to develop inter-industry complexes within their sectors. Ensuring that these strategic programs come to fruition required that the Ministry of Economic Development and the RDB strengthen their roles as co-ordinators of such programs. The Ministry of Economic Development, together with industrial ministries and agencies along with the participation of legislators (members of the Federal Assembly), must propose concrete purpose-oriented programs and investment projects that need the financial support of the RDB.

Currently, the main constraint on the RDB's activities is that it does not have sufficient resources to finance the required industrial projects. At the initial stage of the investment process, it will be necessary to provide approximately US$25 billion in annual investment above that provided from the private sector. The RDB's strategy should be divided into two stages: the initial stage, denoted the "restoration strategy", and the subsequent stage denoted the "strategy of innovative development". The second stage will commence once depreciated fixed capital has been replaced. Currently, Russia's financial and credit resources are less than half that required for replacing assets that have depreciated and many times less than the level of investment necessary to modernise Russian industries.

Western European countries and Japan passed through the revitalisation stage during the post-war period. Their experience may be useful to Russia because Germany and Japan managed to simultaneously restore industrial capacity and modernise, which subsequently became the driving force of their modern industrial development. The mobilisation of financial resources by the state in Germany and Japan is worthy of note. Both countries established funds for national development banks through the sale of commodities received as aid under the Marshall Plan. Financial support for Russia in the 1990s was primarily provided by international financial institutions in the form of credit with high interest rates. In the last few years, the Russian government has stopped accepting such credit and, thus, has taken a step in the right direction. The participation of Russian banks in smaller international investment projects is more effective and desirable. This form of co-operation makes it possible for Russian banks to accumulate technical experience in financing small business investments and the like.

The German experience is of particular interest because the government did not issue bonds in order raise funds for investment in projects that did not promise fast returns and high profits. Currently in Russia, proposals have been made to attract resources for the RDB by issuing bonds guaranteed by the state. However, such bonds can only be repaid during the subsequent development stage, when industrial enterprises reap the returns to the investment in modernising plant and equipment and, as a result, the state has stable sources of tax revenue that can be used to pay off its obligations.

In the restoration period, the RDB must obtain financial capital from the following sources:

(1) initial capital and budgetary support from the government for purpose-oriented programs;
(2) the participation of the Russian Savings Bank (under the patronage of the State) in purpose-oriented programs;
(3) the utilisation of the Central Bank's reserves for strategically important investments;
(4) the transfer of a portion of commercial banks' reserve funds to the RDB;

Furthermore, a secure investment environment must be developed by:

(5) ensuring the government guarantees and monitors investments made by pension funds;
(6) granting governmental guarantees and division of risk of industrial investments made by commercial banks;
(7) initiating a program to attract Russian capital held in foreign banks for investment in Russian industry (the experience of China in attracting of foreign Chinese capital may be helpful here);
(8) carrying out direct credit distribution via the Central Bank through the RDB for programs designated as having a high priority, combined with measures to protect against run-away inflation.

Industrial and economic ministries and agencies must undertake practical measures and develop sound institutions to fund investment programs in industries that produce non-tradable goods and services. These industries have been particularly disadvantaged in recent years because of their inability to acquire foreign exchange. The widespread use of government loans to priority investment projects combined with private financial resources will sharply increase the growth rate in investments and restore investment to levels required to replace depreciated assets and subsequently to modernise Russia's industrial base. Investment strategies for individual strategic and, hence high priority industrial sectors, will be discussed in what follows.

AN INVESTMENT STRATEGY FOR HIGH PRIORITY INDUSTRIES

According to the instructions of the President of the Russian Federation, industrial ministries and agencies, with the participation of research institutes, have developed alternatives to the industrial strategies of the Russian Corporation "United Power System" (RC UPS) and other firms in the electric power industry. The economic values arising from the research into alternative strategies show that financial resources that can be made available for investment in electrical power engineering and other branches of the fuel and power complex (FPC) may be increased without requiring that the price of the fuel increases or a rise in the energy tariff in excess of moderate inflation rates. Aside from retained earnings out of profits, the FPC needs funds made available from the state that have favourable interest and repayment terms so that they can invest in long-term capital-intensive projects. The Ministry of Power Engineering estimates the FPC's need for fixed capital investment from 2000-2010 to be US$180 billion, including more than US$16 billion for electrical power engineering. At the end of February 2002, the government approved the investment of approximately US$2.6 billion in electrical power engineering for the year. The portion of this investment that will be used to renew the RC UPS's and other companies' fixed capital is unknown. The chairman of RC UPS, A. Chubais, declared in March 2002 at an "Investment Forum" in Hanti-Mansyisk that the RC UPS intended to develop 890 megawatts of new electric power capacity in 2002, which is only 17.8 percent of the average annual additional electric power capacity that came on stream in the 1980s. An assessment of the contents of the reform initiated by the RC UPS shows that its main investment goal is to purchase shares of power companies. It is also supposed to generate considerable funding for portfolio investment by raising power tariffs. In contrast to the alternative strategies, the RC UPS calculates investment needs on the basis of tariff increases, not according to what is required to replace and modernise capital equipment. Hence, the following conclusions can be drawn:

(1) Despite the unprecedented increase in power tariffs, the electrical power engineering industry is not able to independently finance investment programs;
(2) Since raising the electricity tariff in excess of inflation provokes non-payment and contributes to inflationary pressure instead of providing a solution to the lack of investment funds, this practice should be abandoned;
(3) It is important that the electrical power engineering industry finances investment through its own private means, as well as receiving funds from the government.

Mixed financing is also necessary for companies in the oil and gas industry. The only difference is that this industry is governed by laws concerning the use of foreign capital to develop new oil and gas fields and particularly the agreements about the division of produce (i.e. input supplies) (ADP). According to the ADP, the Russian machine-building enterprises must supply 70 percent of the equipment used by the oil and gas industry. According to the RMSIT's estimates, foreign investment under the requirements of the ADP could potentially reach US$10 to 15 billion annually. Actual foreign investment in the fuel industry was more modest in 2000 at US$7.7 billion, even though market conditions (world and internal prices) were very favourable. According to data from the Russian Union of Oil and Gas Equipment Producers, total annual demand for equipment is US$4.8 billion dollars in the oil industry alone. In a study made by the Ministry of Power in 2000, it was estimated that US$17 billion dollars yearly are needed for capital investment in the oil, gas and coal industries (excluding investments stipulated by the ADP). According to our own estimates, and accounting for fixed capital depreciation in the extracting and manufacturing industries, as well as of pipelines and other technologically sophisticated equipment, the need for capital investment is much greater. Thus, the fuel industry should combine internally generated investment funds with financial resources provided through the state, including purpose-oriented investment funds.

In the official statistics, capital investment in pipelines is included as part of the "transportation" section. The transportation sector is the largest single investor in Russia. In 2000, total investment in all forms of transportation was equivalent to US$8.9 billion, including approximately US$2.1 billion of investment in railway transport. At present, increased investment in transportation is generated through price increases. However, the replacement of disabled rolling stock and the renewal of railway tracks and ports require an increased level of investment that cannot be covered by further price increases. Instead, investment needs must be met through a mixture of private and state investment financing.

The housing and community services (HCS) sector occupies third place in terms of fixed capital investment after the FPC and the transportation industry. The total amount of investment by the HCS is US$7.5 billion dollars annually. In order to establish a private housing market, the government has adopted a policy to fund residential construction and to provide the required community services such ad schools and hospitals. However, until now, Russian housing policy has not been linked to industrial policy, which is a serious strategic miscalculation. The co-ordination of housing and community services with industrial and investment policy ought to be structured as follows:

(1) The development of those capital goods that are used to provide residential construction materials and maintenance;
(2) Regulation and control of financial flows in state subsidised HCSs, as well as registration and revaluation of the HCS's fixed capital;
(3) State support of investment by households in housing construction as a measure of anti-inflation policy (i.e. by increasing supply and thus reducing pressure on housing prices and rents) in response to increasing household incomes that will eventually arise as a result of previously outlined investment in capital goods projects;
(4) Adjusting the relationship between the central government budget and the budgets of urban areas.

Accelerating capital goods investment will lead to a revival of the Russian economy causing incomes to grow and the development of a middle class. However, the income of the Russian middle class will initially be lower than those in Western Europe and North America. As a result, it will be impossible for the government to withdraw subsidies from the HCS in the near future. Increasing the HCS's tariffs is senseless because non-payments and tax revenue shortfalls will increase as a result, causing further financial difficulties in the sector. Instead, the government should strengthen state control over the large financial resources used by the sector, which are currently used inefficiently. In the wake of privatisation, HCS financial flows have proven to be extremely complicated. The value of fixed capital in this sector has not been re-valued according to the thousand-fold increases in prices and tariffs since the transition of the Russian economy began. Previously accumulated re-investment funds meant to cover depreciation have been lost and new funds to cover these expenses have not been accumulated. The proper organisation of the HCS's finances will enable it to obtain considerable investment funds to replace fully depreciated fixed capital. Thus, a national strategy to attract and develop investment financing and credit from various sources must be implemented to stimulate new housing construction.

Prior to 1999, government investment policy regarding the engineering industry (i.e. infrastructure excluding transport and power) was virtually absent despite the fact that it is the most important branch of the investment complex. The production of machines and equipment was drastically curtailed and the majority of production capacity remained idle, while the remainder was primarily used to repair and assemble machinery from inventory. Since mid-1999, employment of the engineering industry's capacity and its output of machines began to increase, as well as its exports. However, the growth rate of production in the engineering industry from 1999-2001 was adequate only for current requirements and not to offset any of the accumulated depreciation from years past. With regard to the requirements of the early revitalisation period of the alternative strategic plan, the growth rates in question should be several times higher. By the beginning of 2000, the depreciation of fixed capital in the engineering industry was 52.6 percent. Therefore, increased employment of the industry's production capacities due to growth in investment activity will require financing for an increased output targeted at current period depreciation and expansion, but also to replace and renew the industry's already depreciated fixed capital.

From 1998–2000, fixed capital investment in the engineering industry was less than half the amount from 1995–1996 and several times less than in 1990. In the 1990s, the industry financed 75 percent of its fixed capital investment through retained earnings and the remaining 25 percent was financed through outside investment, including 5 percent from government budgets at all levels. In 2002, the government abolished the industry's exemption from profit taxes on fixed capital investment. Although the tax rate on profits decreased at the same time, the industry's ability to finance its own investments was still reduced.

Taken as a whole, the state of investment financing in the engineering industry is so complicated that it cannot be solved successfully without the development of state programs and the co-ordination of financial and material flows by RMSIT, as well as other ministries and agencies. In part, extensive government support for this industry is required to ensure sufficient demand exists for its firms to reap the cost savings associated with economies of scale. Due to the cost savings associated with the scale effect, enterprises will be able to accumulate sufficient funds to ensure capital renewal. Any outside sources of investment funds should be used to foster innovation, undertake research and development and upgrade human capital so that new technologies and production methods can be mastered. In general, the role of industrial and economic ministries should be to ensure that industries receive sufficient investment support so that firms can attain economies of scale in production. As suggested above, strategies must be also developed to provide financial assistance to power companies and railway transportation. The capital goods sectors of the power generation and transportation industries can also obtain considerable re-investment capital through large scale orders. The state's role in this case is to organise appropriate investment programs, encourage research and development and ensure that investment funds are employed appropriately.

Within the framework of the alternative strategy developed here, the investment capital currently available to buyers of machines, equipment and electronic devices is insufficient for them to achieve economies of scale and, as a result, these industries requires direction and financial support from the government. In particular, during the rejuvenation period, the domestic machine assembly, instrument assembly and electronic industries will need budgetary and financial support. Estimates of the refurbishment of machine assembly plants have been published, showing that 10 percent of these plants have adapted successfully to market conditions and produce high-tech research intensive output. To achieve necessary the scale of production in machine assembly, it is necessary to increase the number plants producing near their capacity, as well as to augment the volume of orders for the 10 percent of enterprises that have preserved their personnel and technologies. As for the instrument making and electronic industries, the need for investment support is more acute.

A serious situation has also developed in the tractor and agricultural machine assembly industries. During the last decade, the agricultural industry lacked the means to purchase technology, and this has not changed. In the US and other modern market economies, farmers receive credit or production subsidies in order to purchase technology. They enjoy other advantages as well, such as machine and tractor stations and co-operative societies. In these countries, the state regulates prices in the agricultural machinery supply industry. In the 1990s, Russian state support for farmers that purchased tractors, combine harvesters and other technologically advanced machinery was negligible. This caused a recession in the production and delivery of agricultural equipment, causing a 50 percent reduction in the stock of agricultural machinery and tractors. Thus, in the near future, extensive breakdowns can be expected given that much of the stock of agricultural equipment is worn out.

From 1999-2001, production and delivery of agricultural equipment increased, causing positive growth rates in the agricultural industry. Financial support for purchases of modern equipment also increased and total purchases in 2001 were US$230 million. However, the required investment in tractors and agricultural machines is now estimated at US$2.6–3.3 billion annually. Therefore, the state must pursue strategies to increase the resources available to finance deliveries of new agricultural equipment in two ways. First of all, considerable financial resources may be obtained through state regulation of input prices. According to experts, the agricultural industry loses US$1–1.3 billion annually due to the increase of tariffs for prime energy sources and transportation services in excess of inflation, as well price increases for inputs obtained from the industrial sectors of the economy. Resources that are currently used to pay these price increases could instead be used to purchase modern equipment. In light of the critical levels of depreciation of agricultural machinery and equipment, the state must step in and expand and improve the distribution of agricultural credit for the leasing of tractors, combines and other equipment. Further, farms should have access to private sector bank credit for purchasing new equipment and technology.

CONCLUSION

Since 1999, the RMSIT and other ministries have followed strategies directed toward increasing the share of scientifically intensive and high-tech production in the engineering industry. The proportion of scientifically intensive output is calculated by dividing the volume of research and development expenditures by the volume of output achieved. If research and development costs are estimated, the value of high- tech production is evaluated instead. The following gradations are specified: if research and development costs exceed 8.5 percent of the output volume, then there is significant level of scientifically intensive production; if they are between 3.5 percent and 8.5 percent, there is a significant level of high- tech production. To design and conduct industrial policy in the scientifically intensive and high-tech sectors of Russian industry, the establishment of federal research centres for science and high technology has been ongoing since 1999. Further, the RMSIT and other agencies are classifying technological knowledge and elaborating strategies to develop competitive macro-technologies (i.e. transformative technologies).

Large-scale production based on scientifically intensive macro-technologies requires considerable resources to equip the new industries that arise. In modern market economies, high tech industries are often fostered and supported through government initiatives. In individual countries, such technological transformations are either directly financed through the budget or receive considerable support from the state. In Russia, state support for scientifically intensive technologies is still insignificant. Hence, there is an urgent need for purpose-oriented credit to be made available by the government for specific large-scale programs in this sector, such as the development of civil aviation, the nuclear power industry and the like. The volume of investment in scientifically intensive macro-technologies could increase to dozens of billion of US dollars annually, but this will only occur once stable economic development has been achieved.

Chapter 8

INTERNATIONAL TRADE POLICY AND REINVESTMENT IN THE RUSSIAN ECONOMY

James D. Gaisford and Inna Iourkova

ABSTRACT

Protectionism exists in all countries. In Russia, the industrial sector feels particularly threatened by foreign competition for a variety of reasons – underinvestment, technological obsolescence, poor quality – and, hence, is prone to seeking protection. The question is how politicians should respond to these predictable pleadings of vested interests. The case for a tariff-based trade regime that provided moderate levels of protection that does not discriminate among sectors is made. In particular, the benefits that a relatively open and stable trade regime can have in assisting in the process of transition are outlined. The obligations, constraints and opportunities arising from accession to the World Trade Organization are also presented.

INTRODUCTION

Under President Putin, Russia has set very ambitious goals for economic growth. At the same time, greater attention and effort has been expended on Russia's bid to join the World Trade Organization (WTO). While the Russian economy grew at a rate of about six percent annually between 2000 and 2006, this growth was supported by strong international energy prices. About two thirds of the Russian exports consist of oil, gas and other fuels. In this situation, any future weakening of world oil prices would likely reduce growth and could lead to another serious recession for the Russian economy. Should Russia work to reduce or, by contrast, consolidate its dependence on international markets? After the shocks associated with privatization, price liberalization and the economic crisis of 1998, the Russian government is determined to try to prevent further shocks to the Russian economy. Likewise, there is a strong domestic opposition to trade liberalization on the "wrong" economic terms.

Why should Russia bother about international trade or worry about the formulation of international trade policy? What are the appropriate national and transnational aspects of trade policy for a large transition economy such as Russia? In this chapter we argue that an open stable and transparent international policy regime is particularly important for Russia. While standard arguments concerning a more advantageous allocation of economic resources and investment across sectors remain highly important, there is a further highly compelling reason for an open trading regime. By broadening markets and promoting competition, international trade provides an opportunity to lessen transition problems associated with high transaction costs and thin markets, which are a legacy of the former command economy.[39] The pro-competitive effect of international trade not only increases economic activity by reducing the economic distortions associated with market power but also provides a basis for sustained increases in investment over the longer term. In this context, gaining approval for World Trade Organization (WTO) accession would help Russia consolidate many of its previous economic, regulatory and structural reforms. WTO accession would be a significant step on the road to full integration into the world economy that would benefit current WTO members, as well as Russia itself.

GAINS FROM TRADE AND IMPEDIMENTS TO TRADE

International trade provides, of course, potential benefits in the form of mutual gains for participating countries. Comparative advantage is the cornerstone of so called *inter-industry trade* where a country such as Russia exports one good, say petroleum, in return for the import of a different type of good, say automobiles. Comparative advantages and disadvantages exist because countries differ in important respect including natural resource endowments and climates, accumulated capital, know-how and technology, average income-levels and income distributions. Much of the trade between developed and less developed countries is based on comparative advantage because of the large differences in tastes, endowments, technologies and experience. Further, comparative advantage is always a two-way street. If Russia has an advantage in producing petroleum relative to automobiles in comparison with the European Union (EU), then the EU has an advantage in producing cars relative to oil in comparison to Russia. Thus, both countries can gain from exporting in accordance with their comparative advantages.

Intra-industry trade occurs when a country exports and imports different varieties of the same of good. For example, Russia may export some types of steel to the EU, while the EU exports other specialized varieties of steel to Russia. Indeed, much of the phenomenal increase in international trade among modern market economies has been trade of this intra-industry type. The causes of intra-industry trade tend to be linked with varying forms of scale economies. Countries are able to exploit larger economies of scale and scope when they produce for the world market. At the same time that producers are able to rationalize production, consumers have access to more variety because of the availability of imports. So-called *pro-competitive* effects also arise as domestic producers come into competition with foreigners. Thus, international trade also makes markets more competitive and lessens the distortionary effects of market power. For a large former command economy such as Russia,

---

[39] The problems for Russia that arise from high transaction costs and thin markets where there are few buyers and sellers are discussed in detail in other chapters in this book.

the latter pro-competitive benefits are likely to be more significant than greater economies of scale *per se*.

In spite of the pervasive view in most economics textbooks, international trade is not frictionless. The transaction costs and even the transport costs associated with international trade are typically higher than those associated with intra-national trade even for geographically disperse countries such as Russia. The higher are transaction and transport costs, the lower are trade volumes and the smaller are the gains from trade. Transport costs tend to be higher for international transactions simply because the distances involved are typically greater. Weak transportation and communications infrastructure, however, constrains intra-Russian trade as well. Firms also face additional risks in international transactions. Commercial risk is greater and the threat of opportunism is more serious because multiple legal jurisdictions are involved. Additional risk arises from fluctuating currency values. Market economies have been able to develop institutions for reducing risk. Just as there are costs associated with risk, there are costs associated with risk avoidance. Commercial risk can be reduced through the use of intermediaries such as trading houses or financial institutions,[40] and disputes can be resolved via international arbitration. Exchange-rate risk can be reduced by using forward or futures markets to *hedge* or close risky positions arising from the provisions for future payments and receipts in contracts.

Governments, both intentionally and unintentionally, take measures that affect the cost of international transactions. By maintaining fully convertible currencies, governments greatly reduce the costs of international transactions. Although firms do face exchange rate risk when they engage in international as opposed to intra-national trade, they need not resort to *counter-trade* or barter-type goods-for-goods transactions. The limitations of counter-trade are severe because a country is forced to balance its trade on a bilateral basis with each of its individual trading partners. Trade barriers such as import tariffs or export taxes also increase the costs of international trade. Even when explicit barriers are absent, customs and inspection lead to extra brokerage charges on international transactions.

Governments do intervene frequently in trade flows. Tariffs and Non-Tariff Barriers (NTBs) shelter firms in import-competing sectors and export subsidies support firms in export industries. Governments have strong incentives to intervene directly and indirectly in international trade as they pursue domestic political goals such as re-election and related economic goals such as supporting the incomes of various vested interests, stimulating regional development, etc. While the national interest tends to be a secondary consideration in the conduct of trade policy, limited trade restriction by a large country, such as Russia, can work to its overall advantage by increasing the world prices of its exports and reducing the prices of its imports. Since it is natural for countries to intervene, free trade does not represent a policy-equilibrium for the international economy even though it would be an efficient state in the absence of other forms of market failure. While each country's own interventions may further its interests, or at least those of its government, the actions of other countries typically

---

[40] For example, some banks specialize in document collection procedures that require a foreign buyer to make payment before gaining access to the goods. Documentary letters of credit provide for a further reduction in commercial risk for the seller, since payment is insured even if the buyer refuses to take possession (Kerr and Perdikis, 1995).

work in the opposite direction.[41] Consequently, multi-lateral trade liberalization is typically in the interest of most, if not all, countries.

Market-oriented countries have tried to deal with this self-defeating or *prisoners'-dilemma* aspect of protectionist international trade policy through multilateral efforts at the global and regional levels. At the global level, efforts at trade liberalization have been made through the General Agreement on Tariffs and Trade (GATT) and the World Trade Organization. At the regional level there have been many attempts at liberalization. The European Union (EU) and the North American Free Trade Agreement (NAFTA) are among the largest and most far-reaching Regional Trade Agreements (RTAs).

Before considering Russia's potential participation in the WTO and RTAs, it is useful to consider the conduct of Russia's trade policy from a purely national perspective. There are three important dimensions to be discussed. First, the orthodox arguments for tariffs rather non-tariff barriers become even more important for large spatially dispersed transition economies such as Russia. Second, it is in Russia's unilateral interest to pursue a regime of low to moderate tariffs rather than either high barriers or unilateral free trade. Third, it would be desirable to avoid using trade policy to defend losers or promote winners.

AVOIDING NON-TARIFF BARRIERS

For Russia and other transition economies, it is particularly important that the sole instrument of trade policy should be simple *ad valorem* or percentage import tariffs, rather than non-tariff barriers (NTBs) or state trading agencies. There is good reason that so-called "tariffication" along with tariff-reduction has been a core feature of the GATT since its inception. From the business point of view, tariffs facilitate greater trade by providing a much higher degree of transparency than NTBs or state trading agencies. Taking a longer-term perspective, this also provides a stimulus to investment by Russian firms that use imported intermediate goods as well as foreign exporters. From a government perspective, tariffs minimize administrative costs and minimize the possibilities for corruption as well as providing a source of government revenue. In Russia, reducing red tape and arbitrary bureaucratic action in customs administration would be an extremely important step in the process of transition. Tariffs also have other important advantages over NTBs. As economic growth occurs and Russian demand rises, tariffs allow an increase in trade volumes while quantitative measures do not.

Quantitative measures and state trading agencies almost inevitably lead to discrimination among trading partners whereas tariffs can and typically should be non-discriminatory. While non-discrimination is a central tenet of the GATT and WTO largely for reasons of fairness, there are strong economic grounds for non-discrimination as well. By extending the same most favoured nation (MFN) tariffs to all trade partners, whether inside or outside the WTO, Russia can ensure that imports arrive from the most efficient or lowest cost sources and that trade is not artificially diverted to high-cost countries by a discriminatory tariff structure.

---

[41] Johnson (1953), Dixit (1987), and Kennan and Riezman (1988) have examined the formal Nash equilibrium in tariffs for a stylized two-country, two-good world in which each country pursues a simple national-welfare-maximizing goal. Clearly, in the real world of international trade there are many countries trading many goods, pursuing many goals and using many policy instruments. Nevertheless, the central point still remains; in the world at large, with all its complexity, free trade is not a policy equilibrium.

Until Russia's bid to join the WTO is accepted, of course, its international commitments do not require that it grant all countries its lowest MFN tariff rate. Nevertheless, doing so is generally good pre-accession politics as well as good economic practice. As a large country, however, Russia could reasonably consider exceptions where it does not grant MFN status to specific countries because those countries do not afford it MFN status. Unless or until the Commonwealth of Independent States or successor arrangements become effective market-based regional trade organizations with virtually no internal trade barriers, the case for discrimination in favour of former Soviet republics such as Ukraine and Kazakhstan is also weak. This is true regardless of whether this discrimination occurs explicitly within the tariff structure or implicitly via NTB's, state trading agencies or the pricing policies of firms in which the state retains a major interest.

In relation to Russia and other transition economies, a further vitally important problem with quantitative measures, such as import quotas or voluntary export restraints (VERs) agreed to by foreigners, is that they are anti-competitive (Helpman and Krugman, 1989). To take an extreme example, suppose that there is a single Russian firm, but that the world market is competitive because there are many foreign firms. Under a tariff, the domestic firm would trigger a flood of imports if it raised its price above the world price plus the tariff. The domestic firm, therefore, is effectively a price taker, albeit at a price higher than the world price. By contrast, with quantitative restrictions the domestic firm can raise prices with impunity. Since the volume of imports remains fixed no matter how high the price is raised, quantitative measures help preserve market power and prevent competition. Taking a long-term perspective, non-tariff barriers will also lead to greater misallocation of investment.

AVOIDING HIGH TRADE BARRIERS

A trade policy system that is characterized by a low to moderate average tariff is warranted for Russia. This does not mean, however, free trade should be pursued on a unilateral basis. Indeed, an average tariff rate in the range of 15% is probably warranted on international as well as domestic political-economy grounds. For infinitesimally small countries with no market power, free trade is the optimal policy. Russia, however, is sufficiently large that it could exercise some influence over the world market for many products through its trade policy, and for a few products such as petroleum and natural gas it could have a more substantive impact on international prices.[42] The standard rebuttal to a policy of national-welfare-maximizing tariffs is that a country will face retaliation that renders it worse off overall. From a theoretical viewpoint this rebuttal is vacuous. In essence there is a prisoner's dilemma in the trade policy arena where one country cannot forestall the "individually-rational" tariffs of rival countries by not imposing its own "individually-rational" tariffs. Concerns over retaliation, however, point to the advantages of international cooperation over trade policy where low to moderate tariffs can serve as a bargaining chip.

---

[42] Formally, if a large country used tariffs to maximize national welfare, it would set the tariff rate on each good equal to the inverse of the foreign export elasticity. Thus, different goods would have different optimum tariff rates. Nevertheless, it remains impractical to attempt calculate a set of optimum tariffs. Further, even though Russia is large enough to possess pricing power on world markets, the anti-competitive effects of trade barriers on the domestic market strongly suggests that Russia should still avoid high tariff rates.

Such tariffs may be lowered as concessions in Russia's negotiations pertaining to WTO accession and in future trade negotiations as discussed more extensively below.

In public debate, it is often argued that Russia needs high trade barriers rather than low to moderate tariffs because its domestic firms are not (yet?) able to withstand foreign competition. Lack of competitiveness, however, is not itself a problem. Rather, it is a symptom of the underlying structural problems relating to financing, marketing, quality of output, underemployment, etc. Over the long term, foreign competition provides the impetus for domestic firms to deal with many of these underlying problems. Even in the short-term, however, the economy-wide implications of import competition should not be overstated. Numerous firms in many sectors have failed in the course of the transition and painful adjustments will undoubtedly continue. Though foreign competition may be blamed, this is part of the natural process of adjusting to a market economy. Given the uneven debt loads that have been inherited, some well-managed firms will go bankrupt while other more poorly managed firms will remain solvent, at least temporarily. Nevertheless, the very presence of foreign exporters entering Russian markets creates general-equilibrium forces through the balance of payments that ease the pressure on domestic firms. Import growth creates a shortage of foreign exchange that pushes pressure on the Ruble – leading to its depreciation. This in turn makes imports themselves less attractive and domestic goods more attractive.

The so-called *infant-industry argument* could also be used to try to provide a somewhat more sophisticated justification of high levels of tariff protection in Russia. The infant industry argument has been used to justify both import-substituting and export-promoting strategies of developing countries. This argument suggests that an industry would develop a comparative advantage if only it were given assistance to get started or grow. The infant industry could be promoted by a tariff, an export subsidy plus a tariff, or by a domestic subsidy on production, capital investment, etc. Since an export subsidy raises the (non-subsidized) domestic price above the world price, a tariff or non-tariff barrier is needed to prevent the re-entry of exported goods. A practical problem with the infant industry argument is that it leaves an open avenue for rent-seeking activity where firms lobby for support from government. Thus, it is not surprising that many so-called infant industries never grow up. This problem seems to be especially pronounced with the import substitution strategy because of the export barriers that arise with import substitution. Whether because of the absence of export barriers or not, countries that have relied more on export promotion throughout the 1970s and 1980s, such as Korea, appear to have out-performed countries that have relied on import substitution, such as India.

There is a crucial theoretical dimension of the infant industry argument that is not obvious in many public discussions. Since the industry does not start or expand on its own, the expected present value of profits or net private benefits must be negative. In order for it to be socially desirable to have the industry start or expand, the expected present value of net social benefits must be non-negative. Thus, for a true infant industry, there must be some *externality* that causes the net social benefits to exceed the net private benefits. Applications of the infant industry argument in developing countries have focused on externalities arising from imperfections in capital markets and so-called appropriability problems involving the adaptation of technology and marketing (Krugman and Obsfeld, 1994). These types of market failure are also plausible in the case of Russia. If capital markets do not function properly and costly investments are required early on but revenues will materialize later, an industry may grow at less than the efficient rate, or not even start at all. A particular sector may also grow too slowly if it is costly for the initial entrant(s) to appropriate or adapt technology or marketing. These problems are likely to cut across sectors making it particularly difficult to identify specific industries that are deserving of support. Further, the argument clearly does not provide a general argument for high levels of tariff protection that would expand import-competing sectors at the expense of exporting sectors.

In summary, there is a very strong general case against a high degree of protectionism. In the case of Russia, the case is even stronger because of the discipline that international prices impose on domestic markets where competitive forces are frequently weak. The pro-competitive benefits of a low to moderate tariff regime, however, will be more pronounced if there is a high degree of uniformity in tariff rates across goods.

AVOIDING PROMOTING WINNERS AND/OR DEFENDING LOSERS

A third important feature of a sound post-transition trade policy regime is that tariff spikes and tariff escalation should be avoided. All imported commodities that do not enter tariff-free ideally should be subject to an *ad valorem* tariff that is uniform across goods; there should not be discrimination across goods. Otherwise, the import-competing sub-sectors that are favoured with higher than average tariff rates will have an artificial incentive to become too large relative to those with lower than average tariff rates.[43] For similar reasons, exports should neither be subsidized nor taxed. Although a low to moderate uniform tariff rate allows for limited protection to the import-competing sector as a whole, no sub-sectors are favoured or penalized. The fact that world price signals are still manifest under a uniform tariff is particularly important during the post-transition era as Russia emerges from an initial state of highly distorted prices and institutionalized state trading. Over the long-term, such a uniform tariff regime will facilitate re-investment in sectors where Russia has a comparative advantage. A uniform tariff rate also limits the possibilities for rent seeking. This appears very important in the Russia and may other transition countries given the history of non-arms-length connections between firm managers and government officials under the former command regime.

In practice, tariff spikes and tariff escalation are observed across a very large range of countries and may be difficult to avoid or remove. Tariff spikes frequently protect politically sensitive sectors with tariff rates that are much higher than the average. Textiles and apparel, sugar and dairy products are sensitive in many developed countries, rice is sensitive in Japan, beef is sensitive in the EU, sugar is sensitive in the US, poultry is sensitive in Canada, etc. It seems that tariff spikes have frequently come into being innocently enough. In response to shifts in demand and technological changes at home and abroad, certain sectors expand while others decline. Not surprisingly, groups closely associated with sectors that are in decline frequently lobby for protection from foreign competition regardless of whether imports are a significant contributing cause of the difficult adjustments being experienced. In reaction to demonstrable economic hardship, politicians often set trade-related policy to defend groups with vested interests tied to losing or declining sectors.

---

[43] It should be acknowledged that uniform tariffs are not typically second-best, let alone efficient, if the average tariff is to remain positive rather than equal to zero. Nevertheless, the information requirements preclude solving the full second-best problem and appropriately targeting each import-competing sub-sector.

In response to the acute short run adjustment pressures on these groups, a permanent policy that targets support to "losers" is seldom appropriate whereas a temporary policy response that facilitates adjustment is often warranted. Temporary deviations from uniformity may be warranted in the event of terms of trade shocks. Where congestion arises in the infrastructure relating to the training and relocation of labour, there is a strong case for temporary support to declining industries (Leger and Gaisford, 2001).[44] For example, suppose that a sudden sharp decline in steel prices ultimately requires large-scale migration and significant retraining of the migrants. Temporary support to steel production, which is gradually phased out, would avoid excessive congestion of vocational schools and other training facilities and allow an orderly move to lower steel outputs. Such temporary anti-surge or safeguard measures differ from countervailing duties and anti-dumping duties in that there is no presumption that foreign trade practices are unfair.

Picking winners for trade policy support is at least as problematic as defending losers. Many countries use patterns of *tariff escalation* where inputs are subject to lower tariffs than outputs to give extra protection to high-value added sectors. At first it may appear that small deviations from uniformity in nominal tariff rates are inconsequential, the resulting differences in *effective protection* can be more dramatic (Corden, 1966). For example, first suppose that both steel and automobiles are tradable goods and that both are subject to the same nominal tariff rate of 15 percent.[45] In this case, the effective rate of protection on automobiles would be 15 percent since the tariff structure allows for an additional fifteen percent in value added in the domestic industry compared to the world market. Now, by contrast, suppose that steel enters tariff free, while automobiles are still subject to the 15 percent tariff. There is room for additional value added in the automobile industry and the effective rate of protection is in excess of the apparent 15 percent nominal rate because the input is subject to a lower tariff.[46] Such a policy might be warranted if a high-value-added sector were too small on economic efficiency grounds. In the absence of externalities that constrain the size of the sector and in spite of the seemingly positive political appearance, the economic rationale for discriminating in favour of high value-added sectors at the expense of other sectors is extremely weak.

The infant-industry argument discussed above could also be used to try to justify trade policy that targets a few selective Russian industries with higher than average tariffs and/or export subsidies. As we have seen, however, requests for infant industry treatment may become fairly generic and cut across a wide variety of importing and exporting sectors when incomplete capital markets or appropriability problems in technology transfer or marketing arise in developing or transition countries. A strategic trade policy argument, under stringent conditions, may appear to provide a stronger justification for targeting export subsidies (Brander and Spencer, 1985; Helpman and Krugman, 1989). An export subsidy can potentially shift profits from foreign firm(s) to domestic firm(s) in a world oligopoly. Essentially, the export subsidy reduces the effective marginal cost of the domestic firm(s)

---

[44] Leger and Gaisford (1996) argue for temporary production subsidies rather than tariffs to avoid consumption-side distortions. For post-transition countries including Russia, however, government budget considerations may dictate the use of tariffs.

[45] If there are any other tradable inputs into automobile production, we assume that they are also subject to tariffs at the 15 percent rate.

[46] Or, consider the case where steel is subject to a 50 percent nominal tariff rate. Since the input is subject to a higher tariff, it is more difficult to add value in the domestic automobile industry.

allowing a credible commitment to higher output levels. There are a number of general caveats to this argument (Grossman, 1986). The argument is weakened when firms are not wholly domestically owned, when there are many domestic firms, or when there are domestic consumers of the product in question. The argument is reversed or, in other words, becomes an argument for export taxes if the world oligopoly competes in prices rather than quantities. In view of the need to target strategic industries, thereby opening the door for rent seeking activities, many have questioned the general policy relevance of the strategic trade policy argument. As discussed above, the problem of rent seeking makes the strategic trade policy argument particularly problematic for Russia.

JOINING THE WTO

As well as national dimensions to trade policy there are important transnational dimensions. Under this heading we turn first to the question of Russia's potential membership in the WTO. There are at least three important reasons why membership in the WTO is important to Russia. First, the WTO forces some desirable disciplines on member countries and would do the same for Russia. WTO commitments prevent member countries from taking measures that are counter-productive from the standpoint of their own broadly-defined national welfare. In other words, membership in the WTO would reinforce moves that are in Russia's long-term national interest such as tariffication and low to moderate tariffs. The General Agreement on Tariffs and Trade (GATT) and the General Agreement on Trade in Services (GATS), which fall under the WTO, would require that Russia immediately grant Most Favoured Nation status to all other members. Non-tariff measures would also have to be converted to tariffs. These requirements are very desirable in that they will add transparency to trading relationships and prevent discrimination against any trade partner.[47] As discussed above, tariffication itself has desirable pro-competitive effects that diminish the problems of thin markets and high transaction costs, which are a remnant of the command system. WTO members are also *bound* by upper limits on their tariffs. While bound tariffs need not be uniform across goods, it would be possible and desirable for Russia to choose such tariff bindings. Membership in the WTO would also have the desirable effect of preventing the use of export subsidies, except in the agricultural sector where limited use remains possible.

The second key reason why WTO membership should be important to Russia is that it provides guaranteed access to foreign markets on an MFN basis. By joining the WTO, Russia ensures that other members will not discriminate against its exports of goods and services. This benefit from access is of a once-time nature that is not directly related to the benefits of further trade liberalization by foreign countries. On an on-going basis, the WTO provides members with access to dispute settlement procedures. Consequently, Russia would have a means of questioning seemingly contrary policies of its trade partners. It should be emphasized, however, that joining the WTO will not prevent other member countries from applying Anti-Dumping Duties (ADDs), if Russian firms that engage in "unfair pricing," or Countervailing Duties (CVDs), if Russian governments engage in "unfair subsidies." Russia now faces a very large number of anti-dumping actions against exports in sectors such as

---

[47] Further, incentives for rent seeking by foreign firms or governments desiring preferential access to Russian markets would be eliminated by extending MFN status to all trade partners and requiring tariffication. Such rent seeking is, of course, inefficient on a global basis.

steel, chemicals, textile and food. What would change with accession, however, is that Russia could test the allegations of unfairness leveled by foreign countries in WTO dispute-resolution panels.

The third and perhaps most important reason why acceding to the WTO is desirable for Russia is the least obvious in general public debate, but widely discussed among economists. Membership in the WTO is valuable as a commitment and signaling device. By accepting the disciplines of the WTO, it becomes more difficult for any country to back-slide into protecting or promoting individual domestic vested interests on a long term basis. Rent-seeking interests can be resisted more readily and the temptation to defend losers and promote winners is limited. For the Russia, WTO commitments would help consolidate the market-reform process and provide a more certain environment for both domestic and foreign investment. Increased trade broadens markets and lowers information costs.

By almost any conceivable metric, Russia is the largest country in the world that remains outside the WTO. While Russia entered into negotiations to initially join the GATT in 1993, and subsequently to join the WTO with its inception in 1995, more substantive efforts began under President Putin in 2001. Once it was decided to pursue WTO accession more earnestly, it appears that the Russian government became overly optimistic about achieving fast and smooth entry into the WTO. While this may indicate a high degree of commitment on the part of Russian administration to join the WTO, the obstacles to entry were severely underestimated. Unlike China, which joined the WTO in 2001 as a developing country after 15 years of talks, Russia is applying to enter the WTO as a developed country. This has resulted in even more stringent and complicated requirements.

In addition to the advantages, including reduced risks and barriers for Russia's exports and a more favorable climate for foreign and domestic investment, WTO accession will also result in a number of major difficulties and adjustments for the Russian economy. Many domestic goods and services could face serious challenges if they were faced with sudden exposure to intense international competition because of large instantaneous reductions in trade barriers. Where adjustment costs are significant, there is a case for gradualism. Russia has argued for such gradualism in opening the financial service and telecommunications sectors and the liberalization of a number of sensitive manufacturing industries including automobiles, aircraft, and pharmaceuticals. Russia has also insisted on keeping the state monopolies in some sectors.

In spite of the difficulties, tariffs have been, perhaps, the least controversial area of the negotiations. For example, in the auto industry WTO members have proposed tariffs of 10-15 percent, instead of the existing 25 percent. While compromises on the levels of import tariffs and non-tariff barriers on agricultural goods appear more difficult, the most controversial issue in the agricultural talks is that Russia wants to retain the prerogative to substantially increase agricultural export subsidies in the future. This is strongly opposed by Australia, New Zealand, and many other members of the Cairns Group of agricultural producers. While increased export subsidies may placate certain vested interests in the agricultural sector, they definitely run contrary to Russia's overall national interest.

Within the financial services sector, liberalization in both insurance and banking is complicated by overlapping and contradictory regulations that are currently in place. In many cases, relaxing direct restrictions on foreign participation alone may be completely ineffective. For example, removing the 12 percent limit on foreign ownership in banking failed to generate greater foreign participation due to an array of restrictions on the activities and organization of foreign banks. In the telecommunication sector Russia proposed general limits on foreign participation ranging from 25 percent to 49%, while continuing Rostelecom monopoly over long distance and international services until 2010. This offer appears highly problematic because estimates of the current share of foreign participants is higher than those in the Russian offer.

Russia has also insisted that due to the natural advantages in the energy sector, it requires the right to set domestic prices for natural gas at much lower levels than world prices and thereby implicitly tax exports. Since this is an area of potential market power for Russia, there could be an economic rationale for the Russian position. In reality, however, providing indirect support to residential consumers and the weak manufacturing sector seems to have been at the heart of the Russian position. Not surprisingly the EU, as the downstream buyer of Russian natural gas, has argued against such an energy policy. Nevertheless there is some evidence of convergence in positions.

Implementation of the WTO Agreement on Trade Related Aspects of Intellectual Property Rights (TRIPS) is mandatory for all WTO members and poses serious difficulties for Russia.[48] To date, the Russian government has been unwilling and/or unable to seriously control the rampant piracy of music and software. Further, the Russian court system also appears unprepared to adequately handle sophisticated issues concerning patent, copyright and trademark disputes. Consequently, problems with intellectual property rights protection continues to slow the accession process.

In spite of all the difficulties and delays, further integration into the world economy is the next logical step on the road to becoming a market economy for Russia. The long-term strategic advantages of WTO membership outweigh the temporary disadvantages and adjustment costs. President Putin has pushed strongly for accession to the WTO, and the EU and the US are, in principle, in strongly in favour of Russia's accession since it provides an opportunity for trade related benefits over the longer term and political benefits in the shorter term. The prospects for Russian accession to the WTO are now more promising than at any time since the start of negotiations in 1993. Nevertheless, even the most optimistic forecasts expect Russia's WTO accession only near the end of the first decade of the 21st century.

CONCLUSION

An open stable and transparent trade policy regime is in Russia's national interest. By broadening markets and promoting competition, international trade provides an opportunity to lessen transition problems associated with high transaction costs and thin markets, which are a legacy of the former command economy. This is central to encouraging higher levels of investment that will begin to counter the massive problems of capital obsolescence that has arisen over the transition era. Accession to the World Trade Organization should continue to be a high priority. In its pursuit of WTO membership, Russia is moving toward the tariffication of non-tariff barriers and toward more moderate average tariff rates. Unfortunately, Russia is like most other countries in that it has been able to make little

---

[48] The connection between intellectual property rights and investment is discussed in depth in another chapter in this book.

progress toward uniformity in tariff rates across goods and avoiding the defense of losing industries and the promotion of would-be winners.

Beyond membership in the WTO, Russia may contemplate joining existing or future Regional Trade Agreements. For example, a free trade agreement with the European Union could be a worthwhile medium term objective that generates increased investment in Russia in addition to increased trade. As well as providing improved access to lucrative Western European markets, such an agreement would remove much of the trade diversion that has occurred as the European Union has expanded to include the Baltic countries and many Central European countries. In view of the large distortions caused by the EU's common agricultural policy, it would be to the mutual advantage of both parties to partially or fully exclude agriculture from such a trade agreement. While a free trade agreement with the EU could be good for Russia, there appears to virtually no political or economic grounds for Russia to join the EU and thereby integrate more fully with it.

Regional Trade Agreements with the countries that formerly comprised the Soviet Union also make sense over the longer term on both trade and investment grounds. The dismantling of the Soviet Union was accompanied by the birth of the Commonwealth of Independent States. While the CIS and related initiatives have never lived up to expectations as regional trade agreements, the problem is not with the idea of a trade agreement for the region, but rather with the timing. It is not surprising that market-based regional trade has not flourished in the transition era, given that all parties have shared problems of weak price signals, general stagnation, continued state trading agencies, etc. Of course, eventually strong regional trade linkages appear mutually advantageous because transportation costs for intra-regional trade tend to be relatively low in comparison with shipments to Western Europe, North America and the rest of Asia. In terms of geography and to a lesser degree language and culture, therefore, the countries that formerly comprised the Soviet Union will become natural trading partners for one another if they are ultimately successful in establishing market economies.

REFERENCES

Brander, J. A., and Spencer, B. J. (1985). Export Subsidies and International Market Share Rivalry. *Journal of International Economics*, 18, 83-100.

Corden, W.M. (1966). The Structure of a Tariff System and the Effective Protection Rate. *Journal of Political Economy*, 74, 221-237.

Dixit, A.K. (1987). Strategic Aspects of Trade Policy. In T. Bewley (Ed.), *Advances in Economic Theory, Proceedings of the 5th World Congress of the Econometrics Society*. (pp. 329-362). Cambridge: Cambridge University Press.

Helpman E. and Krugman, P.R. (1989) *Trade Policy and Market Structure*. Cambridge MA: MIT Press.

Grossman, G. M. (1986). Strategic Export Promotion: A Critique. In P.R. Krugman (Ed.), *Strategic Trade Policy and the New International Economics*. (pp. 47-68). Cambridge, MA: MIT Press.

Johnson, H.G. (1953). Optimum Tariffs and Retaliation. *Review of Economic Studies*, 21, 142-153.

Kennan, J. and Riezman, R. (1988). Do Big Countries Win Tariff Wars? *International Economic Review*, 29, 81-85.

Kerr, W.A. and Perdikis, N. (1995). *The Economics of International Business*. London: Chapman and Hall.

Krugman P.R. and Obsfeld, M. (2003). *International Economics*, 6th ed. Reading MA: Addison-Wesley.

Leger, L.A., and Gaisford, J.D. (2001). Imperfect Intersectoral Labour Mobility and Welfare in International Trade. *Journal of Economic Surveys*, 15 (4), 463-489.

In: Revitalizing Russian Industry
Eds: J. Gaisford, V. Mayevsky et al., pp. 111-129   © 2007 Nova Science Publishers, Inc.
ISBN 978-1-60021-778-4

Chapter 9

THE ECONOMICS OF FOREIGN INVESTMENT LAW AND BUSINESS PRACTICE IN THE RUSSIAN FEDERATION: "LEARNING TO SHARE THE GOLDEN EGGS AND NOT TO KILL THE GOOSE THAT YOU WERE LENT"

William A. Kerr and Kristal M. Bessel

ABSTRACT

Foreign investment is always a contentious issue. While foreign investment brings a number of benefits, it also may inhibit the development of strong domestic industrial sectors. It is often difficult for policy makers to determine the desirable degree of foreign investment and to put a policy environment in place to achieve that desired level. If policy makers get it wrong, radical changes in foreign investment policies may follow. In the Russian Federation, beyond these policy difficulties, the absence of a well functioning commercial legal system increases the risk levels faced by foreign investors. Progress has been slow in putting an effective legal system in place. In particular, poor enforcement remains a crucial issue. In the face of inconsistent foreign investment policy, vague and evolving laws and poor law enforcement, foreign investment has contributed less to the revitalization of Russian industry than it could have been the case.

INTRODUCTION

The treatment of foreign investment is one of the most hotly debated topics in politics, civil society and economics. It elicits strong emotions even in modern market economies that have long accommodated a considerable degree of foreign investment – witness the strong adverse reaction among civil society groups that surrounded the failed negotiations attempting to establish a Multilateral Investment Agreement (Loppacher and Kerr, 2006a). The issue of foreign investment has always been extremely contentious in developing countries (Amin, 1976; Kerr, 1993; Streeten, 1977; Vernon, 1971) and latterly has come to vex transition economies (Hobbs, et al., 1997). For the Russian Federation, with its vast resources, the role of foreign investment was a subject of considerable debate even during the Soviet era and that debate continues throughout Russia's post-communist reforms (Considine and Kerr, 2002).

Most countries have a love-hate relationship with foreign investment. On the one hand, foreign investment removes a constraint that arises in the domestic market due to a shortage of capital at competitive international rates. There is no reason why profitable investment opportunities should match the domestic supply of investment funds if access to international capital markets is allowed. Investment can be transferred to other countries when the domestic supply of investment funds exceeds profitable domestic investment opportunities at competitive international rates. If domestic capital markets work poorly, savings rates are low, or the transfer of individual savings to lending institutions only takes place at a low rate, capital shortages will be exacerbated and may become a significant constraint on economic expansion. Further, foreign direct investment (as opposed to portfolio investment) may bring with it a range of positive externalities for the capital importing country (e.g. access to up-to-date technology, managerial expertise, training of skilled labour, access to export markets, etc.). Thus, foreign investment is often seen as an integral part of the development process and, if that investment fails to materialise, governments may actively attempt to encourage it.

Foreign investment, however, is often viewed with suspicion. Foreign direct investment, in particular, is viewed as providing unwanted competition by existing or potential rivals operating in the domestic economy. They are often able to play on inherent nationalism of the populace and domestic politicians to equate foreign with "unfair" competition (Loppacher and Kerr, 2006b). Foreign firms often have inherent advantages in access to information, managerial skills, technological sophistication, etc., that give them a competitive advantage over domestic firms. They may also be able to exercise considerable market power. Further, they may be of sufficient size or of sufficient importance in the domestic economy to have undue influence over the political process. Portfolio investment is perceived as "fickle" because it responds quickly to international price signals or signs of poor management of the domestic market at the macroeconomic level. Capital flight is certainly disruptive and provides the harsh discipline of the market for inept or corrupt macro-economic management (Kerr, 1999). Further, actors in portfolio markets, for all their technical slickness, lack sophistication as they are unable to differentiate markets with a sufficient degree of precision to prevent the well known *flu* effect, whereby nearby well-managed economies are penalized for the poor macroeconomic management of their neighbours. It is probably not surprising that portfolio investment is viewed with suspicion by government when good macroeconomic management can be punished along with the bad. In a vast country such as the Russian Federation, regions with reasonably good economic management may be penalized by international capital markets for inept or corrupt management in other regions.

Some of the problems with foreign investment are, however, a function of the domestic economic environment in the host country. If the host country environment is risky for foreign investors, this means that they will require high prospective rates of return. These high rates of return, however, foster impressions that the returns are unwarranted or exploitive and increase the probability that foreign firms' property rights will not be respected. Further, a risky environment may also alter inbound investment in qualitative ways. High levels of risk will attract a larger proportion of *risk lovers* who may be less prudent and who have a predilection to ignore the law and business conventions. The former leads to unrealized expectations among the local population while the latter lowers respect for foreign investors. As a result, their activities and assets may be more at risk. This may kick off a downward spiral of rising risk and declining investor quality that eventually leads to a situation where countries don't want the type of investors they can attract. Thus, high quality foreign investment is inherently dependent on creating a low risk investment environment in the host country. If the investment environment is secure, then investors are able to base their decisions on the degree of risk inherent in the prospective investment itself. The Russian Federation is still struggling to lower the degree of risk in the business environment in which foreign investors must operate.

ECONOMIC INSTITUTIONS AND FOREIGN INVESTMENT

Foreign investment is normally divided into portfolio investment and direct investment. The major difference between portfolio investment and direct investment is that portfolio funds represent a financial contribution without any expectation of an active management role, whereas with foreign direct investment there is an expectation of an active management role. Direct investment does not necessarily imply a financial contribution as the contribution to a joint venture may be in kind; e.g. managerial expertise, a brand name, intellectual property. In most cases, however, direct investment will also involve a financial contribution. Foreign direct investments can take a variety of forms – licensing, franchising, partnerships, purchases of controlling interests through the acquisition of stock, joint ventures, acquisitions, mergers and greenfield investments (Hobbs et al, 1997).

Institutional arrangements to promote portfolio investments hinge on three things – sound macroeconomic management, security against fraud and government capriciousness, and unfettered capital movements. Portfolio investors will be attracted to markets where returns on investment are not obscured by changes in the rate of inflation that cannot be anticipated and where government intervention in the form of exchange controls is unlikely. Those providing funds must be assured that financial statements, prospectuses, and other forms of reporting companies' performance have a low probability of being fraudulent. The legal system also has to work well enough to deter individuals from absconding with the funds provided. There must also be laws and mechanisms in place to prevent confiscation of funds by the whim of government officials either acting officially or individually abusing their positions. Finally, portfolio capital will be attracted to markets that do not tax and scrutinize inbound investment or tax or otherwise fetter outbound flows.

The institutions associated with the management of direct foreign investment are more complex and reflect, in part, the policy conundrum that direct foreign investment presents to policy makers in host countries. The question of the role that foreign firms should play in the transition of the economy of the Russian Federation has proved to be one of the most vexing problems for policy makers. Russian policy makers are faced with attempting to simultaneously satisfy what appear to be two fundamentally conflicting industrial policy goals. On the one hand, there is the goal of creating a modern, domestically owned and operated commercial industrial sector to ensure economic independence. On the other, there is the goal of acquiring foreign technology, expertise and capital to increase the rate of economic growth. The desire to acquire up-to-to date technology and expertise is particularly important given the virtual collapse of Russian research and development capacity and the need to prevent the total depreciation of its high quality capital stock. In particular, expertise from modern market economies is needed to establish effective systems of vertical coordination within Russian supply chains based on markets to replace the *visible hand* of bureaucratic command from the state (Kerr, 1994). Coordination of Russian supply chains has proved a significant obstacle in the transition process and a major source of the Russian Federation's poor international competitiveness. Simply put, transaction costs along Russian supply chains are too high.

The conflict between the goal of establishing a successful domestically owned industry and the need to acquire foreign technology, expertise and capital arises because the most efficient, and sometimes the only, means of assuring the acquisition of up-to-date technology and managerial expertise is through direct investment by transnational firms (Offerdal, 1992). While there are other means of acquiring up-to-date technology such as the purchase of rights to the use of patents and licensing arrangements, in the absence of strong legal protection for industrial processes and intellectual property, these alternatives are unlikely to be available. While the Russian Federation has enacted legislation to protect intellectual property, enforcement is at best weak – and more often nonexistent.

Strong, well-enforced laws to enforce patents and other forms of intellectual property allow the firm to sell the rights and thus capture the gains from research and development. When intellectual property protection is weak, once the process moves outside the direct control of the firm, the potential for diffusion without compensation arises. Hence, individual foreign firms may rationally refuse to sell or license their products and processes. In short, the licence value of a process in the Russian Federation will be less than the profits obtainable from self-operation and self-diffusion of the process.

Developing an internationally competitive industrial sector is an ongoing process. Often, officials and business persons in the Russian Federation act as if they believe that modernization can be accomplished with a one-time transfer of technology. In reality, there are continuous search costs for firms not directly engaged in research and development in the identification and evaluation of technology developed by others. A once and for all technology transfer is much less important than the relatively continuous acquisition of improvements in existing products and, in particular, processes (Archibald and Rosenbluth, 1978).

A significant proportion of new technology originates in private corporations. As it is unlikely that, for the moment, foreign transnationals will undertake a significant amount of research within the Russian Federation, research and development activities can be expected to remain concentrated in the modern market economies. Some tasks, which draw heavily on Russia's abundant supply of technically sophisticated individuals at low cost, of course, may be undertaken within the Russian Federation. It is, however, often very difficult for foreign firms to fully utilize the potential of this group due to the poor enforcement of intellectual property rights. Transnational firms have exhibited a predilection to hire the best and the brightest of the existing Russian research cohort and move them to their research facilities in modern market economies. Officials in the Russian Federation have expressed concern regarding this "brain drain". In the absence of resources to offer competitive compensation for scientists and engineers, the emigration of highly qualified individuals will continue. In a few cases, scientists have been able to form private research groups and successfully bid for research contracts but their aging equipment and poorly maintained facilities have, for the most part, made them uncompetitive. In particular, the almost total breakdown in the supply of spare parts for sophisticated equipment has meant that they have not been able to fulfil research commitments for the contracts they have been able to secure.

As research will continue to take place primarily in modern market economies, a conduit for ongoing transfers of technology is required. Given the reluctance of foreign firms to transfer technology directly to firms in the Russian Federation, allowing the transfer to take place through intra-firm channels that terminate in foreign corporate outlets within the host country may be the only workable alternative. Attempting to restrict the transfers to firm-to-firm market transactions across borders will only inhibit the acquisition of technology.

In theory, transfers of technology between the divisions of a transnational corporation have two positive impacts for the host country: (1) the direct modernization of the affected industries which should improve international competitiveness; and (2) the externalities associated with the demonstration effect and improvements to human capital. Models of technological transfer between local subsidiaries of transnational firms and host country firms have been formally presented by Findlay (1978), and Wong and Blomstrom (1992). Das (1987) suggests that technology transfers by transnational firms create externalities that are a benefit to the host country as a whole. According to Marton (1986):

> ...the most important channel of technology transfer has been through foreign direct investment by multinational enterprises based in developed countries. The growth of corporate multinationalization has been accompanied by technological flows from parent companies to their foreign subsidiaries and affiliates (p. 412).

The view that transnational firms are conduits for technology transfer is supported by the work of Hymer (1960), Streeten (1977), and Vernon (1971, 1975, 1977).

From a political economy perspective, however, these benefits come with a cost. Transnational firms must be allowed a chance at profitable operation in the host country in order to encourage them to invest. This implies that, at any given time, the opportunities for private domestic enterprises are constrained by foreign competition in those sectors where transnational corporations choose to operate. In many cases, it means that domestic firms are forced to compete on an unequal basis with transnational firms. This lack of equality is based on the international firm's superior access to information and human capital and, possibly, its ability to acquire market power. As a result, the development of indigenous industry in the host country is impeded (Amin, 1976; Barnett and Muller, 1974; Biersteker, 1976, Hymer, 1979). Given their superior management, their access to capital markets and their ability to follow relatively unrestricted employment policies, foreign transnationals should be more than a match for existing large-scale enterprises in the Russian Federation.

Profitable opportunities in market economies are not static, but rather ever-changing and evolving. Given opportunities for profit and growth, transnational firms may well expand and eventually dominate the privatized competing firms in various sectors of the Russian Federation. As a result, the goal of ensuring economic independence through the creation of a domestically owned and operated industrial sector will be frustrated. On the other hand, large, privatized enterprises in the Russian Federation may have sufficient market power and or political influence to compete successfully with foreign direct investors. If the competition is too strong, and particularly if it is perceived as being unfair, transnationals will be eliminated or forced to withdraw from the host country. Their absence, however, reduces the flow of technology and, as a result, beneficial externalities and international competitiveness will be reduced. The goal of modernizing the host country economy will be frustrated.

The relative competitiveness of host country firms and transnationals can be influenced by the legal and policy regimes that define the business environment. Those responsible for shepherding the liberalization process in the Russian Federation must attempt to develop and implement policies that provide a stable balance between profitable transnational firms and a viable domestically owned industry. Such a balance has proved illusive.

As the Russian economy evolves, sectors may gravitate toward either: (1) total domination of an industry by foreign firms; or, (2) the withdrawl of foreign investors. If either of these cases, with their politically undesirable side effects (i.e. unacceptable degrees of foreign control or lack of modern technology) are being approached, policy makers may be forced to introduce radical policy measures to prevent the evolution of an extreme situation. In some developing countries, there have even been radical changes in the government followed by radical changes in policy (Kerr, 1993). In the Russian Federation such radical changes in policy, particularly tax policy, have been observed. Strategic changes in tax policy have been chronic at the sub-national republic level (Considine and Kerr, 2002).

Frequent or radical changes in laws, taxation and investment policy are likely to slow the process of industrial modernization. Only in a stable business environment will firms (both foreign and domestic) make productive (as opposed to speculative) and longer term investments. Those investments that are made may be biased toward, for example, export activities where there is security in the product market, leaving the domestic market starved for output (Considine and Kerr, 1993).

As the transition progresses, attaining an acceptable balance between foreign and domestic investment is becoming a central problem for policy makers. As yet, other problems have had a greater priority. The high transaction costs and considerable risks have made it difficult for foreign firms to operate successfully. The risky legal and policy environment has kept profits low for both foreign and domestic investors and as a result, foreign investment has not taken place on a grand scale. As the legal environment improves, and investment grows, so will the policy challenge.

This discussion is, of course, overly simplistic because alternative arrangements exist to wholly owned subsidiaries of foreign firms and domestically owned and operated firms. As suggested above, these arrangements include partnerships between foreign and domestic firms, joint ventures, franchise agreements, licensing arrangements and strategic alliances. These alternative methods of accommodating foreign investment, however, have often led to franchiser-franchisee, licenser-licensee or intra-firm jockeying for strategic advantage that is a microcosm of the larger foreign firm/domestic firm competition that takes place in the marketplace. Failures among these intermediate forms of organisation is high, partly because of the absence of an effective legal system in the Russian Federation and partly because business ethics differ. Foreign firms complain of opportunistic behaviour by entrepreneurs in the former command economies, while Russians complain about excessive rigidity, lack of trust and pervasive secrecy in their dealings with foreign investors.

Much of this leads back to the absence of a fully functioning and stable legal framework for governing, taxing and protecting foreign investors. The legal regime will be a key determinant of the ability to attract high quality foreign direct investment.

THE ECONOMIC ROLE OF THE LEGAL SYSTEM

Opportunistic behaviour, or self-interest seeking with guile (Williamson, 1979), recognises that, at times, economic agents will seek to exploit a situation to their own advantage. It often means being able to alter the terms of an agreement when the other party is in a vulnerable position. The legal regime that, in part, establishes the risk environment that foreign investors operate within will determine four key parameters within which foreign direct investors must operate. First, it will determine the degree to which foreign investors can expect protection from opportunistic behaviour by governments or government officials individually abusing their position to act opportunistically toward foreign investors. This might take the form of altering taxation rates after asset specific investments or positive profits are made, the extraction of bribes, restricting the repatriation of funds, etc. Second, it will determine the degree to which the foreign investor can expect to be protected from opportunism by those with whom they enter into transactions, business partners and unfair competition from competitors. Third, it will determine the degree to which a foreign investor can expect protection from parties not directly involved in the activity that seek to capture assets or appropriate revenues. Examples would be criminal activities such as theft and extortion. In addition, the degree of discrimination against (or in favour of) foreign firms relative to domestic firms over all three of the parameters outlined above alters investment risk. Defining and protecting investors' property rights is central to this process (Kerr and MacKay, 1997).

Legal systems have two major aspects – the law itself, and law enforcement. The law can be comprised of statutes, precedent and legally accepted conventions. Enforcement encompasses investigation, policing, adjudication and punishment. Good laws that are not enforced do nothing to improve the risk environment. The efficacy of enforcement is directly affected by the human capital embodied in the enforcement personnel – police, prosecutors, judges, prison guards. Commercial crime tends to require sophisticated and well trained enforcement personnel. The legal system is a key institution in determining the risk environment for foreign investors in the Russian Federation.

THE RUSSIAN LEGAL SYSTEM

Since the 1991 fall of communism in what was to become the Russian Federation, the country's legal system, as well as its economy, has been in a state of transition. Under the former communist administrations, social protectionism was the norm, and the "collective good" was the focus, often at the expense of civil liberties and personal security (Feldbrugge, 1993). Russian legal traditions, even prior to the communist era, stressed the power and control of the state as the best regulator of most aspects of society. In the post-communist era, democracy has become the vision for the country. The legal traditions of the past have been forced to mesh with conventions common in democratic legal systems to foster a true democracy that places the individual at a higher level of importance in society. Concepts such as due process and presumption of innocence have been introduced, but the process has been arduous. Lack of familiarity with democratic justice systems has resulted in many changes to Russian legislation. As policy-makers and reformers attempt to restructure the Russian legal system, the state of the law remains uncertain. The development of commercial law has taken a back seat to attempts to put a justice system that supports democratic institutions in place. In many ways, however, the process of building a commercial system to support a private market economy parallels that of the wider legal system, including an oft changing regime that itself contributes to the degree of risk in the commercial environment.

With the dissolution of Russia's command economy, new markets have emerged. Foreign investors have tended to view these newly accessible markets as promising due to the potential to garner high returns as the markets grow and flourish, and, hence, have sought to invest in them despite challenges involved in abiding by and remaining up to date on the volatile Russian legal regime (Hobbs, et al., 1997). A foreign investor in the Russian Federation faces the unenviable task of not only putting in place a solid investment in a particular market, but also protecting that investment from devaluation or dissipation in a country where investment laws are being constantly reformed and indifferently enforced. It remains a risky investment environment.

With the interest foreign investors have shown in the Russian Federation, government faces the maintenance of a delicate balance between the conflicting forces discussed previously. While the Russian economy requires foreign investment and technology to grow and to facilitate development, there remains a strong desire for a commercial sector that is domestically owned and controlled by those with Russia's interests in mind (Hobbs, et al., 1997). The economic independence of Russia appears to be a key goal for its long-suffering citizens. Many Russians feel their investments are threatened by the growing presence of foreign investors who they believe have a competitive advantage due to their wealth and size. Governments in Russia have attempted to respond to these concerns by tailoring foreign investment laws to support the growth of the Russian economy, while still protecting the economic autonomy that Russians values so greatly. The results are mixed, and experiences have varied considerably.

The Russian Federation is a civil law society with a legal system based on Romano-Germanic principles of law (Petrova and Zimbler, 2001). The long period of communist rule infused Russian law with a strong socialist character. Changes have taken place in the past decade designed to develop legislation to support a market system but socialist ideas nonetheless remain the underpinnings of various Russian laws. Overcoming the decades of Soviet influence on the legal system remains a daunting task, and is a key factor in why the Russian legal system is so volatile and ambiguous.

Throughout the Soviet era, several constitutions came and went, all of which were based on socialist theory. The Lenin Constitution of 1918, the Stalin Constitution of 1936 and the Brezhnev Constitution of 1977 shaped the Russian legal system for over 70 years (Beard, 1996). The Constitution is the heart of any country's legal system, as it provides an ideological and structural foundation on which all other laws passed within the country must be based. In Russia, prior to 1991, this foundation was one of socialist or communist ideology. This foundation was codified through the three aforementioned Constitutional instruments. The result was a constitutional structure that recognized the diverse nationality of the Soviet Union, but simultaneously granted complete power over this diverse group to a small governing body (Feldbrugge, 1993).

In its years as part of the Soviet Union, the Russian Federation was under a communist regime. Accordingly, in constitutional terms the nation was ruled by a small governmental body acting on behalf of the proletariat that owned all instruments of production and controlled all social systems (Butler, 1999). The state operated under the notion that in order to run a society efficiently and equitably, all aspects of society must be controlled by a government appointed to act in the best interest of the nation as a whole. A definition of Soviet law was settled upon during the "Conference on Questions of the Science of the Soviet State and Law" in 1938, which was held to clarify the role of law in the Soviet system (Butler, 1999). At the Conference, it was agreed that Soviet law referred to:

> ...the aggregate of rules of conduct established in a legislative procedure by the power of the working people expressing their will and application of which is ensured by the entire coercive power of the socialist state for the purpose of the defence, consolidation, and development of relations and procedures advantageous and suitable for the working people, the full and final destruction of capitalism, and its survivals in the economy, domestic life and the consciousness of people, and the building of a communist society." (Butler, 1999).

This general definition sums up the basis and goal of communism – to provide a powerful state that will govern in the interests of the working class to protect them from exploitation prevalent in capitalist societies at all costs. Throughout the 70-plus years of the Soviet Union, this definition was altered only slightly.

This ideology was reflected in the laws present in the Soviet Union at that time. The Soviet Constitution failed to recognize or protect individual rights of any of its citizens out of concern that this would be contrary to the goal of acting in the interest of the society as a whole. The provisions of the Constitution allowed the vast majority of matters to be decided upon by the federal government, leaving the main responsibility of the lower levels of government, the Union Republics such as the Russian Federation, to be the codification of major areas of law such as criminal and civil law (Feldbrugge, 1993). There was rarely much variation among the codes of different republics, and it is thought that although according to the Constitution of the Soviet Union these matters were to be left to the Republics' discretion, there was "central guidance" from the federal government regarding code structure (Feldbrugge, 1993). This "guidance" allowed common goals to be identified in all republics, creating a more unified Soviet state and easier enforcement of laws created to protect socialism due to uniformity (Feldbrugge, 1993).

Federal laws sought to achieve goals of a socialist society attempting to establish communism by governing nearly all activities of the general society. Law enforcement was sporadic, but the expression of views contrary to those of the communist government was discouraged, often with force (Feldbrugge, 1993). If citizens spoke out against the government, they were deemed to be acting contrary to the interests of the nation as a whole, a practice that is frowned upon in communist societies where the public good is the paramount consideration. Due to the fact that human rights legislation was virtually nonexistent in the Soviet Union, there was no means to protect those whose individual beliefs or actions were contrary to the communist ideal. Concern over the results of communism, namely the discouragement of individual identity and prosperity as well as the lack of efficiency it delivered to society, contributed to the eventual downfall of communism in the early 1990's. In contrast to its high sounding principles, the law never provided an effective constraint on the Communist Party and the government officials it appointed. It was referenced when convenient and ignored when it was not. The important point is that it was codified and was the official "law of the land" when the Communist Party was deposed and the Russian Federation began the transition from a Communist dictatorship to a society that accepted democracy and the rule of law as its guiding principles.

In the post-Soviet era, the Russian Federation is attempting to establish the "rule of law". The process has not been easy nor a linear progression. Liberal-democratic legal theory has emerged as the likely contender for adoption in the Russian Federation, and has already shown itself in the 1993 Constitution. The 1993 Constitution focuses on the recognition and protection of human rights and freedoms and seeks to eliminate much of the communist ideology that existed in its predecessors (Butler, 1999). In addition, a series of new laws have been enacted in the Russian Federation since the early 1990's. However, these initiatives have met with varying levels of success and many of the laws have been revised numerous times in the search for more democratic laws with a less state-centric focus.

The Russian Civil Code, along with the Federation's federal laws, outline the main principles of the civil law (Petrova and Zimbler, 2001). It is in these legal instruments that laws regarding business entities such as limited liability companies, securities, tax, currency, and of course foreign investment are set out. In recent years these laws have taken on a market orientation to allow Russia and its citizens to operate successfully in domestic and international markets and to help strengthen the ailing Russian economy (Petrova and Zimbler, 2001). However, creating more market-oriented Russian laws has proved a challenge because Russian law has many sources, ranging from previous Soviet laws to "jus" - law originating from somewhere other than the present ruler, such as from the Will of God (Butler, 1999). Despite this variety of origins, all are in accordance with the Federation's 1993 Constitution.

The modern legal system in the Russian Federation has structural differences from the Soviet system as well. The new system has law-making responsibilities more evenly distributed among the various levels of Russian government. The Federal Assembly, as well as legislative bodies of republics and cities within the Russian Federation, all possess the power to adopt legislation within the jurisdiction granted to them. Referendums, decrees and presidential edicts are also common sources of law. All bind citizens, but are subject to repeal if they are inconsistent with the principles of the Russian Constitution (Butler, 1999). In addition, the international treaties to which the Russian Federation belongs overrule domestic legislation in the event of a conflict between the two (Petrova and Zimbler, 2001).

In contrast to the Soviet system, which frowned upon separation of powers and delegation, the modern legal system is separated into three branches – the legislative, executive, and judicial bodies (Butler, 1999). The federal government no longer has sole control and influence over the legal system of the country, nor is it responsible for all workings of the legal system.

Laws have been rewritten several times as the Russian governments strive to modify laws to allow a transition to a market economy, but still maintain a uniquely Russian approach (Butler, 1999). It has been an arduous process of learning by doing. There are no road maps for how to transform a legal system designed for a communist society into one suited to democracy and markets. Western influences on Russian laws have been obvious, but the Federation has been careful to enact laws in accordance with Russian ideals. Russia remains a civil law country and a Federation with a diverse ethnicity and history. Influences on their laws will, in part, remain unique and will reflect themselves in the way the laws are written and enforced.

Enforcement of laws in Russia has been and remains unpredictable. With several levels of over-burdened courts, Russia's judicial system has been known to be less than consistent in the judgements it renders (Butler, 1999). Russian courts have tended to favour Russian parties, often to the dismay of foreign parties who may have brought a legitimate claim before them (Webster, 2002). As a result of this bias against foreign investors, the degree of which cannot be anticipated, the risk associated with foreign investment in the Russian Federation increases.

The Federal Security Service of the Russian Federation (FSB) and the Ministry of Internal Affairs (MVD) provide law enforcement within the Russian Federation (Butler, 1999). The FSB and MVD have primary responsibilities of providing intelligence and maintenance of public order or policing, respectively (Butler, 1999). In response to the brutish tactics and selective law enforcement sometimes employed by these bodies in the past, they have been subject to new legislation in recent years that seeks to make them more transparent and accountable (Butler, 1999). It appears that this legislation has not achieved one of its major purposes – minimizing corruption. Beyond an immediate shortage of resources, human capital remains a major constraint on enforcement activities. In the Soviet era there was no need for any expertise relating to commercial crime and the violation of private property rights – commercial activity was extremely limited as was private property. Commercial crime enforcement efficacy is dependent to a considerable degree on relatively sophisticated human capital. There is nowhere to formally build that human capital in the Russian Federation and returns to investment in human capital are too small in the public sector to attract individuals who might be willing and able to acquire it. As a result, foreign investors have little recourse even if their case may be legally straightforward.

FOREIGN INVESTMENT LAW AND POLICY

For much the 20th century, the Russian economy was all but closed to foreign investment (Considine and Kerr, 2002). In 1987, however, in response to a faltering economy that many believed was due in large part to the Soviet Union's economic isolation, the economy was officially re-opened to foreign investment (McMillan, 1994). Although this policy reversal began conservatively, with foreign investment limited to certain forms but including limited opportunities for direct investment by private capitalist firms, the Soviet government believed it was a step in involving the Soviet Union in global economic activity. From these modest beginnings, there remains today a widespread faith that foreign investment will continue to be key to the economic recovery of the Russian Federation and its transformation into a market-oriented system (McMillan, 1994).

The Soviet legal system was concerned with state ownership, planning and control, leaving no room for international capital involvement in the Soviet economy (McMillan, 1994). Although the Soviet Union put significant effort into research, it lacked sufficient resources to fund development of many of the discoveries and actively discouraged the entrepreneurship that is often required to turn an invention into an industrial product. As a result, during the early part of the Brezhnev era, the Soviet Union began to consider allowing foreign involvement in the economy through industrial cooperation agreements[49] (McMillan, 1994). This allowed the innovations to be funded more extensively, but prevented foreign bodies from actual ownership. However, these agreements did not result in an economic turnaround for the Soviet Union and were for the most part unsuccessful.

As the Soviet Union moved into the period of Gorbachev's tenure in the 1980s, the floundering economy moved high on the political agenda. Gorbachev promoted a program known as *perestroika*, implemented by a series of governmental decrees in 1987, that sought to revive the Union's economy (McMillan, 1994). With the introduction of this program, participation of foreign capital was now permitted in joint ventures within the Soviet Union. This policy was integral to linking the Soviet Union with global markets and exposing Soviet enterprises to international performance standards. It was expected that this would lead to improved competitiveness in world markets by modernizing the way Soviet enterprises produced goods and organized their transactions (Artisien-Maksimenko and Adjubei, 1996). While it was agreed that the economy needed to be opened, the Gorbachev reforms still reflected Soviet paranoia regarding the potential negative influence of foreign firms in the economy and foreign investment was heavily constrained.

Under Gorbachev's policy, foreign capital participation in joint ventures was limited to a 49 percent equity share, and profit repatriation provisions favoured export-oriented investments due to difficulties in repatriating returns on investment because of the inconvertibility of the ruble (McMillan, 1994). Tax holidays and minimal regulation were used as selling features for Soviet investment, but it was commonplace for a investor to devote money to a Soviet company based on benefits such as these, only to have these benefits removed a short time later as policy changed. Fear of foreign firms being too successful motivated many of these policy changes. At the same time, there was a realization at the macro level that insufficient foreign investment was being encouraged to achieve the modernization goals (Considine and Kerr, 2002) and further liberalization took place.

As foreign investment policy changed in the years following 1987, the restriction on foreign equity in companies was lifted and requirements were softened. A new foreign investment law was passed in 1991 to consolidate the various decrees and regulations that had appeared since 1987. However, following the fall of the communist regime in late 1991, the Russian law regarding foreign investment, which had previously existed simultaneously with the Soviet law, became the new law of the country. Subsequently, progress once again stagnated and the new government allowed "scare tactics", such as KGB searches of premises of joint ventures suspected of having been involved in illegal activities, to be used in law enforcement (McMillan, 1994).

The last Soviet era foreign investment law remained the basic law on foreign investment in the Russian Federation for quite some time, but quickly became largely irrelevant due to inflation and inaccurate terminology (McMillan, 1994). Further, no market-oriented enforcement mechanisms were put in place. Effectively, the foreign investment regime was in limbo and investments were made in *wild west* fashion with no regard for the official rules. The official rules, however, could be used for post-investment opportunism by government officials and, sometimes, private Russian entrepreneurs.

---

[49] These agreements were known as "compensation deals" and resulted in equipment, technology and expertise for projects being supplied by Western parties on a credit basis, with later repayment through export of project output (McMillan, 1994).

Finally, in 1999, the Russian government passed a comprehensive Act regulating foreign investment. The Law on Foreign Investment in the Russian Federation (Foreign Investment Law) requires foreign investments to be subject to the same regulation and treatment as domestic investment, unless Russian interests are threatened and require protection (Terterov, 2001). In addition to guaranteeing national treatment, the Law permitted foreign investment in all forms available in the Russian economy – from stocks and bonds to the acquisition of existing Russian-owned enterprises – unless expressly prohibited by law. There remain few restrictions on foreign direct investment, but those that do exist are for the large part industry-specific. For example, foreign investment in Unified Energy Systems, a Russian electric power company, is capped at 25% (Terterov, 2001).

With the advent of modern legislation in Russia, the official focus appears to be on attracting new foreign investors and guaranteeing their rights (Petrova and Zimbler, 2001). This is consistent with the theoretical perspective that after periods of relative closure to foreign investment, governments go through an opening stage to encourage foreign investment in the name of modernization (Kerr, 1993). The government has sought to guarantee rights by allowing free repatriation and reinvestment of profits – but only after payment of applicable taxes (Petrova and Zimbler, 2001). The 1999 law also includes a tax stabilization clause that applies to companies with greater than 25 percent foreign equity ownership. This clause prohibits increases in import duties and federal taxes on this form of investment for a period of up to seven years to allow initial investments to be recovered (Petrova and Zimbler, 2001).

In 1999, the Russian Federation also passed the Law on Protection of the Rights of Investors on the Securities Market. This law prohibited the sale of shares until they are fully paid for and a report regarding the issue of the shares has been filed with the Securities Commission. The law also introduced joint and several liability for all signatories of a securities prospectus for damages to investors due to misrepresentation (Petrova and Zimbler, 2001).

These legal reforms have resulted in changes in the Russian statutory regime, creating new entitlements such as the right of the investor to compensation for illegal acts and to the use of international tribunals for settlement of disputes with Russian entities (Vecchio and Chessick, 1999). The law has differentiated between various types of investment projects and has allowed for different applications of the law to different investment categories.

The new law and its surrounding legislation are far from perfect. It remains unclear, for example, exactly how to define different investment types. Also, in many provisions, it is specified that certain activities must take place "in accordance with Russian law", requiring further research by potential investors (Vecchio and Chessick, 1999). The current Law on Currency Regulation and Currency Control requires Central Bank approval for certain types of transactions including securities transactions, a process which can result in delays of several months for investors (Petrova and Zimbler, 2001). A Central Bank Directive published in 1999, however, now allows foreign parties to make equity investments in a Russian company in hard currency without obtaining a currency license. Previously, a license was required if investments were not made in rubles through a special type of bank account (LeBoeuf et al., 2000). This directive may not solve any problems however, because although it may decrease delays experienced in foreign capital investment, it exposes investors to currency devaluation.

Although these provisions exist to protect investors, the use and enforcement of these provisions has been inconsistent (Petrova and Zimbler, 2001). Many of the "guarantees" regarding investors' rights may be overridden by the application of so-called "grandfather clauses" contained in the legislation that allow restriction of the law's application on public policy grounds. This clearly allows for post-investment opportunism by government officials. In fact, the new law fails to address many key issues for foreign investors contemplating investing in Russia, such as detailed tax structure, corruption and enforcement.

Few of the "new" provisions differ widely from the provisions of the prior 1991 law or the provisions of the Russian civil code (OECD, 2001). Some provisions have clarified ambiguous portions of prior laws, while others have added more uncertainty due to their language and unclear application. In addition, some provisions create new obstacles for investors by requiring further research into a wide range of Russian laws. Foreign investment law in Russia remains a deterrent to foreign investment, largely due to the immense burden in its interpretation and its poor enforcement. While many foreign investors have had positive experiences in Russia, the ability of Russian governments, government officials and entrepreneurs to act opportunistically remains virtually unconstrained. According to Williamson (1979) the concept of opportunism does not imply that all individuals act opportunistically all the time. Risk is created for those entering into transactions, such as foreign investments, when the *threat* of opportunism is present. As suggested above, for foreign investors, opportunism can arise from governments, government officials abusing their power for personal gain, transaction partners, investment partners and organized crime. Examples of the experiences of some foreign investors in the Russian Federation can illustrate the risk of opportunism.

THE INVESTOR EXPERIENCE

The Russian Federation's economic potential initially made it a popular investment destination. Within five years of the collapse of the Soviet Union, private foreign investment in Russia reached almost US$6 billion (Walker, 1997). However, with vague laws and rampant corruption, being successful as an investor in the Russian Federation is difficult unless an investor properly educates himself as to how to work well within the unique Russian legal system – and even then one is open to a variety of opportunism.

Experiences of foreign investors in Russia have ranged from pleasant and profitable to terrifying and disappointing. The Mafia activity in Russia remains a deterrent for many, particularly following the 1996 murder of a Western businessman by the name of Paul Tatum who had entered the Russian market as a part-owner of a Radisson hotel (Walker, 1997). In June of 2001, a Canadian executive with Norex Petroleum Ltd. who had invested a substantial amount of money in developing Siberian oil fields with partner Tyumen Oil Co. lost his investment when Russian gunmen took over the operations office of the company he had financed (Webster, 2002). These are but a few examples of opportunistic Russian business partners who refuse to play by the rules, often because it is easy to render the rules inapplicable to you if you know how to manipulate the Russian legal system.

Violence is not the most common way that foreign investors in Russian business ventures experience defeat. The Russian law enforcement system is known for its corruption, often demonstrated by judges who interpret vague, disputed foreign investment laws in favour of a

Russian party, or by police who overlook shady dealings of Russian business and selectively enforce investment laws (Webster, 2002). The Canadian company Kinross Gold Corp., which invested nearly US$70 million in a gold mine development in Siberia, is involved in a legal battle with its Russian partner, Geometall Plus, over the validity of Kinross's shares (Webster, 2002). Legal disputes over validity of investments, development licenses, and debt collection have resulted in huge losses for many companies that entered into business dealings in the Russian Federation either independently or in partnership with Russian businesses. With inadequate laws and overabundant loopholes for those who know how to play the system – experienced Russian investors and capitalists – foreign investors can often find that their expectations far exceed their experience.

Many businesses have a very different story to tell. A large number of investors have made a substantial profit in Russia and have had positive experiences. The key appears to be using a high level of due diligence in researching the company you are investing in or partnering with, to examine their profitability, business practices and stability (Terterov, 2001). Many insist that partnering with a reputable Russian investor or company who understands Russian law, corporate structure, bureaucracy and government interaction can allow a foreign investor to avoid the pitfalls that many overeager foreigners seem to experience (Palmer, 2002). Even this degree of due diligence, however, can fail to protect an investor from opportunism from one's business partners.

A large number of Fortune 500 companies have invested successfully in the Russian Federation, including Philip Morris, Coca Cola and Dow Chemical. These companies have found Russia a favourable place to invest and conduct operations in because of the vast amounts of natural resources, large population base, and extensive skilled workforce (Terterov, 2001). To successfully control a business in Russia, it is believed that a share or stake of at least 50% is required, although 75% is preferable (Terterov, 2001). Of course this is much higher than is normally required for effective control of a company in modern market economies. Many successful investors state that it is very difficult to run a successful business without local input, as Russian authorities are traditionally tougher on foreign investors. With a local partner who has an in-depth understanding of Russian administration through experience, a business is likely to be successful. However, success in this case will be dependent on the reliability of the local partner. This is the key reason why due diligence is of utmost importance. However, it may not always be enough.

CONCLUSION

Attracting foreign investment into the Russian economy remains a priority in the economic policy of the Russian Federation. Although the foreign investment environment in the Russian Federation has improved in the last fifteen years, its share in the world's total accumulated direct foreign investment was only 0.3 percent in 1998 (Bumag, 2001). The absence of comprehensive legislative reform during the period in which centralized Soviet management has been abandoned in favour a new market economy has resulted in a high-risk, unstable investment environment. Opportunism, in all its forms, is widely practiced. Small changes in the law, often lacking clarity, have allowed many individuals to use law to their advantage when dealing with foreign investors who do not have the experience, and therefore level of familiarity, needed to understand the law at a similar level of depth. This lack of legal transparency represents a significant transaction cost for foreign investors.

Loopholes in the law have allowed many businesses to set up opportunistic dealings such as joint ventures with foreign investors, only to use legal manoeuvring to force the foreign investor out of the partnership when profit begins to appear. It has become possible for investors to lose millions of dollars in unsavoury business deals with Russian parties due to corrupt law enforcement officials who favour the interests of Russian business. When enforcement bodies lack resources to carry out their responsibilities and vague laws leave the investment regulation process open to corruption and political interference, problems with consistent enforcement arise (Hobbs, et. al., 1997). Further, the poor training of Russian police and lack of experience in other enforcement agencies leaves the door wide open for sophisticated commercial opportunism. Lack of consistency makes it difficult for an investor, foreign or otherwise, to arrange business dealings so as to obey applicable laws and to be aware of the legal ramifications of his or her actions.

Many Russians remain fearful that foreign investment will result in the foreign ownership of the Russian economy, a particularly unsettling thought after Russians spent many years in a battle to wrest power over their country and its economy from communist governments. Starting from this perspective, many Russians see foreign investment as a way to easily fund ambitious business projects but have no intention of sharing profit they believe belongs to Russians. The legal environment allows them to act opportunistically.

Despite all the difficulties and risks, Russia has a huge consumer market and a vast array of natural resources that can be developed if investment exists to fund the ventures needed to utilize them. If an investor is able to keep up to date with the frequent amendments to important legislation and familiarize himself thoroughly with difficult to understand tax laws and accounting procedures, he may be successful. He will also have to diligently research the background and reputation of any potential business associates and network within the Russian Federation to establish contacts to aid in manoeuvring through the bureaucracy and politics of Russia.

These are huge tasks for a potential investor to undertake and can be enough to discourage many from entering the Russian market. Russian legal reform is necessary to keep protection of Russian autonomy in the forefront, yet improve the Russian investment market to strengthen the economy. Through the development of more transparent and efficient laws in the areas of tax, currency, and securities, the process of investing in Russia can become much more simple and accessible. By defining the application and scope of laws, loopholes can be minimized, aiding in the control of corruption and opportunism by providing more accountability and predictability.

All of this requires the building of institutions. One of the major constraints would appear to be the low level of human capital investment in the enforcement sector. This will require direct investment in existing personnel and the recruitment of new personnel with higher levels of human capital through improved compensation. While a good start has been made in reforming the formal legal rights of foreign investors, the problems with enforcement still allows for a large degree of opportunism to be practiced on foreign investors. Reform in this area may be particularly difficult because corruption and opportunities to engage in private opportunism mean that many individuals have a personal stake in the continuation of the existing regime for foreign investment. Thus, the Russian Federation may find itself stuck in a sub-optimal stable equilibrium (Kerr and MacKay, 1997) that prevents its full transition to a market economy. If nothing else a failure to remove the ability to act opportunistically against foreign investors will delay the process of modernization in the Russian Federation because important opportunities for technology transfer will be foregone.

REFERENCES

Amin, S. (1976). *Unequal Development*. New York: Monthly Review Press.

Archibald, G.C. and Rosenbluth, G. (1978). *Production Theory in Terms of Characteristics – Some Preliminary Considerations*. Discussion Paper No. 78-19, Department of Economics, Vancouver: University of British Columbia.

Artisien-Maksimenko, P. and Adjubei, Y. (Eds.) (1996). *Foreign Investment in Russia and Other Soviet Successor States*. New York: St. Martin's Press.

Barnett, R. and Muller, R.E. (1974). *Global Reach, The Power of the Multinational Corporations*. New York: Simon and Schuster.

Beard, R. (1996). *Law and Politics*. Bucknell Russian Studies Program, Lewisburg: Bucknell University, http://www.departments.bucknell.edu/russian/politics.html.

Biersteker, T.J. (1976). *Distortion or Development?: Contending Perspectives on the Multilateral Corporation*. Cambridge MA: MIT Press.

Bumag, R.T. (2001). Investments in Russia Rise for 2000, *The Russia Journal*, 4 (21), http://www.russiajournal.com/printer/weekly4726.html.

Butler, W.E. (1999). *Russian Law*. Toronto: Oxford University Press.

Centre for Co-operation with the Economies in Transition. (1996). *Investment Guide for the Russian Federation, 1996*. Paris: Organisation for Economic Co-operation and Development.

Considine, J.I. and Kerr, W.A. (1993). Russian Re-Centralization of Energy. *Geopolitics of Energy*, 15 (2), 7-10.

Considine, J.I. and Kerr, W.A. (2002). *The Russian Oil Economy*. Cheltenham: Edward Elgar.

Das, S. (1987). Externalities and Technological Transfer Through Multinational Corporations. *Journal of International Economics*, 22, 171-182.

Feldbrugge, F.J.M. (1993). *Russian Law: The End of the Soviet System and the Role of Law*. Boston: Martinus Nijhoff Publishers.

Findlay, R. (1978). Relative Backwardness, Direct Foreign Investment and the Transfer of Technology: A Simple Dynamic Model. *Quarterly Journal of Economics*, 92, 1-16.

Hobbs, J.E., Kerr, W.A., and Gaisford, J.D. (1997). *The Transformation of the Agrifood System in Central and Eastern Europe and the New Independent States*. New York: CAB International.

Hymer, S. (1960). *The International Operations of National Firms: A Study of Direct Investment*. PhD Dissertation, Cambridge MA: Massachusetts Institute of Technology.

Hymer, S. (1979). *The Multinational Corporation: A Radical Approach*. Cambridge MA: Cambridge University Press.

Kerr, W.A. (1993). Domestic Firms and Transnational Corporations in Liberalizing Command Economies – A Dynamic Approach. *Economic Systems*, 17 (3), 195-211.

Kerr, W.A. (2000). A New World Chaos? – International Institutions in the Information Age. *Estey Centre Journal of International Law and Trade Policy*, 1 (1), 1-10, www.esteyjournal.com.

Kerr, W.A., Hobbs, J.E. and Gaisford, J.D. (1994). Privatization of the Russian Agri-Food Chain: Management Constraints, Underinvestment and Declining Food Security. In G. Hagelaar (Ed.), *Management Studies and The Agri-Business: Management of Agri-Chains.* (pp. 118-128). Department of Management Studies, Wageningen: Wageningen Agricultural University.

Kerr, W.A. and MacKay, E. (1997). Is Mainland China Evolving into a Market Economy? *Issues and Studies*, 33 (9), 31-45.

LeBoeuf, Lamb, Greene and MacRae, L.L.P. (2000). *Russian Law News: Foreign Investors May Make Equity Investments in Hard Currency Without a License.* http://www.russianlaws.com/archive/cic.html.

Loppacher, L.J. and Kerr, W.A. (2006a). The GATS Impact on Private Investors: Is it 'Much Ado About Nothing'? *Investment Management and Financial Innovations*, 3 (4), 79-88.

Loppacher, L.J. and Kerr, W.A. (2006b). Rules for Foreign Investment – The US Agenda in Bilateral Trade Agreements. *The Geneva Post Quarterly*, 1 (2), 195-229.

Marton, K. (1986). Technology Transfer to Developing Countries via Multinationals, *The World Economy*, 7, 409-426.

McMillan, C.H. (1994). *Foreign Investment in Russia: Soviet Legacies and Post-Soviet Prospects.* Occasional Paper No. 5, Ottawa: Centre for Research on Canadian-Russian Relations.

Offerdal, E.C.F. (1992). Taxation of Foreign Direct Investment. In V. Tanzi (Ed.), *Fiscal Policies in the Economies in Transition.* (pp. 232-253). Washington, DC: International Monetary Fund.

Organisation for Economic Co-Operation and Development (OECD) (2001). *The Investment Environment in the Russian Federation: Laws, Policies and Institutions.* Paris: OECD.

Palmer, M. (2002). Investing in Russia: First Hand Advice from a One Man Profit Centre. *International Living Magazine*, 17 (11), http://www.escapeartist.com/international/russiainvest.htm

Petrova, E., and Zimbler, B. (2001). *Russian Federation: Brief Review of the Legal System.* LeBoeuf, Lamb, Greene and MacRae, L.L.P. Publication, www.russianlaws.com/publ.html.

Streeten, P. (1977). Self-reliant Industrialization. In C.K.Wilber (Ed.), *The Political Economy of Development and Underdevelopment.* (pp. 34-47). New York: Random House.

Terterov, M. (Ed.) (2001). *Doing Business with Russia*, 2nd edition, London: Kegan Page Ltd.

Vecchio, M.S., and Chessick. P. (1999). *The New Russian Foreign Investment Law: Old Wine in New Bottles.* Moscow: The Russian-American Chamber of Commerce, http://russianamericanchamber.org/newsletter/new_russian_investment_law.html.

Vernon, R. (1971). *Sovereignty at Bay: The Multilateral Spread of US Enterprises.* New York: Basic Books.

Vernon, R. (1975). *Multinational Enterprises in Developing Countries: An Analysis of National Policies.* New York: United Nations Industrial Development Organization.

Vernon, R. (1977). *Storm Over Multinationals: The Real Issues.* Cambridge MA: Harvard University Press.

Walker, M. (1997). Investing in Russia: Not for the Weak at Heart, *Europe*, http://www.eurunion.org/magzine/9703/p08/p08-9703.htm

Webster, P. (2002). Ripped off in Russia: Canadian Companies are Losing their Investments. *Maclean's Magazine*, May 20.

Williamson, O.E. (1979). Transaction Cost Economics: The Governance of Contractual Relations. *Journal of Law and Economics*, 22, 233-262.

Wong, J and Blomstrom, M. (1992). Foreign Investment and Technological Transfer. *European Economic Review*, 36, 137-155.

Chapter 10

PIRACY, PROPERTY AND PRODUCTIVITY: THE CASE FOR PROTECTING THE RESULTS OF INTELLECTUAL ACTIVITY

William A. Kerr and Shari L. Boyd

ABSTRACT

The protection of intellectual property is important for the Russian Federation for two reasons: (1) it is necessary for the long term revitalization of Russian industry because it is the key to technological competitiveness and; (2) it is an essential element for the integration of Russia into the global economy. Under communism, intellectual property belonged to the state and all research was state funded. The state-sponsored research system has all but collapsed during transition and if Russian industry is to have a chance at being technologically advanced mechanisms must be found to encourage private sector research and development. In the short-run technological transfers are possible from modern market economies but only if foreign firms feel that their intellectual will be protected in Russia. While the Russian Federation has been putting the legal framework in place to protect intellectual property, enforcement remains a major problem. Neither the resources nor the investment in human capital have been forthcoming to overcome the deficiencies in enforcement. An effective regime for protecting intellectual property remains a major challenge for the revitalization of Russian industry.

INTRODUCTION

The legal protection of intellectual property is a contentious economic issue. This is particularly the case in developing countries that produce little intellectual property themselves meaning that resources must be expended to provide protection for intellectual property belonging to foreigners. The issue is further complicated because the method used to provide intellectual property protection entails government's endowing the owners of intellectual property with a monopoly – albeit a temporary one – and thus allowing the producers of intellectual property the opportunity to reap monopoly profits. In some cases these monopoly profits mean that people with low incomes are forced to pay high prices for necessities. The protection of intellectual property has been particularly contentious in the area of pharmaceuticals and agricultural inputs for this reason. The result is that individual countries face different incentives to protect intellectual property with those countries that produce the majority of the world's intellectual property wanting strong international protection for intellectual property while countries that do not produce significant amounts of intellectual property show little interest in expending resources to protect intellectual property. The latter group of countries, of course, are typically poor.

One might argue that the reason that countries are poor is that they do not protect intellectual property. While clearly, the failure to protect intellectual property contributes to a country's impoverishment, there are many other determinants of the level of development. Many developing countries lack the scientific establishment and technical sophistication to support modern research and development programs. Developing countries often act as if they can free ride on developed countries research and development efforts.

As a result, a major rift arose between developing and developed countries over the issue of protection for intellectual property during the last quarter of the 20th century (Kerr, et al. 1999). The culmination of that rift was the inclusion of the Agreement on Trade Related Aspects of Intellectual Property (TRIPS) under the administrative mandate of the new World Trade Organisation (WTO) negotiated during the Uruguay Round that was completed in 1994 (Gaisford and Kerr, 2001). The TRIPS provided for strong enforcement of intellectual property internationally and all members of the WTO, including developing countries, had to acquiesce to TRIPS disciplines. Developing countries, however, have continued to chafe at providing protection for, particularly foreign, intellectual property and the issue came to a head at the Doha Ministerial of the WTO over patents on drugs used in the treatment of AIDS and other epidemic diseases.

The reason why the international protection of intellectual property has become so important for developed countries over the last two decades is that the proportion of the value of goods comprised of intellectual property has been rising at a rapid rate (Gaisford, et al. 2001). This is largely a result of the computer revolution including the widespread uptake of the internet but also encompasses biotechnology and electronic media and entertainment technology. Intellectual property is, in short, the foundation of the *knowledge economy* that developed economies have wholeheartedly embraced and expect to be the basis for their future prosperity.

While the granting of temporary monopolies provides the opportunity to capture monopoly profits, the development cost for new technology are often high. Further, the rate at which competing and substitute products are developed is relatively rapid. This means that the product life cycle of any innovation is likely to be short – much shorter than the twenty years provided by patent protection. Thus, to increase the probability of recouping research and development costs, those developing new technology need their property protected in the widest possible markets for their products, including markets in developing countries.

While failure to protect intellectual property has direct effects on the profits of inventing firms it also produces important negative externalities for global economic welfare. Reducing the probability of having a profitable result from investing in research and development causes firms to re-evaluate their investment decisions. This means that fewer resources will flow to research and development activities which will slow the rate of innovation. Less innovation reduces global welfare.

The situation in the Russian Federation is, however, different than that in developing countries. The Russian Federation has significant research capacity and a large pool of individuals with the human capital necessary to undertake research. Admittedly, the physical capital that was a legacy of the Soviet Union is depreciating rapidly and, to a lesser degree and at a slower rate, so is the stock of human capital. The economic disruptions that surround the process of transition have been particularly disruptive to the Russian research establishment because in the Soviet era all funding for research and development was provided by the state. In modern market economies, on the other hand, a considerable proportion of research and development is undertaken within the private sector. Much of the research is done in house within private firms. Declining economic activity has put considerable pressure on government budgets in the Russian Federation and public funding, as a consequence, has been drastically reduced. These cuts have been even deeper for the research establishment as governments scrambled to find the funds to meet current obligations. Research, with future, and often problematic, pay-offs was not a high priority. Privately funded research has not been forthcoming to offset the decline in public funds. This is for two reasons, the macro economic environment has been too volatile to justify long term investments and the market institutions that are required to support a private sector research establishment, including those for the protection of intellectual property, have not evolved. In short, transition has been particularly difficult for the research establishment. Further, there are no "road maps" for how a private sector research establishment can be fostered. Certainly, the protection of intellectual property is central to the transition to a more market based research system but there are a large number of other institutions that will also have to evolve.

THE ECONOMICS OF INTELLECTUAL PROPERTY PROTECTION

As a means of ensuring that innovation will continue, patents have existed for five hundred years. A patent gives exclusive rights to the owner of an innovation to prevent a third party from using, reproducing, selling, exporting or importing the product or process that led to the product. In exchange for these exclusive rights, the patentee must disclose all information relevant to duplicating the product or process to the extent that a knowledgeable person within the field could reproduce the product or process. This is very important in a country like the Russian Federation that has a considerable research capacity. Patent disclosure ensures that other researchers have access to information upon which they can make further advances, often in entirely unrelated industries. The discussion of patent protection often focuses on the protection provided those who create intellectual property but the openness required for receiving protection is extremely important to ensuring ongoing technological progress.

Patents give the inventor a temporary monopoly so that expensive research and development (R&D) costs may be re-cooped and, in return, makes their acquired knowledge available to the public. This "give and take" process offers incentives for investing in R&D in order to develop new products and processes. Without the incentive of monopoly rents, the level of innovation would fall and society would be worse off without the new inventions.

While the reasoning behind granting patents and, thus, giving companies temporary monopolies is quite straight forward – new innovations in exchange for exclusive rights – it receives much scrutiny. Controversy arises due to the nature of monopoly pricing. A monopoly will produce at a sub-optimal level for the corresponding demand for the product, resulting in higher prices. The lower volume of sales coupled with an increase in price allows the monopoly an opportunity to improve its financial position relative to one where it faces competition. The granting of monopoly rights does not, however, guarantee a firm will make a profit – many innovations fail.

Granting a firm a temporary monopoly over their innovation produces a benefit because society gains from new innovations. As suggested above, there is also the positive externality that, as patents also have a stipulation that once a firm is granted exclusive rights they must disclose all information relevant to the innovation to the public, this information can then become the building blocks for new inventions.

Many ideas have been put forward as to how the benefits of granting patents could be attained without assigning monopoly rights. The search for a "win-win" situation for society whereby it benefits from the inventions but does not incur the higher prices, however, has proved illusive. The alternatives to the temporary granting of monopoly rights that are most commonly suggested are: (1) not granting patent protection to innovating firms, thereby leaving a competitive industry; (2) regulating the monopoly so profits are reduced; i.e. implementing average cost pricing for the industry; and (3) guaranteeing normal rates of return through subsidization. The arguments pertaining to each alternative are discussed below.

No Patent Protection

Intuitively, not granting patent protection seems like the obvious answer to eliminating the monopoly distortion. The consequences are, however, that society will no longer benefit from innovation. The reason patents are granted is to provide the stimulus for a positive level of R&D to bring forth a stream of new discoveries. What would happen if patent protection is no longer given to innovators? As shown in Figure 10.1, the innovating firm would incur average costs of production that would include the costs associated with R&D. To make normal profit (meaning it recouped its investment), the firm would have to receive price P1 from the market. While this alternative seems superior to giving monopoly rights, the problem arises when other firms enter into the industry – assuming since no temporary monopoly has been granted and there are no other barriers to entering the market, the industry is now competitive. In Figure 10.1, a new firm can enter the industry but does not have to incur the costs of R&D or the innovating cost – it can simply copy the investing firm's product because there is no patent protection limiting this practice. Copying an innovation (via reverse engineering) is usually much less costly than undertaking the original R&D (Gaisford et al., 2001). Since the "copycat" firm is able to use the technology and operate with lower average costs, they are able to charge a lower price, P2, in the market and still make normal profits. Eventually, the innovating firm is driven from the market because the copycat firm (or firms) charges a lower price and will, therefore, attract all the customers through its ability to price more competitively. As a result, a situation arises whereby everyone wants to be the copycat, however, without an innovator there is nothing to copy. The long-term consequence of this situation is a decline in innovating activity that slows technological progress.[50]

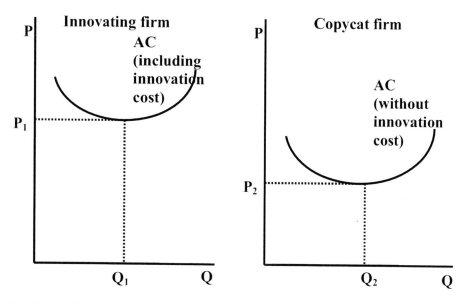

Figure 10.1. Competitive Industry with No Patent Protection.

Regulated the Monopoly or Subsidization

An alternative to granting patent protection without giving a firm a complete monopoly is to regulate the monopoly. The logic behind this alternative is that patents provide the protection from copycats, but society does not incur the higher monopoly prices. This approach also appeals because an incentive to undertake R&D remains and society will still benefit from the new inventions. While this seems like a mutually beneficial option for innovators and society, other factors need to be considered.

As illustrated in Figure 10.2, regulating the monopoly would involve setting the price where the average cost curve intersects the demand curve (point r). At this point the monopoly is making normal profits and will continue to innovate.[51] The problem arises in determining where point r lies.

For some industries, it is possible to derive a reasonable estimate a firm's average cost. This is an extremely difficult problem, however, in the case of innovating firms. The process of invention is not linear or deterministic (i.e., making an investment in research at one point in time does not guarantee that a successful innovation will emerge). The determination of average costs not only has to factor in the R&D costs for the inventions that are eventually marketable, but also all the costs associated with failed projects. Hence, it is not possible to

---

[50] Of course innovation will not cease altogether as some innovation takes place simply due to the challenge it presents to individuals and by accident.
[51] Remembering that in economics models average cost includes among its costs a normal return on investment. It is the cost to the firm of keeping investment resources from moving out of the firm to, other, higher return uses.

simply calculate R & D expenditures for one innovation when determining average cost. Firms that make investments must have the expectation that, on average, they will have a "winning" innovation sufficiently often to offset all of the loses on "failed" innovations. Of course, this means that the "profits" on any "winning" innovation, taken in isolation, are likely to appear very large. The observation of apparently high profits considerably vexes those who worry about the cost of inputs to, for example, poor farmers or those with limited incomes who require pharmaceuticals.

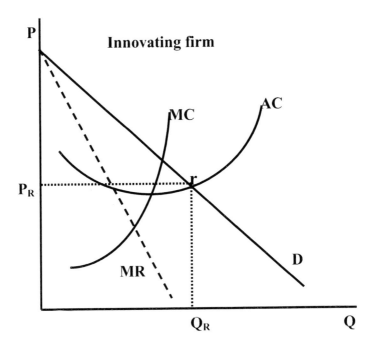

Figure 10.2. Regulated Monopoly Alternative.

Further, under average cost pricing, firms that now have their profits guaranteed by the regulator have considerable incentive to cheat. By making average costs appear higher than they actually are, the firm can make substantial economic profits because the guaranteed price, based on the artificially inflated average cost, exceeds the actual average costs. The result is similar to the unregulated monopoly case. In other regulated industries with costs that are far more standardized that those associated with innovation, firms have been able to hide true costs and excessive profits from their regulators with relative ease (Kwaczek and Kerr, 1989). Approaching the problem of appropriate costs from the enforcement angle, the issue is how to determine how much R&D for innovative purposes should cost.

In addition, for regulated firms, it is important to consider the affect on firms' incentives to be efficient. The current patent system internalizes the efficiency issue into each firm's management decisions. Being inefficient means a reduction in profits. The firm's management (or owners) have an incentive to constantly monitor performance and strive for improvement. However, if profits are regulated and guaranteed, the monopoly's efficiency would not enter into management decisions. Firms know they will make normal profits regardless of what their costs are and have no reason to make adjustments to reduce these costs. Efficiency also comes into play in considering which projects and investments to undertake. Again, if firms are assured normal profits they may engage in unprofitable projects and participate in R&D for unnecessary inventions. As in the case where monopoly rights are not granted, society is again made worse off because firms now are likely to be inefficient and prone to carry out R&D simply because they are assured normal profits.

Directly subsidizing innovation by private firms is fraught with the same difficulties regarding monitoring costs and the design of incentives as attempting to regulate monopoly profits. Hence, while the inefficiencies inherent in the patent system are well known, no socially superior alternative has yet been devised.

WHY PATENTS ARE A CONTENTIOUS ISSUE FOR COUNTRIES WITH LIMITED RESEARCH CAPACITY

Governments and members of civil society in developing countries often express concerns regarding the granting patent protection in their domestic markets. Given that developing countries do not produce many innovations, the reluctance is not without some merit. As Correa (2000, p. 36) explains

> It is the logic of monopoly to charge as high a price as the market can bear, with the purpose of maximizing profits. Price increases shall be a regular feature, and not an accident, with the introduction and/or strengthening of patent protection in developing countries.

As patents inevitably result in higher prices for users of the technology, poor countries and individuals will be more likely to resist the granting of patent protection.

The most apparent reason for the aversion towards patents in developing countries is the degree of poverty. The average annual income in the least developed countries is approximately three hundred dollars per person per year (Sachs, 2001). With large segments of their societies living below the poverty level, it is not difficult to understand why developing countries would object to paying higher prices for, for example, seed developed using biotechnology. While the benefits of genetically modified crops may be apparent, the low incomes of those in developing countries often may not stretch to cover the higher cost of patented seed. This is particularly the case when it is foreigners who hold the rights to the intellectual property and receive the monopoly rents. Since the firms that commercialize innovation, often multinational corporations, are located primarily in developed countries, the net effect is a transfer of rents from poor citizens of developing countries to rich foreigners.

The debate over intellectual property rights creates a further separation of developing countries from developed countries. Developed economies' governments are receiving pressure from corporations to push for strengthened intellectual property rights in international markets. However, developing countries are sceptical as to the effects on their local economy and resist patents on necessary staples. Transition economies are often susceptible to similar arguments because transition has led to widening disparities in income and increases in the proportion of the population living in poverty. Monopoly prices associated with intellectual property protection will impose additional hardship on those citizens. In the case of the Russian Federation, however, unlike most developing countries, the potential to undertake R&D activities is considerable and the short run benefits of free-riding on developed countries' innovative activity needs to be weighed carefully against the effect of poor incentives on innovative activity over the longer term. If the Russian Federation wishes to be a full participant in the knowledge economy it will have to provide incentives to innovate.

Although developing countries raise valid concerns about the consequences of intellectual property rights in poor countries, their reluctance to protect these rights will contribute to serious long run problems. As explained above, patents appear to be a necessary condition to achieving a desirable level of innovative activity. Without protection and enforcement of intellectual property rights innovation will decline. While patents impose the costs associated with monopoly inefficiencies on society, it remains the socially superior choice relative to the alternatives. However, developing countries' actions often do not reflect current patent theories.

Many developing countries have taken the approach of either implementing intellectual property rights but not properly enforcing them or simply not granting protection. The U.S. Trade Representative has identified forty-four developing countries as those that have failed to properly implement or enforce intellectual property rights. This suggests that there is a gap between developing countries' actions and current patent theories.

Multinational firms based in developed countries are major proponents of better intellectual property protection in developing countries and, of course, the right to receive monopoly rents from the commercialization of their innovations. Developing countries wish to have the innovations resulting from R&D, but do not want to protect the foreign property that facilitates the existence of the new innovations. The contentious issue relates to how much protection is needed and what level of profits multinationals should be able to collect? The division between developed countries on one side and developing countries on the other over protection of intellectual property came to a head during the Uruguay Round of international trade negotiation and led to the TRIPS. Developed countries wrested considerable concessions from developing countries with developing countries agreeing to protect the intellectual property of foreigners (and their own domestic innovators) and to accept retaliation in the form of trade sanctions if they did not. Hence, the TRIPS sets out minimum international standards for the protection of intellectual property for every WTO member as well as prospective members such as the Russian Federation.

THE LAW AND PRACTICE OF THE TRIPS

The Agreement on Trade Related Aspects of Intellectual Property Rights (TRIPS) of the World Trade Organization (WTO) provides minimum standards that all member countries signed on to regarding protection of intellectual property. The agreement is one of the three pillars of the WTO – along with the General Agreement on Tariffs and Trade (GATT) and the General Agreement on Trade in Services (GATS) – that came into effect at the end the Uruguay Round of trade negotiations in 1995. It is important to note that to become a member of the WTO a country had to accept all three agreements, even if the prospective member country does not support one of the agreements. As suggested above, the structure and relationship of the agreements allows members to punish countries that do not comply with the TRIPS using trade sanctions under the GATT.

Under TRIPS, members are obligated to provide protection for foreign intellectual property. The method agreed is that countries must put domestic legislation in place to provide intellectual property protection for domestic property in accordance with major international agreements such as the Berne Convention and Paris Conventions administered under the umbrella of the World Intellectual Property Organization that predates the TRIPS, as well as some specific TRIPS provisions. Countries must also allocate resources for enforcement of the legislation. Protection for foreign intellectual property is provided through the WTO principle of *National Treatment* whereby countries agree to treat foreign nationals and firms in exactly the same way as domestic firms.

When the TRIPS agreement came into effect with the creation of the WTO, it was not happily embraced by all members. Many developing countries did not like the agreement, but to become a member of the WTO had to sign on to it. This "all or nothing provision" was a central component of the developed countries' strategy to have all WTO member countries enforce the intellectual property of foreign nationals. As a result of this coercive approach, objections and problems have surfaced. Developed countries often accuse developing countries of not living up to their WTO commitments and developing countries seem reluctant to do so. Several sections and definitions are open to interpretation. The vagueness of the agreement creates problems and disputes among members. For example, Section 27 of TRIPS, that outlines the criteria for patentability as being novelty, non-obviousness and utility, is universally recognized. The definitions of these criteria are, however, not closely specified. The absence of established definitions allows each member to interpret the three criteria in a manner that suits there own interests. Watal (2001), for example, explains how the novelty criterion differs among WTO members. The scope of the search to determine novelty in the US is limited to US borders and contrasts with the European practice of worldwide searches. The utility criterion is also subject to interpretation in the TRIPS agreement. The US uses a broader term than the "industrial applicability" approach used in Europe. While most developing countries have put the legislation required in the TRIPS in place, enforcement remains an issue and they continue to chafe under the agreement's obligations. They are attempting to reduce their commitments at the current Doha (or Development) round of WTO negotiations. For example, protection of intellectual property for pharmaceuticals has been a particularly contentious issue.

Access to medicines in developing countries is a topic that has seen much international debate, culminating in special arrangements being agreed at the Doha Ministerial Meeting of the WTO. Multinational corporations headquartered in developed countries control the development and commercialization of medicines that developing countries need. Developing countries have rallied together to promote access to medicines; i.e. to have their commitments to protect intellectual property abrogated or significantly relaxed.

In a paper presented to the World Trade Organization by a group of developing countries, they stated, "nothing in the TRIPS Agreement should prevent Members from taking measures to protect public health." Developing countries that are members of the WTO are deadly serious about securing access to medicine based on a "flexible" interpretation of the TRIPS objectives and principles. The flexible interpretation outlined by developing countries would allow members to take measures to ensure that intellectual property rights are not abused and do not adversely affect international trade. Such measures would include compulsory licenses in times of emergency where public health is at risk, parallel imports[52] and differential

---

[52] Where the prices of products are lower in a foreign market a Government may decide to allow importation of such products into their national market, so as to allow consumers to purchase at more affordable prices.

pricing. Each of these measures would ensure that intellectual property rights do not overshadow public health issues in developing countries.

At the Doha WTO Ministerial in the fall of 2001 developing countries argued for exemptions to their TRIPS obligations regarding access to medicines during outbreaks affecting public health. In the "Declaration on the TRIPS Agreement and Public Health", developing countries won "flexibilities" giving them the right to defy their TRIPS obligations. In the Agreement members are allowed to grant compulsory licenses[53] in circumstances where public health is in turmoil. Furthermore, it is up to each member to determine what constitutes a public health crisis. Developing countries also received a clause in the agreement that provides for further discussion into a solution in circumstances where public health is at risk. The clause provides for a solution to be established by the end of 2002 in light of a situation where a member country does not have the capacity to manufacture its own pharmaceuticals and would, therefore, have difficulty making use of compulsory licensing (WTO 2001). While developing countries saw the agreement as a way to ensure public health standards, they were difficult for developed countries. This now meant that developing countries could bypass their TRIPS obligations and not enforce intellectual property rights. However, the implication for long-term innovation is less innovation for medicines needed to control public health crisis' in developing countries. While this agreement is a short-run victory for developing countries, there are major implications for the long-term development of pharmaceuticals to treat diseases in developing countries. Unfortunately, developing countries fail to understand the effect their actions have on incentives. This is a lesson that should not be lost on the Russian Federation.

The Russian Federation wishes to join the WTO. To do so it must comply with the TRIPS (Antonyuk and Kerr, 2005). Hence, the TRIPS provides an excellent justification for doing something that a country with significant research potential should do anyway. Accession to the WTO may provide the political justification for providing the resources necessary to protect domestic intellectual property within the Russian Federation. It is an opportunity that should not be foregone.

THE PROTECTION OF INTELLECTUAL PROPERTY IN THE RUSSIAN FEDERATION

In the transition from a command economy to a market economy, Russia's political and legal systems have had to undergo extensive transformation. The centrally planning system that was once the foundation of the Russian economy has now been replaced by a desire to become a modern market economy. Coupled with a new form of government came the requirement to convert the legal system from a private alliance of the communist leaders to one that enforces laws enacted by the new democratically chosen government. Within this new legal framework came the notion of laws to protect intellectual property. Previously, under communist rule everything was owned by the state and personal property was restricted to a few material goods. In this system there was no need for intellectual property rights for

---

Parallel importation may be beneficial to prevent anti-competitive practices where patented products are offered at monopoly prices in the domestic market.

[53] Members are allowed to grant domestic manufacturers licenses to produce generic pharmaceuticals without paying a fee to the patent holders of such a medicine.

individuals because the state controlled all aspects of property. However, in the post-communist Russian Federation intellectual property rights and protection of those rights was recognised as a common institutional arrangement that existed in modern market economies. Laws were passed to reflect, to some extent, those in modern market economies.

After laying out the framework for intellectual property protection in the Russian Federation, the Russian government is now faced with additional challenges. Laws without the ability to enforce those laws are ineffective. Enforcement in Russia is weak even when dealing with "textbook" cases of intellectual property piracy. Intellectual property protection is difficult, expensive and requires specially trained personnel. In an economy such as the Russian Federation that is still in the transition process, the resources that are required to provide a successful enforcement regime are often not forthcoming.

The History of Intellectual Property Rights

Intellectual property rights protection is relatively new to many countries of the former Soviet Union. Under communist rule, all property was owned by the state, thus there was no requirement for laws governing the protection of an individual's intellectual property. Since the fall of communism, Russian legal doctrine has struggled with extending protection to intellectual property rights and enforcing that protection. Even the term "intellectual property" has been a contentious issue from the onset. In the Russian language the word "property" is "ownership" which when translated makes the expression "intellectual ownership". This term is regarded by the Russian legal community as political slang, not a legal concept. Russian legislation has struggled with and subsequently used different terms such as "results of intellectual activity" to avoid using "intellectual property" (Butler, 1999).

Since 1991, the Russian Federation has adopted many laws, decrees and by-laws with regard to intellectual property. The main areas of intellectual property that are now recognized by the Russian Federation are: trademarks, copyright and neighbouring rights and patents. On September 23, 1992, the Russian Federation enacted a package of laws dealing with intellectual property rights: the Patent Law; the Law on Trademarks, Service Marks and Marks of Origin; the Law on Legal Protection of Topologies of Integrated Circuits; the Law on the Legal Protection of Computer Programs and Data Bases (Feldbrugge, 1993). To complete the package of intellectual property laws, the Law on Author's Right and Neighbouring Rights was adopted on July 9, 1993 and the Law on Selection Achievements on August 6, 1993. In additional to each law, a substantial number of subordinate acts were issued by the President and the Government of Russia and many individual ministries and departments (Butler, 1999).

Since 1992, Russia has continued to improve its intellectual property laws to bring the country to the benchmark of modern standards. In 1997, an important change was made to the Federal Law on State Secrets. The Soviet era was characterized by extreme paranoia regarding information – in part because it could threaten the internal control of the Communist Party and in part due to the tensions of the "cold War". The Federal Law on State Secrets was liberalized in 1997 and individuals could gain access to information. The information now available included data on inventions and scientific works that was never before open to the public (Breiter, 1999). By releasing information on inventions and scientific works, others have the opportunity use this information as the building blocks for new inventions. This allows Russia to broaden its knowledge base and create more intellectual property. This was an important step for Russia to continue to open their economy and move away from the closed and secretive practices of the Soviet era.

Rospatent (the Russian Agency for Patents and Trademarks) is the agency that oversees intellectual property rights in the Russian Federation. Rospatent is a Federal body of Executive Agencies and controls all aspects of industrial property[54] as well as the legal protection of computer programs, data bases and topographies on integral circuits. Rospatent also hears conflict cases in its Chamber of Appeals. In 1997, an Interagency Commission on Intellectual Property Rights issues, formed from Rospatent and the Antimonopoly Committee, was created. The Commission is to identify cases of intellectual property violations and report them to the government agencies involved.

Russia's Intellectual Property Regime: Law versus Reality

Russia has progressed a long way since 1991 in terms of laws and legislation covering intellectual property rights, but that alone is not sufficient to having a complete intellectual property regime. Enforcement of those laws and regulations is the other condition that must be met to create a viable system. This seems to be the area regarding intellectual property rights that Russia is having the most difficulty making the transition to a market economy. However difficult it may be to enforce these rights, it is futile to have the laws but not be able to enforce them. The Committee on Intellectual Property Rights (CIPR) (2000) suggests that:

> More than ever, enforcement and implementation are the keys to protecting intellectual property...It is not enough that a country's laws comply with international obligations on paper (p.33).

Although Russia has progressed significantly in passing laws that generally meet present international standards, enforcement of those laws has been inadequate. Piracy, copyright infringement and counterfeiting are common in Russian markets. Russian consumers, knowingly and unknowingly, purchase counterfeit alcohol, food, clothing, pharmaceuticals, household items and pirated CDs and other electronic devises (Breiter, 1999). These items are imported from other countries including, China, Bulgaria and North Korea, in addition to the products produced in Russia.

> The survey of 50 major foreign investors in Russia revealed that counterfeiting, trademark piracy and other intellectual property infringements are costing businesses in Russia an estimated $US1 billion per year. Half of the companies surveyed stated their yearly losses attributed to IPR violations amount to at least $US 1 million, and a third said losses were between $US 5 to 50 million (CIPR, 2000).

Despite the fact that the losses from these infringements are substantial, creating a solid enforcement base is difficult and very expensive.

Many factors contribute to a successful enforcement system including, an uncorrupt police force, strong civil and criminal penalties, an experienced judiciary and adequate

---

[54] Inventions, industrial designs, utility models, trademarks, service marks and appellations of origin.

training and technology. The Russian government is struggling to enforce intellectual property rights as a result of a combination of shortfalls in these areas.

Due to the history of the police force in communist Russia, whose prime objective was to keep the Communist Party in power, there is still a feeling of distrust toward policing institutions by the general public and politicians. As a result the police force is not respected and therefore, holds little authority (Hobbs et al., 1997). Further, because politicians and thus the government distrust the police force, the resources policing receives from the government are minimal. This is particularly the case for the types of sophisticated training required to fight "white collar" crimes such as the violation of intellectual property. According to Hobbs et al., (1997), additional resources for training must be granted if the policing system in the Russian Federation is going to be effective.

Corruption within the police force results from poorly paid officers who lack confidence in their work. Poorly paid workers have little incentive to do their job to the best of their ability, but are also more apt to accept bribes. Bribery not only undermines the manner in which a police force operates but also tends to set the standards for doing business. Bribery creates a vicious circle that is difficult to stop. Once businesses understand that they can participate in illegal acts by bribing the police, then legitimate businesses are comparatively at a disadvantage. Fewer businesses remain incorrupt and bribery becomes a way of doing business.

Intellectual property infringements are difficult to police under the best of circumstances. Intellectual property protection is complicated to enforce due to the nature of the property. Intellectual property includes foreign trademarks, copyrighted documents and patented inventions. It can be difficult to identify a violation of these rights and to make the link to the person(s) involved. A highly trained and sophisticated policing system is required. An intelligent force, however, is not sufficient for effectively combating intellectual property rights infringements. Modern technology and extensive training is key to controlling intellectual property rights infringements.

The police force is not the only arm of enforcement that must ensure intellectual property rights are protected. Investigators, lawyers and judges play an important role in convicting those who infringe on other's intellectual property rights. Investigators may not be willing to devote sufficient time to collecting evidence for a case dealing with intellectual property rights. Other crimes seem more "criminal" and therefore the investigator may unknowingly devote more of their time to those cases. As with the police force, investigators are also inexperienced in the area of intellectual property and lack training in the methodologies used to investigate such cases.

Inexperience is not just limited to the police that carry out the preliminary aspects of enforcement and the investigators who collect evidence when an infringement occurs. Lawyers and judges in the Russian legal system also lack the training and a pool of independent experts to draw information from when dealing with intellectual property rights cases.

A fundamental problem of enforcement is that Russian courts have neither extensive experience, nor sufficient number of judges familiar with IPR cases (Breiter, 1999).

Therefore, even if the police force and investigators successfully identify intellectual property rights abuses the judiciary may not be able to convict or punish the accused.

RUSSIA'S ACCESSION TO THE WTO

In 1995, the same year the World Trade Organization was created, the Russian Federation began accession negotiations. The negotiations initially were concentrated on detailed discussions of Russia's economic system and their trade practices in terms of their alignment with WTO norms and rules.[55] Of course, these negotiations encompass issues dealing with the protection of intellectual property rights covered by the TRIPS.

The TRIPS agreement covers all aspects of intellectual property rights including, standards concerning availability, scope and use, enforcement and dispute prevention and settlement. The forms of intellectual property covered by TRIPS are, copyright, trademarks, geographical indications, industrial designs, patents, layout-designs of integrated circuits, protection of undisclosed information and control of anti-competitive practices in contractual licences.[56] To become a member of the WTO a prospective candidate must develop laws and regulations to ensure each of these forms of intellectual property rights receives protection.

Current State of Russia's WTO Accession Negotiations and TRIPS

As previously mentioned, Russia's accession to the WTO began in 1995. The first meeting of the Working Party on Russia's WTO accession was held in Geneva from July 17-19, 1995. Later in September 1995, the Russian Federation government gathered for a meeting to discuss how negotiations to the WTO were progressing. The meeting concluded with the overall decision to continue accession negotiations. By December of the same year, the Working Party on Russia's accession had had their second meeting at which time specific trade issues were discussed. Among these issues were concerns about trade related aspects of intellectual property rights. As of June 2002 the Working Party dealing with Russia's accession has met on fifteen occasions and dealt specifically with TRIPS in at least five of these meetings.[57]

The 4th Ministerial Conference of the WTO that took place in Doha, Qatar, on November 9-14, 2001 was attended by a Russian delegation. The conference concluded by deciding to initiate a new round of multilateral trade talks covering a number of issues, including difficulties with TRIPS. Under WTO rules, negotiations are open to all WTO members and prospective countries going through the accession process. However, any decisions based upon results from the negotiations can only be accepted by WTO members, not acceding countries. Therefore, Russia has an interest in completing its accession within the time frame to enable it to participate in the negotiations as a full WTO member. However, this does not mean that Russia is prepared to accede to the WTO on any terms. According to the Ministry for Economic Development of Russia, simply because talks are becoming more active does not mean that Russia is ready to accede to the WTO on any terms.

---

[55] See Russia and World Trade Organization, June 2002.
[56] See Annex 1C, Agreement on Trade-Related Aspects of Intellectual Property Rights
[57] See Russia and the World Trade Organization, (a).

The accession terms in all aspects will be based on a realistic situation in the Russian economy, ensure the necessary protection of national producers while keeping an adequate competitive environment.[58]

While Russia has declared it will not accede to the WTO on any terms, it is definite that Russia will not accede at all if the minimum TRIPS standards are not met. CIPR (1999) states that Russia has yet to meet the minimum standards, but is beginning to make progress on intellectual property issues.

Aims, Objectives and Obligations Related to Accession

By acceding to the WTO Russia hopes to gain from the wide range of benefits membership provides. According to The Russian Minister of Economic Development and Trade, each of the goals Russia hopes to achieve with WTO membership should help to contribute to its economic growth and not vice versa.[59] While all goals of accession are important, intellectual property protection could have a major bearing on one of the goals:

> Creation of a more favourable climate for foreign investments as a result of legal system change in accordance with the WTO standards.[60]

The change to the legal system that would directly affect the level of foreign investment is stronger intellectual property rights and protection of these rights. The desire to provide a climate that will attract foreign investment could be impeded if intellectual property protection is not sufficient. A study conducted for the World Bank to consider the relationship between foreign direct investment and protection of intellectual property rights concluded that weak intellectual property rights regimes deter foreign investment in many sectors, but especially in high technology sectors (Smarzynska, 2002). Further, weak intellectual property rights protection discourages investors from undertaking production in the host country and induces them to concentrate on the distribution of imported products. This relationship between intellectual property rights and foreign investment is a further motivation for Russia to strengthen intellectual property laws and regulations, besides the incentive to do so in order to accede to the WTO.

What the Russian Federation Must Do to Comply with TRIPS

Although Russia has made many reforms to its intellectual property regimes, full compliance with the WTO has not yet been attained. A 2002 Special 301 Report published by the United States Trade Representative places Russia on their "Priority Watch List" with regard to the failure to protect intellectual property rights (USTR, 2002). The USTR notes that certain aspects of the Russian Copyright Law and Russia's enforcement of those laws do not seem to be consistent with the TRIPS Agreement. Specifically, protection of well-known

---

[58] See Russia and the World Trade Organization, 2002.
[59] See Russia and the World Trade Organization, (b).
[60] See Russia and the World Trade Organization, (b).

marks, counterfeiting and unauthorized production and export of CDs and CD-ROMs are of utmost importance for the Russian Federation to address to align its laws and regulations with those of the WTO.

> IPR violations are barriers to new investment and impede Russia's effort to join the WTO (CIPR, 2000).

To successfully accede to the WTO Russia must draft new intellectual property laws that are compliant with WTO standards and prove they can implement and enforce those laws.

Russia's Membership to Other International Treaties Pertaining to Intellectual Property

Russia is already party to a number of international treaties concerning intellectual property rights. Russia is a member of the World Intellectual Property Organization along with other agreements including, the Paris Convention for the Protection of Intellectual Property (1883), the Madrid Agreement for the International Registration of Marks (1891), the Universal Copyright Convention (1952) and the Treaty on Patent Cooperation (1970).[61] Most recently, Russia also became a full member of the Berne Convention on March 3, 1995. Russia is also a party to many bilateral agreements on the protection of intellectual property. The United States, Austria, Bulgaria and Sweden all have bilateral agreements with Russia that extend to works published before and after the date the agreements were signed (Terterov, 2001, p.134). None of these agreements on their own can punish a country for not living up to its obligations. Only the TRIPS allows for sanctions and this was one of the major reasons for putting intellectual property rights under the WTO.

CONCLUSION

The need for intellectual property rights in Russia developed only after the fall the Soviet Union. Today, intellectual property rights protection is becoming an integral component of the Russian legal system. The Russian Federation has adopted modern intellectual property laws that are, for the most part, in conformance with international standards. It has also subsequently changed these laws to keep up with current standards in intellectual property law.

It is clear that the Russian Federation recognizes the need for intellectual property rights, if for no other reason than to appear to be a modern market economy. Whether, the central role intellectual property rights play in a modern market economy is well understood, however, is open to debate. In particular, the connection to the rising importance of intellectual property rights in the new knowledge economy may not be well understood. One indication is that the second component of an effective system of commercial law, a strong enforcement regime, has failed to materialise. Laws are ineffective if the enforcement is

---

[61] As a legal successor to the Soviet Union, Russia became a member to the organizations which the Soviet Union held a membership.

absent and penalties for breaking the laws are minimal. The Russian Federation's intellectual property regime is an example of the consequences of adopting laws without the framework in place to enforce them. The result is a weak system filled with corruption. What started as a combination of modern laws that met many international standards is now a set of written documents with no real effect. Of course, the problem of enforcement of commercial law is endemic in the Russian economy and is a major institutional failure in the transition process. It raises the transaction costs of firms, reduces economic activity and deters foreign investment. In the case of intellectual property rights, it condemns the Russian Federation to being a technological laggard.

If the Russian Federation is to gain control of intellectual property matters, attention needs to be focused on creating stronger laws, providing the authority and resources for enforcement and adopting firm penalties for infringements. Russia created a good foundation for intellectual property law but then did not follow through in implementing a complete system. Without the whole package (laws, enforcement and penalties), the system undoubtedly lacks authority and has proved to be flawed.

The international community has expressed concerns concerning the Russian Federation's treatment of intellectual property rights. Foreign firms are uneasy about investing in R&D in the Russian Federation because they cannot be sure their intellectual property will be protected. To further stimulate their economy, Russia needs to be attracting foreign investment, not providing an incentive to invest elsewhere. The Russian government recognizes the benefits of attracting foreign investment, but does not appear to understand the link between strong intellectual property protection and investment. Weak intellectual property rights result in less foreign investment. If the Russian government is serious in their desire to attract investment, a strong intellectual property regime should be a priority.

In the international forum, intellectual property protection is essential. While the Russian Federation has expressed its desire to join the WTO, accession to the WTO requires changes to Russian laws to meet international standards. These changes include altering Russia's intellectual property standards and showing they can realistically be enforced. Once Russian intellectual property rights protection meets the TRIPS standards, the Russian Federation will be one step closer to becoming a member of the WTO.

The Russian Federation needs to be careful that it does not fall into the trap of seeing only the costs associated with granting temporary monopolies to the developers of intellectual property and ignoring the benefits. While this may be understandable in countries with little R&D capacity, and hence will reap fewer benefits, this is not the case in the Russian Federation with its considerable potential ability to engage directly in R&D activities and to act as a host for foreign investment in R&D. Becoming a technological leader is the fastest way for the Russian Federation to make the full transition to a modern market economy. That cannot be accomplished without the effective protection of intellectual property.

REFERENCES

Antonyuk, O.V. and Kerr, W.A. (2005). Meeting TRIPS Commitments in Ukraine: An Important Challenge in the Quest for WTO Accession. *Journal of World Intellectual Property*, 8 (3), 271-282.

Breiter, M., (1999). *Russian Intellectual Property Rights: International Copyright*. Washington, DC: U.S. and Foreign Commercial Service and U.S. Department of State, http://www.tradeport.org/ts/countries/russia/mrr/mark0463.html

Butler, W.E. (1999). *Russian Law*. Oxford: Oxford University Press.

Coalition for Intellectual Property Rights. (2000). Intellectual Property Rights: A Key to Russia's Economic Revival. *Russia Business Watch*. http://www.cipr.org/activities/articles/RBWipr.pdf

Correa, C.M. (2000). *Intellectual Property Rights, the WTO and Developing Countries*. New York: Zed Books Limited.

Feldbrugge, F.J.M. (1993). *Russian Law: The End of the Soviet System and the Role of Law*. Boston: Martinus Nijhoff Publishers.

Gaisford, J.D. and Kerr, W.A. (2001). *Economic Analysis for International Trade Negotiations*. Cheltenham: Edward Elgar Press.

Gaisford, J.D, Hobbs, J.E., Kerr, W.A., Perdikis, N. and Plunkett, M.D. (2001). *The Economics of Biotechnology*. Cheltenham: Edward Elgar Press.

Hobbs, J.E., Kerr, W.A. Kerr and Gaisford, J.D. (1997). *The Transformation of the Agrifood System in Central and Eastern Europe and the New Independent States*. Wallingford: CAB International.

Kerr, W.A., Hobbs, J.E. and Yampoin, R. (1999). Intellectual Property Protection, Biotechnology and Developing Countries: Will the TRIPS Be Effective? *AgBioForum*, 2 (3 and 4), 203-211.

Kwaczek, A.S. and Kerr, W.A. (1989). Canadian Exports of Electricity to the US: International Competitiveness or International Risk Bearing. *World Competition Law and Economics Review*, 13 (1), 19-38.

Russia and the World Trade Organization. (2002). *On the Current State of Russia's WTO Accession Negotiations*, June. http://www.wto.ru/russia.asp?f=dela&t=11

Russia and the World Trade Organization, (a). *Main Stages of Russia's WTO Accession Negotiations*. Geneva: World Trade Organization, http://www.wto.ru/russia.asp?f=etaps&t=10

Russia and the World Trade Organization, (b). *Aims and Objectives of Accession*. Geneva: World Trade Organization, http://www.wto.ru/russia.asp?f=target&t=9

Sachs, J. (2001). *Transcript of the Life-video Presentation, Commission on Macroeconomics and Health*. Novartis Foundation for Sustainable Development Symposium, December 4. http://www.foundation.novartis.com/symposium/speech_jeffrey_sachs.pdf

Smarzynska, B.K. (2002). *The Composition of Foreign Direct Investment and Protection of Intellectual Property Rights: Evidence from Transition Economies*, Policy Research Working Paper 2786. The World Bank Development Research Group, Washington DC: World Bank.

Terterov, M. (2001). *Doing Business with Russia*. London: Kegan Page.

USTR. (2002). *2002 Special 301 Report: Priority Watch List*. Washington, DC: Office of the United States Trade Representative, http://www.ustr.gov/reports/2002/speical301-pwl.htm

Watal, J. (2001). *Intellectual Property Rights in the WTO and Developing Countries*. Cambridge, MA: Kluwer Law International.

WTO. (2001). *Developing Country Group's Paper*, IP/C/W/296,Geneva: World Trade Organization, http://www.wto.org/english/tratop_e/trips_e/paper_develop_w296_e.htm

In: Revitalizing Russian Industry
Eds: J. Gaisford, V. Mayevsky et al., pp. 149-176 © 2007 Nova Science Publishers, Inc.
ISBN 978-1-60021-778-4

Chapter 11

TRANSFORMATION AND REFORM IN THE RUSSIAN ENERGY SECTOR: THE UPSTREAM PETROLEUM INDUSTRY

Jennifer I. Considine

ABSTRACT

The upstream petroleum sector is an extremely important industry for the Russian Federation. This is because it is the major earner of foreign exchange in the economy and thus provides the means to import the technology that is vital to the revitalization of Russian industry. The Russian government wishes both to encourage the development and expansion of this industry, while at the same time allowing the benefits arising from this industry to accrue widely across the economy. This is a question of tax policy – if taxes are too high investment in the industry will be deterred, if taxes are too low the benefits accrue narrowly to owners. The tax problem is made more complex because foreign investment is important for the industry's modernization, yet benefits may flow out of Russia. This chapter examines a number of alternative tax regimes – both those that have been put in place and theoretical alternatives – and forecasts made to 2012. The simulations show considerable variability in the development of the industry leading to the conclusion that "taxes matter".

INTRODUCTION

Throughout its distinguished history, the Russian upstream petroleum industry has been guided by a diverse and colorful array of economic and political influences. No single event or circumstance has been as traumatic as the dissolution of the USSR in 1990. The struggle to complete a successful transformation from a rigid command economy — the unique Stalinist planning model — to a free market based economy has preoccupied the Duma and reformers since the first democratic elections were held in the Russian Republic on June 10, 1991.

While the Russian government has made considerable progress towards the creation of a free market economy, physical and administrative distortions arising from decades of central planning continue to influence the development of the Russian oil industry. These include:

i. The separation of domestic and export markets for strategic commodities including armaments and energy supplies; and
ii. Difficulties associated with the absence of the legal and institutional framework that forms the foundation for a successful, and efficient free market economy.

At the same time foreign direct investment in the Russian Federation upstream petroleum industry has been falling steadily over the past few years – from a peak levels of $1.2 billion reported in 1999 to $441 million in 2000. Progress since 2000 has been strictly limited. According to estimates provided by the United Financial Group (Moscow), the capital-flight-to-GDP ratio has remained virtually constant since late 2000, early 2001 (Granville, 2002, p. 5).

Remarkably, and despite the best efforts of the Duma, full price liberalization in the petroleum sector has yet to be achieved. The failure of what would otherwise appear to be a straightforward economic policy has been attributed to a number of factors, including:

i. The complex (revenue-based) tax system including export duties, the mineral extraction tax, and excise duties.
ii. The absence of a comprehensive and stable legal framework for petroleum taxation, and the licensing and operations of Russian and international oil companies.
iii. The programme of exports for state needs,
iv. The use of "transfer pricing" within vertically integrated oil companies (VICs), and
v. Market distortions created by the non-payments problem.

The main contribution of this Chapter is the use of the Russian Federation crude oil supply curve and "fiscal and pricing" model to aid in the identification of the inefficiencies inherent in the existing petroleum legislation, and to provide an objective framework within which alternative scenarios, or fiscal regimes for petroleum, may be evaluated. The scenarios include:

a) Reference Case: Limited or "Half-Hearted" Reform;
b) Scenario I: The "New Tax Code";
c) Scenario II: No Royalties;
d) Scenario III: Potential Contributions from Production Sharing Agreements (PSAs); and
e) Scenario IV: Potential Contributions from Multilateral Lending Agencies (MLAs).

REFERENCE CASE – HALF HEARTED REFORM

The Reference Case, "Half-Hearted Reform: Maintaining the Status Quo Scenario", represents the conditions existing in the Russian Federation in June 2001 through early 2002. In some respects – specifically given the recent approval of Part II of the Draft Tax Code initially scheduled to go into effect on January 1, 2002 and proposed amendments to existing legislation affecting PSAs – the reference case represents a "worst case" scenario, that will be used to identify inefficiencies inherent in the (2001-2002) tax system.

All prices and costs reported in this chapter are in 2001 (US) dollars, and 2001 roubles. Further, the econometric model is briefly overviewed in the Appendix and discussed in detail in Considine (1999). The assumptions underlying the "Reference Case" Scenario may be summarized as follows:

i. *World Oil Price*: The assumptions concerning future trends in world oil prices have been obtained from the Deutsche Bank study, "Oil Market Outlook: OPEC's Balancing Act."[62] In summary, real (2001) crude oil prices are expected to remain strong, with the price of West Texas Intermediate (WTI) crude oil at Cushing, Oklahoma averaging approximately US$23.00 per barrel throughout the forecast period.

ii. *Domestic Oil Prices*: The successful liberalization of domestic oil prices is a goal that continues to elude Russian policy makers, and progress is achieved only gradually throughout the forecast period. Full price parity – the equality between the supplier's gross wellhead price for domestic oil sales and joint venture exports – is assumed to be attained in the year 2012.

iii. *Transportation Costs*: The reference case assumes domestic transportation charges of US$1.90 per tonne, and export transportation costs – i.e., from the West Siberian Basin to the Black Sea – of US$17.70 per tonne.[63]

iv. *Production Costs*: The reference case assumes crude oil production costs of US$16.50 per tonne, including necessary three-year workover and maintenance charges of US$8.25 per tonne.[64]

v. *Taxes*: The list of taxes and charges includes (a) VAT at 21.5%, (b) Excise Tax at 1.9 Rbls/tonne in 2000-01 and 2.6 Rbls/tonne from October 2001 throughout the remainder of the forecast period, (c) Royalties or Payment for the Right to Use Subsurface Resources at 8%, (d) Geology Fees at 10%, (e) other non-revenue taxes including property tax and social taxes not included in operating costs at 9% of production costs, (f) Profit Tax at 30%, (g) Benefits for the Profits Tax at 20%, and (h) Export duty at 17.1 Rbls/tonne.

---

62 As cited in Sieminski (2002, p.3).
63 See International Energy Agency (2002, p. 80).
64 International Energy Agency (2002, p. 80). Given the structure of the Russian Federation Crude Oil Supply Curve and 'Fiscal and Pricing' model, an increase in crude oil production costs that is accompanied by 'an identical' complementary increase in required three year workover costs will not make a material (or significant) difference to the 'reference' case forecasts. This is primarily attributed to the fact that the portion of crude oil sales that is absorbed by the necessary three year workover costs is re-allocated to the rehabilitation of 'idle' oil wells.

vi. *Direct Investment from the Federal Government*: Federal contributions to the Russian upstream petroleum industry are limited to direct investment funds accruing from the continued collection of the 10% geology fee throughout the forecast period.

vii. *Direct Foreign Investment from Joint Ventures and Production Sharing Agreements*: Foreign direct investment from Joint Ventures is assumed to equal to a conservative US$200 million per annum throughout the forecast period. The level of direct foreign investment from PSAs is limited to the contributions made in the years 1999-2001 throughout the forecast period.

viii. *Loans from Multilateral Funding Agencies*: The implications of new contributions from Multilateral funding agencies and PSAs will be examined separately, in an alternate scenario.

The reference case assumptions concerning taxes, and production and maintenance costs are illustrated in Tables 11.1 and 11.2. The reference case assumptions concerning international and domestic oil prices, transportation and production costs are given in Table 11.3.

Figure 11.1 illustrates the potential implications of these policies and assumptions on the future development of the crude oil production in the Russian Federation. In short, the combination of a continuation of the policies and tax system existing in June 2001 through early 2002, can be expected to have serious implications for the long-term development of the Russian upstream petroleum industry, despite the relative strength in world oil prices.

Reference Case: Half-Hearted Reform: Can the Good Times be Sustained?

> Russia's macro-economic performance during 1999 and 2000 has been surprisingly good and far exceeded expectations. Buoyed by the devaluation of the ruble and a sharp increase in average oil export prices over 1999 levels, real GDP has now surpassed its pre-1998 crisis level – real GDP grew by 3.2 percent in 1999, and is expected to grow by about 7 percent in 2000... Revenues rose to 16.4 percent of GDP in 2000 compared with just 13.4 percent in 1999. Furthermore, all revenues collected at the Federal level since early 1999 have been in cash. (World Bank, 2001, p. 1)

In March 1999, OPEC and a number of major non-OPEC producing companies collaborated to reduce crude oil production, and limit exports to international oil markets.[65] The resulting increase in world oil prices has been sustained beyond reasonable expectations by political altercation, and turmoil in the Middle East, which has included a US$4.00-6.00 'Iraqi' war premium on crude oil prices.[66]

The significant increase in international oil prices – from US$14.36 per barrel of WTI in 1998 to $30.37 in 2000, and $26.07 (est). in 2002 – and sustained economic recovery in the Russian Federation, is expected to send crude oil production soaring to levels as high as 408 million tonnes per annum in 2004 (See Figure 11.1). The bonanza is primarily due to an increase in oil revenues and capital expenditures by domestic producers, and a complimentary reduction in the number of idle oil wells.

---

65 International Energy Agency, 2002, p. 73.
66 Sieminski (2002, pp. 3-31).

The long-term forecast is not so encouraging given the "status quo" reference case scenario, which assumes:

i. No change in the tax system (recall that tax rates are held constant at the levels existing in June 2001 through early 2002 throughout the forecast period) and
ii. Virtually no 'external' investment funds (i.e., the reference case assumes external capital injections of only US$200 million per annum from Joint-Venture producers throughout the forecast period).

As world oil prices recede from US$26.00 per barrel in 2002 to US$23.00 per barrel in 2006 – a level that is maintained for the remainder of the forecast period – the illusive improvement in the Russian oil industry begins to evaporate. Crude oil production from the Russian Federation falls to 304.85 million tonnes in the year 2012, which represents a significant reduction from the 407.77 million tonnes per annum achieved in 2004.

The gains in crude oil production resulting from a slow but steady increase in drilling activity, and the gradual development of new oil wells throughout the forecast period – the total number of oil wells in the Russian Federation rises from 145.1 thousand in the year 2004 to 165.8 thousand in 2012 – is insufficient to offset the reduction in industry productivity that is associated with the idle well problem. The number of idle oil wells rises steadily from 10.91 thousand in 2004 to well over 23.1 thousand in 2012 (see Table 11.4).

The prospects for the Joint Ventures (JVs) and independent producers are equally grim. Despite the continued inflow of foreign direct investment capital, JV production falls steadily in the years of 2004-2012, from 37.68 million tonnes in 2004 to only 21.37 million tonnes in 2012.

The reductions can be attributed to economic distortions, and disincentives, created by the June 2001 tax system. In short, given the inordinately stringent fiscal regime that existed in the Russian Federation in June 2001 through early 2002, Russian production associations, the independent producers, Gazprom and JVs are not able to generate the internal investment funds that are required for the rehabilitation and development of the Russian oil industry.

Figure 11.2 illustrates the prices, taxes and production costs for a tonne of crude oil that has been produced by Russian enterprises for domestic consumption in the years 1993 to 2012, inclusive. Despite the significant reduction in the tax burden from the unusually onerous levels that prevailed in 1994 and 1998 (the height of the post-Soviet Union taxation era), federal and local taxes and crude production costs account for an average of 56 percent of the domestic oil price (the wholesale enterprise price including VAT and transportation costs) throughout the forecast period (2002-2012).

It is important to notice the fact that the domestic oil price shown in Figure 11.2 is the wholesale enterprise price including VAT and transportation costs. As the VAT tax rate on crude oil exports to non-CIS (Commonwealth of Independent States) countries is zero rated (and is assumed to be equal to zero on non-CIS exports throughout the forecast period), domestic prices actually exceed the export price (Urals Blend at the export terminal) slightly in the year 2012. The assumption of parity is reflected in equality between the suppliers gross wellhead price for domestic oil sales and crude oil exports.

Table 11.5 illustrates the net present value of the gross revenues from crude oil sales (including domestic crude oil sales, and non-CIS exports), and the gross tax revenue collected by the Russian government (federal and local) throughout the forecast period. Given the assumptions underlying the reference case, taxes and production costs account for approximately 58 percent of the net present value of gross revenues from crude oil sales in the Russian Federation in the years 2002 to 2012, inclusive.

Given the economic conditions existing in the Russian Federation in June 2001 through early 2002 the assumptions underlying the "Status Quo" reference case may be slightly optimistic in the short-term. To be specific, the Reference case assumes that the 10% Geology tax will be collected by the Federal government and re-invested in the Russian oil industry throughout the forecast period. This condition is based on the underlying assumption that the Russian government will be successful it its attempts to resolve the non-payments problem, non-compliance, and banking crisis existing in the Russian Federation. This has not been the case to date. According to World Bank analyses (World Bank, 2001), the Russian government has been unsuccessful in its attempts to eliminate payment and wage arrears throughout the Russian Federation.

In short, while the recent economic recovery in the Russian Federation has been successful in reducing unemployment, and increasing real wages, so that the percentage of the population living below subsistence fell significantly from 35% in 1999 to 25% in 2000, 'wage arrears have not been completely eliminated. [Many] benefits, such as child allowances, also continue to be plagued by past arrears." (World Bank, 2001, p. 3).

According to International Energy Agency estimates, payments in the gas sector have improved significantly from 1999 levels of 66% of total sales (19% in cash) to 78% of sales in 2000 (71% in cash).[67] While payments in the energy sector have recently been estimated at levels as high as 82%, a significant portion of the recovery has been attributed to an increase in hard currency arising from greater revenue from crude oil exports due to the 'relatively' high level of world oil prices. As mentioned above, the revenues generated from these improvements will not be sufficient to generate a long-term (or sustained) recovery in the Russian Federation upstream petroleum industry.

Sustained recovery in the upstream petroleum industry cannot be achieved without the following necessary prerequisites:

- A significant, and sustained increase in the level of investment capital, both foreign and domestic;
- A revision in the tax system that eliminates onerous 'revenue'-based taxes such as the export duty, royalties, and excises taxes;
- Price liberalization, specifically the achievement full price parity as defined by the equality between the supplier's gross wellhead price for domestic oil sales and the export price.

---

67 Cited in International Energy Agency (2002, p. 33).

Table 11.1. Taxes and Costs of Crude Oil in the Russian Federation – Domestic Use
Crude Oil that is Produced by Russian Enterprises for Domestic Use
1998-2001

Exchange Rate Rbls/US$	June 1998		June 1999		June 2000		June 2001	
	6.16		24.25		28.32		42.49	
	US$/tonne	Rbls/tonne	US$/tonne	Rbls/tonne	US$/tonne	Rbls/tonne	US$/tonne	Rbls/tonne
International Oil Price:[a]	94.98	585.09	130.91	3,174.55	211.42	5,987.36	179.27	7,617.30
Domestic Transportation Costs[b]	6.10	37.58	3.30	80.03	2.90	82.13	1.90	80.73
VAT[c]	12.70	78.25	4.74	115.04	10.71	303.31	12.99	551.84
Wholesale Enterprise Price[d]	59.08	363.95	22.07	535.08	49.82	1,410.77	60.41	2,566.69
Excise Levy	8.00	49.33	2.99	72.49	1.90	53.81	1.90	80.73
Suppliers Price: Gross Wellhead	51.08	314.54	19.08	462.59	47.92	1,356.96	58.51	2,485.96
Royalty[e]	4.07	25.05	1.52	36.82	3.81	108.01	4.66	197.88
Geology Fee	5.11	31.46	1.91	46.26	4.79	135.70	5.85	248.60
Special Purpose Levies[f]	3.54	21.83	1.03	24.96	0.76	21.54	1.48	62.75
Sub-Total: Government Funds and Charges	12.72	78.34	4.46	108.04	9.37	265.25	11.98	509.23
Production Costs[g]	39.60	243.94	11.50	278.88	8.50	240.72	16.50	701.09
Including workover and maintenance charges[h]	11.22	69.09	5.75	139.44	4.25	120.36	8.25	350.54
Producer Balance Profit	(1.24)	(7.63)	3.12	75.68	30.05	850.98	30.02	1,275.65
Benefits for the Profit Tax[i]	-	-	0.62	15.14	6.01	170.20	6.00	255.13
Taxable Profit	-	-	2.50	60.54	24.04	680.79	24.02	1,020.52

Table 11.1. Continued

	June 1998		June 1999		June 2000		June 2001	
Exchange Rate Rbls/US$	6.16		24.25		28.32		42.49	
	US$/tonne	Rbls/tonne	US$/tonne	Rbls/tonne	US$/tonne	Rbls/tonne	US$/tonne	Rbls/tonne
Profit Tax[j]	-	-	0.77	18.67	7.21	204.24	7.21	306.16
Dividend Tax	-	-	-	-	-	-	-	-
Profit for Payment of Dividends	-	-	0.86	20.94	8.41	238.28	8.41	357.18

[a] U.K. Dated Brent f.o.b. Sullom Voe.
[b] Domestic transportation costs, average for the Russian Federation: Source: The International Energy Agency, Russia Energy Survey, 2002, IEA/OECD, 2002, p. 80.
[c] The VAT tax rate is equal to 21.5 percent of the wholesale enterprise price in the years 1998-2001.
[d] Wholesale enterprise price, ex-field gate (excluding VAT/ST). Sources: (i) : The International Energy Agency, Russia Energy Survey, 2002, IEA/OECD, 2002, p. 80; (ii) Energy Intelligence Group, The Almanac of Russian Petroleum 2000, Nefte Compass, EIG, 2000, pp. 1-20.
[e] 8% of wholesale enterprise price minus the excise levy.
[f] Special purpose levies include: Other non revenue taxes including property tax and social taxes not included in operating costs; the Geology Fee for recovery (4%) and the road users tax (4%).
[g] Production costs include exploration, development and lifting costs, depreciation, and current expenses (all variable operating costs). Source: (i) The International Energy Agency, Russia Energy Survey, 2002, IEA/OECD, 2002, p. 80.
[h] Minor workover, and maintenance charges that must be paid every three years to prevent shut-ins. The World Bank, "Staff Appraisal Report, Russian Federation Oil Rehabilitation Project, May 26, 1993, p. 142. Sources: (i) The World Bank, Staff Appraisal Report, Russian Federation Oil Rehabilitation Project, May 26, 1993, p. 7-1,1.(ii) James Smith, "Taxation and Investment in Russian Oil," Journal of Energy Finance & Development, Volume 2, Number 1, JAI Press Inc., 1997, p. 7.
[i] Benefits for the profit tax are assumed to equal 20 percent of the 'producer balance profit.' The rate may be an underestimate. Under existing legislation, oil and gas producers are permitted to reduce their taxable base by up to 50 percent if the profit is allocated to modernization, reconstruction, expansion, and development. Professor Alexander G. Kemp, "The Russian Petroleum Tax System: Evolution, Effects and Prospects," Paper presented to the 15th CERI International Oil and Gas Markets Conference, Sept 30-Oct 1, 1996.
[j] The profit tax is equal to 35% in the years 1998 to February 28, 1999 and 30% thereafter.

Table 11.2. Taxes and Costs of Crude Oil in the Russian Federation - Export Crude Oil that is Produced in the Russian Federation for Exports 1998-2001

Exchange Rate Rbls/US$	June 1998 6.16		June 1999 24.25		June 2000 28.32		June 2001 42.49	
	US$/tonne	Rbls/tonne	US$/tonne	Rbls/tonne	US$/tonne	Rbls/tonne	US$/tonne	Rbls/tonne
Export Price:[a]	82.51	508.28	118.44	2,872.19	198.95	5,634.26	166.80	7,087.53
Export Duty[b]	-	-	4.90	118.83	19.70	557.90	17.10	726.58
Transportation Costs[c]	17.10	105.34	11.00	266.75	10.20	288.86	17.70	752.07
VAT[d]								
Wholesale Enterprise Price[e]	59.08	363.95	22.07	535.08	49.82	1,410.77	60.41	2,566.69
Excise Levy	8.00	49.30	2.99	72.49	1.90	53.81	1.90	80.73
Suppliers Price: Gross Wellhead	57.41	353.64	99.55	2,414.13	167.15	4,733.69	130.10	5,528.14
Royalty[f]	4.57	28.15	7.92	192.16	13.31	376.80	10.36	440.04
Geology Fee	5.11	31.47	1.91	46.26	4.79	135.70	5.85	248.59
Special Purpose Levies[g]	3.54	21.83	1.03	24.96	0.76	21.54	1.48	62.75
Sub-Total: Government Funds and Charges	13.22	81.45	10.86	263.38	18.86	534.04	17.68	751.38
Production Costs[h]	39.60	243.94	11.50	278.88	8.50	240.72	16.50	701.09
Including workover and maintenance charges[i]	11.22	69.09	5.75	139.44	4.25	120.36	8.25	350.54
Producer Balance Profit	4.59	28.26	77.19	1,871.87	139.79	3,958.93	95.92	4,075.67
Benefits for the Profit Tax	0.92	5.65	15.44	374.37	27.96	791.79	19.18	815.13
Taxable Profit	3.67	22.61	61.75	1,497.50	111.83	3,167.14	76.74	3,260.54
Profit Tax[j]	1.28	7.91	19.04	461.73	33.55	950.14	23.02	978.16
Dividend Tax	0.18	1.10	-	-	-	-	-	-

Table 11.2. Continued

	June 1998		June 1999		June 2000		June 2001	
Exchange Rate Rbls/US$	6.16		24.25		28.32		42.49	
	US$/tonne	Rbls/tonne	US$/tonne	Rbls/tonne	US$/tonne	Rbls/tonne	US$/tonne	Rbls/tonne
Profit for Payment of Dividends	1.01	6.25	21.36	517.88	39.14	1,108.50	26.86	1,141.19

[a] Urals Blend at Russian export terminal.

[b] The excise duty--which was abolished on July 1, 1996--was reintroduced by the Primakov government in January 1999. The tax was suspended during the first quarter of 1999 due to the low level of international oil prices. The export tax was set at 2.5 euros per tonne in April 1999 and increased progressively with the price of oil to 42 euros in December 2000. The export tax was cut to 22 euros per tonne on March 17, 2001, increased to 30.5 euros on July 1, 2001, and reduced to 23.4 euros per tonne on September 23, 2001. A draft law on export taxes--currently before the Duma – sets a maximum rate for oil export taxes that is based on world oil prices and varies from zero to a maximum of 53.65 euros per tonne.

[c] Pipeline transportation costs from West Siberia to the Black Sea: Sources: (i) The International Energy Agency, *Russia Energy Survey, 2002*, IEA/OECD, 2002, p. 80; and (ii) Ronald Soligo and Amy Myers Jaffe, "The Economics of Pipeline Routes: The Conundrum of Oil Exports from the Caspian Basin," Paper for the James A. Baker III Institute for Public Policy, May 1998.

[d] The VAT tax rate on exports of crude oil to non-CIS countries is "zero" rated. I.E. Producers are permitted a refund on VAT expenditures. The rate is assumed to equal zero, despite the fact that producers have had difficulty in obtaining refunds. Professor Alexander G. Kemp, "The Russian Petroleum Tax System: Evolution, Effects and Prospects, Paper presented to the 15th CERI International Oil and Gas Markets Conference, Calgary, Alberta, September 30-October 1, 1996.

[e] Wholesale enterprise price, ex-field gate (excluding VAT/ST).

[f] The Royalty is assumed to be equal to 8% of the sales price minus transportation charges and the excise tax in the years 1996-01.

[g] Special purpose levies include: Other non revenue taxes including property tax and social taxes not included in operating costs; the Geology Fee for recovery (4%) and the road users tax (4%).

[h] Production costs include exploration, development and lifting costs, depreciation, and current expenses (all variable operating costs).
Source: (i) The International Energy Agency, *Russia Energy Survey, 2002*, IEA/OECD, 2002, p. 80.

[i] Minor workover, and maintenance charges that must be paid every three years to prevent shut-ins. The World Bank, "*Staff Appraisal Report, Russian Federation Oil Rehabilitation Project*, May 26, 1993, p. 142. Sources: (i) The World Bank, *Staff Appraisal Report, Russian Federation Oil Rehabilitation Project*, May 26, 1993, p. 7-1.1.(ii) James Smith, "Taxation and Investment in Russian Oil," *Journal of Energy Finance & Development*, Volume 2, Number 1, JAI Press Inc., 1997, p. 7.

[j] The profit tax is equal to 35% in the years 1998 to February 28, 1999 and 30% thereafter.

Table 11.3. Reference Case Assumptions: International and Domestic Oil Prices

Year	World Oil Price West Texas Intermediate[A] US$/Bbl	West Texas Intermediate[B] US$/tonne	U.K. Brent Blend (Dated) f.o.b. Sullom Voe[C] US$/tonne	Average Export Price for Russian Federation Export Blend to Urals (32°)[D] US$/tonne	Tanker Costs from the Black Sea to Europe Mediterranean[E] US$/tonne	Average Export Price for Urals Blend At Export Terminal (32°)[F] US$/tonne	Moscow Inter-Bank Auction Exchange Rates Period Average[G] Rbl/US$	Russian Domestic Wholesale Enterprise Price Ex-field Gate Excluding VAT[H] Roubles/tonne
1993	18.45	134.18	128.99	114.18	5.45	108.73	1018	30,430.00
1994	17.19	125.02	119.97	112.58	5.45	107.13	2212	75,000.00
1995	18.42	133.96	128.99	119.85	5.45	114.40	4560	259,000.00
1996	22.20	161.45	157.91	143.85	5.45	138.40	5114.83	385,054.00
1997	20.56	149.53	144.98	135.05	5.45	129.60	5784.92	406,000.00
1998	14.36	104.44	94.98	87.96	5.45	82.51	6.16	363.95
1999	19.30	140.36	130.91	123.89	5.45	118.44	24.25	535.08
2000	30.37	220.87	211.42	204.40	5.45	198.95	28.32	1,410.77
2001	25.95	188.73	179.27	172.25	5.45	166.80	42.49	2,566.69
2002	26.07	189.60	180.15	173.13	5.45	167.68	45.63	3,015.73
2003	21.50	156.36	146.9	139.89	5.45	134.44	45.63	2,444.51
2004	22.00	160.00	150.55	143.53	5.45	138.08	45.63	2,506.79
2005	22.50	163.64	154.18	147.16	5.45	141.71	45.63	2,883.88
2006	23.00	167.27	157.82	150.80	5.45	145.35	45.63	3,275.83
2007	23.00	167.27	157.82	150.80	5.45	145.35	45.63	3,598.08
2008	23.00	167.27	157.82	150.80	5.45	145.35	45.63	3,920.33
2009	23.00	167.27	157.82	150.80	5.45	145.35	45.63	4,242.57
2010	23.00	167.27	157.82	150.80	5.45	145.35	45.63	4,564.82
2011	23.00	167.27	157.82	150.80	5.45	145.35	45.63	4,768.43
2012	23.00	167.27	157.82	150.80	5.45	145.35	45.63	5,855.59

Note: The forecast period is from 2002-2012. All forecast prices are reported in 2001 US$, and/or 2001 Roubles.
[A] Prices for West Texas Intermediate are actual values for the years 1993-2001. [EIA-Weekly Petroleum Status Report, Oil and Gas Journal Energy Database, Pricing Statistics Sourcebook, 4th Edition, 1998. and EIA--Short Term Energy Outlook, September 2002] The forecast values are from Adam Sieminski et. al., "Oil Market Outlook: OPEC's Balancing Act," Deutsche Bank, Global Equity Research, Global Oil and Gas, September 2002.
[B] Barrels are converted to tonnes using a conversion factor of 7.272727 (barrels/tonne), and assuming a gravity for WTI of 34°.

Table 11.3. Continued

C Prices for U.K Brent Blend f.o.b. Sullom Voe are actual values for the years 1993-2001. [EIA-Weekly Petroleum Status Report, Oil and Gas Journal Energy Database, Pricing Statistics Sourcebook, 4th Edition, 1998, and EIA--Short Term Energy Outlook, September 2002.] Forecasts are based on historical WTI-Brent differentials of approximately $9.45 (US) per tonne.

D Prices for the average Urals export price are actual values for the years 1993-1997. [EIA-Weekly Petroleum Status Report, Oil and Gas Journal Energy Database, Pricing Statistics Sourcebook, 4th Edition, 1998.] Forecasts are based on historical Brent-Urals differentials of approximately $7.0182 (US) per tonne.

E Average tanker costs from the Black Sea to Europe Mediterranean are assumed to average $0.75 (US) per barrel of $5.45 (US) per tonne. [Derived from data supplied by the Canadian Energy Research Institute (1995).

F Estimated: Average Urals export price minus tanker costs from the Black Sea to Europe Mediterranean.

G Moscow Inter-Bank Exchange Rate: (i) 1993-1995: The World Bank, Fiscal Management in Russia: A World Bank Country Study, The World Bank, Washington D.C., 1996, p. ix; (ii) Robert Barton Ed., The Almanac of Russian Petroleum: 1998, Petroleum Intelligence Weekly, Moscow, 1998, p. 10-11, (iii) Nick Halliwell Ed., The Almanac of Russian Petroleum 2002, Energy Intelligence Group, Moscow, 2002; and (iv) United Financial Group, *Russian Morning Comment*, Various Issues from January - October 2002, UFG Research Moscow, 2002.

H Prices for the Russian wholesale enterprise price are actual values for the years 1993-1997. [Eugene M. Khatukov, "Russia's Oil Prices: Passage to Market," Ibid., p. 15; and Eugene M. Khartukov, "Low Oil Prices: Economic Woes Threaten Russian Oil Exports," Ibid., p. 6.] Forecasts are based on assumptions price liberalization. I.E. Parity between domestic and international prices is assumed to be achieved in the final year of the forecast period 2012.

Table 11.4. Reference Case: Half Hearted Reform – Production

	Total Crude Oil Production (million tonnes)	Production from Oil Production Associations and Gazprom (million tonnes)	Production from Joint Ventures and Independents* (million tonnes)	Production from Production Sharing Agreements (million tonnes)	Total Crude Oil Exports (million tonnes)	Oil Production Association and Gazprom Exports (million tonnes)	Joint Venture and Independents* Exports (million tonnes)	Total Oil Wells	Idle Oil Wells
1996	310.22	288.60	21.62		98.44	87.37	11.07	139,150	36,606
1997	305.47	280.57	24.90		105.40	91.99	13.41	138,791	36,746
1998	303.53	274.15	29.38		115.90	102.02	13.88	133,274	35,035
1999	305.06	273.23	30.82	1.01	118.16	106.46	11.70	134,872	32,935
2000	324.38	289.50	32.45	2.43	134.63	120.03	14.60	136,528	32,615
2001	348.06	314.17	31.25	2.63	143.98	128.35	15.63	138,238	34,171
2002	376.09	341.56	31.90	2.63	156.19	140.24	15.95	140,069	27,392
2003	395.19	355.43	37.12	2.63	164.00	145.44	18.56	142,704	18,152
2004	407.77	367.45	37.68	2.63	165.82	146.98	18.84	145,093	10,914
2005	374.23	335.73	36.03	2.47	152.31	134.29	18.02	147,607	17,339
2006	350.81	312.65	35.91	2.26	143.01	125.06	17.95	150,106	22,260
2007	338.99	302.32	34.41	2.26	138.13	120.93	17.20	152,628	22,371
2008	326.49	294.12	30.28	2.09	132.79	117.65	15.14	155,173	24,172
2009	319.03	287.18	29.98	1.88	129.86	114.87	14.99	157,739	25,054
2010	311.33	282.02	27.43	1.88	126.52	112.81	13.71	160,352	25,442
2011	301.85	279.08	21.06	1.71	122.16	111.63	10.53	162,997	25,612
2012	304.85	281.97	21.37	1.50	123.47	112.79	10.69	165,804	23,110

* Includes production from Rostopprom, Rostopkompania, Roskonommedra, and geological ennomprises which form part of oil companies.

Sources: (i) 1993-2001: International Energy Agency, Russian Energy Survey (2002); (ii) Petroleum Intelligence Weekly, Almanac of Russian Petroleum (1998 and 2000); (iii) Deutsche Bank Oil Market Outlook – OPEC's Balancing Act, Sept. 2002, and (iv) 2002-2012: Forecast.

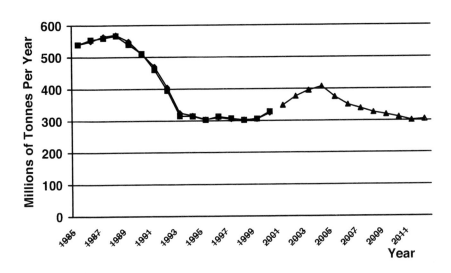

Figure 11.1. Reference Case.

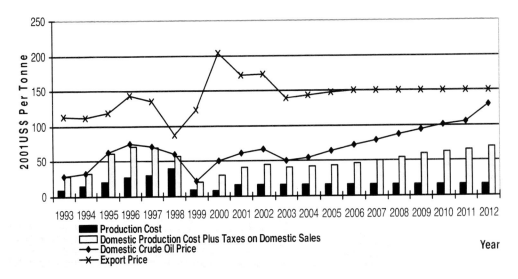

Figure 11.2. Price, Taxes and Production Costs for Crude Oil in the Russian Federation.

ALTERNATE SCENARIOS

The following section presents a number of Alternative Scenarios for the evolution of the regulatory and fiscal (tax) system governing petroleum operations in the Russian Federation. These have been designed to aid in the identification of the inefficiencies inherent in the existing petroleum legislation, and to provide an objective framework within which alternative petroleum fiscal regimes may be evaluated.

Table 11.5. Reference Case: Half Hearted Reform – Gross Revenue and Taxes

	Net Present Value in US$ Millions (2002-2012)					
	Scenario: IEA No Royalty – Excise Tax Maintained for Existing Projects			Reference Case		
	Discount Rate			Discount Rate		
	5%	10%	15%	5%	10%	15%
Gross Revenues From Crude Oil Sales Including Domestic Sales and Exports						
Russian Enterprises	285,592	226,470	184,862	285,592	226,470	184,862
Joint Ventures	31,647	24,925	20,198	31,647	24,925	20,198
Total	317,249	251,395	205,060	317,240	251,395	205,060
Gross Tax Revenue	139,794	109,135	87,943	139,794	109,135	87,943
Payment for the Subsoil	19,687	15,348	12,346	19,687	15,348	12,346
Geology Fee	21,523	16,436	12,971	21,523	16,436	12,971
Total Royalty	41,211	31,785	25,317	41,221	31,785	25,317
Gross Crude Oil Production Costs	48,126	38,136	31,095	48,126	38,136	31,095
Taxes as a Percent of Gross Sales Revenue	0.44	0.43	0.43	0.44	0.43	0.43
Production Costs as a Percent of Gross Sales Revenue	0.15	0.15	0.15	0.15	0.15	0.15

Alternate Scenario I: The "New Tax Code" Scenario

Alternate Scenario I: The "New Tax Code" Scenario examines the potential implications of the "New Tax Code" as specified by a series of legislative initiatives passed by the State Duma and Federation Council and initially scheduled to take effect on January 1, 2002. The "New Tax Code" – essentially Part II of the new Tax Code (including natural resource taxation) – was originally intended to shift the focus of taxation in the Russian Federation from 'gross revenues' to profits.

The rationale behind the new legislation is clear. As a general rule, volume (gross revenue) based taxes tend to be highly distortionary, rather than neutral, and regressive in nature. In the words of Alexander G. Kemp, "The royalty, Mineral Restoration Tax (geological fee) and excise tax are all regressive in nature. They comprise a higher share of profits when these are reduced whether from oil price falls or cost increases. The current Russian tax and royalty system is of course dominated by impositions based on gross revenues rather than profits" (Kemp, 1996, p.3).

In response to these basic principles, the 'original' version (Draft I, Part II) of the new tax code reduced the number of taxes on crude oil significantly, to three main taxes:

1. *A Mineral Extraction Tax*: The royalty, geology (mineral replacement) tax, and excise tax were to be replaced with a 'single' mineral extraction tax (MET). The base rate for the new MET was set equal to 425 roubles ($15 US/tonne) based on a 'current' price of 4,300 roubles ($152 US/tonne) for dated Brent.[1]
2. *A profit tax*: The profit tax was reduced to 24% to be levied on all corporations; and
3. *An excess-profit tax*: The excess profit tax (EPT) – the R-Factor tax – based on the ratio of accumulated revenues to accumulated costs.

Unfortunately these three basic provisions have subsequently been revised 'upward'. The "New Tax Code" scenario assumes the following modifications to the upstream petroleum taxation regime in the Russian Federation:

i. *No Royalty*: The Royalty is abolished in the year 2002.
ii. *No Mineral Restoration Tax*: The mineral restoration tax is abolished in the year 2002.
iii. *The Introduction of a new Mineral Extraction Tax*:
   – The original proposal for the MET is reduced from a base rate of 425 roubles/tonne to 340 roubles per tonne multiplied by a coefficient that is based on changes in world oil prices (dated Brent) in the years 2002-2004.[2]
   – The reduction is justified by the retention of the excise tax at existing (June 2002) rates.[3]
   – The MET is based on 16.5% of the value of dated Brent from the year 2005 to the end of the forecast period.[4]
iv. *The Introduction of a Sliding-Scale Export Duty*: The export duty is set at 35% of the difference between the actual Urals price over a two month period and US$15.00 per barrel.[5]
v. *A Reduction in the Profits Tax*: The Profit tax is reduced to 24% in the year 2002.

All other assumptions including price liberalization, foreign direct investment, and special purpose levies are identical to those assumed by the reference case.

In the years 1991-1999, the development of the Russian oil industry had been repressed by an inefficient, revenue-based tax system. Given the "New Tax Code", this trend can be expected to continue. In short, the introduction of the mineral extraction tax, and sliding scale export duty has effectively increased tax rates throughout the Russian Federation. Specifically, the Duma's efforts to combat transfer pricing schemes within Vertically Integrated Oil Companies (VICs) that result in tax avoidance by replacing royalties and geology fees with a single MET has resulted in a real and significant increase in the domestic tax rate. The results are aggravated by the fact that the 'fixed base' MET is not a fixed rate tax but a 'revenue' based tax that is indexed to the international oil price.

The effects of the new tax code on the future development of the Russian upstream petroleum industry are illustrated in Figure 11.3. The potential implications of the "New Tax

---

1 Cited in International Energy Agency (2002, p. 82).
2 As reported in International Energy Agency (2002, p. 82).
3 As reported in International Energy Agency (2002, p. 82).
4 Cited in Cambridge Energy Research Associates (2002, p. 5).
5 As reported in O'Sullivan (2002, p. 6).

Code" are grim. Russian Federation crude oil flows fall steadily throughout the forecast period, reaching 264.13 million tonnes in the year 2005, a 29 percent reduction from the 374.23 million tonnes reported in the reference case (see Table 11.4). The reduction is wholly attributed to economic distortions, and disincentives arising from the maintenance of an aggressive (still partially revenue based) tax system.

In effect, the new tax burden is so high that domestic producers are not able to generate the internal investment funds necessary to complete mandatory three-year maintenance programmes. Substantial injections of 'external' capital funds will be required to stabilize production at current levels. If these funds are not forthcoming, oil prices are not liberalized, and/or the tax system is not revised, an increasing number of marginal oil fields will be shut-in, foreshadowing a gradual reduction in crude oil flows.

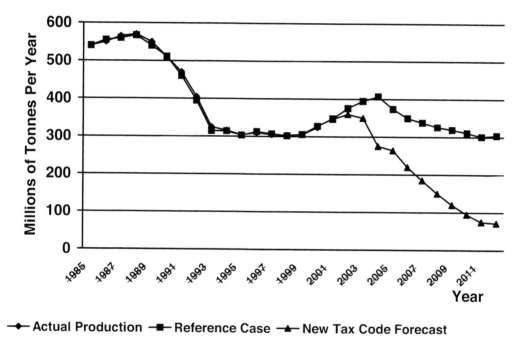

Figure 11.3, The New Tax Code Case.

Alternate Scenario II: The "No Royalty" Scenario

The "No Royalty" scenario examines the potential implications of a shift from revenue-based taxes to profit-based taxes. The excise tax, royalty, mineral extraction tax, and export duties are assumed to be abolished and replaced with a 24% profits tax, and a new R-Factor (excess profits) tax. The removal of royalties and the export duties aids price liberalization policies, and domestic/export price party is achieved in the year 2004.

The excess profits tax (R-Factor tax) has been defined in the following manner: the tax rate for the excess profits tax is determined by an R-Factor schedule where the R-Factor is defined as the ratio of accumulated revenues excluding VAT (since the initial start up date of the project) minus the R-Factor tax paid to date minus the Profits tax paid to date, to accumulated costs:

$$R - Factor \equiv \frac{\text{Accumulated Revenues (excluding VAT)} - (\text{The R - Factor Tax Paid to Date}) - (\text{The Profits Tax Paid to Date})}{\text{Accumulated Cost} + \text{Local Taxes} + \text{The Royalty and Geology Fees Paid to Date}}$$

Where:

i. *Accumulated Revenues* are defined as the accumulated revenues from the sale of hydrocarbons and "shall not include the sums of the VAT, customs duties, excises, costs of transportation to the buyer, as well as costs of transportation for export which include tariffs on pumping and transfer, filling and discharging, costs of port services, transport/forwarding and commission services, and shall be reduced by the sums of EPT [excess profits tax] on the production of hydrocarbons and tax on the income (profits) of organizations or income tax on physical persons;"[6] and

ii. *Accumulated Costs* are defined as costs related to the prospecting, exploration, production and sales of hydrocarbons plus local taxes plus the Royalty plus the Geology Fee.

The base of the Excess Profits (R-Factor) tax is defined as revenues minus operation, development and exploration costs, local taxes and royalties. The R-Factor tax may be deducted from the tax base for the Profits tax. To facilitate the calculation of the R-Factor tax rate it is assumed that the R-Factor tax is deducted from accumulated revenues in the numerator lagged by one year. The schedule for the R-Factor tax is illustrated in Table 11.6.

Table 11.6. R-Factor Tax Schedule

R-Factor	Tax Rate
< 1.0	0%
1.0 to 1.2	15%
1.2 to 1.3	20%
1.3 to 1.4	30%
1.4 to 1.5	40%
1.5 to 2.0	50%
> 2.0	60%

The results of the No Royalty Scenario are illustrated in Figure 11.4. The short-to-medium term forecast is promising. Indeed, under the No Royalty tax regime crude oil production reaches 416.82 million tonnes in 2004. As the level of internal investment funds rises, the number of new projects increases significantly, and the idle well problem is resolved in the 2007. The Russian oil industry is self sufficient until 2010, at which time production declines as the aging of oil fields begin to take a toll on crude oil flows.

The shift to a profit based tax system will have significant positive implications for the level of gross tax revenues collected by the Russian government. Assuming a 10 percent discount rate, the net present value of gross tax revenues rises to US$195.13 billion over the period 2002 to 2012, which represents a 97 percent increase over the level reported in the reference case.

---

6 Cited in Article 436, Tax Base.

It is important to notice that this result has been obtained despite the abolition of the royalty, and excise tax, and a reduction in the profit tax. The potential gains to the profitability of the Russian oil industry from the elimination of revenue-based taxes would appear to outweigh any perceived difficulties arising from the calculation and collection of profit-based taxes.

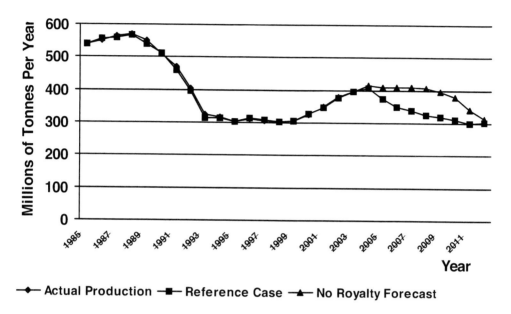

Figure 11.4. The No Royalty Case.

Alternate Scenario III: Potential Contributions from Production Sharing Agreements

In December 1995, the Russian Duma passed the "Law on Production Sharing Agreements" (PSAs). The legislation represents an attractive alternative to the fiscal/legislative regime currently governing the development of Joint Ventures in the Russian Federation. To be specific, the Production Sharing Agreements that are currently under negotiation in the Russian Federation would introduce a number of attractive fiscal provisions, including the right to international arbitration, and the exclusion of all taxes with the exception of those specifically stated in the agreement.

Remarkably, only limited progress has been made since 1995. In short, the original (1995) Federal Law on Production Sharing Agreement contained a number of contradictions to existing legislation.

Unresolved issues include:

i. The development and approval of a new federal law on Production Sharing Agreement Taxes, and the adoption of the PSA chapter of the tax code,
ii. The revision of a number of 'related' petroleum taxation laws, including;
   - amendments to the Cost Recovery and Abandonment acts,

- new acts on implementation, and commercial discovery,
- accounting, reporting, currency and banking instructions,
- the VAT (to provide for a refund mechanism),
- the profits tax (to provide for special rates for PSAs),

iii. A revision of the clause in the 'draft' PSA law that permits the government to revise the terms of a PSA unilaterally in the event an undefined 'substantial change in circumstances' (International Energy Agency, 2002, p. 87).

Tables 11.7 and 11.8 present the PSAs that are being implemented and/or have been authorized by Russian Federation List Laws. It is interesting to note that no 'new' PSAs with a foreign partner had been signed and implemented since that passage of the original PSA law in 1995 and 2002. The three projects listed in Table 11.7 – Sakhalin I, Sakhalin II and the Khar'yaga (Horizons II and III) – were signed before 1995, and have been 'grandfathered' (International Energy Agency, 2002, p. 85).

Alternative Scenario III, which introduces "Potential Contributions From Production Sharing Agreements", assumes that the Russian Federation will continue to make positive progress towards the development and implementation of a comprehensive, and stable, legal framework for PSA investment. According to World Bank estimates, approximately $80 billion in 'external' investment funds is awaiting the passage of PSA legislation (see Table 11.8).

Table 11.7. Production Sharing Agreements Currently Implemented and/or Authorized in the Russian Federation - Grandfathered

Projects that were signed before the passage of the 1995 PSA law and grandfathered			
Project	Foreign and/or Domestic Partner	Location	Estimated "External" Investment (Billions of US$)
Sakhalin I	ExxonMobil (30%), Sodeco (30%), ONGC (20%), SMNG (11.5%), Rosneft (8.5%)	Sakhalin Oblast (offshore) Fields/Blocks: Odoptu, Chaivo &Arkutun-Dagi	$14.00
Sakhalin II	Shell (55%), Mitsui (25%), Mitsubishi (20%)	Sakhalin Oblast (offshore) Fields/Blocks: Piltun-Astokskoye & Lunskoye	$10.00
Khar'yaga Horizons II and III	LUKoil, Nenets Oil, Totalfina-Elf, Norsk Hydro	Nenets Okrug	$2.00

Table 11.8. Production Sharing Agreements Currently Implemented and/or Authorized in the Russian Federation – Legislative Approval

PSA projects that were authorized by 'list laws' passed by the State Duma			
Project	Foreign and/or Domestic Partner	Location	Estimated "External" Investment (Billions of US$)
Sakhalin III I Kirinskiy Block	ExxonMobil (33.3%), Texaco (33.3%), SMNG & Rosneft (33.3%)	Sakhalin Oblast (offshore) Fields/Blocks: Kirinskiy	$6.55
Sakhalin III II Ayyash/East Odoptu	ExxonMobil (66.7%), SMNG & Rosneft (33.3%)	Sakhalin Oblast (offshore) Fields/Blocks: East Odoptinskiy & Ayyashskiy	$0.20
Northern Territories Block	LUKoil, Arkhangelskgeologia	Nenets Okrug	$8.00
Prirazlomnoye	Rosshelf, Gazprom, Wintershall	Barents Sea	$2.00
Usinsk	LUKoil	Komi Republic	-------
S. Lyzhskoye, N. Kozhva (Bl.-15)	Parmaneft	Komi Republic	-------
Yurubcheno-Tokhomskoye	East Siberian Oil	Evenk Okrug (Krasnoyarsk Kray)	-------
Uvat Block	Uvatneft	Khanti-Mansiysk Okrug	-------
Federovo	Okrug Surgutneftegaz	Khanti-Mansiysk	-------
Luginets	Tomskneft (VNK/YUKOS)	Tomsk Oblast	-------
Tyanskoye	Surgutneftegaz	Khanti-Mansiysk Okrug	-------
Vankor	Yeniseyneft, Anglo-Siberian	Krasnoyarsk Kray	-------
Kharampur	Rosneft, Purneftgaz	Yamalo-Nenets Okrug	-------
Komsomol'sk	Rosneft, Purneftgaz	Yamalo-Nenets Okrug	-------
Udmurt Block		Udmurt Republic	-------
Kovykta	RUSIA Petroleum, BP Amoco, EAGC (Korea)	Irkutsk Oblast	-------
Samotlor	TNK, Nizhnevartovskneftegaz	Khanti-Mansiysk Okrug	$1.25
Priobskoye	YUKOS	Khanti-Mansiysk Okrug	$12.00
Krasnoleninskoye	TNK, TNK Nyagan (Kondpetroleum), Yugraneft	Khanti-Mansiysk Okrug	$8.00
Salym Group	Shell, Evikhon	Khanti-Mansiysk Okrug	$4.00

Sources: (i) The World Bank, "Review Paper: Taxation of Oil Production in the Russian Federation," The World Bank, Report No. 16331-RU, Washington D.C., February 24, 1997, p. 31, (ii) IEA, 2002., p. 86, (iii) Dr. Keun-Wook Paik, "Sino-Russian Oil and Gas Cooperative Relationship: Implications for Economic Development in Northeast Asia,' paper delivered to the Northeast Asia Cooperation Dialogue XIII Infrastructure and Economic Development Workshop, Moscow, October 4th 2002, An event organized by the Institute for Far Eastern Affairs, Russian Academy of Sciences & Institute on Global Conflict and Cooperation, University of California; and (iv) Interview with Deputy Minister V. Z. Garipov, *Infotek*, No. 8, 2000 cited in IEA, 2002., p. 84.

As shown in Tables 11.7 and 11.8, this estimate accounts for investment funds for only the major PSA projects. The contributions from the 'smaller' PSAs have not been included. An alternative estimate provided by the World Bank suggests that the smaller PSAs (not listed in Tables 11.7 and 11.8) will provide an additional US$5 billion in external investment capital.[7]

---

[7] Crude Oil Production in the Russian Federation (1997, p. 62).

In Alternative Scenario III, the entire US$85 billion is invested in PSA agreements in the Russian Federation. Seventy six percent, or US$65 billion, of the total is devoted to the development of the upstream petroleum industry. The first installment of PSA investment capital was implemented in December 1998, so that the first crude oil flows from PSAs were brought into production in 1999. After this point, the remaining "external PSA investment funds are distributed gradually throughout the forecast period.

Assuming that US$65 billion in PSA investment is allocated directly to the exploration, and development of new oil wells – and not rehabilitations – the funds will facilitate the completion of 67,010 new oil wells.[8] As these funds are assumed to be distributed gradually throughout the forecast period, the PSA scenario projects the completion of approximately 6,092 new oil wells per annum in the years 2002 to 2012, inclusive.[9]

The tax system that will govern the development of PSAs in the Russian Federation is assumed to follow the basic structure of the Sakhalin II agreement between Mitsui/ Mitsubishi/ Shell and the Russian government.[10] The basic terms of the Sakhalin II agreement are illustrated in Table 11.9.

To minimize the difficulties associated with calculating the State's share of 'Profit Oil' for a large number of PSAs which are assumed to come on stream at different time periods (the exact dates of which have yet to be determined), the reference case assumes that the average State share of profit oil for the entire PSA production effort will equal 10% over the period 2002 to 2004, 50% in 2005 to 2007, and 70% in 2008 to 2012.

Table 11.9. Sakhalin II Production Sharing Agreement

Terms of Agreement	Tax Rate
Royalty	6 Percent
Cost Oil: The agreed terms include the deduction of an allowance for the recovery of costs or "Cost Oil" from license area production.	The deduction of operating and development costs from 100 percent of production.
Profit Oil: The term profit oil is defined as the oil remaining after the deduction of the allowance for costs. "Depending on how "Cost Oil" is defined and what limits may be placed on Cost Oil in any one accounting period, Profit Oil may resemble either traditional accounting profit or net cash flow."[a]	Investor's Share of Profit Oil, after cost: 90% until the internal real rate of return is equal to 17.5% 50% until the internal real rate of return is equal to 24% 30% while the internal real rate of return is greater than 24%
Profit Tax	24 percent
Withholding tax on dividends	5 percent

[a] The World Bank, 'Taxation of Oil Production in the Russian Federation', The World Bank, Report No. 16331-RU, Washington D.C., February 24, 1997, pp. 32-33.

Source: The agreed terms for the Sakhalin II PSA are taken from Smith (1997).

---

8 The estimate for the number of PSA oil wells has been calculated using the average cost for new oil wells assumed in the reference case--$970,000 (US) per new oil well.
9 The assumption that $65 million of available PSA investment capital is devoted to the completion of new oil wells is optimistic. Undoubtedly a portion of these funds will be devoted to natural gas wells, the modernization of production facilities, and the construction of complimentary pipeline and infrastructure.
10 As reported in Smith (1997, p.9).

The PSAs are assumed to be fully self sufficient; all minor workovers and rehabilitations are completed by the project operator, so that the projects are not plagued by the problem of idle oil wells. All other 'internal' investment revenues – specifically the proceeds accruing from profits (and/or) the benefits for the profit tax – are maintained as profits, and not reinvested in the upstream petroleum industry.

Figure 11.5 illustrates the potential implications of "Contributions from PSAs" on the future development of the Russian crude oil industry. The 'superficial' implications of the significant injection of 'external' capital funds are promising. Crude oil production in the Russian Federation reaches 413.78 million tonnes in the year 2004, an increase of 6.01 million tonnes over the 407.77 million tonnes reported in the reference case.

As might have been anticipated, the entire amount of the increase is attributed to new crude oil flows from PSAs. In short, given the strict provisions of the PSA agreements, and the precise specifications concerning the oil and gas fields that are eligible for PSA participation, the PSAs are completely isolated from and have minimal implications for the rest of the Russian oil industry.[11] The volume of crude oil production and exports from joint venture producers, and Russian enterprises (excluding PSA participants) is identical to that obtained in the reference case.

Once again, the long-term scenario is far from encouraging. While the level of PSA crude oil production rises steadily through the forecast period – from 8.64 million tonnes in 2004 to a peak production level of 63.31 million tonnes in the year 2012 – the gains are more than offset by the production declines from Russian enterprises and joint venture producers. Crude oil production from the Russian Federation falls to 366.65 million tonnes in the year 2012, a significant 11 percent reduction from the peak level of 413.78 million tonnes achieved in 2004.

As described in the Reference Case, the reductions can be attributed to economic distortions and disincentives, created by the onerous June 2001 tax system. In short: while the PSAs benefit from an improved fiscal (tax) system, the remaining Russian enterprises and joint ventures continue to operate under a large, and unduly onerous tax burden, and are unable to generate the internal investment funds that are required for the rehabilitation of the (non-PSA) Russian oil industry.

The benefits from the approval and implementation of PSAs in the Russian Federation may be listed as follows:

i. *Increased crude oil production*: PSAs can be expected to add approximately 63.31 million tonnes of production to crude oil flows in the Russian Federation by 2012.);[12]
ii. *Increased Crude Oil Revenues*: Assuming a 10 percent discount rate, the net present value of the gross revenue from crude oil sales in the Russian oil industry is estimated at US$240.3 billion for the years 2002 to 2012 inclusive, which represents a significant 6.0 percent improvement over the US$226.5 billion achieved in the Reference Case. Crude oil sales from PSAs account for the entire increment, US$13.83 billion; and

---

11 A possible exception to this general rule involves the economic distortions that may be created by increased competition for scarce pipeline capacity on the Transneft system.
12 This estimate is virtually identical to estimates obtained by World Bank. In the words of World Bank analysts: "Under the 'free market' scenario, all of the major PSA projects are assumed to go forward, thus producing 65 mt, for a total investment of $65 billion (US)." Crude Oil Production in the Russian Federation (1997, p. 62).

iii. *Increased Tax Revenues for the Government of the Russian Federation*: Assuming adequate tax collection arrangements and compliance by the Russian enterprises, the net present value of gross tax revenue is estimated at US$116.3 billion for the years 2002 to 2012, which is a 7.0 percent improvement over the US$109.1 billion achieved in the reference case. The tax revenues collected from PSAs account for the entire increment of approximately US$7.2 billion.

Despite the benefits, and incentives to both the Russian government and PSA participants, the provision of a favourable tax regime for a limited number of select foreign participants and Russian enterprises, does not address the fundamental problems and challenges currently facing the Russian upstream petroleum industry.

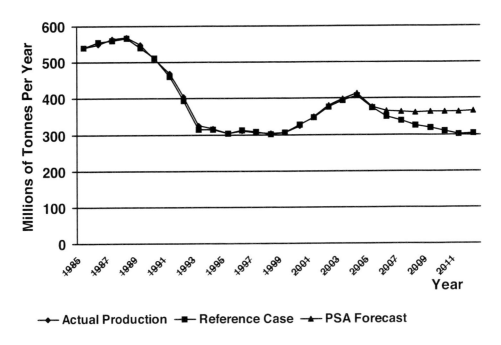

Figure 11.5. The Contributions from PSAs Case.

Alternate Scenario IV: Contributions from Multilateral Lending Agencies

The Multilateral Loan Scenario assumes the implementation of a hypothetical "World Bank Oil Rehabilitation" project, which will provide the external capital funds for: (a) 1,000 new oil wells, and (b) 3,000 rehabilitations. The projects would be completed over a three-year period (2003-2005). All other assumptions are identical to those that applied in the Reference Case. Figure 11.6 illustrates the potential implications of the "Multinational Loan Scenario" on the future development of the Russian oil industry.

The initial impact of a significant injection of 'external' capital funds is promising. Crude oil flows from the oil production associations and Gazprom reach 351.0 million tonnes in 2005, which is an increase of 5.0 percent over the 335.73 million tonnes reported in the reference case. The problem of idle oil wells subsides gradually in the years 2003 to 2005. By

2005 the idle well problem falls to only 8400, which is nearly 9000 lower than the 17,400 reported in the reference case.

The joint venture producers are not so fortunate. Forced to compete with a growing number of subsidized Russian enterprises, exploration success rates, and finding rates, are slightly lower throughout the forecast period. As a result, the level of joint venture crude oil production is slightly lower than that obtained under reference case assumptions throughout the forecast period. Joint venture production reaches only 36.00 million tonnes in 2005, which is approximately 30,000 tonnes lower that the 36.03 million tonnes estimated in the reference case.

Once again, the long-term scenario is not so encouraging. Given the economic distortions and disincentives created by the June 2001 tax system, Russian enterprises are unable to sustain the new found gains in production. Crude oil production from the Russian Federation falls to 313.81 million tonnes in the year 2012, which is a mere 8.96 million tonnes higher than the 304.85 million tonnes attained in the reference case.

The moral of the "Multilateral Loan Scenario" is clear. A continuation of the taxation/legislative regime that existed in (mid-2001) will be detrimental to the long-run performance of the Russian crude oil industry, regardless of the volume of external capital injections that are devoted to rehabilitation and development efforts.

The policies assumed by the "Multilateral Loan Scenario", including the success of price liberalization policies and additional contributions of investment funds from multilateral lending agencies, will be insufficient to reverse the long-term prospects for the Russian Federation oil industry.

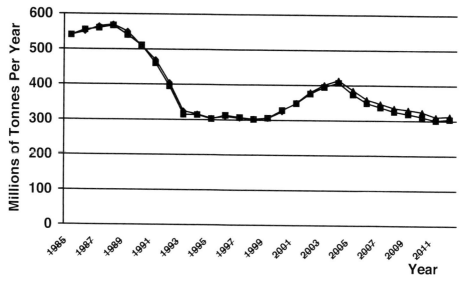

Figure 11.6. The Multilateral Lending Case.

Conclusion

The long-term development (and success) of the Russian oil industry will be enhanced significantly by the implementation of a comprehensive economic reform program – including:

a) The development, and completion, of a stable and comprehensive legal and contractual framework for oil operations, including petroleum taxation and the licensing and operations of the vertically integrated companies (VICs), joint ventures (JVs) and PSAs;
b) The reduction of statutory tax levels, and a shift from revenue to profit based taxation;
c) The elimination of market distortions created by the non-payments problem. This will require the effective coordination of macroeconomic reforms, including monetary and fiscal policy, banking reform, the adoption of reliable institutions for financial intermediation and bankruptcy laws;
d) The abolishment of privatization policies that discourage foreign participation in strategic sectors of the Russian Federation such as the use of 'transfer pricing' within the VICs, the program of exports for state needs, and the loans-for-shares privatization program of 1995;
e) The removal of policies that inhibit the construction of new pipeline capacity on the Transneft export system, for example the abolition of the 'hard currency' component of export tariffs, and the 'removal' of policies providing for the subsidization of inefficient (and obsolete) domestic pipeline systems.
f) The removal of all remaining administrative restrictions on crude oil exports, including:
  – The centralized allocation of export capacity and discriminatory tariff policies;
  – Barriers and confiscatory policies related to the level of tax arrears;

As illustrated by Scenario III: The "No Royalty" Case, the Russian crude oil industry is clearly capable of generating the internal investment funds necessary to maintain (and even increase) contemporary levels of crude oil production. External injections of investment capital, from JVs, PSAs and multilateral lending agencies, are not required to maintain crude oil flows at contemporary levels.

Given the potential for profits or economic rents in the Russian oil industry, an infinite number of petroleum rent schemes may be devised for the collection and distribution of these rents. In the final analysis, the interests of the Russian Federation will be best served by the development of a tax regime that promotes self-sufficiency in the upstream petroleum industry.

APPENDIX: OVERVIEW OF THE RUSSIAN FEDERATION CRUDE OIL SUPPLY CURVE AND 'FISCAL AND PRICING' MODEL

The Russian Federation crude oil supply curve and 'fiscal and pricing' model is developed in detail in (Considine, 1999). It is a variation of the rate of effort approach developed by Zapp, (1962), and Hubbert (1967). The actual 'rate of effort curve' is based on the existence of an 'objective' empirical relationship between drilling activity and discoveries, so that the model is insensitive to political and economic influences. The exogenous driving variable, the number of wildcats, may be determined by central command, the specifications of multi-lateral lending agencies, the level of investment funds devoted to the exploration effort, and/or the principles of perfect competition. A time series representing the evolution of exploration effort and cumulative discoveries for the entire history of the Russian oil industry (1860-2002) is used in the estimation of the parameters.

The Russian Federation crude oil supply forecasting model is sufficiently flexible to model the difficulties encountered in the transition to a free market economy – including the separation of domestic and export markets, barriers to price liberalization such as the non-payments problem, and a variety of assumptions concerning the level and nature of foreign participation in the discovery and development of Russian oil reserves.

REFERENCES

Bartle, R. G. (1976). *The Elements of Real Analysis*, Second Edition. New York: John Wiley and Sons.

Cambridge Energy Research Associates, CERA Advisory Services: Russian Energy (2002). *CERA Executive* Roundtable. London: Cambridge Energy Research Associates, Inc, May 8.

Campbell, C. J. (1996). The Status of World Oil Depletion at the End of 1995. *Energy Exploration & Exploitation*, 14, 247-282.

Considine, J. I. (1999). *The Evolution of the Russian Oil Industry (1860-2012): A Search for a Long-Run Crude Oil Supply Forecasting Model*, Thesis presented for the degree of Doctor of Philosophy at the University of Aberdeen, Aberdeen, Scotland.

Granville, C. (2002). Balance of Payments--Preliminary 3Q02 Data. *Russia Morning Comment*, Moscow: United Financial Group, October 7.

Halliwell, N. (Ed.) (1999). *The Almanac of Russian Petroleum: 2000*, Moscow: Energy Intelligence Group.

Hubbert, M. K. (1967). Degree of Advancement of Petroleum Exploration in the Unites States. *The American Association of Petroleum Geologists Bulletin*, 51 (11), 37-42.

International Energy Agency (2002) *Russia Energy Survey*, Paris: OECD/IEA.

Interview with Deputy Minister V. Z. Garipov (200) *Infotek*, No. 8, cited in International Energy Agency, *Russia Energy Survey*. Paris: OECD/IEA.

Kemp, A. G., and Jones, P. D. A. (1996). *Investment, Taxation and Production Sharing in the Russian and Azerbaijan Petroleum Industries*. North Sea Study Occasional Paper No. 55, Aberdeen: The University of Aberdeen.

Kemp, A. G. (1996). *The Russian Petroleum Tax System: Evolution, Effects and Prospects.* Paper presented to the 15th CERI International Oil and Gas Markets Conference, Calgary, September 30-October 1.

Lyubomirskaya, L. (2002) *Tax on the Use of Mineral Resources, Article 436.* Moscow: Tax Base.

O 'Sullivan, S. (2002). Export Duty Rises From 1 June. *Russia Morning Comment.* Moscow: United Financial Group, Moscow, April 30.

Paik, K-W. (2002) *Sino-Russian Oil and Gas Cooperative Relationship: Implications for Economic Development in Northeast Asia.* paper delivered to the Northeast Asia Cooperation Dialogue XIII Infrastructure and Economic Development Workshop, Moscow, October 4th.

Sieminski, A. (2002). *Oil Market Outlook: OPECs Balancing Act*, Frankfurt: Deutsche Bank, Global Equity Research, September.

Smith, J. (1997) Taxation and Investment in Russian Oil. *Journal of Energy Finance and Development*, 2, (1), 23-35.

The World Bank (1997) *Review Paper: Taxation of Oil Production in the Russian Federation.* Report No. 16331-RU, Washington, DC: The World Bank.

The World Bank (1997) *Crude Oil Production in the Russian Federation.* Washington. DC: The World Bank.

The World Bank (2001). Memorandum of the President of the International Bank for Reconstruction and Development and the International Finance Corporation to the Executive Directors on a Country Assistance Strategy Progress Report of the World Bank Group for the Russian Federation. Russian Federation Country Management Unit, Europe and Central Asia Region, Report No: 21709-RU, January 11, Washington, DC: The World Bank.

Zapp, A.D. (1962). Future Petroleum Producing Capacity of the United States, U.S. Geological Survey Bulletin 1142-H, Washington, DC: U.S. Geological Survey.

In: Revitalizing Russian Industry
Eds: J. Gaisford, V. Mayevsky et al., pp. 177-195   © 2007 Nova Science Publishers, Inc.
ISBN 978-1-60021-778-4

Chapter 12

TRANSFORMATION AND REFORM IN THE RUSSIAN ENERGY SECTOR: NATURAL GAS AND OIL TRANSMISSION

Wilfred Barke

ABSTRACT

Russia has vast reserves of petroleum energy most of which are located far from major domestic centres of population or export markets. This is the case for both natural gas and oil. Hence, pipelines are a key component in Russia's desire to revitalize its industrial base. The transition from a command system to a market-based system has been difficult and is far from complete. This chapter examines the evolving regulatory system for the movement of petroleum energy. While the Russian government appears to be well motivated, there is an inherent conflict between the temptation to try and capture monopoly rents through government controlled transmission companies and the desire to improve the efficiency of the energy transportation system. This conflict has not been satisfactorily resolved

INTRODUCTION

One of the greatest challenges facing the Russian energy sector will be to attract the foreign direct investment necessary to replace aging pipeline infrastructure and to build new export pipelines to Europe, Eastern Siberia and the Far East. To attract the 'missing' foreign direct investment funds, the government of the Russian Federation would be well advised to support initiatives that promote competition in the production, marketing, and transportation of crude oil and natural gas supplies.

The *Russian Federation Energy Strategy* and stated government policy objectives clearly advocate the liberalization of domestic energy prices, and the creation of free markets in the energy industry. However, a number of factors threaten to impede the development of a competitive environment, and inhibit foreign investment in the energy sector. These include, but are by no means limited to: (i) the monolithic Gazprom monopoly, (ii) restricted access to export markets for crude oil and natural gas, (iii) the lack of regulatory and jurisdictional clarity, (iv) inefficient tolling structure and practices, (v) the lack of a requirement for Gazprom to post critical information on pipeline operations in a timely manner, and (vi) the lack of a transparent and equitable system for allocating limited export capacity.

RUSSIA'S PRIMARY POLICY OBJECTIVE

The existence of a viable inter-regional pipeline transmission system is critical for the future development of the natural gas industry in the Russian Federation. Given current technology, high pressure pipeline systems are the only efficient means of transporting natural gas over long distances. These systems form the critical link between remote producing regions such as Western Siberia and areas where markets are located.

In light of the Russian Government's stated commitment to the creation of free markets in the energy industry, a few points are worthy of mention. Pipeline 'toll' and 'tariff'[1] design must support the principles of competitive markets and open access to transmission lines. At the same time regulatory agencies must thoroughly understand and be able to articulate primary government objectives. If regulatory agencies fail to embrace fundamental policy objectives, the industry will be deluged with numerous *ad hoc* approaches to pipeline regulation. The resulting confusion can be expected to hinder the long term development of the natural gas industry.

To cite one example, in the early 1990s the US Federal Energy Resource Commission (FERC) embarked on a comprehensive initiative to redesign North American pipeline tariffs – under Order 436. The primary objective of Order 436 was to create competition in the inter-state pipeline system. Order 436 led to the adoption of a sequence of new Orders and regulations that has significantly changed the manner in which the natural gas sector conducts its business. In short, the restructuring of the inter-state pipeline tariff in North America has played a pivotal role in the creation of a competitive and efficient natural gas industry.

In Russia, the energy sector was restructured in the early 1990s in order to "introduce commercial disciplines" and attract private investment capital. The policies were designed to attract capital, and not necessarily to introduce competition or reduce barriers to entry in the gas industry. Now, over ten years later, the word restructuring has taken on a whole new meaning. The Russian Federation has a put new priority on the creation of a competitive environment in the industry, specifically promoting non-discriminatory access to supply systems.[2]

The primary policy objectives of the Russian Federation for this industry have been clearly articulated by a number regulatory agencies. These may be summarized briefly as follows:

The Ministry of Economy and Trade "MET": According to the MET: "institutional changes in the fuel and power sectors must be accompanied by total organizational and

---

[1] The word toll is defined as the rate that the shipper pays the transmission company for transporting gas in $/Mcf. The word tariff therein shall mean the toll and other regulated service terms under which the Transmission Company agrees to offer transmission service.
[2] IEA (2002). Russia Energy Survey 2002, p. 30.

financial transparency."[3] The new strategy recognizes the importance of price and regulatory reform, in particular:[4]

- The introduction of non discriminatory tariffs for the transportation of gas via trunk gas pipelines and distribution networks;
- The development of the infrastructure required to implement open access to gas pipelines including electronic bulletin boards;
- The creation of guidelines enabling the industry to re-define and publish the amounts of available capacity on the gas pipelines;
- The creation of purchase limits for Gazprom affiliate transactions. The purchase limits will enable gas distribution and independent gas marketing organizations to make direct purchases without the direct supervision of Gazprom.

The Commission on Access to Oil and Gas Pipelines ("CAOGP"): In January 2001 the CAOGP issued a prime-ministerial resolution[5] addressing the regulation of all prices and tariffs for the transportation of natural gas in the Russian Federation. Resolution 1021 provides the framework for predictable and transparent regulated prices, and regulated access to networks and other gas transportation services.

The Ministry of Energy ("ME"): The Main Provisions of the Russian Energy Strategy to 2020[6] have been approved by the Russian government. The Energy Strategy, among other things, clearly reinforces the principles of price and market liberalization in the natural gas sector.

This chapter makes a series of recommendations that are predicated on the belief that the current energy policy objective of the Russian government is to create an environment that enhances competition in the marketing, distribution, transmission and production of natural gas.

DISSOLVING THE GAZPROM MONOPOLY

In its current monopolistic form Gazprom represents one of the greatest challenges facing policy makers in the Russian Federation. Not since the days of Rockefeller's Standard Oil Company has a company enjoyed such a monopolistic hold in the energy industry. In 2000[7] Gazprom:

- produced 90% of total Russian gas output;

---

[3] Strategy of Development of the Russian Federation through 2010, Social and Economic Aspect, Center for Strategic Research, submitted to the government of the Russian Federation on May 25, 2000, Section 3.5.1. Note: This report is known in Russia as the 'Gref plan', after the Minister of Economy and Trade, German Gref.
[4] Strategy of Development of the Russian Federation through 2010, Social and Economic Aspect, Center for Strategic Research, submitted to the government of the Russian Federation on May 25, 2000.
[5] On State Regulation of Gas Prices and Tariff for Gas Transportation in the Russian Federation (Resolution No. 1021, December 29,2000).
[6] The Main Provisions of the Energy Strategy of the Russian Federation to 2020, November 2000.
[7] IEA (2002). Russia Energy Survey 2002, p. 111.

- controlled virtually all the gas transported through high-pressure, large diameter pipelines;
- controlled 100% of the gas exports to Europe and
- provided 20% of federal budget revenues, approximately 20% of convertible currency revenues and nearly 8% of GDP.

In early 2001, an interview with a senior government official confirmed the fact that the liberalization of the natural gas sector is a top priority for the Russian government . However, the official noted, "we should be realistic and realize that there will not be a competitive gas market in this county in the immediate future....What we say is that appropriate conditions should be created... We honestly say that Gazprom is huge and it will be very difficult to make our new players really competitive."[8]

The difficulties are well defined. Monopolies such as Gazprom have a natural tendency to attempt to extract excessive economic rents from new players. Under the current rules of engagement only those players that do not present a risk to Gazprom's core business are allowed participate in the industry. Innovative ideas and discoveries are quickly absorbed by Gazprom and customer choice is limited. As noted by the official cited above the Gazprom monopoly can be expected to inhibit competition in the Russian gas industry for so long as these trends are permitted to continue.

In is interesting to note that the *Energy Strategy of the Russian Federation* does not indicate when, if ever, companies such as Gazprom will be privatized. The Russian government has remained silent on this critical issue. The need for reform is clear. To attract foreign investment the Russian government must be prepared to delineate a timeline and process for reducing Gazprom's dominant position in the market place over time.

It is important to recognize that reducing Gazprom's dominance in the natural gas sector may take several years. As an interim measure the Russian government would be well advised to commit themselves to a corporate unbundling strategy. At the present time, the Russian government's stated strategy is "Management Unbundling", which consists of the financial and organizational separation of Gazprom's pipeline network from its production units. This reorganization can be expected to foster competition in the pipeline industry and encourage non-discriminatory access to transmission capacity.

What is lacking is a detailed timetable for this restructuring strategy.[9] For example, one top priority for the Russian government in the near future might include the unbundling of Gazprom's business segments – including exploration and production activities, upstream capacity services (i.e. processing and gathering), mainline transmission services, distribution, and energy merchant activities – into distinct and independent business entities.

As long as Gazprom's business segments remain integrated it will be impossible for regulatory authorities to ensure the transmission tariffs are applied to third party shippers in a non-discriminatory manner. In short, financial and organizational separation provides the prerequisite framework for regulatory authorities to audit Gazprom's commercial activities.

In defiance of the governments stated policy objectives, Gazprom has implemented a corporate strategy that solidifies its dominant role in the natural gas sector. Over the past few

---

[8] Interview with Vladimir Milso, Section Head, Economic analysis and regulation systems development, Kommersant Daily, January 16, 2001, reported in IEA (2002). Russia Energy Survey 2002, p. 148.
[9] IEA (2002). Russia Energy Survey 2002, p.110.

years Gazprom has acquired more than 50 of the largest distribution network in the Russian Federation and currently owns 10% of the entire distribution network. In addition in October 2000, Gazprom made a take over bid for Siberian-Urals Oil and Gas Chemical Company (Sibur), which owns nine major Siberian processing plants, and purchased 51% of the company's equity.[10] These activities solidify their dominance in the market place and critically impede the ability for new players to enter the sector.

With over 38% of the total outstanding shares, the Russian Federation government is the largest single shareholder of Gazprom.[11] Needless to say, the relationships between Gazprom and the government is extremely close. It is often hard to distinguish government policy from company policy. As the largest shareholder in Gazprom, the Federal Government clearly plays a major role in deciding how quickly existing management should be replaced and by whom.[12] Since the Russian government's stated policy objective is to introduce competition into the gas sector, they should use their influence in Gazprom to ensure that the deregulation process takes place in a timely and orderly fashion.

Notwithstanding the Russian government's stated policy objectives, the economic motivation to maintain the Gazprom monopoly is clear. This conflict of interest cannot continue indefinitely. As the gas sector becomes more competitive, commercial pressure from industry participants will force the Russian government dispose of its interest in Gazprom. In the interim the Russian Federation should use it's voting interest to promote a more competitive gas sector. More competition in the natural gas sector will increase the size of the overall industry pie and will, in the long term, enhance shareholder value.

PROMOTING COMPETITION IN EXPORT MARKETS

Gazexport, a wholly owned subsidiary of Gazprom, is the sole exporter of Russian gas to Europe. The volumes are non trivial and rising. Approximately 130 Bcm was delivered to European nations in 2000. By 2008, Gazexport will deliver up to 200 Bcm under long term contracts, some of which will not expire until 2025. Approximately 80% of currently contracted volumes are long term, the remaining 20% will be sold under annual contracts. Gazprom has a stated policy not to sign any additional long-term contracts with European customers until 2008.[13]

The development of a competitive natural gas sector in the Russian Federation is inhibited by Gazexport's European monopoly. Access to export markets for new players is of critical importance for attracting foreign investment and hard currency reserves. The absence of competition at export points limits the choices for buyers, increases the price volatility due to poor liquidity and hinders price transparency. Sellers to Gazprom become price takers and market clearing signals are distorted. The absence of a liquid market hub generally causes gas to be transacted at price levels that do reflect the current market value of the commodity.

Fortunately, the constraints will eventually force Gazexport to relinquish its monopolistic hold over the export market. Over the next few years the following market trends can be expected to prevail:

---

[10] IEA (2002). Russia Energy Survey 2002, p.119 and p.121.
[11] Gazprom Annual Report 2000, p.25.
[12] IEA (2002). Russia Energy Survey 2002, p.144.
[13] IEA (2002). Russia Energy Survey 2002, p.136.

- European companies and governments will wish to limit their dependence on a single supplier of Russian gas;
- Gas-on-gas competition in Europe will push prices down;
- Traditional long term take or pay contracts will come under significant pressure and more than likely be dissolved;

In light of these market trends, specific government regulations mandating the breakup of Gazexport's long term sales arrangements are not required at this time. Instead, the Russian government should utilize a phased in approach, directing Gazexport to open up access to the export market. This goal could be accomplished by requiring Gazprom to make the annual sales arrangements that come up for renewal each year and made available to other third party producers through an electronic auction bid process. Gazprom, and its affiliates, should be explicitly prohibited from participating in the auction. Finally, preferential access to excess export capacity should be granted to all third party producers who wish to sell into the export spot market.

These measures will introduce gas-on-gas competition in the Russian Federation and will likely place downward pressure on the price of Russian gas supply in the near term.

Gazprom's stated policy, not to sign any additional long-term contracts with European customers until the year 2008 is, in part, due to the company's concern that they will not be able to meet future market commitments through their proprietary production. If competitive market forces in both Europe and Russia render many of the long term marketing arrangements obsolete it may be in Gazprom's economic interest to harvest the imbedded price premium in these long term sales arrangements early. This can be accomplished by selling contracts to other third party producers. These agents may be prepared to take on the risk of the contractual obligations in exchange for direct access to export markets.

THE FEDERAL ENERGY COMMISSION REGULATION OF GAZPROM'S UPSTREAM PROCESSING SERVICES

Gazprom owns all of the major processing plants at Orenburg and Astrakan and Sibur owns nine major Siberian gas processing plants. In October 2000, Gazprom made a takeover bid for Sibur and purchased 51% of the company's equity. As this created a gas-processing monopoly permission for the sale was required from the Antitrust Ministry. It appears to have been forthcoming, albeit with stringent conditions attached. Needless to say, the deal contravenes a key element of the government's Economic Strategy;[14] that is, to prevent Gazprom from gaining control over the processing of casing head petroleum gas.[15]

A similar situation existed in Canada where Duke Energy (formerly "Westcoast Energy Inc.") owned over 85% of the gathering and processing capacity in the Northeast British Columbia (BC) production basin. The Northeast BC basin is a remote location far from market areas, where weather conditions are harsh and the exploration and production activities are challenging and expensive. As Duke (a third party) owns and operates the

---

[14] IEA (2002). Russia Energy Survey 2002, p.122.
[15] Strategy of Development of the Russian Federation through 2010, Social and Economic Aspect, Center for Strategic Research, submitted to the government of the Russian Federation on May 25, 2000, Section 3.5.1.

upstream processing facilities producers are able to reduce their initial capital exposure to the area. At the same time, operating costs are reduced by the increased utilization of existing assets and the achievement of economies of scale.

The Duke processing assets represented a potential monopoly and as a result were regulated by Canada's National Energy Board (NEB). In short, the NEB has determined that the processing assets form an integral part of the natural gas trunk line system and therefore fall under their jurisdiction. The NEB was successful in its attempt to create a competitive industry in Northeastern British Columbia by ensuring that all producers are entitled to non-discriminatory access to Duke's processing facilities.

Although the Antitrust Ministry has imposed stringent conditions on Gazprom, there is no guarantee that these will be successful without constant monitoring and enforcement. The Federal Energy Commission (FEC) should be responsible for regulating Gazprom's processing plants to ensure that producers receive access to processing services on a non-discriminatory basis. In summary, whenever Gazprom and/or its affiliates own upstream processing plants with monopolistic powers over a specific producing region, such facilities should fall under the jurisdiction of the FEC.

STRENGTHENING THE REGULATORY AUTHORITY OF THE FEDERAL ENERGY COMMISSION

In 2001 the Russian Federation was announced that the FEC was to be replaced by a new unified regulatory body. While the name FEC will remain, the responsibilities of the new organization will be substantially increased.[16] Although this is a step in the right direction, more needs to be done. Initiatives to redesign tariffs will fail if the FEC does not have final authority over the movement of natural gas on inter-regional gas transmission systems.

In short, the Russian FEC must have the same regulatory authority over inter-regional transmission systems as the FERC in the United States. To this end, the Russian government must continue to strengthen the independence of the FEC by streamlining and merging the functions of all relevant regulatory authorities, including the Commission on Oil and Gas Pipeline Use and the energy section of the Anti-Monopoly Ministry. Finally, the Russian government should be prepared to provide sufficient funding to allow the FEC to effectively police and enforce tariff regulations.

TOLL AND TARIFF DESIGN

The Elimination of Point-to-Point Distance Based Toll Design Methodology

In the years prior to 2000, there were two transmission tariffs in the Russian Federation:
(i) $9 per thousand cubic meters per hundred kilometers for deliveries to domestic customers and,
(ii) (ii) 80 cents per thousand cubic meters per hundred kilometers for Commonwealth of Independent States (CIS) export customers. These were

---
[16] IEA (2002). Russia Energy Survey 2002, p.121.

reduced to a single tariff in the range of 60 cents to one dollar per thousand cubic meters per hundred kilometers in July 2000.[17]

For independent producers the level of transmission costs is the most important determinant of the "economic radius" of production. That is the distance by which gas can be transported from the point of production to a customer and still sold at a profit.[18] Gazprom's current transmission rate design embraces a distance based point-to-point toll methodology. Although distance based point-to-point toll methodology may be the most equitable toll design methodology because it limits cross subsidization of tolls between shippers, it inhibits the creation of a competitive market.

A point-to-point distance based toll design is counter productive in the Russian Federation where the stated policy objective of the government is to create a competitive environment and physical volumes must be transported over largest distances. Distance based point to-point toll designs creates barriers of entry for small capital players, discourages the development of reserves that are remotely located from market areas, restricts the operational flexibility for the shipper to optimize their exposure to transmission charges and inhibits the creation of liquid transactional hubs. The elasticity of the "economic radius" under a distance based toll methodology favours large scale shippers. This is primarily a result of the fact that large scale shippers have the economies of scale that are necessary to optimize the average distance that a cubic meter of natural gas must physically travel from supply basin to the market area. The transportation costs for paper transactions, diversions, and displacement volumes can be "canceled out" thereby reducing the actual transportation costs that are paid per cubic meter.

In the Russian Federation the natural gas regulators would be well advised to consider a fundamentally different approach to transmission services and pricing such as a pool-to-pool toll design structure whereby costs and services are grouped and segmented by business activity.

Pool-to Pool Tolls: Segmentation of Transmission Services by Business Activity

As mentioned above, in a pool-to-pool toll structure costs and services are segmented by business activity. The "transactional pooling areas" provide the economic and operational framework for players to off-lay the risk of moving gas from production areas to the market. This structure allows for the "segmentation-of-risk". New non-traditional players, such as energy merchant brokers, can enter the market and take speculative positions on behalf of small producers who may not have the tools necessary to manage speculative price risk. The increase in the number of players provides transactional liquidity within the pool and allows a broader range market participants to further diversify price risk. Finally, segmentation shifts the transportation paradigm from a point-to-point structure to a pool-to-pool structure defined by "into the pool", "out of the pool", and "between pool" services.[19]

---

[17] IEA (2002). Russia Energy Survey 2002, p121.
[18] IEA (2002). Russia Energy Survey 2002, p121.
[19] The concept of structuring transportation services around transactional pools was presented to the Canadian Association of Petroleum Producers by this chapter's author in a presentation entitled Revision to WEI

For example, in a point-to-point toll system, a small capital producer has no choice but to hold long haul transport capacity for 100% of their expected production. Under a pool-to-pool tolling system the same small producer has a real option to reduce its holding of long haul capacity and sell their excess production on the day in the upstream pooling area. This is due to the increased liquidity at the primary receipt points (i.e., pooling areas).

Transactional pooling areas enhances foreign direct investment in the natural gas sector by:

- allowing new players to effectively manage investment risk through;
- increasing transactional liquidity;
- providing transparent market based clearing prices close to the well head;
- reducing the cost of unutilized transportation;
- allowing for the creation of synthetic transportation services;

Last but by no means least, the increased transactional liquidity will allow for the creation of sophisticated paper commodity markets including the development of useful financial derivative products such index swaps, options, and long term fixed price instruments.

The transmission services framework must recognize the realities of a competitive and open access transmission system. On an inter-regional pipeline transmission system like Gazprom, business activities will typically fall into three broad categories: (1) the receipt, movement and delivery of gas in and around logically connected supply basins; (2) the receipt, movement and delivery of gas in and around logically connected end use and export market areas; (3) and the long haul transportation of gas between the logical supply and market areas. This will result in the segmentation of the transmission system into three distinct business areas: a Supply Area, a Market Area and a Transmission Area (see Figure 12-1).

The benefits of the pool-to-pool tolling may be summarized as follows; Pool-to-pool tolling:

- Enables the development of independent contracts, prices and services that address the requirements of pipeline customers that are active in each business area;
- Allows the creation of transactional hubs within the various pooling areas thereby:
  - Eliminating the need for certain customers to hold long haul transportation and reducing transportation charges and price risk
  - Promoting competitive market priced transactions for the purchase and sale of natural gas
  - Balancing transactions within various pooling areas
  - Providing customer's with new choices for gas supply options
  - Improving customer's abilities to manage their gas supplies and transportation portfolios
  - Enhancing liquidity system wide

NOMS" dated March 26, 1999. The concept of segmentation as proposed herein was further refined by TransCanada Pipeline in a presentation entitled Transportation Services White Paper dated January 16, 2001.

- Encouraging the entry of new market entrants
- Facilitating the creation of sophisticated commodity markets and synthetic transportation arrangements

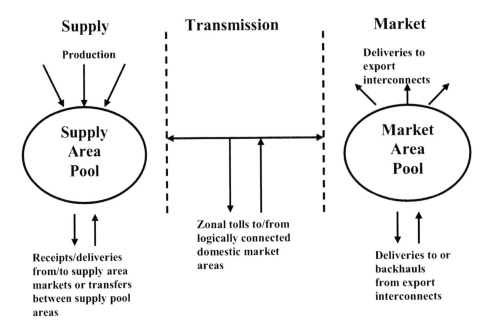

Figure 12.1. Transmission Segmentation by Business Activity.

Finally, the implementation of a pool-to-pool tolling system in the Russian Federation will improve cost accountability not only between segments, but also between different customers within each segment.

Pool-to-Pool Tolls: Cost Allocation

Segmentation of the transmission system into three distinct business areas supports the efficient allocation of costs and service tolls. When establishing tolls for each pipeline segment, each business area – supply, market, and transmission – will have its own cost center so that the direct and indirect costs may be recovered equitably.

Various cost allocation methodologies, such as distance-based, or assets-based, can be used to allocate costs to each pool. An asset-based approach allocates the specific facilities that are located in an area (i.e. pipe, meter, stations, and compression) to that area's cost.

Alternative cost allocation methodologies are required to allocate non-area specific assets (i.e., General Plant and Equipment, Operating Expenses and Corporate Overhead) to each area. The cost allocation methodologies for non-area specific assets should be consistent across all three areas.

When defining the cost pools the degree of cross subsidization for similar services within the pool will have a direct impact on the competitiveness of the business activities related to that pool. As a general rule, the cross subsidization of services within a pool will enhance the liquidity of the pool. To cite one example the tolling system in Alberta, Canada charges receipt tolls into the pool that subsidizes producers that are located in remote locations. Producers are willing to accept this degree of cross subsidization in order to reap the benefits accruing from the increased liquidity of the supply pool.

The tolls designed for each business area will reflect the major functions carried out in each area (i.e., the receipt of gas for delivery to a market, the movement of gas between supply and market hubs and the delivery from the market hub to a customer's delivery point) and the underlying cost structure of each area. As a result, each area will have a specific tolling design.

The separation of cost pools supports a categorization of costs that reflects the underlying cost structure of the business activity while simultaneously improving cost accountability. Separate cost pools allow tolls in each area to be independent of business activity in other areas. The degree of independence will depend on the allocation methodologies used.

Pool-to-Pool Tolls: Financial Model

The FEC would be well advised to establish an efficient and transparent toll design methodology within each cost. As a general rule the objective of toll design is to keep tolls as low as possible. This can be achieved by using a financial model that provides the incentives for transmission companies to:

- adopt cost-effective measures;
- optimize throughput where assets are under utilized;
- introduce new services which enhances the transactional liquidity of the pools, and
- encourage long-term capital investment by transmission companies.

Toll certainty: The stability of the tolling system is of critical importance to producers when analyzing the economics of future production opportunities. To achieve this objective transmission companies should be required to file predefined annual revenue requirements for a minimum term of five years. The established annual revenue requirements will be fixed for the entire period regardless of any changes due to actual costs. The exceptions to this rule include uncontrollable, unforeseen "off-ramp" events, and *force majeure*. Any savings in the actual costs would accrue to the benefit of the transmission company.

Reducing fuel and line loss: According to Gazprom's estimates fuel usage and line loss exceeded 9.0% of total throughput in 1998.[20] This represents a significant cost to producers and can have an adverse impact on competition by rendering marginal projects uneconomic. By way of comparison, TransCanada's high pressure pipeline system's provision for fuel and line loss is less than 5% of the total throughput.

The Fixed Revenue Requirement Model should include a toll incentive mechanism that rewards the transmission companies for reducing pipeline fuel, losses and leakage. This can be accomplished by allowing transmission companies to retain a portion of the fuel and line loss savings for the benefit of the shareholder.

Improving Pipeline Reliability: Gazprom's statistics on pipeline "failure rates" have improved considerably over the past two decades. In 1999, the rate stood at 0.18 failures per thousand kilometers.[21]

---

[20] IEA (2002). Russia Energy Survey 2002, p.126.
[21] IEA (2002). Russia Energy Survey 2002, p.126.

Notwithstanding recent improvements Russian transmission companies should be held accountable for pipeline operations. For example, Russian Federation pipelines should be required to operate at predetermined annual throughput levels that are adjusted for planned maintenance schedules.

If the transmission company is unable to provide a shipper with firm service that is less than the predetermined throughput level, then the shipper should be given a credit to be applied against future pipeline charges. The transmission company should be accountable for failing to meet the predetermined throughput targets.

Reinvesting in pipeline infra-structure: One of the biggest challenges facing the Russian energy sector is the age and condition of its pipeline infrastructure. Of more than 150,000 km of high pressure, large diameter transmission lines, 70% were commissioned before 1985. Approximately 19,000 km of the pipeline system is beyond its design life-span and needs replacement. In short, the investment requirements are significant and can be expected to increase sharply over the next two decades.[22]

These investment requirements can be met quite easily without causing shippers undue financial hardship. The financial toll model can be modified to incorporate the concept of a "Demand Toll Surcharge" (DTS); that is to say shippers can be charged a toll rider that is sensitive to market price.

The purpose of the DTS is to raise the maintenance capital that is required to replace the existing infrastructure. The DTS algorithm is a function of the Commodity Price. For example, the DTS will increase when commodity prices are greater than a predetermined mean reverting average. The DTS would be capped at a predetermined level that is a function of the pipeline depreciation rate. The DTS methodology takes advantage of the fact that producers will be willing to pay increasing transmissions tolls during periods when commodity prices are higher than the long term historical average. The revenues collected through DTS should be used exclusively for replacing aging pipeline infrastructure, and not for pipeline expansion projects.

OTHER INITIATIVES

Creation of an Electronic Public Bulletin Board

At present it is difficult to verify whether spare capacity exists on the vast Gazprom transmission system network. This is critical for the introduction of new independent third party shippers. The transmission company can play a key role in creating a competitive environment by ensuring that market information is disclosed to the public in a non discriminatory and timely manner. The FEC has a clear mandate to compel Gazprom and other transmission companies begin to post the following information on their bulletin boards:

- Daily available physical capacity by segment;
- Daily throughput volumes by segment;

---

[22] IEA (2002). Russia Energy Survey 2002, p.118.

- Operational Notices of any factors or conditions that could affect the available capacity;
- Historical throughput volumes by segment;
- Contracted capacity by segment and by shipper;
- All capacity available for bid;
- Details of capacity awarded through the bidding program;
- Toll and tariff sheets.

Allocation and Access Rules

In an effort to ensure a greater level of competition for excess capacity the FEC should direct transmission companies to develop a daily capacity allocation algorithm. This will ensure that all physical capacity that is not being utilized by "firm" shippers is allocated to "interruptible" shippers who are requesting such service. The administration details of this system should allow the FEC to conduct audits to ensure that the capacity is awarded third party shippers in a non-discriminatory manner. In the event of a system failure, remaining available capacity should be allocated on a prorated basis as a function of total volume of gas initially scheduled.

To ensure open access in a non-discriminatory manner, the following should be mandated – "firm" shippers wishing to assign excess firm capacity to a third party shipper for a term greater than 30 days should be required to post such capacity on the public bulletin board. All shippers should have the opportunity to bid on such capacity, and the bidding program should be conducted as an auction with capacity awarded to the shipper who bid the highest on a per unit of service basis.

Code of Conduct Policy

To safeguard the Russian pipeline system from corruption, the FEC should introduce and enforce an Act that prohibits both unjust discrimination against third parties and preferential treatment of affiliates. The Code of Conduct Policy should:

- Apply the terms and conditions of the tariff in a uniform manner to all shippers and potential shippers;
- Require the transmission company to strictly enforce tariff provisions
- Not give affiliates preference over-non-affiliates in matters relating to transportation service, including scheduling, balancing or curtailment priority;
- Process all requests for transportation service in a similar manner;
- Ensure that no third-party confidential shipper information is disclosed to affiliates;
- Ensure that that all public information is posted contemporaneously;
- Ensure that transmission operating employees and the operating employees of affiliates are separated and function independently;
- Maintain its books of account and records separately from those affiliates; and
- Post on the public bulletin board the names and address of its affiliates.

TRANSFORMATION AND REFORM IN THE RUSSIAN OIL SECTOR

Since the reorganization of the oil industry in the 1990s, competition in the upstream portion of the oil and gas industry appears to be on track with the Russian Governments stated policy objectives. At the present time, the sector includes eleven large Vertically Integrated Companies (VICs). In 2000, these eleven companies accounted for 88% of the total crude oil production in the Russian Federation, and 79 % of refinery throughput. The residual crude oil flows were made up of production from over 100 small independent producers (3%) joint ventures (6%), and Production Sharing Agreements (PSAs) (less than 1%).[23]

The Russian Federation has developed an extensive domestic oil pipeline system, with links to nearly all of the former Soviet republics. The state-owned transmission company, Transneft, manages, services and is responsible for the development of the entire Russian trunkline system. By the end of 1999, the system covered approximately 46,700 km of domestic territory, including 867 oil storage tanks with a total capacity of 12.8 million cubic meters. Including export capacity the Former Soviet Union's (FSU) pipeline network is the largest integrated system in the world with a total length of about 62,000 km.[24]

Transneft classifies its pipelines into three major categories; Export, interregional, and intraregional. Of these three only the export pipelines are approaching full capacity. In 1998, the average throughput in the Russian Federation reached levels as high as 103% of export capacity. In contrast, the average load factor of Transneft's non-export pipelines is approximately 56% of capacity.[25]

Transneft is a regulated fee-for-service carrier. Its export lines are regulated by the Commission for Oil and Gas Pipeline Use, an agency that was established in November 2000 to replace the Inter-Departmental Commission.[26]

Although the Russian government has made significant progress towards the development of competition in the upstream petroleum industry, a number of transmission issues are yet to be addressed. These include:

- Establishing a system to monitor the different quality of crude put into the Transneft pipeline system and to compensate shippers accordingly;
- Establishing a tolling system to fund future pipeline expansion projects;
- Strengthening the role and independence of the FEC;
- Implementing a transparent toll design methodology;
- Establishing a transparent and equitable approach to allocating limited pipeline export capacity to markets;
- Developing programs to maintain pipeline reliability targets.

---

[23] IEA (2002). Russia Energy Survey 2002, p.65.
[24] IEA (2002). Russia Energy Survey 2002, p.88.
[25] Mikhailov (2000, p.3).
[26] IEA (2002). Russia Energy Survey 2002 p.89.

Establishing a Crude Oil Bank

There has virtually been no change in Transneft's general operations since the Soviet era. The pipeline does not segregate crudes, so that the mixing and blending that occurs during pipeline transport produces a generic "Export Blend". At present there is no way to compensate shippers for the differences between the quality of crude that is put into the system and the quality of crude that is actually delivered. The creation of a crude oil banking system would enable Transneft to send the correct signals to producers and compensate them appropriately for the relative value of different types of crude. For example, if an appropriate system of compensation were established, then low quality crude producers would no longer have the incentive to inject their low quality oil into the general export flow, and would be able to re-direct their output towards specialized local refineries.

Tolling Pipeline Expansion Projects

Transneft is responsible for developing Russia's oil pipeline system, which is a task that, without an appropriate toll and tariff system, could well prove to be daunting. Current proposals to expand export capacity, and build new terminals on Russian territory, are expensive. Projects to increase the crude oil export capacity of the Druzhba Pipeline into Eastern Europe are less expensive, but more difficult politically.[27]

In the past, major pipeline expansions such as the Chechnya bypass and the Baltic pipeline have been financed through a special tariff surcharge that is attached to the regular Transneft tariff. As a result, all shippers must help pay for the pipeline system whether they use the pipeline or not. The Russian government was able to justify the Baltic Pipeline by viewing the project as "strategic" and, thereby, liberating Russian producers from an over-dependence on individual transit states.[28]

The definition of a Pareto efficient tolling model for pipeline expansions is that no one can made better off without making someone else worse off. This is a difficult criterion to fulfill. To be specific, there is no clear answer to the question as to whether pipeline expansions should be financed through a rolled-in or incremental toll methodology. In North America, proponents of pipeline expansion projects often argue in favour of having capital costs of the expansion project rolled into the current rate base. The FERC, on the other hand, often requires inter-state pipelines to toll expansion projects incrementally. In Canada, the National Energy Board tends to favour a rolled-in methodology for those pipeline expansion projects that utilize a substantial portion of the existing pipeline infra-structure (i.e., looping, right-of-way, compression).

There is no debate whatsoever regarding "greenfield" pipeline projects, which are financed exclusively by long term contractual commitments. Clearly, greenfield pipeline projects such as the Baltic Pipeline Project should not be financed through a general pipeline levy. If the Russian government's political agenda is strategic in nature and considered vital for the interest of public security, then "strategic projects" should be financed by the government through direct investment or tax relief initiatives.

---

[27] IEA (2002). Russia Energy Survey 2002, p 96.
[28] IEA (2002). Russia Energy Survey 2002, p.90.

The use of a rolled-in tolling methodology for pipeline expansion projects that utilize a substantial portion of the existing infra structure, such as expanding the Druhbza Pipeline into Eastern Europe, represents an efficient solution. To be specific, the rolled-in tolling methodology satisfies two of the FEC's main objectives, the creation of both non-discriminatory and transparent tolling systems.

Implementing a Transparent Toll Design Methodology

The basic tariff methodology utilized in the Russian Federation is a forward looking, cost based model. Prices are set to recover a revenue requirement 'target' that is based on the opportunity costs (including profits and taxes) of meeting planned levels of operations. Tariffs are adjusted periodically to account for inflation. In January 2000, Tranneft introduced a new two-tier tariff with a capacity charge (per tonne), and a pumping charge (per tonne-km).[29]

Russian crude oil transportation costs have been rising significantly since the early 1990s. In 1992 and 1996 Transneft's regular rouble tariffs increased eight-fold in dollar equivalent terms. By March 1996, transportation costs from West Siberia to Novorossiysk reached over $30 per tonne. Two years later in August 1998 the FEC reduced transportation costs significantly as world international oil prices – and Russian export margins – plunged to record lows. Pipeline tariffs were reduced again in real dollar equivalent terms during the financial crisis and severe devaluation of the rouble later that year. Since March 1999, pipeline tariffs have risen again reflecting higher operating costs and crude prices. As in the past, changes in pipeline tariffs appear to be more closely tied to the value of the crude (and the ability of oil companies to pay) than the costs of operation.[30]

If the objective of toll design is to keep tolls as low as possible, then the FEC should adopt a financial model that provides incentives for the transmission companies to:

- adopt cost-effective operating measures;
- optimize throughput where assets are under utilized;
- provide incentives for transmission companies to introduce new services and
- encourage long-term capital investment by transmission companies.

A transparent cost of service methodology that is implemented in a non-discriminatory manner will satisfy all of the above criteria.

As mentioned above, the stability of the tolling system is of critical importance to producers when analyzing the economics of future production opportunities. To achieve this objective Transneft should be required to file predefined annual revenue requirements for a minimum term of five years. The established annual revenue requirements will be fixed for the entire period regardless of any changes due to actual costs. The exceptions to this rule include uncontrollable, unforeseen "off-ramp" events, and *force majeure*. Any savings in the actual costs would accrue to the benefit of the transmission company.

---

[29] IEA (2002). Russia Energy Survey 2002, p89.
[30] IEA (2002). Russia Energy Survey 2002, p.90.

Allocation of Scarce Export Capacity

Not surprisingly, little progress has been made towards the efficient allocation of scarce export capacity in the Russian Federation. Regulations that were introduced during the financial crisis of 1998 are still in place. Specifically, a rigid system of mandated domestic deliveries for both crude and refined products reduces a company's ability to export crude oil supplies. Pre-specified amounts of crude oil must be delivered to domestic refineries according to quarterly balances developed by the Ministry of Energy and of Economy and Trade.[31]

Scarce export capacity is allocated through a simple method of pro-rationing production volumes from the previous quarter. Companies that are dissatisfied with their quotas can apply for additional incremental shipments on a "carrying availability" basis. Producers who find themselves with surplus capacity can loan, transfer or sell it to whomever they deem appropriate. In theory, all companies should be allowed to export 30% of their production. Those with greater lobbying power have been able to increase their access to export markets. This is virtually an identical situation to that prevailing in the period 1992-1995.[32]

In the past, the Russian government had announced plans to introduce an auction system for export quotas as early as the second quarter of 2001. Such a system was advocated by the IMF, among others, as an efficient means of allocating a scarce resource – Russia's limited export capacity – to international markets. Under the new plan, oil companies will bid for quota's at an open auction, with proceeds going to the federal budget. The amount bid for access to export markets would be a function of the price differential between domestic and export oil prices.

The new auction has the following limitations:

- The Russian government has a clear incentive to limit exports indefinitely and keep the differential between export and domestic prices as wide as possible.
- Large oil companies have an incentive to lock up all of the export capacity extracting excessive rents from small to mid-size producers.

The fact that the proceeds of the export auction accrue to the federal government represents a clear conflict of interest, which will motivate the government to act in a manner that will inhibit foreign investment in the oil sector. To eliminate the conflict, all proceeds that are realized through an Export Auction in excess of the regulated rate of return should accrue to Transeft and should be used to maintain the existing pipeline infrastructure.

CONCLUSION

In its current monopolistic form, Gazprom represents one of the greatest challenges facing the energy industry in the Russian Federation. To address this issue the Russian government should delineate a timeline and process for reducing Gazprom's dominance in the

---

[31] IEA (2002). Russia Energy Survey 2002, p.93.
[32] IEA (2002). Russia Energy Survey 2002, p. 93.

market place. By formally addressing this requirement in a timely manner, the government will be able to entice foreign investors to enter the natural gas sector sooner rather than later.

Gazprom's transmission rates are currently assessed on a distance-based, point-to-point tolling methodology. Given the inefficiencies inherent in the point-to-point tolling system, it would be beneficial to consider a fundamentally different approach to transmission services and pricing. In an alternative pool-to-pool tolling structure, costs and services would be grouped and segmented by business activity. The segmentation would effectively shift the transportation paradigm from a point-to-point structure to a pool-to-pool structure with "into the pool", "out of the pool", and "between pool" services (Barke, 1999).

Segmentation, and the creation of "transactional pooling areas", will provide the economic and operational framework that is necessary for market participants to 'lay off' the risk of moving natural gas supplies from major producing areas to the market. The creation of a number of new transactional pooling areas will enhance the prospects for foreign direct investment in the natural gas sector by allowing new players to effectively manage investment risk.

In the oil sector, the Russian government has announced plans to introduce an auction system for export quotas in the second quarter of 2001. Under this system, the vertically integrated oil companies, joint ventures, Production Sharing Agreements and independent oil companies will all bid for quotas at an open auction, with proceeds going to the Federal budget. The amount bid for access to export markets will be determined by the differential between domestic oil sales and world oil prices.

At the present time, the proceeds of the Export Auction are to be received by the Russian government. This represents a conflict of interest, which can be expected to motivate the government to act in a manner that will inhibit foreign investment in the oil sector. The proceeds from the Export Auction program in excess of Transneft's regulated rate of return should remain within Transeft, and should be used to maintain existing pipeline infrastructure and to fund future export pipeline expansion projects.

The promise of an imminent increase in export capacity is guaranteed to attract sufficient levels of foreign direct investment to develop the full potential of Russia's vast, and potentially lucrative, hydrocarbon resource base. It is central to the revitalization of Russian industry in general given energy's importance in industrial production.

REFERENCES

Barke, W. (1999). *Revision to WEI NOMS*, presentation to Westcoast Pipeline Company, Calgary, Canada, March 26.

Barke, W. (2001) *Transportation Services White Paper*, presented to Transcanada Pipeline Company, Calgary, Canada, January 16.

Centre for Strategic Research (2000). *Strategy of Development of the Russian Federation through 2010, Social and Economic Aspect*, Moscow: Center for Strategic Research, submitted to the government of the Russian Federation, May 25.

IEA (2002). *Russia Energy Survey 2002,*, Paris: The International Energy Agency.

Gazprom (2000). *Gazprom Annual Report 2000*. Moscow: Russian Federation.

Governement of the Russian Federation (2001). *Osnovnie Polozheniya Energeticheskiye Strategii Rossii na period do 2020 goda* [Energy Strategy of Russia for the period ending 2002: Main Provisions]. Moscow: Russian Federation.

Governement of the Russian Federation (2001). *On State Regulation of Gas Prices and Tariff for Gas Transportation in the Russian Federation*, Resolution No. 1021, Moscow: Russian Federation, December 29.

Mikhailov, N. (2000). *Russia's Pipeline System and Oil and Gas Transportation Projects*, BISNIS, August, http://www.bisnis.doc.gov/bisnis/bisnis.cfm.

Milso, V. (2001) Interview with Vladimir Milso, Section Head, Economic Analysis and Regulation Systems Development. *Kommersant Daily*, Moscow, Russian Federation, January 16.

Transcanada Pipeline Company (2002). *Transcanda Transportation Services White Paper*. Calgary, Transcanada Pipeline Company, January 16.

Chapter 13

THE ROLE OF HOUSEHOLD DEMAND IN THE EXPANSION OF RUSSIAN INDUSTRIAL PRODUCTION

Alla Chebanova

ABSTRACT

The determination of consumer expenditure is complicated even in normal economic times. The transition process in the Russian Federation cannot be considered "normal economic times" Macroeconomic policies in Russia have acted to both erode incomes and increase consumer risk. Consumer demand is inhibited and hard to predict. As a result, forecasting for purposes of investment decisions in manufacturing firms is difficult. Hence, sufficient inducements for investment in revitalizing Russian industry remain elusive.

INTRODUCTION

The purpose of this chapter is to thoroughly analyse the effect of an increase in household and government demand on stimulating economic activity in Russia. This analysis takes account of current government social policies, as well as policies regarding income and property. It is hoped that it will also contribute to the evolution of the State as an economic agent with particular focus on the system of national accounts (SNA).

METHODOLOGY

In order to analyse the effects of consumer demand on Russian industry, we have researched the behaviour of households (as conventionally interpreted in macroeconomic models) and the state. Our research has shown that the impact of the state (or the public sector of the economy) on industrial production is very complex and diverse because the public sector is composed of two smaller sectors: public enterprises and the public financial sector which includes both the direct purchase of goods and services by government as well as the provision of credit on more favourable terms than can be obtained from the market. Each of these sub-sectors influences the public sectors' total demand for goods and services in a different way.

For this research, the state's total demand for industrial output is limited to the demand of the public financial sector. Of course, public enterprises also affect demand for industrial output. However, demand by public enterprises is for intermediate products and should be treated similarly to demand for intermediate goods by private enterprises. The public sector also supplies industrial commodities and services and in this sense does not differ from other economic actors (in the absence of public policy initiatives). Thus, while it is important to consider role of public enterprises in the formation of industrial policy, there is still considerable controversy surrounding the optimal scale, structure, efficiency and management of public enterprises. This not simply a Russian debate as there is a global tendency to reduce direct state ownership of the means of production (Osborn and Gabler, 1992. At the same time, government budgetary allocations for social programs, infrastructure and the development of industries that produce collective goods have increased in Russia. Thus, by participating in the state's social policies, the public financial sector directly influences final consumer demand (including the demand for industrial output) through three channels: by paying the salaries of civil servants and employees; through direct social transfers; and through income regulation. However, in order to avoid double counting, estimates of the proportion of total consumer demand that can be attributed to the public financial sector must be considered in the context of final household demand.

The public financial sector also influences industrial development by stimulating demand for capital intensive products. It accomplishes this by directly financing investment projects through the budget and other special federal programs. However, due to the scarcity of budget resources, competition arises between these two forms of government support, and a "crowding-out" effect may arise. The analysis of these problems can be based on a study of reciprocal income and expenditure flows between industries (or, more generally, the production sector), on the one hand, and the public and household sectors, on the other. Such an examination of financial flows between different sectors of the economy is the methodology that will be used in this chapter.

A GLOSSARY OF PRINCIPLE CONCEPTS

A glossary of the principle terms and concepts established in a modern market economy is necessary because they may have a very different meaning in transitional economies. There may also be differences in the calculation of certain indicators or in accounting procedures, due to the fact that the time frame in which they are undertaken in a transitional economy may not coincide with that used in a modern market economy, or because transitional economies may not have adopted the same system of national accounting (SNA). Differences in the time frames for calculation may be corrected by estimating adjustment factors. To rectify accounting differences, statistical data must be aggregated and calculation procedures must be simplified. As a result of current accounting practices, quantitative estimates often are only broadly illustrative of economic trends.

In Russia, the current official procedure is to estimate GDP only quarterly, so there is no monthly GDP data available. This is one example of existing differences in the time frame of index calculation between Russia and modern market economies. Having only quarterly estimates is the source of a number of computational difficulties. One such consequence is that research organisations must rely on their own estimates (which usually differ from the government's methods) to adjust official statistics if they wish to undertake their own analysis and/or produce in house forecasts. As a result, quantitative estimates undertaken after such *ad hoc* adjustments differ greatly among organisations and may lead to contradictory conclusions. Therefore, neither the official statistics nor the adjusted statistics are a reliable basis for the development of macroeconomic or industrial policy.

An example of accounting differences is the grouping of economic agents according to the International Standard Industrial Classification of All Economic Activities (ISIC) in most modern market economies and the All-Russian Classification of Principal Industries of National Economy (ARCPINE) used in Russia. For example, when GDP is calculated under the guidelines of the SNA, power, gas and water supply are separated from other industries, while Russian statistics treat them as part of a much broader industrial category.

In order to effectively undertake the research required for this chapter, it was necessary to clearly define industrial and economic terminology, as well as the composition and structure of the sectors of the economy under consideration. However, major methodological and practical difficulties may arise when defining the industrial sector including its composition, structure and major economic players. First of all, there is no single multilateral statistical collection agency that is responsible for the industrial sector within the framework of the SNA. This has not, however, prevented the relatively widespread use of similar classification in theoretical macroeconomic literature, both in modern market economies and in Russia. At the outset of Russia's economic reform, the term "real sector" simply represented a general concept of material production or the productive sector – which is commonly thought of as the industrial sector in market economies. During the time Russia was plagued by economic crises and recession, the interpretation of this term evolved, so that the real sector was viewed separately from the financial sector (meaning financial capital – sometimes denoted "fictitious capita" in Russia). Financial markets became somewhat detached from actual production as the scale of speculative operations with currency (and later with state securities) grew and titles to property changed in the course of privatisation. In the process, a distorted view of the real sector arose, which has hindered efforts to adequately evaluate it. In this study, the real sector will be analysed as a set of the following industrial branches:

1. Agriculture, hunting, forestry, fishing;
2. Mining;
3. Manufacturing;
4. Power, gas and water supply;
5. Construction;
6. Wholesale and retail trade, restaurants (or public catering according to Russian statistical nomenclature);
7. Transport, storage, communications.

Although it would be appropriate to define the real sector of the Russian economy according to the established methods of the SNA, we are confronted by a statistical problem, since the Russian GDP is not classified and calculated according to the SNA. However, there is such a great need for quantitative estimates (even if they are only approximations) of total real production in the Russian Federation that various surrogate indices are also available, besides the official figures. For example, the Goskomstat of the Russian Federation produced an index of the production and service output of basic industries (IBI) to calculate GDP on the basis of data showing the change in production in industry, agriculture, construction, transport, and retail trade. The Ministry of Economic Development and Trade measures economic activity by calculating an index that is equal to the mean of output in industrial production, agriculture, construction and assembly works and retail turnover. Some independent researchers calculate their own statistical indices based on conditions in a branch or several branches of the economy. For example, The Russian Economic Barometer calculates a number of indices based on monthly selective surveys of Russian entrepreneurs (REB Indexes)[1]. Thus, at present, there are many official and unofficial indices, which reflects the need for accurate evaluation of the real sector in the Russian economy. Unfortunately, as a rule, they are not comparable to each other because of the poor development and accuracy of data collection, the statistical base and methods of data processing.

There are similar issues in the identification and definition of the household sector (in terms of its composition and the economic agents operating within its framework) as with the real sector. The main question is whether economic agents that are actively engaged in private enterprises without legal standing belong to the household sector or to the real or financial sector (depending on their activities). On the one hand, services offered by small private entrepreneurs, as well as professional services, do possess purely commercial features (i.e. they are intended for sale), so they cannot be properly categorised as households, nor as private non-profit institutions serving households. On the other hand, according to Russia's tax laws, entrepreneurs are subject to income tax as individuals, and so they may be categorised as households.

Multivariate reciprocal financial flows of incomes and expenditures between the real sector (or in narrower sense, industry) and the public and household sectors can be illustrated through the classification system presented in Table 13.1:

Theoretically, state and household demand for commodities and services produced by the real sector are identical to income (in-going) flows, and one can obtain a quantitative estimate of demand by balancing financial outcomes in any fixed moment of time. However, in transitional economies like Russia's, it is impossible to balance all operations that link the real sector with the state and household sectors. This is because of the lack of legal recognition of certain financial flows, which leads to inadequate reflection of these financial flows in official statistics. The information currently available only allows one to evaluate the major income flows that shape final demand for commodities and services by households and the state.

---

[1] Since December 1991 *The Russian Economic Barometer* has carried out monthly panel surveys of managers of Russian enterprises. A sample consists of 500 industrial and 300 agricultural enterprises and covers many regions of the Russian Federation. Most industrial enterprises are manufacturing enterprises of average size according to Russian standards (i.e. the number of employees is in a range between 500 and 2000 persons). During the period in question the institutional status of many enterprises changed: the number of state-owned units in the sample has decreased from 82 percent to 15 percent. As for agricultural enterprises, half of them specialize mainly in crops, while the other half is involved in cattle farming. Most of them are also average sized enterprises (according to the number of employees).

Table 13.1. The Pattern of External Financial Flows in the Real Sector

Expenses (outgoing)*	Incomes (source)
I. To the public sector: • Taxes and similar payments, as well as payments on sanctions and fines, going towards the government's budget, as well as off-budget funds paid all levels of government; • Interest payments on credit received from the government, as well as repayment of the state's credit resources at the expiration of the lending period; • Transfers of a share of the net profits of either solely state-owned or mixed enterprises (the latter with the state's participation in ownership); • Revenues from privatization of previously state-owned real sector enterprises.	**I. From the public sector:** • Direct budgetary financing from a number of purpose-oriented budget funds (for example, at the Federal level: the Road and Ecological Funds, the Fund of Ministry of Nuclear Industry, the fund of restoration of minerals' base and so on); • Other kinds of direct budgetary financing (besides purpose-oriented funds) in industry, construction, agriculture, fisheries, conservation of the environment, transport and communication; • Provision of credit by the Government; • Payment for state orders and financing of Federal purpose-oriented programs; • Transfer of resources in order to pay for the renewal of government reserves.
II. To the household sector: • • Wages and other forms of payments for work; • • Revenues from enterprises in the real sector intended for final consumption.	**II. From the household sector:** • Payment for commodities and services offered to the population by the real sector and intended for final consumption; • Crediting of the real sector through delinquent arrears of wages in productive industries; • Purchase of corporate shares and bonds using a system of collective institutional investors by households; • Resources for starting own business in the real sector.

* A note about the scheme: There are some differences between accounting and bookkeeping practices regarding the concept of financial flows. For example, income flows are usually associated with a constant time interval between two successive payments, while random movements of incoming resources to the recipient characterise flows to the real sector. A similar distinction exists between outgoing financial flows and expenses. This difference may not seem severe when trying to balance financial assets for a certain time period. However, it can have a negative effect on economic activities within the period in question. Therefore, along with the problem of quantitative concordance of material and financial flows, such flows must also be optimised over time to ensure the circular flow of expenses. The most striking example of the lack of concordance between material and financial flows is the interruption of production due to economic strikes caused by non-payment of wages.

Table 13.2. The Main Components of Financial Flows from the Household Sector to the Real Sector of the Russian Economy (in billions of roubles)

	1996	1997	1998	1999	2000	2001
Volume of retail trade turnover	753.3	862.6	1010.9	1722.8	2306.7	3005.0
Volume of commodity turnover in public catering	31.3	32.8	35.7	59.3	80.7	112.8
Volume of paid services rendered by the real sector of economy including:	145.4	192.3	221.4	307.4	437.3	595.0
• consumer services	37.6	48.9	51.0	71.8	86.3	109.1
• passenger services	50.3	64.4	71.0	94.5	160.4	209.7
• communication services	15.8	23.1	28.4	42.6	65.2	95.0
• utilities	41.7	55.9	71.0	98.5	125.4	181.2
Volume of accumulated delinquent arrears of wages in so called productive industries due to a lack of own resources of enterprises and organizations	36.7	49.1	77.0	38.5	30.9	24.1
Total	966.7	1136.8	1345.0	2128.0	2855.6	3736.7

Sources: Sotzialno-ekonomitcheskoe polojenie Rossii v 1999 g. [The Social and Economic Situation in Russia in 1999], pp. 75-79; Sotzialno-ekonomitcheskoe polojenie Rossii v 2000 g. [The Social and Economic Situation in Russia in 2000], pp. 85, 89, 91, 206, 207; Sotzialno-ekonomitcheskoe polojenie Rossii v 2001 g. [The Social and Economic Situation in Russia in 2001], pp. 97, 106, 108, 221.

Table 13.3. The Volume of Retail Trade Turnover and Accumulated Delinquent Arrears of Wages in Industry (in billions of roubles)

	1996	1997	1998	1999	2000	2001
Volume of retail trade turnover (billion roubles)	753.3	862.6	1010.9	1722.8	2306.7	3005.0
Volume of accumulated delinquent arrears of wages in industry due to a lack of own resources of enterprises and organizations (billion roubles)	10.3	25.4	30.8	15.9	11.4	11.4
Total (billion roubles)	763.6	888.0	1041.7	1738.7	2318.1	3016.4
Share of the GDP (%)	35.6	35.8	38.0	36.5	31.7	33.4

In its analysis, this chapter will concentrate largely on problems of qualitative analysis and quantitative estimates of demand for manufactured goods by the household sector. The issue of stimulating the state's demand will be considered in connection to the present public investment and innovation policy in the Russian Federation. A quantitative analysis of the actual consumer demand over the recent past has also been undertaken in this chapter. Keeping in mind the limitations listed above, namely the absence of the SNA and the lack of official Russian statistics, as well as the highly aggregated nature of the statistics that are available, estimate have been made (in nominal values) of the volume of main financial flows from the household sector to the real sector of the Russian economy between 1996 and 2001 (Table 13.2).

Only two types of financial flows from the household sector to the real sector have a direct bearing on industry: the volume of retail trade turnover and the volume of accumulated delinquent arrears in wages (which may be caused by the lack of privately provided financial capital being available to firms and other organisations), see Table 13.3:

Two major assumptions have been made in the calculation of the values in Table 13.1 because it is not possible to determine these values with certainty: (1) the portion of GDP attributed to international trade or transaction costs and profits of organisations primarily engaged in international trade; and (2) the structure of commodity turnover in both domestic products and imports. The above data shows that financial flows from the household sector to industry as a percentage of GDP peaked during the crisis in 1998 at 38 percent. This was mainly due to the delay in payment of wages because enterprises lacked access to private sector loan capital. These delinquent arrears can be considered a form of credit from households to industry. In subsequent years, financial flows from households to industry declined.

The relationship between income flows from the household sector to the real sector, as well as changes in this relationship from 1996 - 2001 (in current market prices), is shown in Figure 13.1.

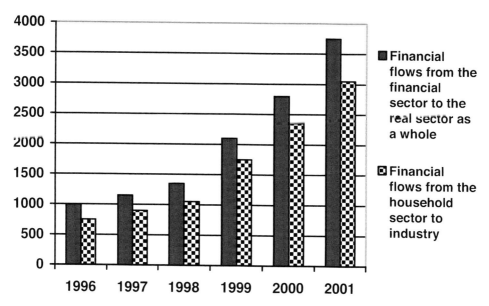

Figure 13.1. Financial Flows from the Household Sector to the Real Sector and Industry.

Table 13.4. The Structure of Retail Trade Turnover from 1997 – 2001

	Foodstuffs	Other commodities	"Preference" coefficient
1997	**49.0**	**51.0**	**0.961**
I quarter	48.2	51.8	0.931
II quarter	50.1	49.9	1.004
III quarter	50,.	49.7	1.012
IV quarter	47.6	52.4	0.908
1998	**49.9**	**50.1**	**0.996**
I quarter	47.5	52.5	0.905
II quarter	49.6	50.4	0.984
III quarter	49.7	50.3	0.988
IV quarter	51.7	48.3	1.070
1999	**48.1**	**51.9**	**0.927**
I quarter	49.2	50.8	0.967
II quarter	48.97	51.03	0.960
III quarter	47,8	52,2	0,917
IV quarter	46,9	53,1	0,883
2000	**46.5**	**53.5**	**0.869**
I quarter	46.8	53.2	0.881
II quarter	46.5	53.5	0.871
III quarter	46.1	53.9	0.855
IV quarter	46.5	53.5	0.868
2001	**46.1**	**53.9**	**0.856**
I quarter	46.4	53.6	0.865
II quarter	46.3	53.7	0.861
III quarter	46.2	53.8	0.859
IV quarter	45.8	54.2	0.844

Note: The index describing retail trade expenditures by the population was replaced on January 1, 1999 by another index. Now, retail trade turnover includes consumer goods sold to consumers whose prices are partially or completely controlled by social agencies. The value of commodities that social organizations receive from the retail trade through transfers without money, as well as the turnover of public catering is excluded from this index. Thus, indices for the volume of retail trade prior to 1999 are not directly comparable to those for more recent years.

Source: These calculations are based on data from Sotzialno-ekonomitcheskoe polojenie Rossii v 1999 g. [The Social and Economic Situation in Russia in 1999], pp. 76-77; Sotzialno-ekonomitcheskoe polojenie Rossii v 2000 g. [The Social and Economic Situation in Russia in 2000], pp. 85-86; Sotzialno-ekonomitcheskoe polojenie Rossii v 2001 g. [The Social and Economic Situation in Russia in 2001], pp. 97, 99-100.

The composition of final consumption by households is also very important for determining the effect of household demand on the development of industrial production. The structure of retail trade turnover (sales volumes for foodstuffs and other commodities) and changes in demand during the period from 1997 – 2001 is presented in Table 13.4.

The "preference coefficient" is the ratio of the amount of foodstuffs demanded by households to other commodities. If this index exceeds 1, it indicates that the population is more likely to buy foodstuffs than other goods, which indicates deterioration in the real disposable income of households and thus a change in the structure of final consumption by households. Quarterly movements in the preference coefficient from 1997 - 2001 are shown in Figure 13.2.

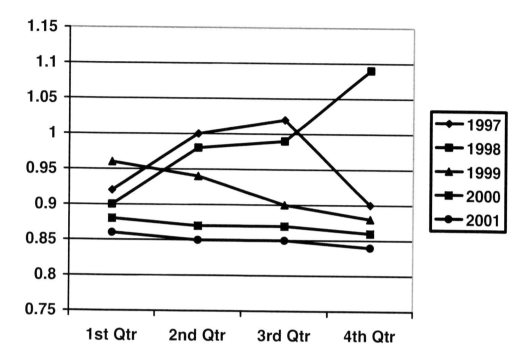

Figure 13.2. Preference Coefient from 1997-2001.

The dynamics of the preference coefficient shown in Table 13.4 and on Figure 13.2 illustrate a sharp drop in the standard of living for an overwhelming majority of the population after the crisis in August 1998. In the fourth quarter of 1998, this coefficient was at its peak during the entire period in question. This crisis in the structure of final consumption by households has been overcome rather quickly. From the first quarter in 2001 onwards, there was a steady decrease in the preference coefficient. In the fourth quarter of 2001, it was 1.27 times less than in 1998, which is a sign of growth in the real disposable income of the population, as well a change in household preference for foodstuffs versus other industrial commodities.

Naturally, factors determining household demand for industrial output influence supply factors in industry. An interesting aspect of industrial growth after the crisis in 1998 is that it occurred mainly through an increased utilisation of available industrial capacity rather new plant and equipment. Even though the profitability of Russian enterprises are improving, the large quantity of surplus industrial capacity explains the absence of demand by Russian industry for external sources of financing and the increasing isolation of the real sector from capital markets.

Each industry and each enterprise has a different level of idle capacity, depending on the type of technologies that are used in production, the intensity of the production downswing, the physical condition of the available equipment and how up to date the technology in use. Generally speaking, however, the growth potential of Russian industry based on available production capacity is still rather high, although continually decreasing[2]. The potential for growth based on available production capacities is shown in Figure 13.3 as the domain between the two curves (this graph is based on the entire set of responses to surveys by the REB) (REB, 2002, p.52).

The REB's figures show that the percentage of enterprises lacking capacity to meet expected demand increased from 3 percent in the third quarter of 1998 to 13 percent by the end of 2000. However, in the fourth quarter of 2001, this percentage decreased to 9 percent and was 10 percent on average in 2001. Nevertheless, one can expect that the reduction of unused capacity will continue in the near future. Thus, according to the REB's data, the percentage of enterprises with excess capacity in relation to expected demand was at its maximum in the third quarter of 1998 (68 percent), after which it followed a downward trend to 42 percent in the fourth quarter of 2001. The persistence of this trend and the depreciating away of old production capacity (and thus the ability to increase output) largely depend on external factors that affect the dynamics of total final demand of both consumers and the state. Thus, in the near future, financial flows from the public sector will determine not only when opportunities to revitalise the existing stock of capital good will be exhausted, but also the succession in which different industries will initiate the process of real sector modernisation. In particular, industries producing final products will initiate real sector modernisation, followed by industries that produce primary products. Hence, these financial flows also affect the volume of demand for foreign investment, which depends on the level of capital intensity of the industries in question.

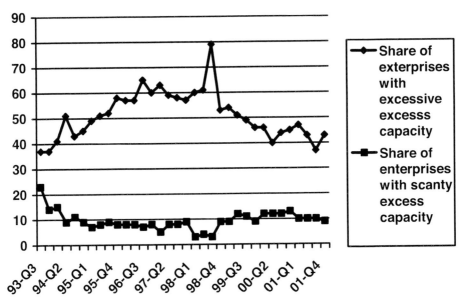

Figure 13.3. The Percentage of Industrial Enterprises with Excessive and Scarce Production Capacities.

---

[2] In further analysis, data obtained in monthly selective panel surveys of Russian managers carried out by the quarterly bulletin of the Institute of World Economy and International Relations (*The Russian Economic Barometer* (REB)) will be used. One should take into account that the conclusions drawn from these surveys are based mainly on the opinions of the respondents. However, there are two reasons to use the REB's information: first, it is possible to detect new trends as they arise (often there is no way to do this using the official statistics); second, the sample is sufficiently representative.

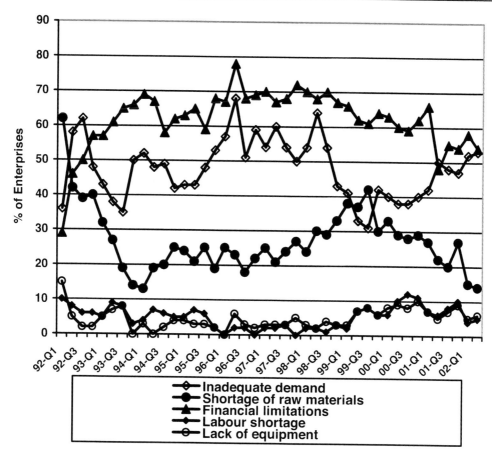

Figure 13.4. Factors Restricting Production in Industry.

In order to stimulate industry by manipulating demand, moderate inflation must be allowed and if necessary fostered in the consumer market. This is because moderate inflation induces consumers to carry out a greater number of transactions and demand more liquid assets (money) while at the same time increasing the marginal propensity to consume, which, *ceteris paribus*, stimulates increased domestic production of consumer commodities and services. Thus, incentives for domestic production are influenced by the state's budgetary, monetary, and institutional policies, which in turn, leads to the increased use of industrial capacity. Let us examine the effect of state policies on production in greater detail. In Figure 13.4, the main factors that currently constrain the growth of industrial output are shown (according to the information taken from the REB's surveys) (REB, 2002).

For analytical convenience, it is advisable to divide the period under examination into several sub-periods: (1) from the outset of reform to 1993; (2) from 1993 to 1998 (inclusive); (3) 1999[3]; (4) from 2000 to 2001. There are a number of conclusions that can be drawn from the changes that occurred in the time interval between 1993 - 2001.

---

[3] One should keep in mind that most changes mentioned below started in the autumn of 1998, but, as the figure is based on subjective estimates by respondents to the REB's surveys, it is necessary to take into account a certain time lag between the receipt of information and its reflection in surveys.

First of all, until mid-2001, the ranking of factors that constrained production by degree of impact was unchanged, excluding the short post-crisis period in 1999 when, according to the REB's data, the negative effect of raw material shortages on production exceeded the impact of inadequate demand. Prior to mid-2001, the absence of credit restrained output to the greatest extent. Inadequate demand for output and a shortage of raw materials, industrial materials and semi-manufactures followed in their impact on output. Shortages of labour and production capacity (e.g. equipment), which tend to occur intermittently have a weak negative impact on output in comparison to the first three factors.

It should be noted that the effect of the restrictions imposed by parameters determining the supply of production resources (raw materials, semi-manufactures, industrial equipment, labour, etc.) had been intensified in the wake of the crisis in 1998, especially by the shortage in raw materials. The latter factor gave rise to hopes that some fraction of the demand for raw materials would be re-oriented towards domestic production and increased demand for domestic agricultural output. However, the negative impact of these factors on output declined after their peak at the end of 2000.

Secondly, the dynamics of each constraining factor underwent significant changes during the post-crisis period. Towards the end of 1999, financial pressure on production, as well as demand constraints, slackened for a number of reasons: (1) expansionary monetary policy; (2) improvements in the collection of payments; (3) the gradual restoration of the pre-crisis level of real income of consumers. However, since the end of 1999, demand factors have exerted a greater influence upon industrial production. By mid-2000, this trend caused the ranking of factors affecting production to change (in Figure 13.4, this can be seen as the point of intersection between the curves reflecting the influence of the shortage of financial resources and the influence of inadequate demand). By the end of the second quarter of 2001, factors connected with inadequate demand had a larger negative effect on industrial production than either of the other factors.

It is still too early to predict whether this will be a sustained trend. For example, according to managers' estimates, during the second half of 2001 the shortage of financial resources was the most significant factor restraining production. However, two things must be considered. First, the proportion of enterprises whose production was impeded by shortages of loan capital during that period was at its lowest over the entire time period under examination. Second, the portion of enterprises that experienced insufficient demand (or surplus productive capacity) was (according to managers' estimates) relatively constant at approximately 50 percent. The problem of surplus capacity needs serious theoretical analysis and solutions must be proposed in the formation of state industrial policy.

THE INFLUENCE OF MACROECONOMIC POLICY ON CONSUMER DEMAND DURING TRANSITION

In order to understand the key factors that affected consumer demand in Russia during the post-reform period, it is necessary to divide past macroeconomic policy into several stages: the first stage (1993-1995), a second stage (1996-July 1998) and the restoration stage (after the crisis in August, 1998)[4]. The restoration period involves several sub-periods, each having its own specific effect on the dynamics of consumer demand. According to available statistics, it was not until December 2001 that the consumers' real disposable income increased compared to 1998. In the first period of the restoration stage internal demand collapsed and the rouble underwent a real revaluation, as a result of the state's rigid monetary and budgetary policies, as well as policies directed towards the expansion of exports. The second period was characterised by a transition towards more moderate policies. The use of the "currency corridor" mechanism made it possible to balance the growth rate of the exchange rate (nominal devaluation) and inflation rates. Thus, the trend in the growth of the real exchange rate (or real revaluation of the rouble) was overcome. However, the introduction of the "currency corridor" mechanism could not alter the collapse of domestic demand and the Russian market continued to be depressed. The absence of domestic demand was not offset by increased exports. In this situation, industrial enterprises that were oriented towards the domestic market survived by financing current production through non-payment all along the supply chain, non-payment of wages and/or delays in wage payments and while not officially firing workers, failing to actively employ and compensate them. It also becomes apparent that incomes were unofficially reduced given the level of non-payment of state pensions and wages in the civil service. As the value of savings was severely eroded, consumers could not use savings to offset their declining incomes. In effect, these reductions in disposable income can be considered as the state's policy.

The reallocation of the population's financial resources to the real sector is one of most important features of the restoration period. Figure 13.1 illustrates the increase of financial flows from the household sector to the real sector of economy (in particular, to industry) during the post-crisis period. The reallocation of financial resources towards the real sector from 1998 - 2001 had different effects depending on the economic policy under which they occurred. Immediately after August 1998, the rapid decline in the exchange rate (the devaluation effect) and the stagnation of wages and salaries increased domestic competitiveness in production and led to an intensive process of import replacement. There was also growth of household demand as a result of measures that had been taken to stabilise the social and economic situation in Russia, thus restoring the real disposable income of consumers. The effect of the increase in real incomes, however, diluted factors important to industrial growth, such as enterprises' low costs on the supply side. Over time enterprises' costs began to rise again as the economic situation stabilised.

The rouble's value has beeen gradually increasing, (in real terms) and households are experiencing growth in real incomes. However, these two trends, although positive in general, have negative impacts as well. The increasing value of the rouble has caused a decline in the competitiveness of Russian industry. This lack of international competitiveness in Russian manufacturing has been masked in the middle of the first decade of the 21st century by high energy prices. Furthermore, consumers tend to prefer imported goods to domestic goods, thus leading to the possibility that the Russian economy may return to a situation in which the growth of trade turnover (i.e. of final demand) is satisfied to an increasing degree by imported products. As a result, the financial position of domestic producers could further deteriorate preventing them from carrying out research and development activities, modernising their

---

[4] The restoration stage may be considered completed after the level of available real income for the population reaches and then exceeds that of the pre-crisis period (the middle of 1998).

equipment, investing in more efficient modern technologies and developing marketing networks. Indeed, these circumstance are very similar to those that gave rise to the crisis in August 1998 and their existence shows that the potential advantages of the post-crisis situation (i.e. the restoration stage) were quickly exhausted. A new macroeconomic policy is necessary so that the increase in real incomes, and thus consumption by the population, can be paralleled by growth in the domestic industrial sector. However, the dynamics of mass consumer demand determines the development of those industries that are oriented towards the domestic market.

THE EXPANSION OF CONSUMER DEMAND WITHIN THE FRAMEWORK OF THE STATE INDUSTRIAL POLICY

This author's opinion is that state industrial policy pertaining to the issue of stimulating demand for domestic output should be based on two main principles. First, the stimulation of demand must involve both dynamic and structural aspects to promote the development of domestic industry. Secondly, problems pertaining to deficient demand cannot be solved separately from other aspects of macroeconomic policy. Due to the interaction among various sectors of the economy, and the fact that prices for some commodities and services are extremely volatile, certain factors that are exogenous to consumption must be addressed in order to realise all of the benefits of a policy geared toward the expansion of domestic demand for domestically produced goods. These exogenous factors will be outlined below and referred to as "boundary" factors.

If the savings rate remains constant and if domestic commodities are competitive with similar imported goods, then household consumption expenditures, or aggregate consumer demand, for domestic goods is a function of a number of factors. These factors are divided into three groups, according to their effect on consumers' demand for final manufactured goods produced by Russian industries:

(1) Factors that are related to disposable income;
(2) Factors that significantly influence household expenditure, although they are not functions of disposable income (these factors may be further divided into quantitative and structural factors);
(3) Factors reflecting specific relationships in the transitional economy.

Consider first the dynamic and structural factors influencing household demand that will influence the Russian market for industrial goods from the near future to the medium-term. In general, household demand is a function of disposable income. Disposable income may be used either for consumer expenditures or savings. It can be theoretically postulated that, *ceteris paribus*, and assuming constant levels of consumption and saving, the dominant factor determining the level of consumer expenditures and their savings level is the size of disposable income. The relationship between income, consumption and savings has been studied on the microeconomic and macroeconomic levels. Major economic studies in this domain were carried out (based on long term US data) by Nobel prize winner, Simon Kuznets (Kuznets (1946) and Raymond Goldsmith (Goldsmith, 1955), as well as by Colin Clark (based on British statistics) (Clark, 1957). The functional relationship between total consumption and total income was established and analysed within the framework of the theory of the market economy in the seminal work by J.M. Keynes published in 1936, *The General Theory of Employment, Interest and Money*. Before Keynes, there was a little analysis of aggregate demand. Keynes also formulated the foundations of the modern theory of consumption functions in macroeconomics.

In its most general form, a consumption function relates consumption expenditures and disposable income. From this function, one may derive the consumption schedule to illustrate the effect of changes in disposable income on consumption, *ceteris paribus*. It is important to identify whether income stems from the industrial sector or from the government. In modern Russia, the government exerts the greatest influence on domestic industry. Therefore, any social, property and labour payment policies directed towards the systematic medium- and long-term growth of total disposable income, *ceteris paribus*, create incentives for the development of domestic industrial production. Among such measures are the following:

- An increase of the minimum wage to the subsistence level for the able-bodied population (with adjustments for annual inflation and changes in average wages);
- An increase in salaries in the civil service;
- An increase in the real value of pensions and other government grants (in particular increases of the average size of undergraduate student and postgraduate grants, social security payments and other government transfers to individuals);
- An increase the pay of the military

These measures may have positive effect on domestic production of consumer goods. The proportion of the population whose incomes are either relatively low (i.e. at, or slightly exceeding, the subsistence minimum) or in the middle range will exert the greatest amount of influence on industrial development.

At present, the relatively low level of total disposable income in the Russian Federation is associated with a high average propensity to consume. Therefore, demand can only exert a short-term stimulating influence upon domestic industry. The low average propensity to save further supports the necessity of government supplied credit expansion in the first stage of the state's industrial policy. Once households have surpassed a certain threshold value of income, they will spend relatively less on consumption and save relatively more. In essence, the growth in income alters the structure of household consumption towards an increase in spending on consumer goods. This qualitative pattern of behaviour implies that as income increases (decreases), general consumption of all goods increases (decreases), but the rate of increase (decrease) in consumption will vary for different groups of commodities and services. This result was discovered by a Prussian statistician in the nineteenth century, Ernst Engel and is now called Engel's law. This law states that as incomes increase, the structure of household consumption tends to be biased away from necessities and toward what are termed "higher order goods". Under certain conditions, the highest order good is saving. Thus, after passing a certain threshold, households will spend relatively less on consumption and save relatively more. In the context of macroeconomic policy, this means that in the second stage of the state's industrial policy, it will be possible to abandon wide-scale government provided credit expansion and rely on more conventional sources of investment, such as domestic savings.

The structural factors of the proposed industrial policy are ranked below according to their stimulating influence on production:

1. The Reduction of Poverty and Social Inequality

In the framework of this portion of industrial policy, measures should be taken in order to:

- Reallocate social allowances and social aid to those in the society with the fewest means.
- Increase per capital incomes for population groups with the fewest means relative to those who are better off in order to accelerate the purchasing power of those whose incomes are lower than the subsistence minimum.

Measures such as these will increase demand for domestically produced goods from the most disadvantaged groups in the population. The reduction of poverty and inequality is a powerful factor in the stimulation of consumer demand, mainly for domestic foodstuffs, particularly in the short run. The short-term influence of this factor arises because there is no capacity constraint in the consumption-oriented branches of industry. If there were a domestic capacity constraint, even a minor restoration of real disposable incomes would lead to rising prices and a shift towards "cheap" imports.

2. An Increasing Propensity of Consumers to Purchase New Commodities and Services that at the Beginning of their Product Life Cycle were Considered Luxuries[5]

With the current level and structure of household demand in the Russian Federation, it is difficult to determine which commodities and services may emerge as luxuries in the future. Instead, it can be argued that the stimulating effect of this facet of consumption will tend to be zero. However, in Russian conditions, the observed consumption patters may indicate a change in preferences as incomes increase. It will exert a dynamic influence on household demand towards higher order (i.e. those which are not considered necessities) consumer goods throughout the duration of the State Industrial Policy (SIP). This trend can be measured through changes in the "preference coefficient", which reflects the relationship between foodstuffs and other goods in retail turnover (see Table 13.4 and Figure 13.2). The evolution of consumer preferences over time will first shift from foodstuffs toward other goods in general, then towards durable goods and finally to goods which signify physical wealth, such as real estate. This trend in consumer expenditures will lead to an overall expansion of consumption in Russia.

---

[5] A discussion and demonstration of this hypothesis was previously presented in *Forecasting Postwar Demand* by American economists A. Smithies (1945), S.M. Livingston (1945) and J.L. Mosak (1945).

3. The Stimulation of Additional Consumption in Connection with the Accumulation of Wealth or Property (in Net Value, Free of Debts) due to the Growth in Real Incomes

Here "wealth" implies both real estate and household financial assets (cash, deposits in commercial banks, securities, insurance policies and pensions). In the long run, the wealth of a developing society increases, creating incentives for additional consumption, because the need for saving decreases for a given level of disposable income. The foundations of this idea were developed in a modified model by prominent American economist and 1981 Nobel Prize winner, J. Tobin (1951). Increases in wealth will have a widespread effect upon households' demand only in the long run. As for the short- and medium-term (i.e. during the first stage of the SIP) its effect will be limited to a narrow group of consumers, mainly wage earners, whose pay is stable and exceeds average levels of income.

4. The Negative Effect of Accumulated Consumer Arrears on Households' Decisions Concerning Current Consumption

This factor may adversely affect the growth of domestic industry only in the long run. At present and in the near future, the restoration of the system of consumer credit will positively influence certain segments of domestic industrial production.

5. The Growing Prevalence of Households with Relatively High Incomes

The behaviour of the "average" consumer most likely depends on the relative size of one's income rather than the absolute size of one's income. On standard hypothesis regarding the behaviour of an "average" consumer in an economic slump, is that his/her level of consumption is, at least in part, determined by their highest ("peak") income level in the recent past, rather than by their current income. In other words, they will draw down savings to maintain existing levels of consumption. Thus, consumption patterns act as a kind of built-in stabiliser during recessions. A more detailed discussion of these issues is undertaken by American Economist J. Duesenbury (1949) in his work on the theory of "achieved peak income". This aspect of consumer behaviour may have a gradual stimulating effect on demand in the long-run, as general welfare will increase and income inequality is reduced.

6. The Factor of Social Stratification

The level of total demand in general, and demand for domestic industrial output in particular, depends on the structure of income distribution among various social and economic groups in connection with their relatively different marginal propensities to consume (MPC). In a market economy, a society is stratified according to the source and form of income received. There are those who receive their income by selling their labour and those who derive their income from their property. According to S. Weintraub (1958), the main strata are workers, renters and those who receive their income as profits. In the Klein - Goldberger (Klein and Goldberger, 1955) econometric model, the main strata are farmers, owners of other enterprises and those who receive wages and salaries. In general, those who receive wage incomes have a much higher propensity to consume than those who derive their incomes as owners of property. It is also true the latter have a higher propensity to save than the former. It has been also ascertained that this rule holds when the behaviour of consumers in different countries is compared, so that countries with a high proportion of income derived from property holdings have a higher level of savings.

In the Russian Federation, consumption by wage earners predominates in the structure of total consumption in the short- and medium- term, because they have a higher propensity to consume than those who own property. Currently, wages and salaries compose more than 60 percent of total income. This will lead to growth in the demand for domestic output. The state's current methods for the stimulation of small business development (including legal reforms) will support increased domestic production as well. However, it seems improbable that the structure of society during the implementation of the SIP will be modified sufficiently so that the total marginal propensity to consume will be reduced.

Now, let us consider the factors affecting demand that are not functions of disposable income, and yet exert significant influence upon household demand. These factor link social and property policies to other tools of public macroeconomic policy, so we may call them "boundary factors". The balance between these factors will determine whether social and property policies will reinforce macroeconomic policy or have, at best, limited impact. The main factors comprising this group are prices, inflation and changes in taxation. Let us consider each of these factors in turn.

The price factor: During the future period of accelerated growth in household real incomes and/or the purposeful development of individual sectors of the domestic market, it will be necessary to moderately dampen the rouble's appreciation in order to preserve the price competitiveness of domestic industry and prevent the reorientation of an increasing proportion of consumer demand towards the import sector. This policy will allow domestic goods to replace imports. Furthermore, in the short run it may promote the expansion of national exports and offer a partial solution to the current account imbalance and an adjustment in the external liabilities of the Russian Federation.

The inflationary factor: There are two contending theories of consumer behaviour. On the one hand, the decision to consume or to save may be largely based on the "standard" level of consumption established during the previous peak income period. On the other hand, these decisions may be influenced to a significant degree by expected changes in the level of current and future income, price levels, etc. In the latter case, expected future price increases are perceived as a destabilising force because they cause current expenditures to increase and savings to decrease, leading to production expansion in the short run. An expected reduction in prices and incomes and reduction in the trade deficit may cause consumption to fall in favour of saving. Improvement in the position of households is dependent on expectations of rising future money incomes and stable prices. Keeping inflation within moderate levels while increasing real disposable incomes will facilitate moderate growth in the production of consumer products.

In the context of inflationary expectations, divergence between the consumption function in the long run and short run may be explained partially by the division of personal income into two components: transitory income, which is a function of short-term factors, and permanent income, which is a function of long-term factors. Each component is characterised by a separate marginal propensity to consume (MPC). In particular, MPC is larger for permanent income than transitory income. The foundations of this theory were put forth by prominent American economist and Nobel Prize winner Milton Friedman (1957) and subsequently were elaborated on by his colleagues from the Chicago School of Modern Monetarism.

Finally, although changes in taxation are exogenous to the aggregate consumption function, they may exert considerable influence on consumption. It is obvious that tax increases reduce gross income and determine, *ceteris paribus*, the size of disposable income.

Certain aspects of aggregate demand reflect specific relationships in the transitional economy and have theoretical, as well as practical, significance for the formation of the SIP with regard to the expansionary effects of demand on the domestic market for industrial goods. The composition and combination of these factors and the intensity of their influence differ across transitional economies. In post-reform Russia, it appears as if the dominant factor influencing domestic output remains the non-payment of wages. The Institute of the Study of the Economy gave much attention to the legal and some of the economic aspects of this issue in the transitional period[6].

From an economic point of view, the persistence of the non-payment (and/or delays in payment) problem for earners of wages and salaries exerts an odd combination of influences on the development of domestic industry. On the one hand, at the microeconomic level, arrears in wage payments are a latent and non-voluntary mode of credit from employees to employers; on the other hand, at the macroeconomic level, this factor is detrimental to aggregate demand and, hence, to domestic industry as a whole. Thus, arrears in wage payments to employees of government organisations that have accumulated considerably in the post-reform period exert an overall negative influence on domestic production. Such arrears cause deferred demand by the portion of the population whose incomes come from the government and associated organisations. The situation is complicated by the fact that the main sources of this non-payment are regional authorities which are not participants in the SIP.

The Russian Constitution restricts interference of the Federal government in the financial affairs of regional authorities. Thus, regional authorities have the right to use their own resources, as well as transferred federal resources, as they wish. In essence, federal transfers are not used as purpose-oriented tools. Thus, the Federal government possesses only a narrow range of measures for exerting influence upon the financial expenditures and activities of sub-national governments. The reduction or discontinuation of federal transfers is a possibility, but for the present, such measures are nothing more than abstract threats.

Wage arrears in the budgetary sphere are a local government's debt to its employees and are analogous to Russian citizens' borrowing from themselves individually and collectively. These wage arrears are distinct from legitimate forms of budgetary obligations on the part of citizens officially recognised in the Budget Code of the Russian Federation in the following ways:

---

[6] See, for example, R.Entov, A.Zolotareva, O.Lugovoy. "Factori vozniknovenija i nakoplenija neplatejey v rossiiskoy ekonomike i regionah" ["Factors of Emerging and Accumulation of Non-payments in Russian Economy and Regions". *Regionalnaya ekonomika* (sbornik statey) [Regional Economy (a collection of articles)]. Moscow, Consortium on issues of applied economic research, 2002, pp. 196 -200.

(1) The wage arrears are absolutely non-voluntary.
(2) There is no documentation or registration of these arrears, leading to many opportunities for manipulation and abuse. There is also an increased probability than an employee may lose the right for total compensation of overdue wages in cases when he/she leaves a job.
(3) The interest-free nature of such "obligations" makes such involuntary "loans" profitable for debtors (regional authorities). During the emergence of the problem of non-payment, the possibility of introducing fines and other extra charges for delayed payment of wages was raised. However, it was unrealistic to introduce such penalties because of the widespread occurrence of such non-payments. For example, in 1997, wage delays occurred in 73 regions of the country; in 1998, this number increased to 83 regions, and by the middle of 2002, it had occurred in 51 regions. Moreover, due to high inflation, there was a reduction in the real value of previously accumulated arrears, so it is necessary to discuss wage arrears in terms of negative interest rates. For example, at the height of the August 1998 crisis, total wage arrears increased nominally by 7.7 percent, while in real terms, they decreased by approximately the same magnitude (i.e. they were absorbed by inflation).
(4) Open-ended repayment schedules for accumulated wage arrears owed by sub-national governments. For example, at the end of 1998, the average period of arrears was approximately 3 months. This period exceeded 4 months in fifteen regions, and in Altai Territory, it was 8 months.
(5) The open-ended nature of wage repayments indirectly illustrates the relative lack of protest by society against such actions. This is due to the fact that the largest portion of overdue arrears is owed to two categories of employees in the public sector: teachers and physicians[7]. It is typical of individuals in these professions to be highly tolerant, and to refuse not to execute their official duties as a form of protest when presented with a great ethical dilemma. Thus, the neglect of their rights on the part of local governments is particularly objectionable.

The accumulation of wage arrears by regional governments passed through several phases that were closely correlated with the division of revenues and expenses between the Federal government and regional governments as well as the macroeconomic stabilisation policy undertaken by national financial authorities. The first phase occurred from 1992/1993 to mid -1995. At the beginning of this period, the delayed payment of government wages became a widespread phenomenon. Employees in the government were affected negatively by two main factors in the country's economic and political development: a sharp fall in economic activity, which entailed an equally sharp reduction of government revenues at all levels of state administration, and confusion about the fiscal powers and responsibilities of the Federal governments, regional government and municipal administrations. Furthermore, some

---

[7] By January 1, 2002 the share of employees in health and education organisations that were owed wage arrears varied across regions: from zero in Ust-Orda Buryat Autonomous Area, Kaluga Region and Kaliningrad Region to 100 percent in Vladimir Region, where all arrears of wages fell on teachers. In six other regions of the Russian Federation, arrears of wages in health and education exceeded 90 percent of total arrears of wages: 97.9 percent in Novosibirsk Region, 96.5 percent in Komi Republic, 96.3 percent in Moscow Region, 93.3 percent in Republic of Karelia, 91.9 percent in Chelyabinsk Region and 91.8 percent in Kamchatka Region. For most Russian regions having wage arrears, the share of arrears in the education and health sphere varied from 60 percent to 90 percent. Arrears were present in 56 regions by the end of 2001 averaging 81.3 percent).

governments and related authorities elected to withhold wage arrears in commercial banks and/or used them for speculative investments on currency markets. This sort of activity was widespread, as double-digit monthly inflation and high interest rates made it profitable to invest somebody else's money in such risky ways. The use of public finances for non-budgetary aims led to serious violations of accounting regulations and repayments of wages and salaries.

The second phase in the progression of the wage arrears problem began near the end of 1995, when there was a change in the state's strategy concerning mechanisms to reduce the government deficit. Progress regarding the repayment of wages resulted from an explicit shift from expansionary monetary policy to increasing internal borrowing and a tight monetary policy. Further, the progressive shifting of expenditure powers between the Federal government and regional governments came to an end, and the doctrine widely recognised internationally became the norm: a budgetary service ought to be financed at the place where it arises, no matter whether it is under the federal, regional or municipal jurisdiction. Thus, the budgets of sub-national governments were increasingly burdened by civil, legal and social budgetary obligations. Often these responsibilities were ignored. It should be noted that at present, the proportion of federal government contributions to sub-national governments' budgets differs across regions, as well as across categories of expenditures. For example, federal payments fund a larger part of public health than education due to the existence of universal medical insurance. However, in general, federal funding is a relatively small part of total expenditures, especially the share intended for the wages of employees of regional governments.

As a result of the tighter monetary policy there was a pronounced increase in non-monetary transactions and barterization both at the sub-federal government and in local government institutions. Barter and non-monetary forms of wage payments were not, however, an option for governments and other related employers. Hence, there was increasing tension regarding wage payments in every level of government in the Russian Federation during the second phase of the non-payment problem. The second phase ended in August 1998. However, the problem of accumulated wage arrears by regional government had taken on crisis proportions long before August 1998.

The increasingly acute nature of the arrears problem became evident during its third phase covering the period August 1998 to mid-1999. At this time the first systematic statistical data appeared regarding government sector wage arrears across regions that had arisen as a consequence of the realignment of budgetary responsibility among different levels of government. During the first and second phases, one could judge the scale of such arrears only through indirect and very rough estimates. The new statistical data showed a continuous increase in wage arrears at the end of 1998. In October, arrears totalled 14 billion roubles; in November, 15.2 billion roubles (an increase of 8.6 percent); and by December equalled 16 billion roubles and two and a half times the monthly allotment for wages and salaries of employees. Action by the Federal government fostered a decrease in these arrears to 13.8 billion roubles by the end of the year, but the total increase of the arrears in 1998 was more than 2.2 times previous levels. The only six regions in which there were no wage arrears were Moscow, Saint Petersburg, Samara Region, the Yamalo-Nenets Autonomous Area, the Taimyr Autonomous Area and the Krasnodar Territory. In comparison, according to reports of the Ministry of Finance of Russian Federation, in 1997 there were only 15 regions that did not have accumulated wage arrears.

The fourth phase in the evolution of wage arrears began in mid-1999. By the end of 2000, only five regional governments were free of wage arrears: the Chuvash Republic, the Krasnodar Territory, the Astrakhan Region, the Orel Region and Moscow. In 2001, only six regional governments completed the financial year without arrears: the Chuvash Republic, Krasnodar Territory, the Nenetz Autonomous Area, the Ivanovo Region, the Smolensk Region and Moscow. Of course, in the post-crisis period the problem became less acute, so the scale of the problem of wage arrears has fallen in Russia.

By December 2001, the absolute size of wages and salaries arrears in regional government's budgets declined by approximately 6 percent in comparison to December 2000. In two main areas of government expenditure, public education and public health, this reduction was approximately 6.3 percent and 4.4 percent, respectively[8]. By the end of 2001, the wage arrears to educators and public health workers were 66.9 percent of the total amount required for payment of their wages. Surprisingly, budgetary arrears for wages and salaries have not dissipated even in the face of economic revival. Furthermore, at the end of 2001 and in early 2002, there was a resurgence in arrears, largely due to the decision by the Federal government to raise the wages and salaries of its employees by the end of 2001. However, sub-national government were unable to clear the accumulated arrears. According to media sources, by the middle of 2002, 51 percent of the Federation's population had arrears in wages and salaries, and in many cases there appeared to be little prospect of any forthcoming payments.

CONCLUSION

The direct and indirect effect of macroeconomic policy has negatively impacted consumer demand in the Russian Federation. Both disposable incomes and expectations have been negatively affected while the traditional cushions against disruptions in demand – savings and access to credit have been severely eroded or have failed to develop. In particular, wage arrears are a major inhibitor of consumer spending. The permanency of the problem of arrears in wages in Russia may be explained by the following circumstances. The general turn around in economic performance in the Rusisan Federation has been accompanied by increasing differentiation in the social and economic development of Russian regions, due in part to differences across industries and, as a result, some regions are not able to fulfil obligations arising from the decisions of Federal authorities. The method used to standardise the level of government services received by the citizens of the Russian Federation is far from perfect. It is impossible to eliminate arrears of wages and salaries of government employees through transfers from the Federal Fund of Financial Support of Regions and other subsidies because sufficient funds are not available. Further, the autonomy of sub-national governments and the absence of a legal method to influence their behaviour towards employees mean that the Government of the Russian Federation does not have the authority to correct the problem. Given the disarray in consumer spending it is difficult for the managers of Russian firms to plan production, particularly over the payback period of

---

[8] It is interesting that in December 2001, unpaid wages and salaries in the education sector in Russia's regions exceeded 7 percent of the annual required expenditure on teachers pay, and in public health it exceeded 4.6 percent for medical workers.

industrial investments. As a result, these investments are inhibited, slowing the process of revitalizing Russian Industry.

REFERENCES

Clark, C. (1957). *The Conditions of Economic Progress*. London: Macmillan.
Duesenberry, J.S. (1949). *Income, Saving and the Theory of Consumer Behavior.* Cambridge MA: Harvard University Press.
Friedman, M. (1957). *A Theory of the Consumption Function*, Princeton: Princeton University Press.
Goldsmith, R.W. (1955). *A Study of Saving in the United States*, Vols. 1 and 2. Princeton: Princeton University Press.
Keynes, J.M. (1936). *The General Theory of Employment, Interest and Money*.Cambridge: Cambridge University Press.
Klein, L.R. and Goldberger, A.S. (1955). *An Econometric Model of the United States, 1929-1952*. Amsterdam: North Holland.
Kuznets, S. (1946). *National Product Since 1869*. New York: National Bureau of Economic Research.
Livingston, S.M. (1945). Forecasting Postwar Demand II. *Econometrica*, 13 (1), 15-24.
Mosak, J.M. (1945). Forecasting Postwar Demand III. *Econometrica*, 13 (1), 25-53.
Osborn, D. and Gaebler, T. (1992). *Reinventing Government: How the Entrepreneurial Spirit Is Transforming the Public Sector*. New York: Addison-Wesley.
Smithies, A. (1945). Forecasting Postwar Demand I. *Econometrica*, 13 (1), 1-24.
Tobin, J. (1951).*Relative Income, Absolute Income and Saving*. New York: Macmillan.
The Russian Economic Barometer, 11 (1) (2002).
Weintraub S. (1958) *An Approach to the Theory of Income Distribution*. Philadelphia: Chilton.

Chapter 14

FROM FARM TO FORK: FOOD SUPPLY CHAINS IN THE RUSSIAN FEDERATION

Jill E. Hobbs and Shari L. Boyd

ABSTRACT

Privatization and the freeing of prices cannot alone lead to a modern market-oriented industry. Nowhere is this more evident than in the Russian food industry. A range of market institutions common in modern market economies were entirely absent in the Russian food system – spot markets, auctions, enforceable contracts, etc. As a result, instead of competitive markets (and prices) evolving, privatization led to monopolization along supply chains. The need for transaction cost reducing institutions all along food supply chains from farms through food processing, wholesaling to retailing is explained. The major remaining constraints are discussed and the prospects for the Russian agri-food sector outlined.

INTRODUCTION

After the fall of the Soviet Union in 1991, the process of privatization began in the Russian food supply chain. In the new Russian Federation not only did former state-controlled farms become privately owned, but downstream food processing and distribution sectors also began to change. During the Soviet period downstream enterprises were organized as state monopolies. Each sector was fundamentally controlled as a sub-division of a branch ministry or another central institution (OECD, 1998). However, this system was plagued with difficulties. The extensive planning system was supposed to match supply with demand in all sectors, but the two were constantly in disequilibrium. In the 1990s during the early stages of transition, problems in the agri-food sector threatened some sectors of Russian society with starvation. The lack of food sources was not attributed to a problem with food production, but to massive failures in the food supply chain. Harvesting, distribution channels and inadequate storage facilities – essentially downstream links in the supply chain – were to blame (Leitzel, 1995).

During the Perestroika (restructuring) period attempts had been made to rectify the system. In 1988 and 1989 the legal status of downstream state enterprises was changed. Management and employees of individual enterprises were allowed to rent the enterprises, which eventually were converted into joint stock companies. This proved to be an important step in the long-run privatization of the downstream agri-food chain.

BUILDING FOOD SUPPLY CHAINS BEGINS WITH PRIVATIZATION

Formally, the Russian privatization program began in mid-1992. General principles of this program were then applied to the agri-food sector – including downstream enterprises. Under the general principles most of these downstream enterprises fell in the mandatory privatization category of the general program guidelines. In the Presidential Decree of December 4th, 1994 it was declared that,

> In order to protect agricultural producers against monopoly power of processing industries and "service suppliers"…downstream enterprises should be privatized through corporatization according to the first option[1] of preferences given to employees and all remaining shares should be sold at closed auctions to agricultural producers (OECD, 1998, p.95).

This decree led to substantial changes in downstream agri-food operation in Russia. The Russian government was stepping away from the command system and encouraging employees to buy shares in companies. However, as will be discussed the rate at which each sector of the supply chain became privatized was not uniform, which led to further complications.

MARKETING CHANNELS IN THE RUSSIAN AGRI-FOOD SECTOR

With the privatization of the agri-food system, marketing channels are gradually emerging and it is the success of these channels that will complete the transition from a command economy to a free market economy. Marketing channels perform a number of roles within a successful supply chain. They facilitate the price-seeking mechanism of a market economy whereby the forces of demand and supply yield an equilibrium price. Marketing channels also aid in bringing potential buyers and sellers together and through the exchange of products provide information on consumers' requirements in the form of price signals (Hobbs et al, 1997).

While freely operating marketing channels are crucial to the success of a market economy, they were not present in centrally planned economies. Marketing channels were not necessary because there were no markets. While products did move from producers through to consumers this was not in response to price signals within a marketing channel, but the

---

[1] Option 1 of the three options of employee preferences in the Russian privatization program states, employees (workers and managers) were given 25 percent of non-voting shares free of any charge. In addition, workers were entitled to buy for cash or vouchers another 10 percent of voting shares at closed subscription. These shares were to be sold to them at a 30 percent discount of the January 1992 book value and could be paid in installments over three years. Moreover, up to 5 percent of voting shares could be sold to management at nominal prices.

result of decisions made by central planners. This system could be viewed as a completely internal vertically integrated system because each component was required to pass its output to the next designated link in the chain. Since the entire chain was mapped out, marketing was not an important aspect of the supply chain.

Freely operating marketing channels only became necessary once privatization began. Previously, producers, processors, distributors or retailers did not have to think strategically about marketing channels. In modern market economies marketing channels evolved over a long period of time and in the process have developed and adapted to each industry. The sudden privatization of the Russian agri-food industry did not allow for a gradual progression of new marketing channels. As a result, those that emerged tended to be fragmented, poorly organized and inefficient.

Appropriate infrastructure for working marketing channels to emerge has been slow to develop. A lack of institutions such as commodity exchanges, wholesale markets and auctions has impaired the transition to a functioning market economy whereby clear market signals are apparent.

> The agro-food market in Russia still lacks both horizontal and vertical coherence, and an effective private marketing system has yet to emerge (Arnold et al, 2001).

If the Russian agri-food industry is to continue to develop into a modern market-oriented sector, marketing channels must be efficient and competitive. An absence of effective marketing channels will result in market prices that are not truly representative. There are a number of ways of organizing transactions at the producer-processor interface. These include auctions, dealers/agents, direct sales to processors and forms of joint marketing. Alternatively, farmers markets bring producers of agricultural output into direct contact with consumers. Each of these has its respective advantages and disadvantages, resulting in different levels of transaction costs depending on the presence of facilitating institutions in the Russian economy.

Before discussing the economic merits of different marketing channels for agricultural produce in the Russian Federation, it is useful to consider the concepts of operational efficiency and pricing efficiency. *Operational efficiency* refers to the efficiency with which products move physically through the supply chain from farmers to consumers. In essence, it is a measure of the value of output as a proportion of the cost of inputs. A change in technology that increases the quantity of goods moved through a supply chain or that increases the speed with which perishable products move through the chain, for a less than proportionate increase in resource use, would represent an increase in operational efficiency (Hobbs et al., 1997.

Pricing efficiency refers to the accuracy with which price signals are transmitted from consumer to producers though market prices that reflect the true value of products to the end user. Improvements in the extent to which prices accurately reflect the value to consumers of a good enable a more efficient allocation of resources (Hobbs et al., 1997).

Marketing channels span a spectrum of vertical coordination possibilities. At one end of this spectrum lies spot markets in which transactions occur in the current time period between multiple buyers and sellers. Price signals coordinate the movement of products through the channel and the allocation of resources. Vertical integration lies at the other end of the spectrum, wherein one firm integrates forwards (backwards) into downstream (upstream) processing/marketing (supply) functions. Products move along the supply chain as a result of within-firm managerial decisions. In between spot markets and vertical integration lie a myriad of alternative coordinating relationships, including contracts, strategic alliances and joint ventures. Transaction Cost Economics posits that the vertical coordination mechanism that emerges will be the one that minimizes the sum of production and transaction costs (Williamson, 1979).

Farmers' Markets

Farmers' markets provide a central location to which a number of farmers bring their produce to sell directly to consumers. As a marketing institution, they are relatively simple and, in a sense, epitomize the spot market transaction, with (usually) large numbers of buyers and sellers conducting single period transactions. Small-scale private farmers often find farmers' markets a useful outlet for produce, particularly in the early stages of industry development given the small quantities of products they have for sale. In general, however, they are not a suitable marketing channel for large former state or collective farms due to the much larger volumes of output. After privatization, land ownership in Russia remained mainly large-scale enterprises. While old state-farms were liquidated and broken up into smaller production units[2], these still tended to be relatively large-scale. Highly perishable products (e.g. fresh milk) or products requiring further processing are not suited to sale through farmers' markets due to problems of time and physical asset specificity.

Although useful in the early stages of industry development, farmers' markets have tended to become less important as an economy matures and as the infrastructure and institutions that facilitate more sustainable long-term supply chain relationships evolve. Farmers' markets exhibit low levels of operational efficiency; they are time consuming and relatively inefficient at smoothing out fluctuations in supply and demand over time and space. A supply glut in one region due to an exceptionally good harvest will result in lower prices at the local farmers market as supply outstrips demand. There is usually no means by which product can be easily shipped to another region where a supply shortage may exist due to unfavourable harvest conditions (Hobbs et al., 1997).

The direct contact between producers and consumers at a farmers' market enhances pricing efficiency in as much as a farmer will quickly realize whether a product is selling well or not selling at all, and adjust prices (and presumably production decisions) accordingly. On the other hand, the price discovery process is highly duplicative, with numerous bilateral negotiations between sellers and buyers (Hobbs et al., 1997). Consumers incur sorting costs in determining the quality of products. The use of grades as quality signals is not common in farmers' markets so that duplicative sorting activity by buyers occurs as numerous consumers sort each product. Farmers' markets have become obsolete in modern market economies as a mainstream method of food distribution, although remaining a peripheral marketing channel in some urban areas for the sale of 'specialty' agricultural produce or where there may be utility benefits to some consumers from purchasing products directly from farmers.

---

[2] A variety of ownership structures were created, including owner-operated family farms, agricultural cooperatives and joint stock companies.

Auction Markets

Auction markets are another form of spot market but one in which the seller is relatively passive, and without the *tâtonnement* or recontracting process of bilateral price negotiations between buyer and seller that occurs in a farmers' market. Buyers bid on a visual assessment (or in the case of electronic auctions, a written description) of a product and the rule of *caveat emptor* (buyer beware) applies. For auctions to function efficiently as a transaction mechanism, the characteristics of the product of importance to buyers must be ascertained easily through a visual inspection. An adequate number of buyers are essential to avoid a thin market problem. If markets are thin, prices are not determined competitively and the possibility exists for collusion among buyers. If these two conditions exist, auctions can be an efficient price-discovery and market clearing mechanism. Auction prices are usually public information and represent an important source of market price information to assist price discovery in parallel direct sales relationships between producers and processors. Thus, auctions can reduce price information costs for farmers and processors even if they do not use the auction market directly (Hobbs, 1997).

The auctioneer, or auction company, is a private entrepreneur who earns a commission from the seller on the auctioned items (usually a percentage of the value). As such, the incentive is for the auctioneer to ensure a sufficient number of buyers attend a sale to obtain a higher price for the commodity. The auction company acts as the intermediary between buyer and seller, helping ensure that the seller receives payment. The farmer usually receives payment from the auction company for the auctioned commodities (less commission) immediately following the sale. The auctioneer then collects payment from the buyer. In this way, auction companies can be an important industry development mechanism in fledgling industries when processors are prone to defaulting on payments and farmers face high transaction costs in evaluating the reliability and financial stability of a potential buyer.

The flip-side of this is that auction companies must shoulder much greater risks in a transition economy than in more developed market economies where there is less uncertainty. Higher risk will result in higher commissions to reflect the larger risk premium that sellers must pay for protection against buyers defaulting on payment. Strengthening bankruptcy laws to protect creditors is an important institutional development in ensuring the effective operation of auction markets. An auction system also needs to be backed by an effective and enforceable commercial legal system that confers upon buyers a legal obligation to pay for commodities purchased at the auction.

Auctions involve additional transportation and handling of agricultural produce, which must be shipped to the central auction location by sellers, then transported to the buyer's place of business[3]. In this sense, they are not as operationally efficient as other (direct) marketing channels. Although auctions are a transparent and – provided there are a sufficient number of buyers – competitive method of price discovery, they may impede the efficiency with which price signals are transmitted from consumers to producers. As quality must be determined on the basis of a visual inspection, the price cannot reflect other quality dimensions that can only be determined during the early stages of processing. For example,

---

[3] The is not the case for electronic auctions, which usually involve buyers bidding on the basis of a written description (or video) of the animal or product and shipment direct from the farm to the buyer after the completion of the auction.

carcass quality in livestock is difficult to determine in a live-ring auction prior to slaughter; the baking qualities of wheat are difficult to determine on the basis of a visual inspection of the kernel. The methods used to produce the animal, or the wheat, may affect final processing quality but are not be disclosed by the auction process. In these situations, the auction does not exhibit strong pricing efficiency. Partly for these reasons, auctions have diminished in importance at the farmer-processor interface in the livestock industries of many market economies such as the US, Canada and the UK.

Despite these limitations, auctions still play a critical role in other agricultural sectors, for example, in the fresh flower markets of the Netherlands and in many early morning fresh fish markets. The speed of the auction process and its market-clearing function is critical for highly perishable products that cannot be stored and offered for sale at a later date[4]. Creating the institutional environment necessary for the operation and maintenance of viable auction markets would be a valuable industry development initiative for the Russian agri-food sector.

Direct Sales through the Spot Market

Direct sales between farmers and processors can occur through the spot market or through a longer-term contractual relationship. When selling on the spot market, both buyers and sellers incur transaction costs in locating suitable trading partners and in discovering prices. If the institutional mechanism of an auction market is not available to assist in transparent price discovery, prices are determined solely as a result of bilateral one-on-one bargaining. Final price determination may be on the basis of some objective measurement of product quality, such as deadweight carcass grades or grain quality grades. Direct spot market sales can leave one party to the transaction at a bargaining disadvantage if the other party has significant market power or if an asset specific investment has been made. Thus, the competitiveness of the agricultural production and processing sectors influence whether direct spot market sales are an efficient, sustainable transaction medium.

Producers of perishable agricultural products tend to be in a vulnerable bargaining position due to the time specificity of their produce. The ability to store products and choose the timing of marketing strategically is an important feature of many North American grain markets and provides grain producers with more flexibility vis-à-vis marketing than their dairy counterparts.

Where auction markets exist in parallel to direct spot market sales as an alternative vertical coordination mechanism, buyers and sellers may use the published auction prices as a basis for price determination. In other cases, industry associations have collated and published price information to assist in transparent price discovery for their members[5]. Mandatory price

---

[4] The Dutch auction method is used for fresh flowers. The auctioneers' clock counts down the time remaining in a sale, with the first buyer to bid being awarded the sale. Thus, lots are auctioned extremely quickly. Cattle tend to be sold using the English auction method, where the auctioneer calls out a starting price and drops the price until the first bid is received. Bids then rise until no more bids are forthcoming, and the sale is awarded to the last bidder at the last price bid. Sellers can specify a reserve price below which the commodity will not be sold. The English auction provides more information to buyers with respect to the prices that other buyers are willing to bid for a commodity, although not the upper limit on a buyer's willingness to pay (Hobbs et al, 1997).

[5] For example, CANFAX in Canada collects deadweight slaughter cattle price information from producers and disseminates the information to member ranches. The Meat and Livestock Commission in the UK (a quasi-

reporting to a central regulatory authority may enhance the transparency of the price discovery process, however, care must be taken to protect the commercial confidentiality of the information on an individual enterprise level. Recent moves to introduce mandatory price reporting in US cattle markets have been extremely controversial.

Contracts

Moving along the vertical coordination spectrum, contracts represent more formal, longer-term supply relationships. Contracts in the agri-food sector tend to be of varying degrees of complexity, with different obligations on each party. The simplest contracts are market-specification contracts in which the buyer agrees to provide a market for the seller's product. Price, or the method of determining price, may be specified in advance. Control over the production process and the risks associated with this process remain with the seller, whereas the buyer takes on the responsibility and risk of finding a market for the product.

Production management contracts give more control to the buyer over elements of the production process, such as input usage and sometimes the right to inspect production practices. Again, the buyer agrees to purchase (and find a market for) the final product. Resource-providing contracts are the closest contractual form to full vertical integration. The buyer supplies key inputs (e.g. in the case of livestock this may include the young animals, feed, medicinal supplies), supervises production and provides a market for the output. The buyer assumes all of the production risk, with the supplier often paid on the basis of volume of output per unit of input, or some other measure of operator efficiency (Mighell and Jones, 1963).

Similar problems of price discovery attend market specification and production management contracts as is the case with direct sales via a spot market, although the method of price determination may be specified clearly in a contract[6]. Operational efficiency is likely to be higher than under an auction, given the removal of the additional product handling and transportation step. There is potential for improved pricing efficiency if prices can be linked to an objectively determined and credible measure of product quality.

The challenge lies in designing complete (fully contingent) contracts in the environment of uncertainty that permeates business transactions in the Russian Federation, and given relatively weak legal institutions for the enforcement of contracts. As a result, high transaction (monitoring and enforcement) costs may lead to under-investments in production or processing capacity. Producers (or processors) will be reluctant to make the asset-specific investments necessary to expand production to meet the needs of a contractual party if there is a risk that the other party could opportunistically renege on that contractual agreement.

A study of the fruit and vegetable sector in the Russian Federation reveals the general distrust of contracts that is an inevitable consequence of an economic environment characterized by uncertainty and weak institutional enforcement:

---

governmental organization) collects price information from processors and publishes average price information by carcass grade for cattle, hogs and sheep.

[6] For resource-providing contracts the method of determining the return to the contractee, rather than price discovery per se, is the relevant issue.

> There is no trust of contracts, which are largely unenforceable ... State farms and newly privatized farms are uncertain what to plant because they feel vulnerable without guaranteed outlets. They do not trust the vegetable bases to honour contracts and the feeling is mutual (Jones, 1993, p.22).

The unenforceability of contracts remains a major impediment to closer vertical coordination along agri-food supply chains and deters investment at all levels of the sector. Without ongoing investment in updated production and processing facilities, improvements in food quality and food safety are not attainable and the Russian agri-food sector will become increasingly uncompetitive relative to imports.

Collective Bargaining and Cooperative Marketing

The emerging private farm sector must grapple with downstream market power in the form of monopsonistic of oligopsonistic buyers – particularly where privatization of existing food processing facilities has created regional monopsonies. Market power in the first-stage agricultural processing sector has long been a contentious issue in many western market economies. Joint marketing of individual farmers' produce has been a key feature of some sectors, with the right to market collectively enshrined in (or sometimes mandated by) legislation[7].

The role of group marketing as a countervailing bargaining strategy deserves closer attention. Lang (1980) showed how the introduction of collective bargaining in US crop and horticulture sectors was able to shift the risk of product quality deterioration from farmers to processors who were more easily able to control quality. The result was an improvement in product quality due to a reduction in organisational slack and X-inefficiencies. Appropriately aligning incentives with the abilities of a party to reduce joint risks by making them the residual claimant to a transaction leads to a net gain in economic welfare. An effective commercial legal system is necessary for the enforcement and long-term viability of collective bargaining agreements in the agricultural sector.

Farmers may also form voluntary agricultural marketing cooperatives with the objective of securing a long-term market and obtaining a higher price for their products. Traditional cooperatives with an open membership and a one-member, one-vote principle are vulnerable to the free-rider problem; any increase in average industry prices benefits both members and non-members, reducing the individual incentive to join. Conflicting member objectives with respect to decisions over long-term reinvestment in cooperative assets versus short-term return to members have also been problems (Cook, 1995). More recently so-called "New Generation Cooperatives", characterized by restricted membership and more focused goals, have emerged in the agricultural sectors of modern market economies. The development of

---

[7] The creation of supply management marketing boards in Canada is one example. Compulsory marketing of all produce through producer-controlled marketing boards provides countervailing bargaining power, however the marketing boards have also been the subject of much criticism due to the market-distortions they create that are welfare-reducing in aggregate. In the UK, marketing boards (without supply management powers but through which all milk had to be marketed) were at one time key mechanisms for enhancing the countervailing bargaining power of dairy farmers. Voluntary farmer marketing cooperatives have subsequently replaced these marketing boards. The Capper-Volsted Act in the US is another example; the Act provides an explicit exemption from anti-trust legislation to cooperative marketing arrangements among farmers.

agricultural marketing cooperatives in the Russian Federation is probably hampered by negative connotations associated with compulsory collective activities in the command economy era. Education will be an important tool in promoting an understanding of the voluntary cooperative model, its advantages and its pitfalls as a means of organizing marketing transactions. Allowing horizontal cooperation among agricultural producers may also require a specific exemption from anti-trust regulations.

THE FOOD PROCESSING AND DISTRIBUTION SECTOR

During the rapid dismantling of the command economy institution in the Russian food industry some sectors were not prepared for the change and did not adapt well. The food processing and distribution sector had little experience with the methods and organization of production under free market conditions (Arnold et al., 2001). Processing plants lacked adequate equipment and distribution channels were unorganized and inefficient. The processing and distribution links of the supply chain became fragmented and unstable. Small-scale middle-men were constantly entering and eventually leaving the market, which led to further instability. Many processing facilities had previously been part of vertically integrated farm production-food processing units. Privatization and restructuring changed this relationship, thus processors no longer had the guarantee of an 'in-house' supply. They became disorganized but remained relatively large compared to the rest of the supply chain, wielding considerable market power vis-à-vis the private farm sector.

Food Processing

The free market system posed a number of adjustment problems for the Russian food processing sector. In the command economy food processing enterprises did not have to operate in competitive markets; there was no incentive to produce high quality food. Prices were administratively determined rather than determined competitively. Equipment and technology became outdated in the absence of competitive pressure and without the need for product differentiation. Processing plants continually churned out low quality, high priced, homogeneous products. Typically, production units were large scale and regionally based. While this offered the potential for economies of scale benefits, generally technology was obsolete and the plants tended to be highly labour-intensive relative to modern food processing plants.

When the Russian food industry began the transition to an open market economy, processors were faced with competition – both domestically from other regions and from imports. In general the imports were of higher quality and were cheaper than domestic products. Domestic processors, no longer cushioned by the command economy system, initially were not able to compete:

> On the whole, the privatization of food processing plants has not been beneficial; privatized enterprises have failed to modernize or attract financing for the development of their production (Arnold et al., 2001, p.105).

While inefficient processors with outdated technology struggled to compete, Russian consumers benefited from the access to higher quality food, lower prices and additional variety provided by imported food.

When privatization began, the food industry had the largest number of industrial enterprises, but the smallest number of employees per enterprise, compared to other industries. As seen in Table 14-1, by 1997, 92 percent of the Russian food processing industry had been privatized.

Table 14.1. Privatization in the Russian Food Processing Industry

	Privatized firms (%)	Firms with government part ownership in the total number of privatized firms (%)	Privatized firms in which the controlling package of shares belongs to agricultural producers (%)
Processing, total Including:	92	18	14
Meat	92	16	9
Dairy	92	18	16
Flour	90	35	14
Flax	83	32	11

Source: Granville and Oppenheimer, 2001.

These newly privatized enterprises produced 93 percent of food products and employed 91 percent of the labour force in the food industry (OECD, 1998). In just four years food processing evolved from complete state ownership to 92 percent of processors being privately owned. As in other sectors of the economy, however, many enterprises became only semi-privatized. The government retained an ownership share in almost 20 percent of food processing enterprises in total and over a third of enterprises in some food sectors. Typically, these newly privatized food processing enterprises tend to be large-scale and wield considerable (regional) monopoly power vis-à-vis agricultural producers (OECD, 1998).

In addition to the initial privatization process that began in 1992, the Ministry of Agriculture and Food enacted "second stage privatization". This second stream proposed that small-scale dairy plants, grain storage elevators and some small scale processing enterprises situated in remote areas issue shares to farmers so they become majority shareholders. This second stage privatization resulted in the creation of more new food processing plants in Russia. Table 14-1 shows that agricultural producers held controlling shares in 14 percent of food processing establishments in 1997. In many cases, these food processing enterprises are the result of the break-up of former state-farms that were vertically integrated forwards into processing, and have been privatized, with ownership shares distributed among former managers and workers of the enterprise.

Growth in the Russian food processing and distribution sector is dependent on a number of factors, including investment in new technology, access to credit, the quality of inputs, and the development of a reliable cold chain distribution system. Updating food processing technology is a priority. Technological advances reduce average (and marginal) costs of production, allowing processors to be more price competitive in output markets. Hygiene improvements and advances in packaging technology increase the shelf-life of food products, allowing processors to reach a larger market and reducing the time-specificity of their products, thereby leaving them less vulnerable to opportunistic behaviour on the part of downstream distributors or retailers. Whether it is cheaper to invest in new plants with new technology, or retrofit existing plants probably needs to be considered on a case-by-case basis. Although it is likely to be cheaper to modernize a plant in the short-run, in the long-run the plant may be less competitive relative to a newly constructed plant purpose-built to accommodate the latest food processing techniques.

A major constraint to re-investment in the food processing sector is access to credit. Typically, shareholder investments are an important source of internal credit in modern market economies. Weak and poorly enforced rules of corporate governance and questionable accounting and auditing practices plague shareholder-manager relationships in the Russian Federation and deter investment. Given these problems, access to external sources of credit, for example, through loans from the commercial banking system becomes even more important. The maintenance and further development of a competitive commercial banking system is a critical institutional development in this regard, as is strengthening bankruptcy laws to ensure adequate protection of creditors.

Direct investment by foreign food processing firms is an alternative source of financing, as well as a means of importing new technological know-how. Foreign direct investment may take the form of wholly-owned subsidiaries, franchise operations or joint ventures with Russian food processors. Investment joint ventures involve a commitment of investment funds by both parties, with the division of profits dependent on the level of respective risk assumed. Macro-economic instability, under-developed legal and financial institutions and fluctuating rules have been obstacles to foreign investment in the Russian Federation (Hobbs et al., 1997).

Marketing and technical joint ventures involve less risk for the foreign partner, and provide the Russian firm with access to the technological know-how and/or marketing expertise of the foreign joint venture partner. These types of joint ventures can be an effective way for Russian food processing firms to upgrade their human capital skills and their technological capacity. The foreign firm benefits from the local knowledge (and perhaps, political influence) of the Russian partner.

For both parties, a joint venture arrangement carries with it the risk of creating a future competitor. The marriage of two different managerial styles from vastly different corporate cultures and economic environments is probably the biggest challenge to establishing and maintaining a successful joint venture partnership between a Russian and a foreign food processing firm. A common source of joint venture failure is disagreement over the division of risk and profits. Policies that stabilize the macro-economy and strengthen the institutional environment, enhancing the transparency of business transactions, will be important in reducing the potential for this type of conflict between joint venture partners, thereby facilitating investment in the food processing sector.

Access to a reliable supply of high quality inputs on a timely and consistent basis is a challenge for the food processing sector. If the supply of raw materials is patchy – available in abundance in some weeks and not available others – processing plants are alternately operating at excess capacity, or unable to process perishable agricultural products on a timely basis. Cost efficiencies decline, as does product quality. Thus, finding a reliable supply of inputs, where scheduling of supply can be agreed in advance, is important. This has implications for the efficacy of different supply chain relationships with agricultural producers as discussed earlier (auctions, contracts, etc.).

Finding a consistent quality input supply is also important. If quality varies, processors are faced with additional sorting at the processing plant and their ability to deliver an end-product of a consistent quality is diminished. Grading or classification schemes reduce buyer measurement costs and provide the incentive (through price premiums linked to specific grades) for consistent quality inputs. The establishment of nationally-recognized grading schemes for agricultural produce is one piece of the institutional jigsaw puzzle in building a competitive food processing sector. The government or a credible independent industry association could play a role in establishing and ensuring the integrity of agricultural commodity grading schemes. Grades must accurately measure the quality characteristics of importance to the market and be trusted by both buyer and seller as a credible and objective measure of quality. Linking price signals directly to product quality strengthens pricing efficiency.

Food Wholesaling

The food wholesaling industry in Russia underwent an extensive reorganization after the fall of the Soviet Union. Wholesaling was an important step in the vertically integrated supply chain of the command economy. In this system about 70 percent of food products were channeled through state-operated wholesaling agencies. The remainder was distributed through co-operatives and *kolkhoz* markets, 25 percent and 5 percent, respectively. The state-operated wholesalers and co-operatives were strictly regulated. The *kolkhoz* markets were less regulated and were supplied by household plots. These markets were small and controlled their own prices, unlike the state-operated agencies in which the central planner set the prices. When privatization began, the role of wholesalers in Russia changed from being command economy functionaries to being agents of their shareholders. They now perform activities typical of a western wholesaling operation, including supplying inputs, searching for markets, connecting buyers with sellers and even carrying out research and development activities.

Inadequate cold-chain distribution infrastructure remains a challenge in the wholesaling sector. It is a challenge that needs to be addressed to facilitate growth and further investment in food processing. Poor cold chain facilities result in product wastage and increase average costs of production. Product development is constrained to food formats that are not temperature sensitive, for example, canned and smoked meats and fish. Cold chain improvements enable food to be shipped over a wider geographic area, thereby weakening regional monopolies and providing consumers with access to a wider variety of food products from competing manufacturers.

Food Retailing

Food retailing is the final stage in the supply chain from primary agricultural producers to consumers. Retailing serves two functions; first, it provides an outlet where consumers can purchase products. Second, retail outlets are the point at which the agri-food supply chain interacts with the final consumer. The retailer is the collection agency for information from consumers, which can then be transmitted further upstream in the supply chain. Under the command system, retailers did not have a role in providing information to other linked segments of the agri-food industry. Since all decisions regarding what to produce and in what volumes, were made by central planners, retailers were not needed to facilitate the flow of information. In fact, there was little or no communication from the consumer back up the food chain.

The food retail sector did not enjoy a smooth transition from a centrally planned system to a competitive market environment. In large part, this was due to a monopolistic food processing and distribution sector both prior to and immediately following privatization. While the privatization of the food processing sector did not begin until 1992, many retail outlets across Russia were liberalized before that time. Furthermore, privatization of existing large-scale processing enterprises created regional monopolies. Food retailers were at a severe bargaining disadvantage in the food supply chain. Many retailers were unable to compete and were driven from the market (Gardner and Brooks, 1993).

Relative to agricultural production or food processing, food retailing requires relatively little capital investment, and as such is likely to attract entry by small-scale entrepreneurs. While a sector characterized by a large number of small firms will be relatively competitive, it may also be undercapitalized and at a bargaining disadvantage vis-à-vis larger (perhaps monopolistic) processors. In this situation, retailers will have little ability to ensure supplies of consistent quality and quantity. The existence of (initial) economic profits and ease of entry may lead to an influx of entrants and a situation of destructive competition. There are too many firms, few are profitable and further investment is deterred (Schumpeter, 1950). These conditions appear to have been present in the Russian food retailing sector during the first years of transition.

Privatization of food retailing occurred through two processes. New retail outlets were established and state-owned co-operative shops, restaurants and vendors were liberalized. For the most part the state-owned outlets were taken over by their employees, however, most lacked the human capital skills necessary to manage a retail outlet during the turbulent times and uncertain environment of transition. As a result, retail outlets frequently failed and were subsequently purchased by other individuals or bought by existing retail chains. As this process of economic natural selection continued and some macro-economic stability returned to the Russian economy, food retailing (particularly food service) gradually became more profitable and attractive for foreign investors. Many international fast food chains have since invested in food service outlets in the Russian Federation including, McDonalds, Kentucky Fried Chicken and Pizza Hut (OECD, 1998). As the process of old, state-owned outlets being converted to new retail stores continued the food retailing industry within Russia became a more influential link in the food chain.

Access to credit, training in basic business management skills and customer service, and the enactment and enforcement of competition regulations to deter anti-competitive behaviour by monopolistic (oligopolistic) food processors will be important in ensuring the long-term sustainability of the retailing sector and in creating the necessary stability for further investment. During the early stages of transition, when the food distribution system was fragmented and disorganized, horizontal buying alliances emerged. Groups of retailers joined together to buy directly from processors, circumventing the state wholesalers. Economies of scale advantages from buying in bulk and the establishment of their own distribution and wholesaling facilities to counteract the bargaining power of suppliers were also motivations

(Hobbs et al., 1997). Horizontal retailer buying alliances are likely to continue to play a role in the Russian food distribution system given the bargaining power and economies of scale advantages they confer. Indeed, they are prevalent in modern market economies, such as the SPAR group of food retailers in Europe that operates under a common logo (Hobbs et al., 1997).

The reform of food retailing has vastly improved the shopping experience for consumers. In the command system shopping was not a pleasant experience. Retail outlets were stark, and uninviting. Customers were separated from the products by store clerks who selected the goods, thus, consumers could not perform their own quality checks. Quality was highly variable and supply was inconsistent (Hobbs et al., 1997).

Effective consumer protection regulations are an important role of government policy. Regulations that prevent false or misleading labelling regarding the content of food products are necessary in the presence of information asymmetry. Credence attributes, which cannot be detected even after consumption, create an asymmetry of information between the food supplier and the buyer (consumer). Market failure occurs when the supplier of a low quality product does not have an incentive to reveal the true quality of a credence good to the buyer. The 'lemons' problem assures that only low quality goods are offered for sale. Food safety, nutrition content, genetically modified foods and other 'process' attributes are all examples of credence attributes that create an information asymmetry between buyer and seller. If consumers lack confidence in domestically produced food, demand will be lower, reducing market prices and reducing the expected profitability of further investments in the food sector. Labelling regulations, food safety and product standards regulations all have a place in maintaining consumer confidence and in redressing the information asymmetry problem. Mandatory labelling requirements and other industry standards impose a cost on businesses, therefore, an assessment of the relative costs and benefits of policy interventions should be a pre-requisite for actions to correct market failure.

CONCLUSION

The Russian agri-food chain has progressed significantly from the command economy system that once characterized the Soviet Union. Although the transformation has moved the Russia Federation into the category of a free market economy, and the speed at which it has done so is impressive, it is by no means complete. The agri-food sector, particularly food processing, is still dominated by large-scale enterprises with market power and often with regional monopolies.

If liberalization is to continue it is important that marketing channels are developed that result in price signals being clearly transmitted back to agricultural producers. Presently, Russia lacks the infrastructure needed to create efficient, competitive marketing channels. Under-investment in the institutions needed to facilitate transactions has led to incomplete marketing channels. The development of commodity exchanges, auction markets and wholesaling markets and the provision of publicly available price information from these institutions would enhance price discovery. At the same time, tightening of the commercial legal system to enhance the enforceability of contracts would assist in building direct supply chain relationships through contracts as an alternative to short-term spot market transactions.

If the Russian agri-food sector is to expand and become a profitable industry the downstream sectors must adapt to the new economic environment. Competition from higher quality (and in some cases, lower priced) imported products has proved a major challenge to the Russian food sector but has provided much-needed competitive pressure. To compete, the Russian food sector needs to adopt a consumer-driven mentality, rather than the production-driven approach of the past. Consumers in general are demanding high quality goods, product variety, better service and reasonable prices. For domestic companies to succeed they must provide these qualities or they will lose markets to imported products. In this sense, the Russian food sector is no different from that in other modern market economies, grappling with a dynamic consumer market and the need to deliver a variety of high quality products at competitive prices.

Finally, while the privatization and liberalization of the Russian food supply chain has resulted in many challenges, a number of the problems of the past have long since disappeared – to the benefit of consumers. Food shortages and the long queues of consumers snaking out of food stores as they waited to pick up meat, bread or other staples – the classic visual manifestation of life in the command economy system – are gone. Price has replaced food queues as the rationing mechanism through which resources are allocated.

> Like the rest of the world, Russia manages to get goods to the market (Nelson and Kuzes, 1994, p.40).

Many of the challenges facing the Russian agri-food sector are symptomatic of wider problems in the economy. Access to credit, an effective commercial legal system, obsolete technology, lack of business management and other human capital skills, weak rules of corporate governance and distortions created by monopolistic/monopsonistic market power are issues that also affect other sectors. Tackling these challenges through strengthening the institutions that facilitate commercial transactions and encourage investment is an ongoing responsibility of government. Growth in the agri-food sector will also be dependent on the development of sustainable marketing channels for agricultural produce. Attracting foreign direct investment to the food processing sector may also provide a means by which the Russian food sector can leap-frog ahead technologically, as well as providing a much-needed injection of financial capital. Finally, establishing an appropriate institutional environment to govern food quality, food safety and labelling will be important in facilitating accurate quality signals, protecting consumers and ensuring the integrity of the domestic food supply chain.

REFERENCES

Arnold, S., Chadraba, P. and Springer, R. (2001). *Marketing Strategies for Central and Eastern Europe*. Ashgate: Burlington.

Cook, M. (1995). The Future of U.S. Agricultural Co-operatives: A Neo-Institutional Approach. *American Journal of Agricultural Economics*, 77 (5), 1153-1159.

Gardner, B. and Brooks, K.M. (1993). *How Retail Food Markets Responded to Price Liberalization in Russia After January 1992*. Agriculture and Rural Development Department, Washington DC: World Bank. http://www-wds.worldbank.org/servlet/

WDSContentServer/WDSP/IB/1993/05/01/000009265_3961004175126/Rendered/PDF/multi_page.pdf

Granville, B. and Oppenheimer, P. (2001). *Russia's Post-Communist Economy*. Oxford: Oxford University Press.

Hobbs, J.E. (1997). Measuring the Importance of Transaction Costs in Cattle Marketing. *American Journal of Agricultural Economics*, 79 (4),1083-1095.

Hobbs, J.E., Kerr, W.A. and Gaisford, J.D. (1997). *The Transformation of the Agrifood System in Central and Eastern Europe and the New Independent States*. Wallingford: CAB International.

Jones, S. (1993). The Future for Fruit and Vegetable Distribution in Russia. *British Food Journal*, 95 (7), 21-23.

Lang, M.G. (1980). Marketing Alternatives and Resource Allocation: Case Studies of Collective Bargaining. *American Journal of Agricultural Economics*, 62 (4),760-765.

Leitzel, J. (1995). *Russian Economic Reform*. New York: Routledge.

Mighell, R.L. and Jones, L.A. (1963). *Vertical Coordination in Agriculture*. USDA ERS-19, Washington DC: United States Department of Agriculture.

Nelson, L.D. and Kuzes, I.Y. (1994). *Property to the People: The Struggle for Radical Economics Reform in Russia*. New York: M.E. Sharpe.

OECD (1998). *Review of Agricultural Policies: Russian Federation*. Centre for Co-operation with Non-Members, Paris: Organisation for Economic Cooperation and Development.

Schumpeter, J.A. (1950). *Capitalism, Socialism and Democracy*. New York: Harper and Brothers.

Williamson, O.E. (1979). Transaction Cost Economics: the Governance of Contractual Relations. *Journal of Law and Economics*, 22, 233-262.

Chapter 15

THE ROAD AHEAD FOR INDUSTRY IN THE RUSSIAN FEDERATION

William A. Kerr and Jill E. Hobbs

ABSTRACT

The Russian industrial sector has not completed the transition process to being a modern market-oriented sector – and it is not clear when or if that objective can be accomplished. The required institutions are not yet in place and some of those that inhibit progress such as corruption appear well entrenched. Openness to both ideas and competition appear to be key to successfully concluding the process of transition.

INTRODUCTION

The economic performance of the Russian industrial sector in the period of transition has been disappointing. Productivity remains low and under-investment is chronic. In market economies, market failures are legitimate topics for discussion. In Russia, it is not clear whether many markets have actually developed; if this is true, can one discuss market failure? The failure in Russia over the last fifteen years has been the poor development of institutions to support markets. The government has been unable or unwilling to take seriously questions pertaining to property rights, enforcement of commercial law and restraint of corruption. As a result, it is possible to question whether transition will end with Russia being a modern market economy. The alternative is likely to be some form of licensing economy where transactions costs are high and economic benefits will accrue to the few while the general population will not be able to escape poverty. If this comes to pass then the changes set in motion with the end of central planning and resource allocation by command will have largely been for naught.

THE ROAD AHEAD

While it is unlikely that central planning will ever be re-instituted, there may be a temptation for the government to intervene to allocate resources directly because markets have not developed sufficiently to undertake that role effectively. This is not intervention to correct market failure, as is common in modern market economies, but rather to correct for an absence of markets. It should be noted that this type of intervention is not the same as those associated with discussions pertaining to the degree to which governments should be responsible for investment in the economy. Economists and policy makers in modern market economies also argue over the extent of government's responsibility for investment activity. Direct intervention in the allocation of resources through government ministries or through nationalized firms as in the Russian energy industry may lead to significant misallocation and, as well, prevent markets from developing. Direct intervention is, however, simple to understand and can be easily portrayed/construed as evidence of political decisiveness and economic competency.

Building market institutions on the other hand is a long-term process that garners little political capital and seldom fires the imagination of policy makers. It requires a steady hand and a willingness to stay the course when mileposts cannot be easily discerned. Still, after more than fifteen year of transition, a period of relative economic calm has arrived in Russia. Unlike the early years of transition where the degree of disequalibrium was large and changing rapidly, and, hence, institution building was very difficult, a period of stability will facilitate institution building. An open economy is one of the keys to building market institutions. One of the lessons from Central Europe that seems clear is that the openness required to accede to the EU accelerated the process of institutional development both as a result of the experience Central European firms could gain from dealing with fully developed market institutions and from the need to provide a competitive set of market institutions to attract foreign firms and investment.

Until market institutions function well, there is likely to be a shortage of private investment funds available to Russian industry. Hence, there may be a role for government investment funds. Russian industry requires modernization. The government, however, should be wary of thinking it can "pick winners" when providing funds for investment. Commercial criteria, strict enforcement of bankruptcy laws and open competition for those funds are likely to yield better results than attempting to pick winners. It will also assist in fostering the development of private market supporting institutions. A transparent investment environment arising from the development of transaction cost reducing institutions provides the best chance to revitalize Russian industry and to ensure the completion of full transition of the Russian Federation into a modern market economy.

CONCLUSION

The high international prices for oil and natural gas in the first decade of the 21st century has given the Russian economy a breathing space to undertake the remaining reforms that are required for broad-based revitalization of Russian industry. As yet, there is little evidence that the government has chosen to use this period of grace wisely. The road ahead is relatively clear – other transition economies have progressed much further along the way to becoming modern market economies than the Russian Federation. Openness and competition provide the key to unlocking the potential of Russian industry.

INDEX

A

access, 28, 42, 43, 44, 49, 50, 51, 73, 83, 88, 95, 98, 99, 105, 108, 112, 115, 133, 139, 140, 141, 178, 179, 180, 182, 183, 185, 189, 193, 194, 203, 218, 230, 231, 232
accidents, 47
accountability, 126, 186, 187
accounting, 22, 30, 49, 50, 88, 89, 92, 126, 168, 170, 198, 199, 201, 217, 231
accounting fraud, 49
accounting standards, 88
accuracy, 200, 223
achievement, 154, 183
acquisitions, 113
activation, 88
adaptation, 39, 102
adjustment, 104, 106, 107, 198, 214, 229
ADP, 92
Africa, 12, 14, 18
age, 188
ageing, 37
agent, 197
aggregate demand, 211, 215
aging, 85, 114, 166, 177, 188
agrarian, 15
agricultural market, 228
agricultural sector, 78, 105, 106, 226, 228
agriculture, 23, 32, 78, 82, 86, 108, 200, 201
AIDS, 132
Albania, 2
alcohol, 22, 35, 142
alcohol abuse, 22
algorithm, 188, 189
alternative, 7, 8, 11, 14, 16, 17, 26, 36, 42, 47, 67, 85, 87, 88, 91, 94, 115, 116, 134, 135, 137, 149, 150, 162, 167, 169, 194, 224, 226, 231, 234, 237
alternatives, 87, 91, 114, 134, 138, 149

alters, 117, 211
amalgam, 40
ambivalent, 42
amendments, 89, 126, 151, 167
amortization, 76
animals, 227
apparel, 103
arbitration, 47, 48, 53, 58, 61, 99, 167
argument, 102, 104
Asia, 108, 169, 176
assessment, 52, 71, 92, 225, 234
assets, 6, 9, 22, 25, 30, 34, 39, 40, 42, 43, 46, 49, 50, 51, 52, 58, 60, 71, 74, 75, 90, 91, 113, 117, 183, 186, 187, 192, 201, 213, 228
assumptions, 41, 62, 65, 68, 151, 152, 154, 160, 164, 172, 173, 175, 203
asymmetric information, 53, 61
asymmetry, 42, 234
auditing, 49, 50, 231
Australia, 106
Austria, 146
authoritarianism, 38
authority, 10, 16, 20, 22, 143, 147, 183, 218, 227
automobiles, 98, 104, 106
autonomy, 118, 126, 218
availability, 22, 33, 51, 77, 98, 144, 193
average cost pricing, 134, 136
average costs, 134, 135, 136, 232
averaging, 151, 216
aversion, 137
avoidance, 29, 99, 164
Azerbaijan, 40, 175

B

balance of payments, 25, 102
bank failure, 19, 27, 52, 53
banking, 22, 23, 27, 28, 31, 35, 37, 52, 53, 74, 75, 81, 87, 89, 106, 154, 168, 174, 191, 231

bankruptcy, 28, 35, 49, 51, 174, 225, 231, 238
banks, 23, 28, 30, 31, 34, 35, 52, 53, 75, 87, 88, 89, 90, 99
bargaining, 42, 58, 60, 61, 66, 68, 101, 226, 228, 233
barriers, 51, 99, 100, 101, 102, 106, 107, 134, 146, 175, 178, 184
barriers to entry, 178
barter, 99
base rate, 164
beef, 103
Belarus, 2, 40
beliefs, 119
bias, 121
bilateral relations, 58, 59, 60, 63, 71
biotechnology, 132, 137
birth, 77, 108
birth rate, 77
black hole, 33
black market, 20, 23
Black Sea, 151, 158, 159, 160
blame, 221
Bolshevik Revolution, 13
bonds, 33, 61, 75, 80, 90, 123, 201
Boris Yeltsin, 26
borrowers, 89
borrowing, 28, 30, 31, 33, 37, 75, 83, 88, 215, 217
brain, 114
brain drain, 114
Brazil, 88
breakdown, 115
breathing, xi, 239
bribes, 9, 12, 13, 14, 16, 20, 27, 40, 117, 143
Britain, 15
budget deficit, 25, 27, 31, 33, 79
building blocks, 134, 141
Bulgaria, 142, 146
bureaucracy, 9, 14, 49, 125, 126
business environment, 40, 113, 116
business ethics, 116
business management, 233, 235
buyer, 12, 13, 42, 59, 99, 107, 166, 225, 226, 227, 232, 234

C

cabinets, 35
California, 169
campaigns, 31
Canada, vii, xii, 103, 182, 187, 191, 194, 226, 228
capital cost, 191
capital expenditure, 152
capital flight, 19, 36
capital goods, 80, 81, 85, 87, 93, 94

capital intensive, 198
capital markets, 50, 73, 75, 87, 102, 104, 112, 115, 205
capitalism, 7, 119
capitalist system, 12
carrier, 190
cartel, 52
cash flow, 24, 43, 170
categorization, 187
cattle, 200, 226, 227
Central Asia, 2, 176
central bank, 28, 29
Central Europe, 108, 238
central planning, 1, 12, 14, 16, 19, 20, 25, 73, 150, 237, 238
certainty, 42, 187, 203
certification, 44
channels, 115, 198, 221, 222, 223, 225, 229, 234, 235
Chechnya, 31, 191
China, 2, 11, 17, 54, 88, 91, 106, 142
Chinese, 91
circular flow, 201
civil law, 7, 47, 118, 119, 120
civil liberties, 117
civil servants, 198
civil service, 37, 209, 211
civil society, 111, 137
classification, 199, 200, 232
closure, 123
clusters, 40
coal, 78, 92
codes, 119
coercion, 10, 16
cognitive abilities, 42
coherence, 223
cohort, 114
Cold War, 5
collateral, 30, 49
collective bargaining, 228
collusion, 225
command economy, 5, 19, 20, 39, 41, 58, 71, 73, 98, 107, 118, 140, 149, 222, 229, 232, 234, 235
commerce, 16
commercial bank, 28, 29, 31, 33, 34, 35, 37, 52, 54, 88, 89, 91, 213, 217, 231
commodities, 90, 103, 150, 198, 200, 201, 203, 204, 205, 207, 210, 211, 212, 225
commodity, 43, 44, 181, 185, 186, 188, 202, 203, 223, 225, 226, 232, 234
commodity futures, 43
commodity markets, 43, 185, 186
common agricultural policy, 108

Commonwealth of Independent States, 26, 40, 101, 108, 153, 184
communication, 43, 201, 202, 233
communication systems, 43
communism, 7, 26, 117, 119, 131, 141
communist countries, 11
Communist Party, 9, 21, 26, 35, 119, 141, 143
community, 15, 71, 80, 93, 141, 147
community service, 93
comparative advantage, 98, 102, 103
compensation, 25, 27, 78, 114, 122, 123, 126, 191, 216
competency, 238
competition, 7, 8, 9, 10, 24, 30, 51, 53, 58, 59, 71, 74, 82, 97, 98, 101, 102, 103, 106, 107, 112, 115, 116, 117, 134, 177, 178, 179, 180, 181, 182, 187, 189, 190, 198, 229, 233, 237, 238, 239
competition policy, 58, 71
competitive advantage, 112, 118
competitive markets, 41, 43, 57, 178, 221, 229
competitive process, 51
competitiveness, 49, 74, 79, 81, 82, 102, 114, 115, 116, 122, 131, 186, 209, 214, 226
competitor, 89, 231
complement, 48
complexity, xii, 42, 48, 59, 100, 227
compliance, 13, 15, 48, 59, 71, 145, 154, 172
complications, 62, 71, 222
components, 45, 54, 214
composition, 199, 200, 203, 215
concentrates, 41
concordance, 201
concrete, 90
confidence, 23, 25, 27, 36, 45, 50, 52, 53, 75, 143, 234
confidentiality, 227
configuration, 17, 62, 65, 66
conflict, 25, 114, 120, 142, 177, 181, 193, 194, 231
conflict of interest, 181, 193, 194
confrontation, 10
confusion, 178, 216
Congress, 9, 108
consciousness, 119
consensus, xii
conservation, 201
consolidation, 119
Constitution, 15, 17, 118, 119, 120, 215
constraints, 7, 8, 21, 27, 36, 52, 53, 62, 74, 82, 97, 126, 181, 208, 221
construction, 23, 26, 83, 93, 170, 174, 200, 201
consumer expenditure, 27, 197, 210, 212
consumer goods, 21, 37, 204, 211, 212
consumer markets, 44

consumer protection, 234
consumer surplus, 61
consumers, 20, 23, 25, 37, 44, 98, 105, 107, 139, 142, 204, 206, 207, 208, 209, 213, 214, 222, 223, 224, 225, 230, 232, 234, 235
consumption, 25, 43, 104, 153, 201, 203, 204, 205, 210, 211, 212, 213, 214, 215, 234
consumption function, 211, 214, 215
consumption patterns, 213
control, 9, 10, 12, 13, 14, 25, 30, 33, 36, 37, 38, 46, 49, 58, 71, 74, 89, 93, 107, 114, 116, 117, 120, 121, 125, 126, 139, 140, 141, 144, 147, 182, 227, 228
convergence, 107
conversion, 159
corporate governance, 41, 45, 49, 50, 53, 54, 231, 235
corporations, 49, 87, 114, 137, 139, 164
corruption, 5, 12, 13, 14, 16, 19, 21, 27, 35, 38, 40, 46, 47, 49, 51, 53, 59, 100, 121, 124, 126, 147, 189, 237
cost curve, 62, 64, 135
cost saving, 94
costs, xi, 5, 7, 8, 11, 12, 14, 16, 35, 39, 40, 41, 42, 43, 44, 45, 46, 48, 52, 53, 58, 59, 60, 61, 62, 65, 66, 68, 69, 70, 71, 88, 95, 99, 100, 106, 107, 108, 114, 119, 132, 133, 134, 135, 136, 137, 138, 147, 151, 152, 153, 156, 158, 160, 164, 165, 166, 170, 183, 184, 186, 187, 192, 194, 209, 224, 225, 227, 230, 232, 234, 237
costs of production, 230
Council of Ministers, 24
counter-trade, 99
coverage, 3
covering, 142, 144, 217
credibility, 33, 40, 44, 46, 48, 51
credit, 20, 23, 27, 28, 30, 31, 33, 35, 37, 44, 51, 53, 73, 75, 76, 78, 82, 86, 87, 88, 89, 90, 91, 93, 95, 96, 122, 188, 198, 201, 203, 208, 211, 213, 215, 218, 230, 231, 233, 235
creditors, 36, 51, 225, 231
crime, 10, 16, 35, 117, 121, 124
criminal justice system, 10
criticism, 228
cronyism, 38
crops, 137, 200
crude oil, 21, 150, 151, 152, 153, 154, 158, 163, 165, 166, 170, 171, 173, 174, 175, 177, 178, 190, 191, 192, 193
crying, 21
Cuba, 11
culture, 108

currency, 23, 25, 33, 37, 77, 83, 99, 120, 123, 126, 168, 180, 199, 209, 217
current account, 27, 198, 214
customers, 10, 22, 61, 89, 134, 181, 182, 183, 185, 186
Czech Republic, 2, 11, 17, 52, 53

D

dairy products, 103
danger, 48, 50, 54
data base, 142
data collection, 200
data processing, 200
death, 21
debt, 19, 30, 31, 33, 34, 37, 77, 80, 102, 125, 215
debt servicing, 33
debtors, 216
debts, 15
decay, 20
decentralisation, 24
decision makers, 46
decision making, 14, 16
decisions, 22, 28, 42, 46, 48, 53, 62, 66, 68, 113, 132, 136, 144, 197, 214, 218, 223, 224, 228, 233
declining industries, 104
decreasing returns, 62
deduction, 170
defense, 108
deficit, 79, 217
definition, 7, 15, 50, 54, 119, 191, 200
deflation, 19
degradation, 12
delivery, 46, 95, 185, 187
demand, 12, 20, 25, 28, 63, 64, 75, 80, 83, 87, 92, 94, 100, 103, 134, 135, 197, 198, 200, 202, 203, 205, 206, 207, 208, 209, 210, 211, 212, 213, 214, 215, 218, 221, 222, 224, 234
demand curve, 63, 64, 135
democracy, 117, 120
democratic elections, 149
Department of Agriculture, 236
deposits, 25, 27, 32, 37, 52, 213
depreciation, 2, 27, 28, 75, 80, 82, 86, 87, 92, 93, 94, 95, 102, 114, 156, 158, 188
deregulation, 181
designers, 15
desire, 19, 49, 113, 118, 140, 145, 147, 177
desires, 6
destruction, 26, 119
devaluation, 30, 33, 37, 77, 80, 83, 118, 123, 152, 192, 209

developed countries, 15, 74, 79, 98, 103, 115, 132, 137, 138, 139, 140
developing countries, 11, 14, 24, 59, 67, 102, 112, 116, 131, 132, 133, 137, 138, 139, 140
development banks, 88, 89, 90
differentiation, 218, 229
diffusion, 114
direct foreign investment, 113, 125, 152
direct investment, 83, 112, 113, 114, 121, 126, 152, 177, 191, 231
disappointment, 26
discipline, 31, 33, 51, 54, 103, 112
disclosure, 49, 133
discount rate, 166, 171
discrimination, 100, 103, 105, 117, 189
disequilibrium, 221
dispersion, 40, 58
displacement, 184
disposable income, 204, 205, 209, 210, 211, 212, 213, 214, 215, 218
dissatisfaction, 31
distortions, 40, 52, 98, 104, 108, 150, 153, 165, 171, 173, 174, 228, 235
distribution, 9, 29, 41, 45, 46, 51, 66, 74, 88, 91, 95, 145, 174, 179, 180, 181, 221, 224, 229, 230, 232, 233
divergence, 43, 87, 214
diversity, xii, 35
division, 23, 58, 71, 89, 91, 92, 138, 214, 216, 221, 231
Doha, 132, 139, 140, 144
domestic demand, 83, 209, 210
domestic economy, 112
domestic factors, 82
domestic industry, 104, 210, 211, 213, 214, 215
domestic investment, 82, 88, 106, 112, 116, 123
domestic markets, 21, 103, 137
dominance, 41, 180, 181, 193
double counting, 198
draft, 146, 158
drugs, 10, 44, 132
due process, 117
Duma, 35, 85, 87, 89, 149, 150, 158, 163, 167, 169
dumping, 104, 105
durable goods, 212
duration, 212
duties, 82, 104, 123, 150, 165, 166, 216

E

earnings, 24
ears, 53
earth, 15

East Asia, 54
Eastern Europe, 1, 8, 14, 18, 40, 54, 55, 72, 127, 148, 191, 192, 235, 236
economic activity, 10, 16, 26, 27, 98, 121, 133, 147, 197, 200, 216
economic change, 26
economic crisis, 97
economic development, 26, 77, 80, 96, 218
economic efficiency, 104
economic goods, 9
economic growth, 2, 8, 9, 14, 21, 36, 37, 39, 41, 42, 45, 46, 47, 48, 52, 53, 54, 74, 86, 87, 97, 100, 113, 145
economic growth rate, 86
economic indicator, 40
economic institutions, 7
economic performance, xi, 40, 152, 218, 237
economic policy, xi, 36, 74, 125, 150, 209
economic problem, 74
economic reform, 19, 21, 26, 36, 38, 174, 199
economic reforms, 19, 26, 36, 38
economic rent, 10, 174, 180
economic resources, 98
economic stability, 38, 233
economic systems, 5, 6
economic transformation, 5
economic welfare, 228
economics, xi, 6, 42, 53, 99, 111, 135, 187, 192
economies of scale, 94, 98, 183, 184, 229, 234
education, 11, 216, 217, 218
Education, 229
educators, 218
EIA, 159, 160
elaboration, 78
elasticity, 101, 184
elderly, 32
elderly population, 32
election, 99
electrical power, 75, 82, 86, 91, 92
electricity, 37, 92
embryo, 10
emigration, 114
emotions, 111
employees, 32, 189, 198, 200, 215, 216, 217, 218, 222, 230, 233
employment, 28, 32, 94, 115
energy, xi, 19, 27, 34, 36, 37, 38, 78, 81, 82, 83, 92, 95, 97, 107, 150, 154, 177, 178, 179, 180, 183, 184, 188, 193, 209, 238
engagement, 180
entrepreneurs, 7, 9, 116, 122, 124, 200, 233
entrepreneurship, 121

environment, 2, 6, 10, 21, 22, 24, 39, 40, 41, 42, 44, 45, 46, 47, 48, 49, 51, 52, 53, 54, 59, 74, 88, 89, 91, 106, 111, 112, 116, 117, 118, 125, 126, 133, 145, 177, 178, 179, 184, 188, 201, 226, 227, 231, 233, 235, 238
epidemic, 13, 132
equality, 115, 151, 153, 154
equilibrium, 7, 8, 11, 14, 16, 17, 34, 41, 50, 51, 54, 65, 66, 67, 99, 100, 102, 126, 222
equilibrium price, 222
equipment, 3, 42, 75, 76, 78, 79, 80, 81, 82, 83, 86, 91, 92, 94, 95, 114, 122, 205, 208, 210, 229
equity, 15, 49, 52, 76, 122, 123, 181, 182
erosion, 23, 25
estimating, 198
Estonia, 40, 45
ethics, 13
ethnicity, 120
EU, 98, 100, 103, 107, 108, 238
Europe, 1, 53, 75, 128, 139, 159, 160, 176, 177, 180, 181, 182, 234
European Union, 2, 98, 100, 108
evolution, xi, 11, 116, 162, 175, 197, 212, 218
examinations, 3
excess demand, 22, 25
exchange controls, 113
exchange rate, 24, 27, 28, 30, 32, 33, 34, 37, 77, 99, 209
exchange rate target, 33
exchange rates, 24
exclusion, 167
execution, 7
exercise, 9, 58, 101, 112
expenditures, 29, 95, 136, 158, 200, 204, 210, 211, 214, 215, 217
expertise, xii, 46, 53, 112, 113, 114, 121, 122, 231
exploitation, 119
export promotion, 102
export subsidies, 99, 104, 105, 106
exporter, 181
exports, 21, 24, 25, 27, 83, 88, 94, 97, 98, 99, 103, 105, 106, 107, 150, 151, 152, 153, 154, 158, 171, 174, 180, 193, 209, 214
exposure, 16, 47, 106, 183, 184
external liabilities, 214
external shocks, 40
externalities, 102, 104, 115, 116, 132
extraction, 9, 14, 117, 150, 164, 165
eyes, 13

F

failure, 2, 14, 25, 35, 45, 47, 49, 50, 53, 127, 132, 145, 147, 150, 187, 189, 231, 234, 237
fairness, 100
faith, 5, 121
family, 10, 23, 224
Far East, 169, 177
farmers, 95, 136, 214, 223, 224, 225, 226, 228, 230
farms, 95, 221, 224, 228, 230
fast food, 233
federal government, 119, 120, 193, 217
federal law, 89, 120, 167
federalism, 37
Ferdinand Marcos, 12
finance, 21, 32, 49, 52, 74, 75, 76, 80, 82, 88, 90, 92, 94, 95
financial capital, 82, 87, 88, 91, 199, 203, 235
financial crises, 33
financial crisis, 52, 192, 193
financial institutions, 2, 44, 45, 99, 231
financial intermediaries, 49, 51, 52
financial markets, 34, 87
financial resources, 76, 81, 87, 88, 89, 90, 91, 92, 93, 95, 208, 209
financial sector, 197, 198, 199, 200
financial stability, 225
financial support, ix, 78, 82, 83, 90, 94
financial system, 28, 33, 45, 74, 76, 77, 78, 79, 80
financing, 22, 25, 31, 33, 51, 52, 53, 75, 76, 78, 79, 81, 82, 86, 87, 88, 89, 90, 92, 93, 94, 102, 198, 201, 205, 209, 229, 231
fires, 238
firms, 6, 14, 22, 24, 27, 28, 30, 31, 40, 41, 42, 46, 50, 51, 52, 53, 54, 57, 58, 59, 60, 61, 62, 65, 66, 67, 68, 69, 70, 73, 75, 78, 81, 82, 88, 89, 91, 94, 99, 100, 101, 102, 105, 112, 114, 115, 116, 117, 121, 132, 133, 134, 135, 136, 137, 138, 139, 147, 197, 203, 218, 230, 231, 233, 238
fiscal policy, 32, 174
fish, 226, 232
fisheries, 201
fishing, 12, 199
fixed rate, 164
flexibility, 184, 226
flight, 27, 34, 112, 150
float, 34
floating, 27, 30, 32, 37
flood, 101
fluctuations, 224
focusing, 22
food, 23, 25, 27, 43, 44, 78, 83, 106, 142, 221, 222, 223, 224, 226, 227, 228, 229, 230, 231, 232, 233, 234, 235
food industry, 221, 223, 229, 230, 233
food processing industry, 230
food production, 221
food products, 230, 232, 234
food safety, 228, 234, 235
Ford, 47
forecasting, 175, 197
foreign banks, 53, 75, 83, 91, 107
foreign direct investment, 112, 113, 115, 116, 123, 145, 150, 153, 164, 177, 185, 194, 235
foreign exchange, 34, 80, 91, 102, 149
foreign exchange market, 80
foreign firms, 14, 101, 105, 112, 113, 114, 115, 116, 117, 122, 131, 238
foreign investment, 27, 34, 38, 47, 59, 76, 80, 92, 106, 111, 112, 113, 116, 118, 120, 121, 122, 123, 124, 125, 126, 145, 147, 149, 177, 180, 181, 193, 194, 206, 231
foreign nationals, 139
France, 90
franchise, 116, 231
fraud, 30, 50, 113
free market economy, 150, 175, 222, 234
free trade, 99, 100, 101, 108
free trade agreement, 108
freedom, 11, 16, 40
frustration, 14
fuel, 49, 75, 78, 81, 82, 91, 92, 178, 187
full capacity, 190
funding, 86, 92, 133, 152, 183, 217
funds, 2, 24, 30, 36, 49, 75, 79, 80, 81, 88, 89, 90, 91, 92, 93, 94, 112, 113, 117, 133, 152, 153, 165, 166, 168, 169, 170, 171, 172, 173, 174, 175, 177, 201, 218, 231, 238
futures, 99

G

gasoline, 35
GATS, 105, 128, 138
GATT, 100, 105, 106, 138
GDP, 25, 27, 28, 29, 33, 40, 52, 53, 74, 75, 77, 79, 86, 150, 152, 180, 198, 199, 202, 203
GDP deflator, 79
General Agreement on Tariffs and Trade, 100, 105, 138
General Agreement on Trade in Services, 105, 138
geography, 40, 58, 108
geology, 152, 164
Georgia, 22, 26

Germany, 2, 17, 74, 89, 90
Gini coefficients, 40
global economic welfare, 132
global economy, 2, 131
global markets, 122
goals, 21, 89, 97, 99, 100, 113, 119, 122, 145, 228
God, 120
gold, 21, 29, 37, 77, 125
goods and services, 10, 12, 91, 105, 106, 197
governance, 20, 29, 49, 88
government budget, 93, 94, 104, 133, 198
government expenditure, 35, 78, 218
government intervention, 113
government policy, 43, 78, 177, 181, 234
government revenues, 216
government securities, 30, 31, 34
grades, 224, 226, 232
grading, 44, 232
grants, 88, 211
graph, 206
gravity, 159
Great Britain, 75
gross domestic product, 40
grouping, 58, 71, 199
groups, 10, 15, 87, 103, 104, 111, 114, 210, 211, 212, 213
growth, 10, 14, 20, 23, 33, 35, 37, 40, 47, 54, 73, 74, 76, 77, 86, 87, 88, 91, 94, 95, 97, 102, 115, 118, 205, 207, 209, 211, 213, 214, 232
growth rate, 47, 76, 77, 86, 91, 94, 95, 209
guidance, 119
guidelines, 179, 199, 222
guiding principles, 120

H

hands, 9, 30, 49
hard currency, 24, 29, 33, 80, 83, 123, 154, 174, 181
harm, 7
hate, 112
health, 21, 32, 82, 139, 140, 216, 218
health care, 32, 82
height, 153, 216
higher quality, 21, 23, 229, 230, 235
hip, 58, 59, 60, 63
hogs, 227
hospitals, 93
host, 14, 112, 113, 115, 116, 145, 147
hostility, 23
House, 12, 128
household income, 93
household sector, 28, 198, 200, 201, 202, 203, 209

households, 23, 27, 93, 197, 200, 201, 203, 204, 205, 209, 211, 214
housing, 27, 28, 37, 76, 82, 85, 86, 93
hub, 181, 187
human capital, 42, 94, 115, 117, 121, 126, 131, 133, 231, 233, 235
human rights, 119, 120
Hungary, 11, 40, 53
hunting, 199
hydrocarbons, 166
hyperinflation, 19, 27, 29, 35, 80
hypothesis, 212, 213

I

identification, 114, 150, 162, 200
identity, 119
ideology, 118, 119, 120
imagination, 238
IMF, 27, 30, 31, 35, 37, 193
implementation, 45, 59, 73, 74, 142, 168, 171, 172, 174, 186, 214
import substitution, 102
imports, 20, 21, 24, 35, 76, 78, 80, 83, 98, 99, 100, 101, 102, 103, 139, 203, 212, 214, 228, 229
in transition, 14, 40, 46, 53, 60, 61, 62, 198, 200
incentives, 20, 45, 46, 49, 50, 99, 105, 132, 133, 136, 137, 138, 140, 172, 187, 192, 207, 211, 213, 228
incidence, 7
inclusion, 132
income, 2, 5, 9, 11, 20, 22, 28, 32, 40, 43, 77, 93, 98, 137, 166, 197, 198, 200, 201, 203, 209, 210, 211, 213, 214, 215
income distribution, 98, 213
income inequality, 213
income tax, 166, 200
increased competition, 171
independence, 113, 115, 118, 183, 187, 190
India, 9, 10, 13, 14, 17, 88, 102
indication, 146
indicators, 198
indices, 200, 204
indigenous, 115
indirect effect, 77, 218
individual rights, 119
Indonesia, 9, 10, 13, 14
industrial policy, 74, 78, 80, 85, 86, 87, 88, 89, 93, 95, 113, 198, 199, 208, 210, 211, 212
industrial production, 35, 36, 74, 81, 194, 197, 200, 203, 208, 211, 213
industrial sectors, 85, 91, 95, 111
industry, xi, 2, 3, 13, 14, 20, 28, 29, 37, 42, 43, 48, 51, 57, 73, 74, 76, 77, 78, 79, 80, 81, 82, 85, 86,

87, 88, 89, 90, 91, 92, 93, 94, 95, 96, 98, 102, 104, 106, 111, 114, 115, 116, 123, 131, 134, 149, 150, 152, 153, 154, 164, 166, 167, 170, 171, 172, 173, 174, 175, 177, 178, 179, 180, 181, 183, 190, 193, 194, 197, 200, 201, 202, 203, 205, 207, 209, 212, 215, 221, 223, 224, 225, 226, 228, 232, 233, 234, 235, 238, 239
inequality, 40, 212
infancy, 28
infant industries, 102
infinite, 62, 174
inflation, 20, 23, 25, 27, 28, 29, 30, 31, 32, 33, 36, 37, 77, 79, 83, 87, 91, 92, 93, 95, 113, 122, 192, 207, 209, 211, 214, 216, 217
information asymmetry, 42, 43, 47, 53, 234
infrastructure, 2, 42, 58, 71, 88, 93, 99, 104, 170, 177, 179, 188, 193, 198, 223, 224, 232, 234
inhibitor, 218
initial state, 103
initiation, 90
injections, 31, 153, 165, 173, 174
innovation, 79, 86, 87, 88, 94, 132, 133, 134, 135, 136, 137, 138, 140, 202
instability, 27, 33, 229, 231
institution building, 238
institutional change, 5, 6, 7, 12, 86, 178
institutional reforms, 54, 87
institutions, xi, 2, 6, 7, 11, 14, 15, 29, 39, 41, 42, 43, 44, 45, 46, 49, 50, 53, 54, 74, 88, 89, 91, 99, 112, 113, 118, 126, 133, 143, 174, 200, 217, 221, 223, 224, 227, 234, 235, 237, 238
instruments, 33, 62, 118, 120, 185
insurance, 28, 36, 43, 52, 88, 106, 213, 217
integrated circuits, 144
integration, 98, 107, 131, 223
integrity, 232, 235
intellectual property, 107, 113, 114, 131, 132, 133, 137, 138, 139, 140, 141, 142, 143, 144, 145, 146, 147
intellectual property rights, 107, 114, 137, 138, 139, 140, 141, 142, 143, 144, 145, 146, 147
intelligence, 35, 121
intensity, 205, 206, 215
interaction, 7, 71, 125, 210
interactions, 11
interest rates, 31, 34, 37, 75, 77, 81, 90, 216, 217
interface, 41, 223, 226
interference, 126, 215
intermediaries, 61, 99
International Bank for Reconstruction and Development, 54, 176
International Chamber of Commerce, 47
international financial institutions, 90

international investment, 90
International Monetary Fund, 128
international standards, 138, 142, 146, 147
international trade, 59, 62, 97, 98, 99, 100, 107, 138, 139, 203
internet, 132
Internet, 43
interval, 32, 201, 207
intervention, 2, 238
interview, 180
intra-regional trade, 108
inventions, 133, 134, 135, 137, 141, 143
investment capital, 94, 154, 169, 170, 174
investors, 30, 32, 36, 37, 46, 49, 51, 81, 87, 88, 111, 112, 113, 115, 116, 117, 118, 121, 123, 124, 125, 126, 142, 145, 194, 201, 233
isolation, 121, 136, 205

J

Japan, 34, 74, 88, 90, 103
jobs, 32
joint ventures, 24, 113, 116, 122, 126, 171, 174, 190, 194, 224, 231
judges, 117, 124, 143
judiciary, 40, 45, 46, 142, 143
jurisdiction, 120, 183, 217
justice, 15, 117
justification, 28, 102, 104, 140

K

Kazakhstan, 40, 101
Keynes, 211, 219
knowledge economy, 132, 138, 146
Korea, 102, 169

L

labour, 2, 8, 12, 22, 104, 112, 208, 211, 213, 229, 230
labour force, 2, 230
labour market, 12
lack of control, 24
land, 9, 12, 15, 46, 119, 224
language, 108, 124, 141
law enforcement, 111, 117, 121, 122, 124, 126
laws, 7, 14, 15, 35, 44, 45, 46, 48, 51, 71, 87, 92, 111, 113, 114, 116, 117, 118, 119, 120, 121, 124, 126, 140, 141, 142, 144, 145, 146, 147, 167, 174, 200, 225, 231, 238
lawyers, 46, 143

leakage, 187
learning, 6, 120
legal protection, 49, 114, 131, 142
legislation, 24, 28, 48, 49, 74, 90, 114, 117, 118, 119, 120, 121, 123, 124, 126, 138, 139, 141, 142, 150, 151, 156, 162, 163, 167, 168, 228
lending, 23, 30, 31, 53, 74, 89, 112, 173, 174, 175, 201
lending process, 89
lethargy, 21
letters of credit, 99
liberalisation, 22, 26, 27
liberalization, 15, 16, 50, 97, 100, 106, 116, 122, 150, 151, 154, 160, 164, 165, 173, 175, 177, 179, 180, 234, 235
licenses, 9, 13, 14, 24, 35, 50, 52, 125, 139, 140
lifetime, 16, 27
limited liability, 120
links, 190, 221, 229
liquid assets, 207
liquidity, 23, 52, 181, 184, 185, 187
livestock, 226, 227
living standard, 8, 23, 29
living standards, 8, 23, 29
loans, 22, 30, 52, 53, 79, 81, 91, 174, 216, 231
lobbying, 193
local authorities, 30, 31, 37
local government, 41, 215, 216, 217
location, 182, 224, 225
long distance, 107, 178
love, 112
low risk, 113
lower prices, 224, 230
lying, 65

M

machinery, 21, 80, 85, 86, 94, 95
macroeconomic management, 57, 112, 113
macroeconomic models, 197
macroeconomic policies, 3
macroeconomic policy, 208, 210, 211, 214, 218
macroeconomic stabilisation, 216
macroeconomic stabilisation policy, 216
macroeconomics, 211
Mainland China, 18, 55, 128
malaise, 2, 19
management, 19, 22, 31, 43, 49, 51, 52, 112, 113, 115, 125, 136, 181, 198, 222, 227, 228
manipulation, 50, 216
manufactured goods, 21, 202, 210
manufacturing, 77, 78, 92, 106, 107, 197, 200, 209
marginal cost curve, 62

marginal revenue, 62, 63, 64, 65
market discipline, 28
market economy, 1, 2, 5, 6, 16, 17, 19, 24, 25, 38, 39, 41, 52, 53, 54, 74, 76, 102, 107, 118, 120, 125, 127, 140, 142, 146, 147, 198, 211, 213, 222, 223, 229, 237, 238
market failure, 5, 27, 43, 52, 73, 99, 102, 234, 237, 238
market value, 181
marketing, 47, 102, 104, 177, 179, 182, 210, 222, 223, 224, 225, 226, 228, 229, 231, 234, 235
markets, xi, 5, 6, 8, 20, 22, 23, 24, 28, 43, 57, 58, 59, 70, 71, 83, 87, 88, 97, 98, 99, 101, 102, 105, 106, 107, 108, 112, 113, 114, 118, 120, 122, 132, 137, 142, 150, 152, 175, 177, 178, 181, 182, 190, 193, 194, 199, 217, 222, 223, 224, 225, 226, 230, 232, 234, 235, 237, 238
marriage, 231
Massachusetts, 127
measurement, 43, 44, 226, 232
measures, 34, 35, 40, 43, 59, 71, 83, 88, 91, 99, 100, 101, 104, 105, 116, 139, 182, 187, 192, 200, 209, 211, 212, 215
meat, 235
media, 43, 132, 218
medical care, 28
medicine, 139, 140
Mediterranean, 160
membership, 2, 74, 83, 105, 107, 108, 145, 146, 228
memory, 17
men, 229
mergers, 113
metallurgy, 37, 76, 81, 82
metaphor, 11
middle class, 93
Middle East, 152
migrants, 104
migration, 104
military, 21, 74, 81, 211
milk, 224, 228
minimum wage, 211
mining, 32
minorities, 10
minority, 49, 50
mixing, 191
mobility, 11
modeling, 62, 69
models, 89, 135, 142
modernisation, 78, 80, 81, 82, 83, 85, 87, 88, 206
modernization, 73, 114, 115, 116, 122, 123, 127, 149, 156, 170, 238
Moldova, 2, 22
monetary expansion, 74

monetary policy, 75, 208, 217
money, 9, 25, 27, 28, 29, 30, 31, 32, 33, 34, 48, 74, 77, 80, 87, 88, 122, 124, 204, 207, 214, 217
money income, 214
money supply, 25, 31, 33, 74, 77, 87
Mongolia, 11
monopoly, 9, 37, 42, 51, 52, 58, 59, 60, 65, 71, 107, 132, 133, 134, 135, 136, 137, 138, 140, 177, 178, 180, 181, 182, 183, 222, 230
monopoly power, 222, 230
monopoly profits, 132, 137
monopsony, 64, 65
moral hazard, 31, 43, 47
moratorium, 34
morning, 226
Moscow, vii, ix, xi, xii, 83, 128, 150, 159, 160, 169, 175, 176, 194, 195, 215, 216, 217, 218
motion, 1, 237
motivation, 145, 181
movement, 15, 177, 183, 185, 187, 223
multinational corporations, 137
multinational enterprises, 115
murder, 124
music, 107

N

NAFTA, 100
Nash equilibrium, 60, 65, 66, 67, 68, 69, 100
nation, 13, 100, 118, 119
national stock exchanges, 75
nationalism, 112
nationality, 118
natural advantages, 107
natural gas, 101, 107, 170, 177, 178, 179, 180, 181, 183, 184, 185, 194, 239
natural resources, 125, 126
natural selection, 233
neglect, 216
negotiating, 8, 43
negotiation, 22, 41, 44, 46, 52, 138, 167
net social benefit, 102
Netherlands, 226
network, 89, 126, 180, 181, 188, 190
New York, 17, 18, 55, 72, 127, 128, 148, 175, 219, 236
New Zealand, 106
newspapers, 36, 43
Nigeria, 13, 17
Nobel Prize, 213, 215
normal development, 79
normal profits, 134, 135, 136
North America, 93, 100, 108, 178, 191, 226

North American Free Trade Agreement, 100
North Korea, 11, 142
Northeast Asia, 169, 176
novelty, 139
nutrition, 234

O

obligation, 225
OECD, 33, 40, 41, 50, 51, 52, 53, 55, 124, 128, 156, 158, 175, 221, 222, 230, 233, 236
Office of the United States Trade Representative, 148
oil, 14, 34, 37, 49, 77, 78, 81, 85, 92, 97, 98, 124, 150, 151, 152, 153, 154, 156, 158, 161, 163, 164, 165, 166, 167, 170, 171, 172, 173, 174, 175, 177, 190, 191, 192, 193, 194, 239
oil production, 153, 171, 172, 173, 174
oil revenues, 152
oil storage, 190
Oklahoma, 151
oligopolies, 57
oligopoly, 59, 104
open economy, 238
openness, 133, 238
operator, 171, 227
opportunism, 42, 43, 48, 59, 60, 65, 99, 117, 122, 124, 125, 126
opportunity costs, 192
oppression, 10
optimism, 11, 80
optimum output, 64
organization, 41, 107, 183, 227, 229
organizations, 10, 101, 146, 166, 179, 202
orientation, 120
oversight, 53
ownership, 9, 15, 37, 41, 45, 49, 50, 106, 121, 123, 126, 141, 198, 201, 224, 230
ownership structure, 41, 49, 224

P

packaging, 230
paper money, 15
paranoia, 122, 141
Pareto, 7, 48, 191
Pareto optimal, 7
partnership, 125, 126, 231
partnerships, 113, 116
passive, 225
patents, 114, 132, 133, 134, 135, 137, 138, 141, 144
payback period, 218

penalties, 142, 147, 216
pensioners, 24
pensions, 16, 27, 28, 32, 36, 88, 209, 211, 213
perfect competition, 175
permit, 7, 8, 59, 71
pessimism, xi
pharmaceuticals, 78, 106, 132, 136, 139, 140, 142
Philippines, 12
piracy, 107, 141, 142
planned action, 35
planned economies, 8, 9, 222
planning, 2, 8, 12, 19, 22, 24, 25, 82, 89, 121, 140, 149, 221
plants, 94, 181, 182, 183, 229, 230, 231
Poland, 11, 29, 40, 45, 52, 75
police, 7, 10, 16, 29, 117, 125, 126, 142, 143, 183
policy initiative, 57
policy instruments, 100
policy makers, 28, 111, 113, 116, 151, 179, 238
policy reform, 40, 53
political instability, 14, 40
political power, 26
politics, 101, 111, 126, 127
pools, 87, 88, 184, 186, 187
poor, 12, 14, 29, 31, 51, 53, 57, 74, 75, 97, 111, 112, 114, 124, 126, 132, 136, 137, 138, 181, 200, 237
poor performance, 31
population, 21, 23, 25, 27, 29, 32, 35, 36, 38, 40, 113, 125, 137, 154, 177, 201, 204, 205, 209, 210, 211, 212, 215, 218, 237
population group, 212
portfolio, 25, 92, 112, 113
portfolio capital, 113
portfolio investment, 92, 112, 113
portfolios, 185
ports, 93
positive externalities, 112
potatoes, 23
poultry, 23, 103
poverty, 15, 36, 137, 212, 237
power, xi, 2, 9, 10, 11, 15, 16, 20, 21, 26, 29, 36, 37, 43, 47, 57, 58, 62, 76, 78, 85, 91, 92, 93, 94, 96, 98, 101, 107, 112, 115, 117, 118, 119, 120, 123, 124, 126, 143, 178, 193, 199, 226, 228, 229, 233, 234, 235
power generation, 85, 94
power plants, 37
predictability, 126
preference, 189, 204, 205, 212
preferential treatment, 189
premiums, 40, 232
present value, 102, 153, 166, 171, 172
president, 36

President Vladimir Putin, 38
pressure, 19, 23, 71, 81, 92, 93, 102, 133, 137, 178, 180, 181, 182, 187, 188, 208, 229, 235
presumption of innocence, 117
prevention, 144
price competition, 9
price signals, 103, 108, 112, 222, 223, 225, 232, 234
price taker, 62, 101, 181
prices, xi, 6, 8, 9, 12, 16, 19, 20, 22, 23, 24, 25, 27, 29, 34, 36, 37, 39, 43, 60, 74, 77, 86, 92, 93, 95, 97, 99, 101, 103, 104, 105, 107, 132, 134, 135, 137, 139, 151, 152, 153, 154, 158, 159, 160, 164, 165, 177, 179, 182, 185, 188, 192, 193, 194, 203, 204, 209, 210, 212, 214, 221, 222, 223, 224, 225, 226, 227, 228, 232, 234, 235, 239
pricing policies, 101
primary products, 206
private banks, 87, 88
private benefits, 102
private enterprises, 198, 200
private investment, 46, 178, 238
private ownership, 30, 37, 41, 49
private property, 8, 9, 11, 12, 15, 121
private sector, 29, 40, 46, 47, 48, 53, 88, 90, 95, 131, 133, 203
private sector investment, 46
privatisation, 27, 29, 30, 37, 87, 93, 199
privatization, 19, 39, 40, 41, 42, 43, 49, 50, 51, 52, 54, 97, 174, 201, 221, 222, 223, 224, 228, 229, 230, 232, 233, 235
probability, 59, 112, 113, 132, 216
producers, 24, 44, 77, 78, 80, 98, 106, 132, 145, 152, 153, 156, 158, 165, 171, 173, 182, 183, 184, 187, 188, 190, 191, 192, 193, 209, 222, 223, 224, 225, 226, 229, 230, 232, 234
product life cycle, 132
product market, 116
production, 6, 20, 21, 22, 23, 24, 25, 28, 35, 41, 57, 58, 59, 66, 67, 70, 71, 79, 81, 82, 83, 86, 94, 95, 96, 98, 102, 104, 118, 134, 145, 146, 151, 152, 153, 154, 161, 165, 166, 170, 171, 173, 177, 179, 180, 182, 184, 185, 187, 190, 192, 193, 198, 199, 200, 201, 205, 206, 207, 208, 209, 211, 212, 214, 215, 218, 224, 226, 227, 228, 229, 232, 233, 235
production costs, 24, 151, 152, 153, 154
production function, 6
productive capacity, 77, 208
productivity, 2, 12, 20, 22, 25, 57, 153
profession, xi
professions, 216
profit, 20, 22, 23, 66, 68, 76, 94, 115, 122, 125, 126, 134, 156, 158, 164, 165, 166, 167, 170, 171, 174, 184, 200

profitability, 24, 88, 125, 167, 205, 234
profits, 13, 22, 28, 59, 67, 68, 69, 70, 88, 89, 90, 92, 94, 102, 104, 114, 116, 117, 123, 132, 134, 136, 137, 138, 163, 165, 166, 168, 171, 174, 192, 201, 203, 214, 231, 233
program, 21, 26, 27, 30, 34, 37, 78, 91, 122, 174, 189, 194, 222
proliferation, 59, 71
property rights, 5, 7, 8, 9, 10, 12, 14, 15, 16, 17, 22, 40, 41, 42, 45, 46, 49, 53, 54, 112, 117, 137, 138, 140, 141, 142, 143, 144, 145, 146, 147, 237
proposition, 87
prosperity, 119, 132
protectionism, 103, 117
public education, 218
public enterprises, 197, 198
public finance, 217
public health, 139, 140, 217, 218
public interest, 51
public investment, 2, 202
public policy, 88, 89, 124, 198
public sector, 32, 36, 43, 52, 89, 121, 197, 198, 201, 206, 216
public service, 14
punishment, 117
purchasing power, 23, 28, 36, 212
pure monopoly, 65
Putin, 36, 37, 38, 97, 106, 107

Q

quality assurance, 44
questioning, 43, 105
quotas, 27, 101, 193, 194

R

radio, 11, 43
radius, 184
range, 8, 10, 24, 36, 74, 101, 103, 112, 124, 145, 184, 200, 211, 215, 221
rash, 60
rate of return, 170, 193, 194
rationality, 33, 42
raw materials, 21, 208, 231
real estate, 9, 212, 213
real income, 11, 77, 208, 209, 214
real terms, 29, 32, 209, 216
real wage, 25, 154
reality, 20, 34, 36, 86, 107, 114
reasoning, 134
recall, 47, 49, 153

recession, 29, 77, 95, 97, 199
recognition, 120, 200
reconstruction, 156
recovery, 36, 79, 121, 152, 154, 156, 158, 170
redistribution, 5, 41
reduction, 15, 22, 34, 35, 49, 62, 65, 70, 71, 77, 95, 99, 100, 136, 152, 153, 164, 165, 167, 171, 174, 206, 212, 214, 215, 216, 218, 228
reflection, 10, 27, 200, 207
reforms, 8, 11, 16, 19, 21, 22, 23, 24, 25, 28, 29, 30, 31, 34, 35, 37, 38, 52, 71, 80, 112, 122, 123, 145, 174, 214, 239
regional, 13, 26, 37, 41, 49, 58, 59, 99, 100, 101, 108, 178, 183, 185, 215, 216, 217, 218, 228, 232, 233, 234
regulation, 12, 15, 17, 20, 43, 44, 74, 95, 122, 123, 126, 178, 179, 180, 198
regulations, 6, 7, 59, 90, 106, 122, 142, 144, 145, 146, 178, 182, 183, 217, 229, 233, 234
regulators, 136, 184
regulatory oversight, 49, 53
rehabilitation, 151, 153, 171, 173
relationship, 11, 20, 28, 39, 46, 47, 59, 60, 93, 112, 138, 145, 175, 203, 210, 212, 226, 229
relationships, 42, 44, 46, 47, 49, 50, 53, 57, 60, 61, 105, 181, 210, 215, 224, 225, 227, 231, 232, 234
relative prices, 24
relative size, 213
relaxation, 80, 81, 82
relevance, 105
reliability, 29, 40, 43, 125, 190, 225
rent, 9, 10, 12, 14, 40, 42, 102, 103, 105, 174, 222
repair, 94
reputation, 47, 48, 126
reserves, 29, 33, 34, 37, 77, 81, 89, 91, 175, 177, 181, 184, 201
resistance, 14
resolution, 106, 179
resource allocation, 1, 12, 20, 21, 26, 237
resources, 2, 8, 9, 12, 14, 16, 41, 42, 44, 46, 49, 58, 71, 74, 76, 81, 83, 85, 88, 89, 90, 95, 96, 112, 114, 121, 126, 131, 132, 135, 139, 140, 141, 143, 147, 198, 201, 202, 208, 209, 215, 223, 235, 238
restaurants, 199, 233
restructuring, 30, 78, 178, 180, 222, 229
retail, 22, 23, 25, 199, 200, 202, 203, 204, 212, 232, 233
retained earnings, 92, 94
retaliation, 62, 101, 138
retention, 164
returns, 77, 83, 90, 112, 113, 118, 121, 122
revaluation, 93, 209

Index

revenue, 20, 22, 31, 32, 33, 62, 64, 66, 91, 93, 100, 150, 151, 153, 154, 156, 158, 163, 164, 165, 167, 171, 172, 174, 187, 192
rewards, 187
rice, 103
rigidity, 116
rings, 111
risk, 40, 48, 51, 52, 53, 59, 71, 82, 88, 89, 91, 99, 111, 112, 117, 118, 121, 124, 125, 139, 140, 180, 182, 184, 185, 194, 197, 225, 227, 228, 231
risk assessment, 40
rolling, 93
royalty, 163, 164, 165, 167
rule of law, 40, 46, 54, 120
rust, 3

S

safety, 234
sales, 22, 24, 29, 33, 37, 134, 151, 153, 154, 158, 166, 171, 182, 194, 203, 223, 225, 226, 227
sample, 200, 206
sanctions, 50, 138, 146, 201
satellite, 11
savings, 20, 23, 24, 27, 87, 88, 94, 112, 187, 192, 209, 210, 212, 213, 214, 218
savings rate, 112, 210
scale economies, 98
scarcity, 9, 198
scheduling, 189, 231
school, 32, 93, 104
search, 43, 46, 89, 114, 120, 134, 139
searches, 122, 139
searching, 43, 232
securities, 31, 33, 34, 37, 75, 87, 88, 120, 123, 126, 199, 213
Securities and Exchange Commission, 50
security, 33, 45, 46, 52, 113, 116, 117, 191
seed, 137
segmentation, 58, 71, 184, 185, 194
selecting, 51
self-interest, 7, 12, 14, 15, 41, 42, 43, 49, 117
separation, 120, 137, 150, 175, 180, 187
separation of powers, 120
sequencing, 86
series, ix, 27, 35, 47, 72, 120, 122, 163, 179
shape, 200
shareholder value, 181
shareholders, 41, 43, 49, 50, 51, 89, 230, 232
shares, 29, 30, 37, 51, 92, 123, 125, 174, 181, 201, 222, 230
sharing, 126
sheep, 227

shelter, 99
short run, 52, 104, 137, 212, 214
shortage, 14, 28, 102, 112, 121, 208, 224, 238
Siberia, 125, 158, 177, 192
side effects, 116
sign, 5, 139, 181, 182, 205
signals, 11, 44, 46, 58, 71, 181, 191, 223, 224, 235
signs, 71, 112
skills, 8, 42, 112, 231, 233, 235
small firms, 233
smoked meat, 232
smoothing, 39, 224
smuggling, 10
social benefits, 61, 102
social expenditure, 28
social infrastructure, 85
social organization, 204
social policy, 74
social security, 211
social security payments, 211
social services, 82, 86
socialism, 7, 119
society, xi, 7, 9, 11, 13, 14, 111, 117, 118, 119, 120, 133, 134, 135, 137, 138, 212, 213, 214, 216, 221
software, 107
solvent, 102
sorting, 44, 224, 232
sovereignty, 22
Soviet Union, 1, 8, 12, 14, 19, 20, 21, 24, 25, 26, 27, 28, 40, 55, 108, 118, 119, 121, 122, 124, 133, 141, 146, 153, 190, 221, 232, 234
Spain, 75
spare capacity, 188
specialisation, 23
specificity, 42, 45, 47, 224, 226, 231
spectrum, 41, 223, 227
speculation, 33
speech, 148
speed, 13, 37, 223, 226, 234
spillover effects, 53
sports, 83
spot market, 45, 182, 221, 223, 224, 225, 226, 227, 234
stability, 19, 36, 39, 59, 71, 125, 187, 192, 233, 238
stabilization, 123
stages, 50, 54, 60, 75, 86, 89, 90, 208, 221, 224, 225, 233
standard of living, 35, 205
standards, 27, 49, 53, 81, 87, 122, 138, 140, 141, 143, 144, 145, 146, 147, 200, 234
starvation, 221
state control, 20, 23, 32, 88, 93, 141
state enterprises, 7, 20, 28, 29, 49, 52, 222

state innovation, 78
state intervention, 38
state planning, 20, 74, 90
state-owned banks, 23
state-owned enterprises, 25
statistics, 23, 27, 28, 29, 85, 93, 187, 199, 200, 203, 206, 209, 211
statutes, 89, 117
steel, 59, 98, 104, 106
stimulus, 28, 100, 134
stock, 30, 36, 49, 50, 60, 73, 75, 77, 81, 82, 85, 86, 93, 95, 113, 114, 133, 206, 222, 224
stock markets, 49
storage, 47, 199, 221, 230
strategies, 44, 50, 51, 81, 82, 83, 91, 94, 95, 102
strength, 15, 50, 152
strikes, 201
structural reforms, 98
structuring, 184
subsidization, 134, 174, 184, 186
subsidy, 102, 104
subsistence, 154, 211, 212
substitutes, 65
substitution, 81, 102
success rate, 173
suffering, 118
sugar, 23, 103
summer, 33, 36, 37
supervision, 51, 179
supervisors, 22
suppliers, 24, 28, 43, 46, 49, 51, 61, 153, 222, 233
supply, 20, 21, 23, 25, 29, 43, 44, 45, 46, 47, 51, 53, 57, 58, 63, 64, 70, 92, 93, 95, 112, 114, 150, 175, 178, 182, 184, 185, 186, 187, 199, 205, 208, 209, 221, 222, 223, 224, 227, 228, 229, 231, 232, 233, 234, 235
supply chain, 44, 45, 51, 53, 57, 58, 70, 114, 209, 221, 222, 223, 224, 228, 229, 232, 233, 234, 235
supply curve, 63, 64, 150, 175
supporting institutions, 238
surplus, 23, 25, 60, 62, 65, 66, 68, 82, 193, 205, 208
surprise, 15
surrogates, 31, 32
survival, 47
sustainability, 52, 233
sustainable growth, 76
Sweden, 146
Switzerland, 74
symptom, 102
systems, 5, 6, 8, 17, 28, 43, 44, 45, 47, 48, 58, 70, 71, 114, 117, 118, 140, 174, 178, 180, 183, 192

T

tactics, 121, 122
Tajikistan, 2
takeover, 49, 182
tanks, 85, 190
targets, 20, 21, 30, 36, 104, 188, 190
tariff, 59, 71, 79, 92, 97, 100, 101, 102, 103, 104, 105, 106, 107, 174, 178, 183, 184, 189, 191, 192
tariff rates, 101, 103, 104, 107
tax base, 166
tax collection, 25, 29, 32, 36, 172
tax increase, 215
tax policy, 116, 149
tax rates, 153, 164
tax system, 31, 150, 151, 152, 153, 154, 164, 165, 166, 170, 171, 173
taxation, 22, 116, 117, 150, 153, 163, 164, 167, 173, 174, 214, 215
teachers, 216, 218
technological advancement, 21
technological change, 43, 103
technological progress, 82, 133, 135
technology, 21, 80, 81, 95, 98, 102, 104, 112, 113, 114, 115, 116, 118, 122, 127, 132, 134, 137, 143, 145, 149, 178, 205, 223, 229, 230, 235
technology transfer, 104, 114, 115, 127
telecommunications, 43, 106
telephone, 43
television, 10, 11, 43
temperature, 232
tension, 217
tenure, 2, 30, 36, 38, 122
term plans, 22
terminals, 191
territory, 24, 190, 191
Texas, 151, 159
textbooks, 99
theft, 117
theory, 6, 115, 118, 120, 193, 211, 213, 215
thinking, 6, 238
Third World, 17
threat, 47, 54, 60, 99, 124
threats, 215
threshold, 211
Tiananmen Square, 11
timber, 37, 78
time, 1, 10, 26, 28, 29, 32, 36, 44, 46, 48, 52, 53, 61, 86, 87, 89, 94, 97, 98, 105, 107, 114, 115, 119, 122, 124, 135, 143, 144, 149, 150, 166, 170, 175, 178, 180, 182, 183, 190, 194, 198, 199, 200, 201, 207, 208, 209, 212, 217, 223, 224, 226, 228, 231, 233, 234

time frame, 144, 198
time periods, 170
time series, 175
timing, 86, 108, 226
tolls, 184, 186, 187, 188, 192
tourism, 83
trade, 20, 22, 23, 24, 27, 30, 33, 38, 59, 71, 83, 97, 98, 99, 100, 101, 102, 103, 104, 105, 106, 107, 108, 138, 144, 199, 200, 202, 203, 204, 209, 214
trade agreement, 108
trade deficit, 214
trade diversion, 108
trade liberalization, 59, 71, 97, 100, 105
trade policy, 59, 71, 97, 99, 100, 101, 103, 104, 105, 107
trademarks, 141, 142, 143, 144
trading, 33, 59, 71, 98, 99, 100, 103, 105, 108, 226
trading partners, 33, 99, 100, 108, 226
tradition, 32
training, 104, 112, 126, 143, 233
transaction costs, xi, 5, 7, 8, 15, 16, 17, 39, 41, 42, 45, 47, 52, 53, 54, 57, 58, 59, 60, 61, 62, 65, 66, 68, 69, 70, 71, 98, 99, 105, 107, 114, 116, 147, 203, 223, 224, 225, 226
transactions, 7, 12, 17, 39, 41, 43, 44, 45, 46, 50, 52, 53, 57, 58, 66, 70, 99, 115, 117, 122, 123, 124, 179, 184, 185, 207, 217, 223, 224, 227, 229, 231, 234, 235, 237
transfer pricing, 150, 164, 174
transformation, 17, 33, 87, 121, 140, 149, 234
transformations, 96
transition, ix, 1, 2, 3, 5, 6, 8, 11, 16, 17, 19, 30, 39, 40, 41, 43, 44, 45, 47, 50, 51, 52, 53, 54, 58, 59, 61, 67, 70, 71, 73, 74, 85, 93, 97, 98, 100, 101, 102, 103, 104, 107, 108, 112, 113, 116, 117, 120, 126, 131, 133, 137, 140, 141, 142, 147, 175, 177, 197, 209, 221, 222, 223, 225, 229, 233, 237, 238, 239
transition countries, 2, 40, 45, 51, 53, 103, 104
transition economies, xi, 2, 40, 43, 59, 61, 67, 100, 101, 112, 239
transition period, 2
transitional economies, 198, 215
transmission, 177, 178, 179, 180, 183, 184, 185, 186, 187, 188, 189, 190, 192, 194
transnational corporations, 115
transparency, 49, 59, 71, 79, 100, 105, 126, 179, 181, 227, 231
transport, 82, 93, 99, 166, 185, 191, 200, 201
transport costs, 99
transportation, 17, 37, 58, 59, 71, 85, 86, 93, 94, 95, 99, 108, 151, 152, 153, 156, 158, 166, 177, 179, 184, 185, 186, 189, 192, 194, 225, 227

treaties, 120, 146
trend, 43, 86, 164, 206, 208, 209, 212
trust, 52, 72, 75, 116, 228, 229
trustworthiness, 46
turnover, 23, 75, 200, 202, 203, 204, 209, 212

U

U.S. Geological Survey, 176
UK, 226, 228
Ukraine, 2, 40, 101, 147
uncertainty, 33, 39, 42, 44, 45, 47, 48, 53, 54, 124, 225, 227
undergraduate, 211
underproduction, 57
unemployment, 19, 28, 32, 37, 47, 77, 154
unemployment rate, 28
uniform, 40, 70, 103, 105, 189, 222
United Kingdom, vii
United Nations, 128
United Nations Industrial Development Organization, 128
United States, 15, 17, 75, 145, 146, 176, 183, 219, 236
universities, 32
urban areas, 93, 224
Uruguay, 132, 138
Uruguay Round, 132, 138
USDA, 236
users, 46, 137, 156, 158
USSR, 24, 149

V

vacuum, 10
validity, 125
values, 24, 62, 91, 99, 118, 159, 160, 203
variability, 149
variable, 22, 60, 61, 69, 70, 156, 158, 175, 234
variable costs, 22
variables, 40, 47
variation, 119, 175
VAT, 151, 153, 156, 158, 159, 165, 166, 168
vegetables, 23
vertical integration, 224, 227
Victor Chernomyrdin, 29
violence, 10
vision, 39, 85, 117
voice, 31
volatility, 181
voting, 181, 222
voucher privatization, 41

vouchers, 29, 222
vulnerability, 60

W

wage payments, 209, 215, 217
wages, 16, 20, 22, 23, 25, 28, 32, 201, 202, 203, 209, 211, 214, 215, 216, 217, 218
war, 31, 40, 88, 90, 152
weakness, 58, 74
wealth, 5, 8, 9, 28, 30, 46, 118, 212, 213
weapons, 78, 81
welfare, 100, 101, 105, 133, 213, 228
wells, 151, 152, 153, 170, 171, 172
Western Europe, 2, 90, 93, 108
Western Siberia, 178
wheat, 226
wholesale, 22, 153, 156, 160, 223
winning, 33, 136
winter, 23, 25
workers, 8, 9, 22, 23, 24, 28, 31, 41, 51, 87, 143, 209, 214, 218, 222, 230
workplace, 22
World Bank, 35, 40, 43, 45, 46, 49, 50, 52, 53, 54, 55, 145, 148, 152, 154, 156, 158, 160, 168, 169, 170, 171, 172, 176, 235
World Development Report, 55
World Trade Organization, 97, 98, 100, 107, 138, 139, 144, 145, 148
worry, 97, 136
WTO, 74, 83, 97, 98, 100, 102, 105, 106, 107, 108, 132, 138, 139, 140, 144, 145, 146, 147, 148

Y

Yabloko, 26
yield, 33, 34, 37, 222, 238